THE FUTURE OF FOREIGN DIRECT INVESTMENT AND THE MULTINATIONAL ENTERPRISE

RESEARCH IN GLOBAL STRATEGIC MANAGEMENT

Series Editor: Alan M. Rugman

Recent Volumes:

RESEARCH IN GLOBAL STRATEGIC MANAGEMENT
VOLUME 15

THE FUTURE OF FOREIGN DIRECT INVESTMENT AND THE MULTINATIONAL ENTERPRISE

EDITED BY

RAVI RAMAMURTI

Northeastern University, College of Business Administration, Boston, USA

and

NIRON HASHAI

The Hebrew University, Jerusalem, Israel

United Kingdom – North America – Japan
India – Malaysia – China

Emerald Group Publishing Limited
Howard House, Wagon Lane, Bingley BD16 1WA, UK

First edition 2011

Copyright © 2011 Emerald Group Publishing Limited

British Library Cataloguing in Publication Data
A catalogue record for this book is available from the British Library

ISBN: 978-0-85724-555-7
ISSN: 1064-4857 (Series)

Emerald Group Publishing
Limited, Howard House,
Environmental Management
System has been certified by
ISOQAR to ISO 14001:2004
standards

Awarded in recognition of
Emerald's production
department's adherence to
quality systems and processes
when preparing scholarly
journals for print

INVESTOR IN PEOPLE

CONTENTS

PART II: NEW MULTINATIONALS

PART III: THE CHANGING ROLE OF MULTINATIONALS

PART IV: MNEs AND THE STATE

LIST OF FIGURES

LIST OF TABLES

LIST OF CONTRIBUTORS

Yair Aharoni	Faculty of Management, Leon Recanati Graduate School of Business Administration, Tel Aviv University, Tel Aviv, Israel
Paloma Almodóvar	Strategic Management Department, Complutense University of Madrid, Madrid, Spain
Tamar Almor	School of Business Administration, The College of Management Academic Studies, Rishon Lezion, Israel
Joshua B. Bellin	Accenture Institute for High Performance, Boston, MA, USA
Peter J. Buckley	Centre for International Business, University of Leeds, Leeds, UK
Timothy M. Devinney	Faculty of Business, University of Technology, Sydney, Australia
Fragkiskos Filippaios	Faculty of Business, Kingston University, Surrey, UK
Rebecca Firth	Locum Consulting, Manchester, UK
Jens Forssbaeck	Lund Institute of Economic Research, Lund, Sweden
Pervez N. Ghauri	Department of Management, Kings College London, London, UK
Stéphane J. G. Girod	Accenture Institute for High Performance, London, UK
Niron Hashai	The Hebrew University, Jerusalem, Israel

Seev Hirsch Faculty of Management, The Faculty of Management, Leon Recanati Graduate School of Business Administration, Tel Aviv University, Tel Aviv, Israel

Arie Y. Lewin Fuqua School of Business, Duke University, Durham NC, USA

Lilach Nachum Baruch College, City University of New York, New York, USA

Lars Oxelheim Lund Institute of Economic Research, Lund, Sweden; The Research Institute of Industrial Economics, Stockholm, Sweden

Marina Papanastassiou Department of International Economics and Management, Copenhagen Business School, Frederiksberg, Denmark

Ruth Rama Spanish Council for Scientific Research, Institute of Economics and Geography – CSIC, Madrid, Spain

Ravi Ramamurti College of Business Administration, Northeastern University, Boston, MA, USA

Alan M. Rugman School of Management, Henley Business School, University of Reading, Reading, UK

Karl P. Sauvant Vale Columbia Center on Sustainable International Investment, Columbia University, USA

ACKNOWLEDGEMENTS

This volume grew out of a symposium organized at Tel Aviv University in May 2010 to honour Yair Aharoni, who had just received the prestigious Israel Prize for Administrative and Management Science. The papers presented on that occasion by the co-editors and others became the nucleus of what developed quickly into a broad-based exploration of FDI and MNEs – and a Festschrift to Yair Aharoni. We thank Asher Tishler, dean of the Faculty of Management, Tel Aviv University, for organizing the symposium. Above all, we thank the distinguished authors for enthusiastically joining us in this project, and for their thoughtful and timely contributions.

Ravi Ramamurti would like to thank Dean Tom Moore of Northeastern University for his steadfast support, which made possible this book and everything else he has accomplished in recent years, including founding and growing the Center for Emerging Markets. Tom's professional, ethical, and transparent leadership and selfless service to the university will be sorely missed. Ramamurti would also like to thank Senior Associate Dean Bill Crittenden for his encouragement and guidance over the years. His research benefited greatly from funds provided by the Jeff Bornstein Senior Fellowship and grants provided to the Center for Emerging Markets by the Liberty Mutual Foundation and the BIE Program of the US Department of Education. Like everything else, this project could not have been completed without the support of his wife Meena and their three children – Bharat, Gita, and Arjun. In this instance at least, he showed his appreciation by treating them to a memorable week of sightseeing and relaxation in Israel following the TAU symposium!

Niron Hashai would like to thank Shira Tupiol for her excellent assistance in the coordination of the editing the book chapters. Last but not certainly not least, he is grateful for the patience and support of his wife, Einat and three kids – Ido, Gil and Assaf.

Finally, it has been a pleasure to work with Kim Foster and Rebecca Forster of Emerald Publishing, particularly their responsiveness to our many questions and the speed with which the manuscript was turned into a finished product.

DEDICATION TO YAIR AHARONI

(Photograph by Dan Porges, reproduced with permission)

This book is dedicated to Yair Aharoni, professor emeritus at Tel Aviv University. Since receiving his doctoral degree in 1961, he has authored more than 100 journal articles and book chapters, 150 case studies, 7 books in Hebrew, 6 books in English, and edited 6 more books in English – all pertaining to international business, strategy, and public policy. His seminal work, *The Foreign Investment Decision Process* (1966), was based on his 1961 dissertation at Harvard Business School and presaged what came to be known as the behavioral theory of the firm. An eclectic and original thinker, he wrote about a wide range of topics that affected managers and policy makers. Aharoni was among the first to theorize about state-owned enterprises, multinationals from small countries, the globalization of services, and the political economy of multinational enterprises. His research built on existing theories and frameworks but dared to incorporate new variables and perspectives when necessary, based on his deep understanding of real-world issues.

Aharoni is a fellow of the Academy of International Business and of the International Academy of Management. For his academic achievements he was awarded the Landau Prize in 2007 and the Israel Prize for Management and Administrative Science in 2010.

The chapters in this book, written by a distinguished group of scholars, many of whom are also his friends and admirers, build on Aharoni's lifelong contributions to the study of foreign direct investment and multinational enterprise. In keeping with his contributions, they attempt to peer into the future and address important new trends and issues in these areas.

ABOUT YAIR AHARONI

Yair Aharoni is professor emeritus at Tel Aviv University, where he was earlier the Daniel and Grace Ross Professor of International Business and the Issachar Haimovic Professor of Business Policy. In addition, Aharoni has served as the Thomas Henry Carroll Ford Foundation Visiting Professor of Business Administration at Harvard Business School (1978–1979) and the J. Paul Sticht Visiting Professor of International Business at Duke University (1987–1995), where he was also director of Duke's Center of International Business Education and Research (1992–1995). Professor Aharoni has also held visiting appointments at Boston University, the City University of New York, Columbia University, Copenhagen Business School, Helsinki Business School, IMEDE, New York University, Odense University, Stanford University, and the University of California at Berkeley.

Aharoni's books in English include *Accounting Practices in Israel* (1964); *The Foreign Investment Decision Process* (1966); *Business in the International Environment* (1977); *Markets, Planning and Development* (1977); *The No-Risk Society* (1981); *The Management and Evolution of State-Owned Enterprises* (1986); *Israel's Political Economy: The Dreams and the Realities* (1991). His books in Hebrew include *The Functions and Role of Directors* (1963); *Accounting for Management* (1974, 1978, 1980); *Structure and Conduct in Israeli Industry* (1975); *State Owned Enterprises in Israel and Abroad* (1979); *Business Strategy* (1982); and *The Political Economy of Israel* (1992).

In addition, Aharoni has edited the following six books or special issues: *The Emerging International Monetary Order and the Banking System* (1976); *State-Owned Enterprises in the Western Economies* (1981) (with Raymond Vernon); *Coalitions and Competition: The Globalization of Professional Business Services* (1993); *Global Strategic Alliances Among Service Organizations,* special issue of *International Studies of Management and Organization* (1996) (with John Forsyth); *Changing Roles of State Intervention in Services in an Era of Open International Markets* (1997);

Globalization of Services: Some Implications for Theory and Practice (2000) (with Lilach Nachum).

Throughout his distinguished academic career, Aharoni has also been an institution builder in Israel. He served as the first Dean of the Faculty of Management at Tel Aviv University, was instrumental in establishing the Israel Institute of Business Research, and helped start the Top Executive Program of which he was the first Director. He was also Chief Executive Officer of the Jerusalem Institute of Management and served for five years as the rector of the College of Management in Rishon LeZion, Israel.

INTRODUCTION: RESEARCH ON FDI AND MNEs IN A CHANGING WORLD

Niron Hashai and Ravi Ramamurti

ABSTRACT

This chapter focuses on the four topics pertaining to foreign direct investment (FDI) and multinational enterprises (MNEs) that are the focus of this volume: (1) managerial decision-making processes that result in FDI and internationalization; (2) the changing national origin of MNEs, particularly those spawned by emerging markets; (3) the changing scope of MNEs, as they fine-tune and globally disperse their value chains, expand into new services, and rely increasingly on networks, alliances, and offshoring to enhance global competiveness, and speed up internationalization to the point of being "born global"; and (4) the changing relationship between MNEs and home and host countries. After surveying Yair Aharoni's significant contributions in each of these areas, the chapter offers a preview of the volume's contents on each topic. It concludes with an agenda for future research by international business scholars.

Keywords: Managerial decision making; origin of MNEs; scope of MNEs; MNE-state relations

The Future of Foreign Direct Investment and the Multinational Enterprise
Research in Global Strategic Management, Volume 15, 1–19
ISSN: 1064-4857/doi:10.1108/S1064-4857(2011)0000015007

Almost 50 years ago the seminal work of Yair Aharoni opened up several fascinating questions about how and why firms internationalize. Looking back at his lifetime of scholarship, one is struck by how often he was ahead of most scholars in writing about important new trends in international business. He was among the first to explore the role of multinationals from small countries, among the pioneers to work on state-owned enterprises and their internationalization, among the earliest to explore the globalization of services, and at the forefront of exploring the complex relationship between multinational enterprises (MNEs) and home/host governments. It is only natural therefore that a volume dedicated to Yair Aharoni should try to peer into the future, looking for important new issues and trends in foreign direct investment (FDI) and MNEs. Taking on this challenge are a group of very distinguished international business scholars, most of who have known and admired Aharoni's work for many years.

To be sure, this is also a historic moment at which to contemplate the future of FDI and MNEs. In the short run, the global financial crisis of 2008–2009 significantly curtailed FDI flows. Given the central role of international finance in facilitating foreign trade and investments, the financial crisis and the resulting credit crunch hurt the growth rate of many countries (OECD, 2009; UNCTAD, 2009). In turn, this blunted the motivation for cross-border investment; hurt the profitability of international operations; and created fears of protectionist trade policies, government rescue packages for domestic firms, and restrictions on foreign capital (UNCTAD, 2009). Official statistics confirm that outward FDI did fall quite dramatically after the crisis – by fully 47 percent between 2007 and 2009, from more than US$2 trillion to just US$1.1 trillion. Furthermore, the fall was surprisingly asymmetrical, with developed countries experiencing an average decline of 53 percent, and developing countries experiencing an average decline of only 15 percent. Interestingly, outward FDI from China kept growing even through the global recession, fueled by the massive reserves accumulated by the government and the bargain prices at which assets could be acquired abroad (Sauvant & Davies, 2010). Data from the second half of 2009 and the first half of 2010 indicated that a modest recovery in global FDI outflows may have been underway. Accordingly, UNCTAD (2010) projected global outward FDI flows to rise to US$1.2 trillion in 2010, US$ 1.3–1.5 trillion in 2011, and approach US$1.6–2.0 trillion in 2012. These FDI projections were fraught with risks and uncertainties arising from the fragility of the global economic recovery and the possibility of a double-dip recession. However, historical data reassures one that global FDI flows tend to ebb and flow with the ups and downs of the global economy, and that they tend to recover robustly after periodic slumps, as was the case most recently after the dot-com bubble burst in March 2000.

Perhaps the more interesting and important questions for international business scholars are secular trends in the origin, role, and strategy of MNEs. One such trend, well established by the turn of the 21st century, was the relative decline of MNEs from developed countries, such as the Netherlands, France, Germany, and the United Kingdom (UK), which had their heyday before World War I, or from the United States, which had their heyday in the early decades after World War II. The relative rise and fall of Japanese outward FDI occurred over a shorter period, between 1980 and 2000. In the last decade, the most significant change in the national origin of MNEs has been the rise of such firms in emerging economies. At the same time, the information revolution has caused technology-intensive products and services to become more important than nontechnology intensive ones and turned nontradable services into tradable services (Aharoni & Nachum, 2000). Likewise, small and medium enterprises (SMEs) internationalized more vigorously than before, sometimes even at birth (Oviatt & McDougall, 1994; Knight & Cavusgil, 2004). And, as noted earlier, MNEs from emerging countries, such as Brazil, Russia, India, and China, became active players in the global economy, even acquiring MNEs in the developed countries (Ramamurti & Singh, 2009; Sauvant, 2008).

All in all, the global system as we have known it since World War II, that is, a system driven largely by US hegemony manifested both in its military and political power and in its dominance of technology-intensive multinationals (Vernon, 1966), seemed to be undergoing dramatic change in the 2000s. The aim of this volume is to explore those changes and to understand what they imply for the future of FDI and MNEs.

The famous Danish physicist Neils Bohr once noted that "It's hard to make predictions, especially about the future." Nevertheless, we gathered a group of leading international business and strategy scholars and urged them to speculate on the future of FDI and MNEs in their areas of expertise. Building on Aharoni's work, the chapters that follow look at four aspects of FDI and MNEs:

- The role of managers and the decision-making process that lead firms to internationalize and make overseas investments;
- The changing national origin of MNEs, with the rise of new MNEs from both large and small emerging economies;

- The changing focus of MNEs from natural resources and manufacturing to a variety of services, along with a greater tendency to disperse the value chain globally and to offshore services to third parties, coupled with the growing propensity of smaller firms to become multinational players;
- The changing relationship between MNEs and the state, at home and abroad, and the new challenges governments face in harnessing MNEs for the greater good.

AHARONI'S CONTRIBUTIONS TO INTERNATIONAL BUSINESS

It is rare to find a scholar who has contributed to as many fields of international business as Yair Aharoni. He has touched multiple subjects that have significantly contributed to our understanding of FDI and MNEs and that are still relevant. Without claiming to review Aharoni's contributions comprehensively, we summarize below his main works in the four areas being explored in this volume.

The Decision to Internationalize

Aharoni's (1966) seminal book, *The Foreign Investment Decision Process*, based on his 1961 doctoral research, has been one of the most influential works regarding the decision of firms to engage in FDI. In this book, as well as in subsequent work (see, for instance, Aharoni, Maimon, & Segev, 1978; Aharoni, 1993), Aharoni highlights the decision to engage in FDI as a special case of a strategic decision. He emphasizes the complexity of taking such a decision, given the multiple attitudes and opinions within and outside an organization. An important observation is the critical role of a "champion" within the firm who is emotionally invested in the decision to invest abroad, and who presents compelling arguments for foreign expansion and highlights the negative consequences of inaction. Without someone fighting this battle, it can be very difficult to persuade key decisions makers that foreign investment is within the organization's "feasibility zone."

Thus, Aharoni notes that the successful implementation of an FDI decision is dependent upon multiple factors, including the correct identification of the organization's feasibility zone and its leverage points. In this respect Aharoni identifies the complex interrelationships between changing attitudes, opinions, and social relationships, as well as the role of past experience, present events, and perception of the future as critical factors affecting the decision to invest abroad. This path-breaking work laid the foundation for a stream of work in the 1970s and 1980s about the internationalization process (Czinkota, 1982; Johanson & Vahlne, 1977; Reid, 1981) and FDI (Dunning, 1988, 1993). It is important to note that Aharoni's doctoral thesis of 1961 was in fact one of the first examples of a behavioral theory of the firm, made popular by the contemporaneous study of Cyert and March (1963).

National Origin of MNEs

Aharoni has also contributed much to the shift of scholars' focus from large industrial MNEs based in developed countries to smaller MNEs, often based in small countries. In a series of works (e.g., Aharoni, 1992, 1994, 2000b, 2009; Aharoni & Hirsch, 1996) Aharoni explained how small MNEs from small countries, such as Israel, could overcome their inherent scale disadvantages relative to large MNEs based in large home markets. Among the strategies he identified were the following: focusing on well-defined segments to avoid direct competition with large MNEs that often serve mainstream markets; specializing and customizing products and services in innovative ways to meet specific customer needs and to capture premium prices; reducing marketing costs by engaging in large transactions, which often means targeting business-to-business (B2B) rather than business-to-customer (B2C) transactions; reacting quickly to customer needs by being technologically flexible; and providing superior pre- and postsale service. This line of work has contributed significantly to the understating of the born-global phenomenon (Oviatt & McDougall, 1994; Knight & Cavusgil, 2004). Many of these ideas have relevance also for explaining the strategies of new multinationals from developing countries, which too suffer from being small, from needing to avoid head-on conflicts with Western MNEs, and which start with a limited set of competitive advantages (Ramamurti, 2009).

Scope of MNEs

Yair Aharoni was one of the first scholars to identify the growth of MNEs in services, as opposed to industrial MNEs that develop, produce, and sell goods. In a series of studies, Aharoni noted the difficulties of supplying services abroad due to the intensive interaction that is required between the service provider and its customers (Aharoni, 1993; Aharoni & Nachum, 2000). He analyzed the general phenomenon of FDI in services while paying close attention to specific services, such as accounting (Aharoni, 1999) and airlines (Aharoni, 2004). Among the insights from this line of work was recognizing the role of reputation in enabling firms to provide services abroad (Aharoni, 2000a) and recognizing that alliances with local firms may be necessary to build relationships and credibility with customers, suppliers, regulators, and other local institutional actors (Aharoni, 1993). Aharoni (1996) further emphasized that integration and centralization of global operations is an important determinant of the ability of foreign service providers to successfully compete abroad, because it allows firm-specific knowledge to be transferred efficiently to foreign subsidiaries. Since efficient knowledge transfer often requires standardization and automation of firm-specific knowledge, internationalizing services providers must make tough decisions about which parts of their knowledge base to transfer outside the home country, including to strategic partners. Both choices are likely to be highly influenced by the strategy and organization structure in place to support such transfers. Such choice should allow for efficient knowledge transfer without giving away the firm's core competencies or its competitive advantages.

MNEs and the State

Aharoni has also made several notable contributions to the literature on business–government relations, starting with the special case where government itself is in business – through state-owned enterprises (SOEs). Aharoni recognized, like writers at the time, that SOEs could be instruments of social and economic policy (Aharoni & Vernon, 1981), but he was astute enough to recognize also that SOE managers worked assiduously to increase their autonomy vis-à-vis bureaucrats and politicians, sometimes by playing one master in government against another (e.g., Aharoni, 1981, 1982, 1986; Aharoni, Maimon, & Segev, 1981). Aharoni also studied SOEs' motivations for internationalization and their competitive advantages in doing so, thus becoming one of the first scholars, along with Raymond Vernon, to study this new breed of MNEs (Aharoni, 1980; Aharoni & Seidler, 1986).

The bulk of Aharoni's work on business–government relations focused on the firm's relation with its home government, rather than host governments. Given the structure of the Israeli economy, when most of the country's important enterprises were owned either by the government or the Histradut (the largest workers' union), Aharoni's interest in state-owned and collectively-owned enterprises is not surprising. He published several studies on the structure and conduct of the Israeli economy (e.g., Aharoni, 1975), including one comparing decision-making by the boards of the three types of organizations in the Israeli economy (Aharoni, 1963). He presaged research in two topics that were rarely studied at the time: the use of lobbying or "political strategy" by firms to promote their economic interests, and the tendency of firms to diversify into new businesses in order to grow, forming what we call "business groups" today. He also analyzed all the official and unofficial cartels in Israel in which most large ownership groups participated and interacted.

In other words, Aharoni regularly crossed traditional academic boundaries to study the interplay between firms, markets, bureaucrats, and politicians, frequently in an international setting (Aharoni, 1977, 1981b, 1986, 1991a). In the 1980s and 1990s, he built on his knowledge of SOEs to study how governments privatized these firms and deregulated their industries (Aharoni, 1988, 1991b, 1997). As many privatized firms and new start-ups internationalized aggressively in the "flat world" of the 2000s, Aharoni wrote on that phenomenon as well (e.g., Aharoni, 2009).

AN OVERVIEW OF THE VOLUME

We turn next to the chapters in this volume in each of the four areas of focus (see Table 1). Most articles were written specially for this volume, keeping in mind its focus and the goal of exploring emerging issues in FDI and MNEs.

The Decision to Internationalize

The first chapter of the book is the only previously published piece to be included in this volume. Authored by Aharoni for a volume by Devinney et al. (2010), it is reproduced here because it offers a fascinating and comprehensive review of behavioral elements in FDIs, echoing in a contemporary context many of the issues raised in *The Foreign Investment Decision Process* (1966). Aharoni calls again for more attention to behavioral models of managers, highlighting in particular the critical impact of cognitively limited managers and warns against relying too much on economic models based on rational, omniscient decision makers (e.g., Dunning, 1988, 1993).

Table 1.   Key Topic Areas and Papers in this Volume.

Chapter	Author(s)	Title	Sample of Aharoni's Works
Part I: The Decision to Internationalize			
2	Yair Aharoni	Behavioral elements in foreign direct investment	Aharoni (1966, 1993) Aharoni, Maimon & Segev (1978)
3	Timothy Devinney	Bringing manager's decision models into FDI research	
4	Jens Forssbaeck and Lars Oxelheim	FDI and the role of financial market quality	
Part II: New MNEs			
5	Yair Aharoni and Ravi Ramamurti	The evolution of multinationals	Aharoni (1993, 1996, 1999, 2000a, 2004) Aharoni & Nachum (2000)
6	Ravi Ramamurti	New players in FDI: Sovereign wealth funds, private equity, and emerging-market MNEs	
7	Stephane Girod and Joshua Bellin	Revisiting the modern multinational enterprise theory: An emerging-market multinational perspective	
Part III: The Changing Role of MNEs			
8	Peter Buckley	The impact of globalization and the emergence of the global factory	Aharoni (1992, 1994, 2000b, 2009) Aharoni & Hirsch (1996)
9	Alan Rugman and Paloma Almodóvar	The born-global illusion and the regional nature of international business	
10	Niron Hashai, Tamar Almor, Marina Papanastassiou, Fragkiskos Filippaios, and Ruth Rama	Unraveling the relationships between internationalization and product diversification among the world's largest food and beverage enterprises	
11	Arie Lewin	Trade in services: The global sourcing of business services	

Table 1. (*Continued*)

Chapter	Author(s)	Title	Sample of Aharoni's Works
12	Lilach Nachum	Governance of foreign affiliates as a distinctive choice between networks, market and hierarchy	
13	Niron Hashai	Global service multinationals from a small open economy: The case of Israeli high-tech services providers	
Part IV: MNEs and the State			
14	Seev Hirsch	If Teva changes its "nationality," would Israel's economy be affected?	Aharoni (1963, 1975, 1977, 1980, 1981a, 1981b, 1982, 1986, 1991a, 1991b, 1997, 2000c) Aharoni & Vernon (1981) Aharoni et al. (1981); Aharoni & Seidler (1986)
15	Pervez Ghauri and Rebecca Firth	The impact of foreign direct investment on local countries: Western firms in emerging markets	
16	Karl Sauvant	The regulatory framework for investment: Where are we headed?	

Aharoni's concern is echoed in the chapter by Devinney, who presents a structure for incorporating managerial decision models into management research in general and FDI research in particular. Devinney argues that contemporary international business research should be more deliberative in its understanding of the decision-making processes of managers, and aspire for a tighter linkage between theoretical structures and empirical modeling. He demonstrates possible ways of achieving such goals via formalization of FDI and internationalization decisions.

In the final chapter of Part I, Forssbaeck and Oxelheim analyze the role of financial factors in undertaking cross-border acquisitions. Using a more traditional economic approach, they propose that financial firm-specific advantages drive international acquisitions, while taking into account the sophistication of the home-country's financial markets. Forssbaeck and Oxelheim find that the cost of equity is consistently and significantly more powerful in explaining cross-border acquisitions than alternative explanations. The stand-alone effect of debt costs, on the other hand, is indeterminate. However, when conditioned by home-country financial development, both cost of equity and cost of debt matter. Forssbaeck and Oxelheim further show that the effect of cost of capital on FDI is significantly stronger for firms from countries with relatively underdeveloped financially sectors.

New MNEs

The next part looks at how and why the nationality of multinationals has been changing over time. Aharoni and Ramamurti look at this issue over the last century, starting with European MNEs, which internationalized at the beginning of the 20th century, followed by US multinationals in the post-World War I period, then Japanese MNEs in the 1980s, and, most recently, emerging-market MNEs (EMNEs), led by the BRIC (Brazil, India, China, and Russia) economies. They see this evolution as being the result of changes in government policy, technology, capital markets, and social networks. Among the consequences are the greater diversity in the national origin and industrial distribution of MNEs, and a speeding up of the pace of internationalization. The growth of EMNEs has prodded developed-country MNEs to engage more actively in knowledge- and strategic-asset-seeking FDI, rather than the traditional resource- or efficiency-seeking FDI. Aharoni and Ramamurti anticipate that in the future MNEs will be much more diverse, differentiated by national origin, size, and motivation for FDI. The one-size-fits-all approach to MNEs just will not suffice in this new era.

Given this point of view, in the following chapter, Ramamurti looks at three "new" players in FDI, including sovereign wealth funds (SWFs), private equity (PE) firms, and EMNEs. He notes that SWFs have been around for decades, although they gained prominence in the 2000s as their resources swelled, either because of high commodity prices (e.g. oil exporters) or large current account surpluses (e.g. Asian exporters). However, he concludes that SWFs have been, and will continue to be, unimportant players in FDI, despite their high visibility, with the possible exception of SWFs from China and Abu Dhabi, which may follow Singapore's example and take significant equity positions in foreign enterprises. Most others lack the expertise to select and manage large equity stakes in individual foreign companies. As for private equity firms, he expects their role in FDI to be highly volatile, ranging from very important when capital markets are flush with resources to unimportant when the opposite is the case. In contrast, EMNEs are steadily gaining in importance as sources of FDI and will continue to do so as these countries become engines of the world economy. Ramamurti further contends that EMNEs will contribute significantly to inclusive and sustainable growth, because they are better placed than developed-country MNEs to meet the needs of low-income customers and to adopt "green" technologies, such as wind and solar energy or electric vehicles.

This part concludes with a study by Girod and Bellin that explores the ability of EMNEs to both integrate their organizations globally and yet be locally responsive. It aims to delve deeper into the phenomenon of EMNEs and identify their prospective strategy and structure. Girod and Bellin investigate three EMNEs – one in Asia and two in an African country, in the telecommunications and energy sectors – and find that distinctive aspects of their national competitive context cause them to conduct global and local business differently than developed-country MNEs. Based on these findings, they assert the need for a new theoretical lens to conceptualize the global-integration and local-responsiveness strategies of EMNEs. They inductively develop such a theory that accounts for the evolution of organizational capabilities and global strategy in EMNEs.

The Changing Role of MNEs

This part starts with Buckley's analysis of the structure of the future global system. Buckley analyzes the rise of the "global factory" – a globally integrated network centered on a focal MNE. The main argument made by Buckley is that this type of global system emerges as a response to the increased volatility of the global economy and is driven by the need for flexibility in the location and control of "fine-sliced" activities, the avoidance of monopoly, and the evolution of new management skills. Given this point of view, FDI becomes only one strategy among several utilized by globally integrated MNEs.

Given this broader view of the future global system, the following chapters investigate different types of MNEs that are likely to exist in this global system. These MNEs may be distinguished by their size and focus on products versus services. Rugman and Almodóvar re-examine the focus of Aharoni on small MNEs in light of the greater availability of firm-level data today. More specifically, they concentrate on the "born-global" firm, claiming that the born-global literature misuses the word "global." Their main point is that globalization is associated with economic integration, modernity, and cultural commonalities. Yet obviously there remain barriers to economic integration in the form of discriminatory national and regional trade and investment regulations. Modernity is largely confined to relatively higher income groups and is denied to poorer people, while cultural and religious differences appear to be robust (Rugman, 2005). Therefore, Rugman and Almodóvar argue, born-global firms are more likely to operate on a regional basis where more commonalities are likely to exist and hence should be termed "born regional." Those small and young firms that are trying to act on a global basis are doomed to suffer from an initial "born-global illusion" and become overly taxed by their liabilities of foreignness, which are likely to hamper their performance.

In contrast, Hashai, Almor, Papanastassiou, Filippaios, and Rama examine a totally different type of MNE that is still likely to play a dominant role in the future global system–the world's largest food and beverage enterprises. Hashai et al. are interested in the growth mechanisms employed by large industrial MNEs and more specifically examine the interrelationships between internationalization and product diversification of such firms. Based on the argument that food and beverage enterprises enjoy economies of scope when moderately diversifying into new countries and product areas, but encounter resource constraints when extremely diversified and internationalized, Hashai et al. expect to find an inverted U-shaped relationship between the two strategies. Nevertheless, the authors find that the relationships between the two strategies show both an inverted U-shaped (when geographic diversification is the dependent variable and product diversification the independent one) and a U-shaped pattern (when product diversification is the dependent variable and geographic diversification the independent one). These results imply that the relationships between internationalization and product diversification among food and beverage enterprises are more complex than currently conceived. The authors argue that differences in the efficiency of managing a multinational organization versus the efficiency of running a multibusiness organization may explain the observed different relationships.

In terms of the expected increased propensity of service MNEs, the next chapter presents Lewin's analysis of the global sourcing of services. The chapter reviews the recent development of trade in business services that involves the demand for and the emergence of a global outsourcing industry for many types of business services. It highlights the dramatic increase in the offshoring of business services in the last two decades and, echoing the work of Aharoni on managerial behavior, models the managerial decision to engage in the offshoring of services.

Given the increased propensity of global sourcing of services, two issues come to the forefront. One is the choice of such MNEs between market and hierarchies and the second is the factors affecting the extent of internationalization of service MNEs. The following chapter by Nachum uses a sample of international law firms to analyze how the foreignness and multinationality of their overseas affiliates affects their choice between networks, markets, and hierarchy as alternative modes of governance. She shows that market relationships are the preferred mode of foreign affiliates for at least this category of professional service providers, challenging the view that hierarchical ties to the parent and other affiliates is the major source of advantage for foreign affiliates. Her study reinforces Buckley's view of direct investment and hierarchy as only one of many entry strategies available to MNEs.

In terms of the distinct factors affecting the level of internationalization of service MNEs, Hashai investigates how technological knowledge affects the internationalization of firms from a small open economy, Israel. He finds an inverted U-shaped relationship between the level of technological know-ledge and extent of foreign services provision. This relationship is arguably the joint outcome of the facilitating and inhibiting effects of technological knowledge on the ability to provide services abroad. Hashai further shows that standardization and automation moderate this relationship positively.

MNEs and the State

The section on the relationships of MNEs and their home and host countries starts with a fundamental question posed by Hirsch: does the nationality of MNEs matter? He does so through a case study of Israel's leading MNE, Teva, the world's largest generic drug producer, and asks what difference its nationality would make to Teva's strategic behavior. The paper explores the proposition that even in a world in which national borders and physical distance matter less than ever, the extra costs of doing business abroad – termed "distance premium" by the author – continue to favor home country over host country locations and intraorganizational over interorganizational value adding activities. The paper concludes that, with the exception of stockholders whose welfare is generally not affected by change of nationality, other stakeholders in the new country adopted by the MNE as its "home" would gain at the expense of stakeholders in original home country.

In the next chapter, Ghauri and Firth take a more focused view and investigate the impact of FDI on local firms in host economies. Given the increased propensity of service MNEs, discussed in the previous section, it is only natural that Ghauri and Firth specifically focus on the service sector. They examine both backward and forward linkages and their effects on domestic firms. Their results indicate that the main factors which facilitate linkage formation are subsidiary related variables, and more specifically the mode of entry into the local market, subsidiary autonomy, level of embeddedness, and subsidiary role. They further find that over time the impact of FDI on local firms is positive with increased employment, productivity, and significant upgrading of skills and competencies. This study confirms the importance of the subsidiary in linkage formation and exemplifies how the externalities occurring from linkage formation in the service sector may benefit local firms and subsequently aid local economic development as a whole.

In the concluding chapter of this section, Sauvant takes a macro view of the benefits countries derive from inbound FDI. He critically examines the motivations of host country governments for liberalizing national regulatory frameworks for FDI and establishing a strong international investment law regime. He argues that governments are re-evaluating their stance toward FDI, or at least certain types of it. Sauvant calls for a re-evaluation of such policies and pushing toward regulatory changes that lead to a regime that places more emphasis on maintaining policy space for host country governments while still protecting the interests of foreign investors.

CONCLUSION

This volume builds on and echoes many of the themes of Yair Aharoni's work and highlights opportunities for future research by international business scholars. An illustrative list of promising research questions, emerging from the chapters in this volume, is presented in Table 2.

One important direction for future research is incorporating to a greater extent the role of managers in determining FDI and internationalization decisions. As Aharoni points out in Chapter 2, international business scholars often fall into the trap of assuming (incorrectly) that all measurable variables are more important than all hard-to-measure variables. We need a more thoughtful and rigorous approach to understanding the role of

Table 2. Questions for Further Research.

Theme	Research Questions
The decision to internationalize	• How do managers and organizational decision-making processes affect FDI and internationalization? • What mix of rational considerations and rationally-bounded managerial judgments determine a firm's internationalization and FDI decisions?
New MNEs	• What type of MNEs are likely to dominate the future global system in terms of size, national origin, sector, and motivation for FDI? • Are extant theories of the MNE (e.g., the OLI framework) adequate to explain the rise of emerging-market MNEs? • Under what conditions will emerging-market MNEs compete effectively with or triumph against developed-country MNEs? • What types of strategies and organizational structures are likely to be adopted by emerging-market MNEs, and why?
The changing role of MNEs	• Which types of foreign market servicing modes combinations are likely to dominate in the future global system? • To what extent are "born-global" firms really global, and why? • What are the dominant factors affecting the internationalization of service MNEs? • What are the dominant factors affecting the entry mode choice of service MNEs? • How do firms aspiring to grow choose between product vs. geographic diversification, and how does that affect firm performance? • Why are MNEs moving away from hierarchy to networks (alliances) or arm's-length market relationships, including offshoring? • Which services can MNEs offshore, and what challenges arise in managing and integrating offshored activities with the rest of the organization?
MNEs and the state	• Does the nationality of an MNE affect which value chain activities it carries out at different locations, and what returns stakeholders earn in different countries? • Is an MNE more likely to carry out high value-added activities at home than abroad? • What spillovers are generated in host countries by FDI in services? • Given the fierce competition among countries for FDI, how should governments encourage inbound FDI while still retaining flexibility to do what is best for the host country?

managers in strategic decision-making, not a blind and single-minded pursuit of formal, rational models.

A second important direction for research is studying the growing diversity of MNEs. The one-size-fits-all approach, shaped largely by the experience of the United States and a few other countries, just will not suffice in a world with diverse MNEs. We know MNEs are heavily influenced by home-country characteristics, especially in the early stages of internationalization, and as the national origin of MNEs broadens, we need frameworks that can incorporate key national differences into a general theory of MNEs. Extant theory is a great starting point for a general theory, but only a starting point. Much more work is needed, for instance, to see if EMNEs can be understood adequately with theories developed from the study of developed-country MNEs.

A third promising direction for future research is to extend theories of MNEs, often based on manufacturing or extractive firms, to service firms. We also need to understand more fully how MNEs are reconfiguring their value chains in a "flat world," and how they are managing the resulting organization. Offshoring of business services is another important topic for inquiry, both when it is done through captive units and through third parties. We are still a long way from fully understanding the reasons why MNEs choose certain internationalization paths or entry modes. We also need to understand why firms sometimes choose to grow by diversifying into new products and at other times by diversifying into new geographies, which is riskier or more profitable, and when. Once again extant theory is a useful starting point, but it should be refined and modified as needed to account for new types of MNE, using new types of strategies, in a new global context. A particularly interesting case here is the "born-global" or "born-regional" firm.

Finally, we need to do a better job of understating the interplay between MNEs and governments, and between public and private interests. The basic question of how the nationality of MNEs might affect their strategic behavior and impact on countries is still not well understood. We also need research on how host governments can best harness MNEs, whether by maximizing spillovers to local suppliers, customers, and competitors, or by retaining greater policy leeway to capture gains from inbound FDI while still protecting the interests of MNEs.

Our understanding of FDI and MNEs has come a long way since the path-breaking work of scholars like Yair Aharoni. But as the chapters in this volume show, there is still much we do not understand, and much we need to rethink as the world in which MNEs operate changes.

REFERENCES

Aharoni, Y. (1963). *The functions and roles of directors* (in Hebrew). Tel Aviv: Israel Institute of Productivity.

Aharoni, Y. (1966). *The foreign investment decision process.* Boston, MA: Harvard University, Graduate School of Business Administration, Division of Research.

Aharoni, Y. (1980). The state-owned enterprise as a competitor in international markets. *Columbia Journal of World Business, 15*(1), 14–22.

Aharoni, Y. (1975). *Structure and conduct in israeli industry* (in Hebrew). Tel Aviv: The Israel Institute of Business Research and Gomeh Publications.

Aharoni, Y. (1977). *Markets, planning and development.* Cambridge, MA: Ballinger.

Aharoni, Y. (1981a). Performance evaluation in state-owned enterprises: A process perspective. *Management Science, 29*(11), 1340–1347.

Aharoni, Y. (1981b). *The no risk society.* London: Chatham House Publishers, Inc.

Aharoni, Y. (1982). State-owned enterprise: An agent without a principal. In: Leroy Jones, et al. (Eds), *Public enterprise in less-developed countries* (pp. 67–76). New York: Cambridge University Press.

Aharoni, Y. (1986). *The evolution and management of state owned enterprises.* Cambridge, MA: Ballinger.

Aharoni, Y. (1988). Why do governments privatize. In: J. Forsyth, B. Obel & R. Burton (Eds), *Organizational responses to the new business conditions: An empirical perspective* (pp. 7–23). Amsterdam: Elsevier.

Aharoni, Y. (1991a). *Israel's political economy: The dreams and the realities.* London: Routledge Press.

Aharoni, Y. (1991b). On measuring the success of privatization. In: R. Ramamurti & R. Vernon (Eds), *Privatization and control of state-owned enterprises* (pp. 73–85). Washington, D.C: World Bank.

Aharoni, Y. (1992). The role of small firms in an interdependent world. In: R. M. Burton, B. Obel & J. Forsyth (Eds), *Strategies for players in a larger world: The effect of regulatory and information changes* (pp. 11–32). Amsterdam: Elsevier.

Aharoni, Y. (1993). The internationalization process in professional business service firms: Some tentative conclusions. In: Y. Aharoni (Ed.), *Coalitions and competition: The globalization of professional business services* (pp. 280–285). London: Routledge.

Aharoni, Y. (1994). How can small firms achieve competitive advantage in an interdependent world? In: T. Agmon & R. Drobnick (Eds), *Small firms in global competition* (pp. 9–18). Oxford: Oxford University Press.

Aharoni, Y. (1996). The organization of global service MNES. *International Studies of Management and Organization, 26*(2), 6–23.

Aharoni, Y. (Ed.). (1997). *Changing roles of state intervention in services in an era of open international markets.* Albany, NY: SUNY Press.

Aharoni, Y. (1999). Internationalization of professional services: Implications for accounting firms. In: D. Brock, M. Powell & C. R. (Bob) Hinings (Eds), *Restructuring the professional organization* (pp. 20–40). London: Routledge.

Aharoni, Y. (2000a). The role of reputation in global professional business services. In: Y. Aharoni & L. Nahum (Eds), *Globalization of services: Some implications for theory and practice* (pp. 125–141). London: Routledge.

Aharoni, Y. (2000b). Globalization and the small, open economy. In: T. Almor & N. Hashai (Eds), *FDI, international trade and the economics of peacemaking papers in honor of Seev Hirsch* (pp. 90–116). Rishon Lezion: College of Management Academic Division.

Aharoni, Y. (2000c). The performance of state owned enterprises. In: P. A. Toninelli (Ed.), *The rise and fall of state-owned enterprise in the western world* (pp. 49–72). Cambridge: Cambridge University Press.

Aharoni, Y. (2004). The race for FDI in services – The case of the airline industry. In: P. Ghauri & L. Oxelheim (Eds), *European Union and the race for foreign direct investment in Europe* (pp. 381–406). Amsterdam: Elsevier.

Aharoni, Y. (2009). Israeli multinationals: Competing from a small open economy. In: R. Ramamurti & J. V. Singh (Eds), *Emerging multinationals in emerging markets* Chapter 12, (pp. 352–396). Cambridge, UK: Cambridge University Press.

Aharoni, Y., & Hirsch, S. (1996). The competitive potential of technology-intensive industries in developing countries. In: M. Svetlicic & H. W. Singer (Eds), *The world economy challenges of globalization and regionalization* (pp. 99–118). Hundmills, London and New York: Macmillan Press Ltd. and St., Martin Press Inc.

Aharoni, Y., Maimon, Z., & Segev, E. (1978). Performance and autonomy in organizations: Determining dominant environmental components. *Management Science*, *24*(9), 949–959.

Aharoni, Y., Maimon, Z., & Segev, E. (1981). Interrelationships between environmental dependencies: A basis for tradeoffs to increase autonomy. *Management Science*, *28*(2), 197–208.

Aharoni, Y., & Nachum, L. (2000). *Globalization of services: Some implications for theory and practice*. London: Routledge.

Aharoni, Y., & Seidler, L. (1986). Foreign subsidiaries of state-owned enterprises: Host country response. In: A. T. Negandhi, H. Thomas & K. L. K. Rao (Eds), *Research in international business and international-relations* (pp. 151–176). Connecticut: JAI.

Aharoni, Y., & Vernon, R. (1981). *State owned enterprises in the western economies*. London: Croom Helm Publishers, Inc.

Aharoni, Y. (2010). Behavioral elements in foreign direct investment. In: T. M. Devinney, T. Pedersen & L. Tihanyi (Eds), *The past present and future of international business and management* (pp. 73–111). Bingley: Emerald.

Czinkota, M. R. (1982). *Export development strategies: US promotion policies*. New York: Praeger.

Cyert, R. M., & March, J. G. (1963). *A behavioral theory of the firm*. Englewood Cliffs, NJ: Prentice Hall.

Dunning, J. H. (1988). The eclectic paradigm of international production: A restatement and some possible extensions. *Journal of International Business Studies*, *19*(1), 1–31.

Dunning, J. H. (1993). *Multinational enterprises and the global economy*. Reading, MA: Addison-Wesley.

Johanson, J., & Vahlne, J.-E. (1977). The internationalization process of the firm – A model of knowledge development and increasing foreign market commitment. *Journal of International Business Studies*, *8*(1), 23–32.

Knight, G., & Cavusgil, T. (2004). Innovation, organizational capabilities, and the born-global firm. *Journal of International Business Studies*, *35*, 124–141.

OECD. (2009). Status report: Inventory of investment measures taken between 15 November 2008 and 15 June 2009. OECD Secretary General.

Oviatt, B. M., & McDougall, P. P. (1994). Toward a theory of international new ventures. *Journal of International Business Studies*, *25*(1), 45–64.

Ramamurti, R. (2009). What have we learned about emerging-market MNEs? In: R. Ramamurti & J. V. Singh (Eds), *Emerging multinationals in emerging markets* Chapter 13, (pp. 399–426). Cambridge, UK: Cambridge University Press.

Ramamurti, R., & Singh, J. V. (Eds). (2009). *Emerging multinationals in emerging markets.* Cambridge, UK: Cambridge University Press.

Reid, S. D. (1981). The decision-maker and export entry and expansion. *Journal of International Business Studies, 10,* 101–112.

Rugman, A. M. (2005). *The regional multinationals. MNEs and global strategic management.* Cambridge: Cambridge University Press.

Sauvant, K. P. (Ed.) (2008). *The rise of transnational corporations from emerging countries – Threat or opportunity?* Cheltenham, UK: Edward Elgar.

Sauvant, K. P., & Davies, K. (2010). Le Defi Chinois. *Project Syndicate,* December 2. Available at http://www.project-syndicate.org/commentary/sauvant4/English

UNCTAD. (2009). *Assessing the impact of the current financial and economic crisis on global FDI flows.* New York: United Nations publication.

UNCTAD (2010). *World Investment Report.* Geneva: UNCTAD.

Vernon, R. (1966). International investment and international trade in the product cycle. *Quarterly Journal of Economics* (80), 190–207.

PART I
THE DECISION TO
INTERNATIONALIZE

BEHAVIORAL ELEMENTS IN FOREIGN DIRECT INVESTMENT DECISIONS [☆]

Yair Aharoni

ABSTRACT

The success of multinational enterprises (MNEs) is at least as much a function of management ability and behavior as it is of industry characteristics or environmental factors. These managers display human limitations that affect judgment. Yet International business (IB) researchers tend to ignore management in their research, treating the firm as a black box. To the extent top management team (TMT) is considered, rational behavior in classical economic sense is assumed. Behavioral elements were studied by others in different fields. Clearly, managers behave according to different rules than those assumed in much of the IB literature. Further, managers are not part of a herd but unique. The result of such a lacuna is that theory fails to predict actual behavior and does not allow best guidance for policy options. The chapter summarizes research on behavioral decision making and calls for its application in future research in international business.

[☆] An earlier version of this chapter was originally published in "The Past, Present and Future of International Business and Management," *Advances in International Management* (Vol. 23, pp. 73–112).

The Future of Foreign Direct Investment and the Multinational Enterprise
Research in Global Strategic Management, Volume 15, 23–60
ISSN: 1064-4857/doi:10.1108/S1064-4857(2011)0000015008

Keywords: Managerial decision-making; bounded rationality; behavior; multinational enterprise; foreign direct investment; environmental uncertainty; judgment; heterogeneity; top management teams

Nothing is more fundamental in setting our research agenda and informing our research methods than our view on the nature of the human beings whose behavior we are studying. It makes a difference. A very large difference. (Simon, 1985, p. 303)

There is no general principle that prevents the creation of an economic theory based on other hypotheses than rationality. (Arrow, 1987)

INTRODUCTION

In 1960 I was a young doctoral student. I was distressed by the apparent failure of less developed countries (LDCs) to attract U.S. manufacturing investments. Specifically, I noted that the fervent attempts to encourage foreign direct investments (FDI) by enacting the Law for Encouragement of Capital Investments did not in fact materialize. Therefore, I resolved to study the way foreign investment decisions are made by U.S. manufacturing firms. I hoped that by finding out the considerations business persons took into account in making FDI decisions I could unearth ways and means to increase FDIs in LDCs. I assumed that tax incentives permit a higher rate of return and therefore can make otherwise unpromising investments attractive. The conferral of tax benefits will induce foreign investors to initiate projects which they would not otherwise have undertaken. The problem seemed to be straightforward: how large should the incentives be?

I soon found out that the tax incentives did not play the decisive role I expected them to play. Moreover, the picture emerging from my field research seemed to be one of utterly irrational behavior and a complete lack of economic logic. The decision process had very little in common with the classical economic theory of capital investments. It was necessary to look at the system as a whole, recognizing that decisions are made under uncertainty within an organization and a social system. Once I changed the lens what seemed irrational made sense.

I submitted my doctoral thesis in 1961. Sometimes thereafter, a spate of publications appeared that bore many similarities to the major themes of my thesis. One important contribution that laid out a conceptual basis for looking at the decision-making process was *a behavioral theory of the firm* by Cyert and March (1963). I incorporated these contributions and others when I wrote the Foreign Investment Decision Process (1966a).

Many things have changed since then. These changes made some theories obsolete and modified the nature of the multinational enterprise (MNE). *New technolog*ies impacted quite a few firms. Major new products created totally different markets and new industries. Search engines, dial up modems, and internet browsers – all mitigate transaction costs; connect people and the dispersed components of MNEs worldwide. The rapid coverage of the world with internet facilities changed fundamentally the ways people communicate across borders and the time it takes to respond to a message (Kogut, 2003). One result has been an increased offshore outsourcing of business services – leading Thomas Friedman (2005) to declare that the world is flat. Another result is the surge of electronic trade. In addition, in a growing number of industries, that is, aerospace, telecommunications, or pharmaceuticals, even the largest national market is too small to amortize the enormous research and development expenses associated with new products. The firm must expand into many national markets (Mytelka & Delapierre, 1999).

International operations have grown also because of fundamental changes in the *international political environment*. World exports have increased from $60 billion in 1950 to $16,070 billion in 2008. The multilateral trading arrangement under the auspices of GATT and later World Trade Organization (WTO) has been a necessary precondition to enable this growth. The General Agreement on Services opened up many avenues for FDIs in services – an area not long ago regarded as nontradable. World trade in commercial services grew from $365 billion in 1980 to $3,778 billion in 2008. In the 1960s, managers of international oil firms were able to maintain market share agreements even during periods of oil glut – generating oligopoly rents through political behavior and collusion (Jacoby, 1974; Moran, 1987; Penrose, 1968). Other firms were able to survive by enlisting political support to prevent imports of more efficient firms. A "political strategy" was an important ingredient to gain competitive advantage (Yoffie & Milner, 1989). Stopford and Strange (1991, p. 1) argued that "Firms have become more involved with governments and governments have come to recognize their increased dependence on the scarce resources controlled by firms." As a result, states have become increasingly dependent on MNEs to achieve technological competitiveness. In some countries, "social partnerships" appear to have been operating without serious frictions, allowing firms to collude to allocate market share (Katzenstein, 1984). However, a collusion strategy may be less successful in some cultures than in others (Eckbo, 1976). Deregulation of many infrastructure services has also created opportunities for more international investment. These changes stemmed to a large extent from *changing beliefs*. More and more intellectuals – and then government officials – became ardent believers in the efficiency of free markets or at least disillusioned with the ability of governments to plan and direct the economy. These beliefs led to an almost universal urge to contain the extent of government intervention in the management of resource allocation and to coordinate economic policies, recognizing the fragility of the international financial system. As a result of globalization, the options open to national governments are severely constrained.

In 1960, U.S. MNEs invested to jump tariff walls and many other national restrictions on trade. Since the 1990s, it is generally accepted that open and competitive markets are necessary to ensure economic growth. The Berlin Wall crumbled in November 1989. Since then, the former Soviet Empire disaggregated, its different components moved toward liberal economic policies. Most economies moved from import substitution policies and protection of domestic firm to policies aimed to achieve export-led growth through reduction of government's intervention. These policy changes forced domestic firms to upgrade their products and services, trim costs, and benchmark themselves against best-in-class global competitors. Several of these firms also ventured abroad, in search of markets, lower costs, and resources. To be sure, many economic activities, for example, agriculture or airlines are still highly protected. Capital is being globalized, but national authorities try hard to limit movements of labor across borders. Further, confidence in free market economics, until recently virtually impregnable, has been undermined by the financial crisis of 2007–2008.

The macro economic environment has also changed dramatically. The direct convertibility of the U.S. dollar to gold and the Bretton Woods fixed exchange regime were abandoned. Currencies in the developed world moved to a full float, followed by two oil crises in 1973 and 1979, a decade of high interest rates in the United States, and a debt crisis in many developing countries. The Plaza Accord in 1985 realigned the value of the major currencies and Japanese FDIs zoomed. The Euro Zone was created in 1998; in 1999 the Euro was born (as electronic currency, becoming a cash currency in 2002), and soon rivaled the U.S. dollar as the currency of choice for international business. A financial crisis gripped Thailand, spreading to many Asian countries (Kaufman, Krueger, & Hunter, 1999). All these changes also led to a shift in the distribution of economic and political power in the world. As one example, in 2008 China became the world's largest manufacturing exporter.

The prevailing views on MNEs were also altered fundamentally. In the world of neoclassical economics, FDI had little place (Kindlebeger, 1969). During the 1990s, intrafirm trade (trade within the same MNE) accounted for one-third of all world trade. These transactions are not determined by the market and are valued by the MNE using transfer prices – based on tax and tariff considerations. Another third of world trade is accounted for by the exports of MNE parent firms and foreign affiliates to unaffiliated firms. Thus, nearly two-thirds of international trade in the 1990s was shaped by MNEs (UNCTAD, 1995, p. 193; 1996, p. 121). By 2007, the share of trade within the MNEs, according to WTO, reached 27.5%. In addition, the sales of MNEs' overseas affiliates (international production) are almost double that of world exports. In the 1960s, MNEs were perceived as new forms of colonialism or imperialism and as an arm of American Hegemony (e.g., Levitt, 1970; Saari, 1999, p. 2). Many scholars portrayed national governments as pawns in the hands of powerful MNEs, impotent and incapable of achieving national goals (Barnet & Müller, 1974). Some observers even claimed that the "nation-state is just about through as an economic unit" (Kindlebeger, 1969, p. 207) and would be finished off by powerful MNEs (see Gilpin, 1975, p. 220) that would make the state impotent. (For a description and rebuttal of these arguments, see Wolf, 2004, chap. 11.) In the 1970s, such fears led to nationalizations and expropriations of MNE assets, and to efforts to amend the world economic order. The growing anxiety about the possible dominance of MNEs over countries led also to a request by the United Nations to study the role of MNES and their impact on the process of development. The result was the first systematic efforts at data gathering by the United Nations, identifying 7,276 parent MNEs in the world in 1969 with book value of global FDI stock at U.S.$108.2 billion. Eight of the 10 largest multinational corporations were based in the United States (UN, 1973, p. 77).

Since the 1980s, MNEs have been increasingly recognized as a prime engine to foster long-term economic development. FDIs potential to inject capital without debt servicing obligations, create jobs, transfer technology (including management skills), enhance exports, and raise productivity is now widely acclaimed. The possible disadvantages of FDIs or the possible conflict of power between the MNEs and the nation-states seem to have been forgotten or assumed to be manageable. It is now widely agreed that the advantages of MNEs are less based on factors vulnerable to rapid obsolescence and more on the capability to innovate, generate new technologies, and manage knowledge across a global network of subsidiaries.

The MNE is therefore courted as a major engine of development in a knowledge-based global economy. Different nations compete intensively with each other to get MNEs to locate value-added activities within their borders (Oxelheim & Ghauri, 2004, chap. 1).

MNEs themselves are constantly changing. First, their numbers are growing – to a large extent as a response to changing environment. From 7,276 firms in 1969, the number of MNEs worldwide mushroomed by 2008 to 82,053 parent corporations with 807,353 foreign affiliates (UNCTAD, 2009, pp. 222–223). Second, the home country is now spread. Today MNEs come from almost all countries. In 2008, only 2,418 parents were from the United States, while 21,425 parents were from developing countries (Aharoni & Ramamurti, 2008). Third, MNEs were dominated by resource seeking and manufacturing MNEs. Later, MNEs from the service sector have been steadily increasing their share. In 2008, there were 26 service MNEs among the top 100, compared to 14 in 1993. Fourth, in the 1970s, multinationals were regarded as giants, with sales that dwarfed the GNPs of most countries. This is still true of the largest MNEs. The 100 largest MNEs accounted since 2000 for about 4% of world GDP and to about 9% of foreign assets and 16% of foreign sales of all MNEs. However, the vast majority of firms counted by UNCTAD as MNEs are small in size. Fifth, MNEs are increasingly recognized as market seekers or efficiency seekers and more and more they are strategic asset seekers – looking for new ideas attempting "to innovate by learning from the world" (Doz, Santos, & Williamson 2001, p. 1). Sixth, MNEs shifted from hierarchical organizations to horizontally networked alliances, most of which are not based on equity links. While in the past FDI has been distinguished from portfolio investment by the element of control – assumed to be a function of ownership – today, in Dunning's (1994) terms, hierarchical enterprises are being replaced by alliance capitalism – that do not appear in official statistics. One reason is that MNEs decompose their supply chain, outsourcing operations that can be digitized and decomposed into a cheap labor location and distributing other activities to the best location across the world. They also interconnect all markets and knowledge centers. FDI inflows according to UNCTAD (2009) reached a historic high of $1,979 billion. As a result of the world recession, it went down to $1,697 billion in 2008 and further declined in 2009.[1] Again, these figures do not include alliances and other nonequity forms of cooperation. MNEs have become centers of knowledge and innovation. Managers of MNEs orchestrate assets, coordinate development of new products, eradicate inefficiencies, and allocate resources within the firm. New theories of MNEs indeed emphasized learning, capabilities, and innovation (Kogut & Zander, 1993; Augier & Teece, 2007; Pitelis, 2007). More recently MNEs were recognized as networks rather than as markets or hierarchies. Knowledge within MNEs flows now in all directions within the network and MNEs are knowledge-seekers, not just transferring knowledge from home to their foreign affiliates in host countries (Gupta & Govindarajan, 2000).

The growing sophistication and shrinking costs of transportation and of information and communication technology (ICT) facilitates global integration of operations. To be sure, the world of business is still mainly a domestic one and most production is domestically oriented. Large firms operating in a huge domestic market remain in that market as long as they find enough growth opportunities within it. The larger this market, the more can a domestic firm grow and prosper without ever extending its operations to other markets. Firms from small countries (and those operating in large scale, expensive R&D industries) do not enjoy such a luxury. They must enter lucrative foreign markets in order to grow – and the new technologies allow such a strategy. New technologies also foster a major enhancement of cooperation among firms in diverse locations in different parts of the globe. Rangan and Sengal (2009) convincingly argue that MNEs employing more ICT exhibit a reduced propensity for transnational integration. Instead, they cede ownership to foster decentralized value creation. The most recent transformation is the flurry of FDI in the acquisition of farmland (Von Braun & Meinzen-Dick, 2009; Cotula, 2009).

The changes summarized above were of course noted by international business (IB) scholars. Unfortunately, I cannot identify any seminal papers that *predicted* any of these changes. IB scholars did propose adaptations for theories that became obsolete because of the rapid changes. As one example, Vernon's product life theory (1966) assumed demand led innovations from the home developed country. This and other parts of his model were discredited with time. Vernon himself acknowledged the impact of some changes in Vernon (1979). Cantwell (1995) has shown that the hypothesis that innovation is concentrated in the home country is not true anymore. In fact, clusters of distinctive innovations occur in many centers and the greater capability of many MNEs manifests itself not just in the wider geographical dispersion of their investments, but in the broader degree of cross-border specialization that they are able to manage. Today, many of the innovations by MNEs originate from subsidiaries rather than from headquarters. Teece (1986) analyzed how an inventor can profit internationally from his new invention. He not only suggested the need for what he termed "appro-priability regime" – or available patent protection – but also the possession of complementary assets and capabilities. Recently, Hennart (2009) pointed out that theories are too MNEs centric – assuming the choice of entry is unilaterally determined by the MNE. He called for recognition of the need to bundle firm-specific advantages (FSA) of MNEs with complementary local assets. His model also predicts how entry modes evolve with time. Despite quoting Teece (1986), Hennart assumes that the source of innovation is the MNE, knowledge is transferred from its headquarters and local firms enjoy domestic market position. In fact today MNEs FSA can be in distribution and the innovator is a local firm. MNES search actively for technologies, ideas, and products from outside the firm. Procter and Gamble expects half of its future products to be based on technologies and concepts it will acquire from third parties (Huston & Sakkab, 2006; Jones, 2005).

In the field of strategy, since the seminal Chandler (1962), the theoretical literature has been growing exponentially. By incorporating ideas and concepts developed by industrial economics (IO) to strategy. Porter (1979, 1980, 1985) blazed a new trail in strategy. He made examination of industry structure a cornerstone of identifying the key factors required for success. He was followed by many who attempted to connect industry's structure and performance of firms – including their international operations. Another strand – the resource-based view (RBV) offered an explanation for interfirm variations in performance. Its central tenets are path dependence and firm heterogeneity. Firms are able to sustain competitive advantage because of the ownership of firm-specific resources that must be valuable, rare, and inimitable and nonsubstitutable (VRIN) (Barney, 1991). As the external environment changes, firms need to renew their stock of VRIN resources. Dynamic capabilities are needed to cope with changing environment (Teece & Pisano, 1994). These capabilities and the strategic decisions are made by top management teams (TMTs) – the study of which builds on upper-echelon theory (Hambrick & Mason, 1984). These studies influenced also the IB field. Many recent IB studies stressed the salience of experience, knowledge, as well as path dependence – an evolution of the firm that depends on its past history. Indeed, Jones and Khenna (2006) convincingly argued that "history matters."

One thing did not change: lack of information about alternatives and the impossibility of foreseeing the future makes managers of MNEs "satisficers." Their rational behavior is bounded by the cost of obtaining information, by their cognitive ability and because they are working under uncertainty within a social system. A whole new field of economics was developed – stressing behavioral elements, cognitive bias leading to a search in a relatively familiar domain and other seemingly irrational behavior, including the malleability and context dependence of preferences and behavior. Yet, despite the rich findings of behavioral economics, behavioral marketing, and behavioral finance, it is quite amazing that "the role that managers play in achieving certain internationalization positions is, to a great extent, under-developed in the IB literature ... One important commonality is that they do not leave much scope for discretionary management decision-making" (Hutzschenreuter, Pederson, & Volberda, 2007, pp. 1056–1057). Most IB researchers assumed perfect rationality in their models and managers do not have any role (Kogut, Walker, & Anand, 2002). To the extent individual managers are incorporated into conceptual frameworks, it is assumed they act based on their own self-interest or, if appropriate governance mechanisms is in place, in accordance with interests that are aligned with that of the MNE's owners (see Carpenter, Geletkanycz, & Sanders, 2004; Werner, 2002 for reviews). It is tempting to speculate why IB did not incorporate bounded rationality, decision-making biases, and judgments by managers in their models. It may be more constructive to enumerate these findings, hoping that future researchers would consider their meaning. In the following sections I shall summarize my findings on the foreign investment decision process and the important advances in behavioral theories. I shall then demonstrate the relevance of behavioral findings in prescribing policies and enumerate future research implications

THE FOREIGN INVESTMENT DECISION – A COMPLEX PROCESS

The foreign investment decision process is not a single, identifiable act. Rather, it is a complex succession of acts. It is "a dynamic social process of mutual influences among various members of an organization, constrained by the organization's strategy, its resources and the limited capacity, goals and needs of its members, throughout which choices emerge" (Aharoni, 1966a, p. 15). The foreign investment decision process is made by a group of individuals in an organization all of which are busy. It is a long process, involves different organizational levels. The process is made under uncertainty both because of lack of information and because of the limited capacity of the human mind. The decision process starts because of an outside force that causes a *decision to look abroad*. The strength of this force determines the *investigation process* – throughout which decision makers accumulate psychological commitments toward other organizations and individuals. The more committed they become, the higher the probability of a *decision to invest*. In this sense, the *decision to invest* is not necessarily the last part of the decision process. Thus, if the force that caused the look abroad is strong enough, the decision to invest abroad is already made and the investigation process may concentrate on minimizing the size of the investment and the risks involved. The process is changing with the accumulation of experience and the result of organizational modifications such as the creation of an international division.

Any decision process includes several elements. First, any choice made by an organization depends on the *social system*. The social elements focus on the decision maker's relations with other individuals both within and outside the MNE, such as customers, suppliers including financial suppliers, government agencies in host and home countries and competitors. Second, the process takes a long *time*. Third, decisions are made under *uncertainty*. Therefore, the decision maker's perception of uncertainty is a major element. This perception changes as a result of experience and knowledge. Decision makers also vary regarding how comfortable they are with uncertainty surrounding the decision. Fourth, organizations have *goals*. Finally, there are many constraints on the freedom of action of the decision makers.

The decision-making process is spread over a long period of time. Implicit and explicit negotiations, both inside the organization and with outsiders, may drag on for years. During that period there are many changes, it is often found that certain factors were not taken into account or proved to be unpredictable. These changes invariably require more modifications, more approvals, and sometimes new round of negotiations has to be started.

When a series of investment decisions are examined another important factor emerges: "the accumulation of experience by executives in various echelons regarding foreign investments creates profound changes in the organization itself ... Gradually, organizations may evolve into multinational corporations, vigorously looking for opportunities abroad" (Aharoni, 1966a, p. 174). Organizations learn and with learning the perception of uncertainty in foreign operations changes. Investments previously perceived as risky become acceptable. When the process is put in a historical perspective it may be found that the firm received an export order long time in the past. The foreign market was developed by a foreign agent with top management paying little or no attention to foreign development. With the growth of export business, sometimes even without any deliberate action from headquarters, an export department may have been created. This in turn forms a group of people in the company who feel obligated, driven by their vested interest, to expand the international operations. The very existence of an international division gives a momentum to international operations and these operations are expanded. The assignment of a group of executives to an international division creates several institutional as well as individual commitments. The cost of investigation in an international division is generally lower: knowledge has been accumulated from previous investigations. Further, both because of their role and because of their experience the international executives perceive the risk of foreign operations to be lower. They have more knowledge about remote control operations. With time, foreign investments become a substantial part of total operations. The level of the international division in the firm's hierarchy is much higher and the involvement of top management increases. When the expansion of existing foreign operations is considered, the investigation is much more expeditious.

The location pattern also evolves: very often Canada was the first country selected for foreign operations. The Canadian subsidiary exported to the British Commonwealth. "Most United States investments in Asia and Africa have been made by companies which have had considerable experience in foreign operations in more developed countries. This phenomenon may perhaps be attributed to the idea of 'experience first': companies may have preferred to get their feet wet in safer water" (*ibid*, p. 180). Because of path dependence, the history of the firm is an important variable.

The population I studied was U.S. firms. A similar incremental process of learning and experience as well as the choice of familiar countries first was found by Johanson and Vahlne (1977) in their observations of Swedish firms. Firms are inhibited by lack of knowledge about markets. Therefore, firms proceed in small steps adjusting as they gain knowledge through experience. The internationalization is evolutionary, continuous process from export, to joint venture representation, to sales subsidiary, to resource development subsidiary. Further, based on experience and knowledge acquisition firms enter new markets with successively greater psychic distance. These explanations are considered at the firm – not the individual – level. "In our model, we consider knowledge to be vested in the decision-making system. We do not deal explicitly with the individual decision maker" (Johanson & Vahlne, 1977, p. 26)

In subsequent work, Johanson and Vahlne (1990, 2009) expanded the notion of knowledge development to include knowledge gained through relationships with other bodies on the foreign market. They posit markets as networks of relationships among firms. Insidership in relevant networks is necessary for successful internationalization. Relationships offer potential for building trust and commitments, which in turn shapes a firm's market knowledge.

IB theory developed significantly since the early attempts to understand the foreign investment decision process, the modes of operations and the sequence of entry to different locations. An extensive academic literature used cross-sectional design to study the choice of modes of operation. Brouthers and Hennart (2007) have documented about 100 empirical studies in the last 15 years. Most of these theoretical developments relied heavily on the pioneering efforts of Coase (1937) to explain the existence of firms. Coase stressed the relative costs of internalizing transactions versus operating in external markets. Williamson (1975) developed the transaction costs approach to a general theory of the firm. Buckley and Casson (1976) combined internalization with location effects – portraying the MNE as an internal market operating across borders. Other researchers followed Williamson's transaction cost theory (Hennart, 1982; Anderson & Gatignon, 1986). Dunning (1980) offered a theory attempting to combine the role of ownership and location advantages in explaining why an MNE would engage in FDI – thus demonstrating (I) advantage – rather than exports. This theory was later presented as paradigm – that was updated many times. (For the latest version see Dunning & Lundan, 2008.) Later, influenced by resource-based theory and premised on the idea that organizations learn from experience (Levitt & March, 1988), the MNE was recognized as knowledge-based (Kogut & Zander, 1993). Organizational learning theory is primarily concerned with experience accumulation. It also addresses knowledge articulation and knowledge codification (Zollo & Winter, 2002).

These theories were all based on some – often implicit – assumptions about human behavior. Williamson, for example, relied heavily on bounded rationality and also assumed opportunism, defined as self-interest seeking with guile (Williamson, 1985). Indeed this assumption was the major reason for rejecting the application of TCE to practice (Ghoshal & Moran, 1996). Other theories ignored managerial behavior totally. As pointed out by one of the founders of internalizing, Mark Casson, "Transaction cost analysis … explains the boundaries of the firm very well…. What lies inside the boundaries of the firm is not explained so well because this is not the focus of the theory" (Casson, 2000, p. 118). It seems that many of the IB scholars were willing to assume managers are omnipotent, possessing all the information needed to make rational decisions. As a minimum, it is assumed "that the decision-maker can identify a set of options, and has an objective by which these options can be ranked, and an ability to identify the top-ranked option and select it" (Buckley & Casson, 2009, p. 1568). Thus, the vast literature on entry mode choice tends to assume that firms will move their transferable FSA to locations enjoying country-specific advantages (CSAs). Based on the relative strengths of the CSA the MNE would choose both the initial and the subsequent modes of entry. It is taken for granted that all the relevant information is known. To be sure, relevant does not imply complete. "A rational decision-maker will collect only sufficient information to make the risks surrounding the decision acceptable" (Buckley & Casson, 2009, p. 1568). What is sufficient, how is the information collected and evaluated, how the decision maker knows which information to collect, and what is an acceptable risk are left unanswered. The OLI paradigm also assumes rationality in the classical economic sense. The behavioral elements in decision making were unfortunately ignored. Theoretical developments, clearly demonstrating departures from rationality both in judgment and in choices were extensive – as will be shown in the next section.

THEORETICAL DEVELOPMENTS ON BEHAVIOR

In 1955, Herbert Simon received the Nobel Memorial Prize for his ideas on behavior of bounded rational actors. Simon criticized the classical economists' rational choice model and the reliance of economists, following physics, on equilibrium as unrealistic. Simon pointed out that because of their cognitive limitations; bounded-rational actors do not attempt to maximize profits or utility. The rationality of individuals is limited by the information they have, the cognitive limitations of their minds, and the finite amount of time they have to make decisions. Decision makers lack the ability and resources to arrive at the optimal solution; they instead apply their rationality only after having greatly simplified the choices available (Simon, 1947, 1955; March & Simon, 1958).

Since Simon, behavioral theories have undergone steady developments in different fronts. One has been information processing psychology, using computer simulation. Extensive empirical evidence demonstrates that problem solving involves selective search, based on rules of thumb or "heuristics." Over time these rules of thumb change as outcomes are evaluated. The same process was shown in decisions on investments in securities or medical diagnosis and in many other case studies of organizational decision making (Newell & Simon, 1972).

Another major field has been the empirical refutations of the theory that human beings maximize subjective expected utility (SEU) – reported mainly by Kahneman and Tversky but also by Kunreuther and his colleagues (1978) in studies of individual decisions to purchase or not to purchase flood insurance. Kahneman and Tversky (1979 – Tversky & Kahneman, 1974), based on a series of experiments in different countries, developed a theory they termed prospect theory. It distinguishes two phases in the decision-making process: an *editing* phase, which is a preliminary analysis of the offered prospects, and an *evaluation* phase, which is when the prospect with the highest value is chosen from among the edited prospects. They also demonstrated a *certainty effect* – meaning people overweight outcomes that are certain, relative to outcomes that are merely probable even when the expected value of each is the same. People tend to avoid a loss, even if it means taking even greater risks. *Loss aversion* might depend on *framing* the safer option as the *status quo* and the complexity of the suggested alternatives.

In order to simplify the choice between alternatives, people frequently disregard components that the alternatives share. They focus on those that distinguish them. Since different choice problems can be decomposed in different ways, this can lead to inconsistent preferences. Kahneman and Tversky (1979) call this phenomenon the *isolation effect*. Prospect theory replaces the notion of utility with value. Whereas utility is usually defined only in terms of final assets or net wealth value is defined in terms of gains and losses relative to a reference point (*framing effect* – Tversky & Kahneman, 1981). Decision makers may be more risk averse when they frame a strategic decision as potential for loss and less risk averse than when a decision is framed as potential for gain (March & Shapira, 1987; Miller & Chen, 2004). Attitude of persons toward risk are very different when gain is concerned than when loss is anticipated. For losses the value function is convex and relatively steep, for gains it is concave and not quite so steep. Second, the value of each outcome is a function of "decision weights." These weights do not always correspond to probabilities. Specifically, prospect theory postulates that decision weights tend to overweigh small probabilities and underweigh moderate and high probabilities. Reference points are selected based upon internal capabilities and external conditions considered over time (Shoham & Fiegenbaum, 2002). Decisions have two elements – judgment and choice. Judgment research deals with the processes people use to estimate probabilities. Choice deals with the processes people use to select among actions, taking account of any relevant judgments they may have made. Judgment was shown to be based on extrapolation, overconfidence, and optimism.

In their 1992 paper, Tversky and Kahneman developed an updated form of prospect theory, which they termed *Cumulative Prospect Theory*. The theory incorporates rank-dependent functional that transforms cumulative, rather than individual, probabilities and satisfies stochastic dominance, which the original form of prospect theory does not.

Prospect Theory helps to illuminate experimental results that show individuals often make divergent choices in situations that are substantially identical but framed in a different way. Therefore, managerial choice is not determined uniquely by the objective characteristics of the problem situation. Rather, it depends on the particular heuristic process that is used to reach the decision. Prospect theory has had an enormous influence across a range of disciplines, including economics, marketing, finance, and consumer choice.

Several theories of business firms incorporated bounded rationality. Cyert and March (1963) and Cyert and DeGroot (1974) incorporated adaptive learning and Nelson and Winter (1973) stressed evolution. In these theories profit maximization is replaced by goals defined in terms of targets. A mechanism of some sort, for example, "organizational slack," prevents maximization. Organizational learning could help reaching maximization equilibrium but only if the environment remains unchanged for a very long time. Even if the environmental conditions are identical, different decision mechanisms can produce different results.

More than 40 years after the publication of *A behavioral theory of the firm*, *Organization Science* published a special issue (Organization Science, 2007). It reports the most recent research in this area. None of the papers in that issue – not even any of the hundreds of papers cited – is in international business! The most direct descendents of Cyert and March's work are presented as the organizational learning (Argote, 1999) and evolutionary economics (Nelson & Winter, 1982). In both fields, process-oriented models are important, "In these fields, much theorizing concerns how certain events and experiences set in motion processes of decision making, routine, development, or routine selection that change organizational behavior" (Argote & Greve, 2007, p. 338). Lessons learned are captured by routines such that the lessons are accessible to organizational members. Both used the behavioral theory as a tool for providing basic concepts on which they could build a theory of change. Organizational learning theory has helped to explain the formation, performance, and likelihood of survival of international joint ventures (Barkema, Shenkar, Vermeulen, & Bell, 1997; Parkhe, 1991).

Behavioral economists, too, challenged conventional economic analysis, modifying unbounded rationality, unbounded willpower, and unbounded selfishness, adding significant behavioral findings to today's mainstream economics (for reviews, see Camerer, 2000; Camerer, Loewenstein, & Rabin, 2003; Fudenberg, 2006; Rabin 1998, 2002; Sunstein & Thaler, 2008; DellaVigna, 2009). In 1997 a special issue of the *Quarterly Journal of Economics* was devoted to behavioral economics. Areas of research by behavioral economists include *anchoring* (a cognitive bias one relies too heavily on one trait or piece of information), availability *heuristic* (when people predict the frequency of an event based on how easily an example can be brought to mind. One result is people tend to overstate risks and a result purchase unnecessary insurance, or governments pursuing social goals at the expense of other more fruitful ones), *representativeness heuristic* – where people judge the probability or frequency of a hypothesis by considering how much the hypothesis resembles available data, *Status quo bias* when people are very likely to continue a course of action since it has been traditionally the one pursued and *herd mentality* – where people are heavily influenced by actions of others. It also includes *loss aversion* (Tversky & Kahneman, 1991), *quasi hyperbolic of intertemporal choice* (Laibson, 1997), *cognitive dissonance* (Akerlof & Dickens, 1982), *endowment effect* (the tendency to place a greater value on an item when it might be given up from one's possession than when it is not in one's possession – Knetsch, 1989; Knetsch & Sinden, 1984; Kahneman, Knetsch, & Thaler, 1990), social preferences (Gneezy & Rustichini, 2000a, 2000b), fairness (Kahneman, Knetsch, & Thaler, 1986), and mental accounting (Thaler, 1999). Rabin demonstrated that people cooperate in ultimatum games – in which a proposer suggests to a respondent how much of a given sum each should get. If the respondent rejects the offer both get nothing. If the respondent accepts both get what was offered. Economic theory would predict the proposer would offer a token amount. Experiments show respondents reject offer of less than 20% – because of "fairness" (Rabin, 1993). As another example Camerer, Babcock, Loewenstein, and Thaler (1997) studied New York cab drivers. The profit maximizers should work hard in good days and quit early on bad days. Instead the cabbies had a target earning treating shortfalls from target as a loss. They thus quitted early in good days and work longer on bad days.

Arieli, Loewenstein, and Prelec (2003) followed reference ideas of Kahneman and Tversky and similarly provided some reference values to their subjects and then asked them what compensation they would require to hear an unpleasant sound for certain duration. The subjects quoted arbitrary values linked to the reference values. When the subjects were asked to quote the price they would want for longer duration the subjects quoted values consistent with the initial price. When the initial price is arbitrary and the subsequent price consistent with the initial price, the behavior is termed coherent arbitrariness. We do not value goods (or shares) based on "fundamentals." The experiments show that this combination of coherent arbitrariness (1) cannot be interpreted as a rational response to information, (2) does not decrease as a result of experience with a good, (3) is not necessarily reduced by market forces, and (4) is not unique to cash prices. The results imply that demand curves estimated from market data need not reveal true consumer preferences, in any normatively significant sense of the term.

A famous study conducted by Solomon Asch clearly shows peer social pressure can make a person say something that is obviously false. These errors and mistakes that human beings are subject to are well summarized by Sunstein and Thaler (2008). They also coined the term choice architecture – or the way in which decisions are influenced by how the choices are presented. The book asserts that "the notion that each of us thinks and chooses unfailingly well, and thus fits within the textbook picture of human beings offered by economists" is false (Sunstein & Thaler, 2008, p. 6) Unlike members of *homo economicus*, human beings make predictable mistakes that are the result of widely occurring biases, heuristics, and fallacies, and because of the way they are influenced by their social interactions. Behavioral research raises "serious questions about the rationality of many judgments and decisions that people make" (Sunstein & Thaler, 2008, p. 7).

In the last decade or two, a new branch of economics termed neuroeconomics attempts to combine economics, behavior, and scanning of the brain or use eye tracking and pupil dilation in order to compare the roles of the different brain areas that contribute to economic decision making. (For reviews see Camerer, Loewenstein, & Prelec, 2004, 2005.) In one study, Rubinstein (2008) found different patterns of choice among fast and slow respondents among subjects who were asked to express their preferences in the context of the Allais Paradox. He suggests that we try to identify types of economic agents by the time they take to make their choices. For him, one potentially important task for the neuroeconomics approach is to identify "types" of economic agents, namely to determine characteristics of agents that predict their behavior in different choice problems. It is difficult to do this simply by observing behavior.

Behavioral economists attempt to merge psychology and economics. Most of their studies concentrate on the behavior of individuals. Behavioral finance experts study behavior of individual investors. Many behavioral studies were carried out by marketing experts – trying to understand how consumers make choices. Organization science experts attempted to integrate prospect theory into organizational literature and behavioral decision theory (Slovic, Fischhoff, & Lichtenstein, 1977). Significant attention is paid to issues of managerial decision making (Miller & Chen, 2004; Schwenk, 1995) and commitment (Schwenk, 1986) and for a search of new and increasingly complex biases and heuristics (e.g., Gilovich, Griffin, & Kahneman, 2002; Kahneman, 2003).

One important issue is the consequences of the rapid pace of technological change. Industries, institutions, and the knowledge and skills that constitute core capabilities are under a relentless onslaught and unremitting assault of change. Firms have difficulties in adapting and core capabilities may become core rigidities. These difficulties are clearly a result of behavior of managers – not of rational economic calculations. Thus, Christensen (1997) demonstrates in a study of the disk drive industry the difficulties managers face in changing strategy when what he termed – disruptive as opposed to sustaining – technologies are discovered. Trispas and Gavetti (2000) analyzed how managers in Polaroid coped with the arrival of digital imaging. They provide an example of where mental filters impede evolution of core capabilities in face of radical technological change. As the digital image technology evolved, Polaroid were successful in developing digital image technology but stayed with their original business model and failed to develop manufacturing and product development capabilities, which prevented them from competing efficiently in this new market (Trispas & Gavetti, 2000). In all of these cases and many others, managers' mental models can reduce the companies' ability to react to changes in their environment (Foster & Kaplan, 2001). Managers develop an implicit mental success model and use it as a mental filter to sort information and make decisions in their daily work (Ansoff & McDonnel, 1990). When the environment in which the company is acting is changing a new mental filter must be developed. As long as signals of change in the environment are handled according to an old mental filter the acceptance of new realities will be delayed, which could affect the information system, decision-making process, executive capabilities, and control system (Foster & Kaplan 2001; Ansoff & McDonnel, 1990). In the world of the 21st century, characterized by a relentless pursuit of new technologies and dynamic markets, mental processes that facilitate rather than hinder adaptation to new environment are of great importance. When managers face fading product-market domains they are often inertial in their response to such decline Martin and Eisenhardt (2004) call for a corporate entrepreneurship response whereby managers move their businesses into new market opportunities as the value of current-market domains inevitably begins to fade. They emphasize exiting from declining markets while simultaneously capturing and exploiting opportunities in more promising markets.

Managers are often overconfident (Biais, Hilton, Mazurier, & Puget, 2005; Kőszegi, 2006) and their forecasts suffer from hubris (Hayward & Hambrick, 1997). They therefore fail to consider adequately the possible impact of rare but earth-shattering events (Taleb, 2007). In fact, delusional optimism is one of the forces that drive capitalism.

To summarize, studies of the psychology of decision-making acknowledge human limits on computational power, willpower, and self-interest. They posit functional heuristics for solving problems that are often so complex that they cannot be solved exactly by even modern computer algorithms. They show decision makers are influenced by a wide range of factors, such as personal goals, evaluation criteria, and identity. They sometimes make choices that are not in their long run interests and are often willing to sacrifice their own interests to help others. They may make mistakes because of several factors. First, cognitive biases impair decision makers' abilities to select optimal choices (Barnes, 1984; Schwenk, 1984; Clapham & Schwenk, 1991). Second, they transform intractable decision problems into tractable ones by using routines that short-circuit individuals' autonomous judgments (Nelson & Winter, 1982; Teece, Pisano, & Shuen, 1997). Third, managers are dominated by superior logic that orients behavior and result in blind spots and escalation of commitments (Prahalad & Bettis, 1986; Coff, 1999; Staw & Ross, 1987) and may be dominated by inertia. Further, organizations may develop more blind spots even beyond any individual constraints. Research to date emphasized individual behavior – and less so organizational responses (Das & Teng, 1999).

Two streams of research should be briefly mentioned: TMTs and MNE governance. Both recognize the influence of executives, for example, in determining international strategies. TMT research builds on upper-echelon theory (Hambrick & Mason, 1984) to explore the role of TMT in making international business decisions. The upper-echelon perspective focuses on executive cognition, perceptions, biases, and values and their influence on strategic choice. Managers face information overload, ambiguous cues, and competing demands. Complex decisions require reliance upon simplification heuristics, making cognitive processes increasingly important (Einhorn & Hogarth, 1981). In upper-echelon studies, biases and heuristics are assumed to be relatively consistent across similar demographic characteristics such as age, functional background, and educational experience. Empirical research has linked upper-echelon characteristics and experience with strategic choices such as internationalization (Carpenter et al., 2004). However, there are significant problems with using individual-level demographic variables as indicators of decision making in TMTs (e.g., Lawrence, 1997). Markóczy (1997), for example, suggests that individual demographic characteristics are poor measures of managerial cognition. Kilduff, Angelmar, and Mehra (2000) found no evidence of any effect of demographic diversity on cognitive diversity. Similarly, Priem, Lyon, and Dess (1999) encourage TMT researchers to eschew demographic variables in favor of measures that are more difficult to capture. Others have added that, even if demographic characteristics are representative of cognitive constructs, they cannot be treated independently because executives embody a bundle of attributes that continuously interact with each other (Harrison, Price, & Bell, 1998). A few studies of TMT deal specifically with internationalization. Thus, Herrmann and Datta (2005) examine the relationships between TMT characteristics and international diversification among large, internationally diversified US-based manufacturing firms. Findings indicate that firms with higher levels of international diversification are likely to have TMTs characterized by higher educational level, shorter organizational tenures, younger executives, and greater international experience. In addition, findings indicate that the relationships between TMT characteristics and international diversification are more dominant in better-performing than in lower-performing firms. Glunk, Heijltjes, and Olie (2001) found that the national diversity of TMTs in Sweden and the Netherlands have not progressed in proportion to the level of internationalization of the companies.

An alternative perspective to upper-echelon research is offered by agency theory. The managers – the agents – have substantial discretion as to the actions they take because the principals – the shareholders – are dispersed and cannot coordinate to share monitoring and control costs (Jensen & Meckling, 1976). The managers pursue private benefits. The divergence of interests is greater the lower the managers' equity stake and the lower the likelihood of them getting caught and punished for nonvalue maximizing behavior. Another problem identified by agency theory is that of entrenchment: top executives with high-equity stakes enjoy more freedom to misallocate resources (Stulz, 1988). These executives cannot be removed in a proxy fight or cast out by hostile raiders attracted by low share prices. Jensen and Meckling (1976) argue that ownership gives TMT an incentive to assume risk and aligns their goals with those of other firm owners. They have less incentive to misallocate corporate resources. Stulz (1988) argues that higher equity stakes gives insiders more freedom to misallocate resources, on the corporate decision-making process.

In these studies managers are portrayed as motivated by their own gains – at the expense of the owners of the firm. They ignore studies that clearly demonstrated that fairness is an important motivator. It may well be that managers are motivated by ego and want to do better than the competitors. They demand higher remuneration or a larger bonus only because they compare their paycheck to those of others (see Arieli, 2008). Further, most of these studies are based on the United States with its separation of ownership and control. Morck, Wolfenzon, and Yeung (2005) review a very large body of studies. They point out that 'outside the United States and the United Kingdom, large corporations usually have controlling owners, who are usually very wealthy families. Pyramidal control structure, cross shareholding, and super voting rights let such families control corporations without making a commensurate capital investment" (p. 655). Their paper reviews many studies of different countries. They offer several conclusions. First, corporate governance problem in most countries is that of a conflict between the controlling shareholder and public shareholders – not a conflict between atomistic shareholders and professional managers. Second, the highly concentrated control leads to a range of market power distortions and may curtail investment in innovations. Finally, public policy is much influenced by the power of the rent-seeking controlling groups. Clearly, if one looks for viable policy prescriptions, it is crucial to base public policies on a coherent understanding of behavioral elements that affect the decision process.

RELEVANCE OF BEHAVIORAL FINDINGS TO PRESCRIPTIONS OF POLICIES

Ceteris paribus, better predictions are likely to result from theories with more *realistic* assumptions. Policies should be tailored to influence actual, as opposed to an assumed, behavior. To quote Douglas North, "the uncritical acceptance of the rationality assumption is devastating for most of the issues confronting social scientists and is a major stumbling block in the path of future progress. The rationality assumption is not wrong, but such an acceptance forecloses a deeper understanding of the decision-making process in confronting the uncertainties of the complex world we have created" (2005, p. 5). Thaler and Benartzi (2004, p. 167) suggest that "before writing a prescription one must know the symptoms of the disease being treated." Indeed, many mistakes made that led to the recent financial crisis could have been avoided if the decision-making process would be considered when policies were implemented.

One example is policies designed to attract FDIs – or some types of specific FDIs. Economic theory would have a clear and straightforward prescription: grant some type of tax exemption or reduction. The rationale is straightforward: if the rate of return on investment is low and the risks involved are very high tax incentives may change the rate of return. However, my doctoral study showed that the granting of income tax exemptions is not an important factor in the foreign investment decision process. The reasons for this conclusion were detailed in Aharoni (1966a, pp. 234–242) and will not be repeated here.

Based on the behavioral findings, a much better use of taxpayers' funds is to market the country (Aharoni 1966b), to reduce perceived risk and create the decision to look abroad. The marketing program should acquaint the consumer with the product. In our case – acquaint the investor with the foreign country. It should supply up to date, accurate, and adequate information and neutralize the basic apprehension of uncertainty. It should also suggest concrete projects for considerations and demonstrate the advantage to the firm of investing in these projects. Above all, the program should be well integrated and should aid the investor throughout the decision process. The cost of investigation should be minimized – mainly by supply of relevant information and perhaps by sharing the investigation costs.

My ideas seem to have been ignored by IB scholars. The only study I unearthed on the same marketing theme is Wells and Mint (1990, revised 2000).These authors define promotional techniques to consist of (a) providing information to potential investors; (b) creating an attractive image of the country as a place to invest; and (c) providing services to prospective investors. Both the original paper and the revised one appeared as a Foreign Investment Advisory Service (FIAS) occasional papers – not in an academic journal. In the real world many countries established investment promotion agencies to facilitate FDIs. Today there are 228 such agencies from 156 countries that are members of the World Association of Investment Promotion Agencies (WAIPA) – established in 1995. These agencies directly aim at encouraging FDIs – generally inward FDIs but in many cases also outward FDIs. The effectiveness of these agencies in attracting FDI was studied by Morisset and Andrews-Johnson (2003) – again as an FIAS occasional paper. These authors found that agencies with some kind of participation from the private sector do better than those that are purely governmental. They also provide evidence to suggest that, at least for many countries, a dollar spent on investment promotion yields a better return than a dollar provided as a subsidy or given up through a tax. I did not find even one paper on these agencies in the IB academic journals.

Many more examples of policy prescriptions may be cited from behavioral economics that proposed design of institutions that would help people make better choice. As one example, Shefrin and Thaler (1988) portray the life cycle of savings as much different as classical economic theory. They take account of households' lack of self-control and procrastination (tendency to postpone unpleasant tasks). Procrastination, in turn, produces a status quo bias. Samuelson and Zeckhauser (1988) found that the median number of changes, made by TIAA-CREF participants in the asset allocation over the life time, was zero. Since then, several researchers studied retirement account portfolio behavior – relating it to various demographic variables and other participant characteristics such as age, gender, marital status, time in the 401(k) plan, salary, and time on the job (Agnew, Balduzzi, & Sundén, 2003). Of course, a policy that will achieve a desired result should take into account the behavioral elements. In the specific case of savings behavior, the elements are bounded rationality, self-control, procrastination, and nominal loss aversion. Based on consideration of these elements, a plan was designed to increase savings rate and recognizing, households may lack the self-control to reduce current consumption in favor of future consumption (Thaler & Shefrin, 1981). The plan allows workers to commit themselves now to increase their savings rate each time they get a pay increase in the future (Thaler & Benartzi, 2004).

Recognizing that decisions are driven by emotions, Sunstein and Thaler endorse what they term libertarian paternalism, claiming it is not an oxymoron. Sunstein and Thaler state that "the libertarian aspect of our strategies lies in the straightforward insistence that, in general, people should be free to do what the like – and to opt out of undesirable arrangements if they want to do so." The paternalistic portion of the term "lies in the claim that it is legitimate for choice architects to try to influence people's behavior in order to make their lives longer, healthier, and better" (Sunstein & Thaler, 2008, p. 5). Sunstein and Thaler (2008) use their notion of nudge within the context of choice architecture to propose policy recommendations that they believe are in the spirit of libertarian paternalism in a variety of policy programs. They examine how people can be nudged into making better decisions for themselves on a range of issues, such as buying more healthy food or opting to save more. IB researchers up to now rarely offer such policies.

FUTURE RESEARCH IMPLICATIONS: WHAT ARE THE THINGS WE DO NOT KNOW AND HAVE TO STUDY

We have shown that psychological aspects of decision making were largely ignored by IB researchers. Further, structured experiments are virtually unknown.[2] Of course, a theory susceptible of mathematical measurement is much more elegant and may win applause for sound and profound thinking. However, as March points out, "Variables that can be measured tend to be treated as more 'real' than those that cannot, even though the ones that cannot be measured may be more important" (2006, pp. 203–204). It is quite unlikely that researchers ignored behavioral elements because they have considered them to be wrong or too deterministic.[3] Therefore, IB theory should acknowledge heuristics and other aspects of bounded rationality, incorporate a theory of search, and include dynamic aspiration levels that would change with experience. It must also take account of the social and legal structures within which market transactions are carried out. Studies of actual cases of FDIs may also substantiate the salience of commitment to different stakeholders, including policymakers, accumulated during the investigation process. In fact, each of the areas discussed in IB literature offers ample opportunities for a fruitful future research by using the insights gained by behavioral decision-making and behavioral economics and apply them to different issues of international business. Several examples may be illustrative. Thus, a study of the trade-offs between competition and cooperation in networks should borrow from explanations of fairness. Note that many MNEs achieve competitive advantage by cooperation with other firms rather than by internalizing operations. Further, nonequity forms of FDI, for example, subcontracting, management contracts, turnkey arrangements, franchising, licensing, or product sharing as well as different forms of strategic alliances all increased in importance, even if they are not recorded as FDI. In many service industries, nonequity forms are much more important than equity investments. In professional services, the ownership advantage of the firm are reflected in intangible assets such as reputation or organizational capabilities, information processing, or managerial skills and knowledge (Aharoni, 2000b). For very different reasons, airlines are globalizers that are not allowed to globalize. Inward FDI in airlines has been constrained by ownership requirements in bilateral Air Service Agreements (ASAs). They therefore are forced to use various forms of strategic alliances to augment international competitiveness (see Aharoni, 2002, 2004).[4] These developments affect any discussion of modes of entry: the choice is not only about the degree of ownership, but also about cooperation with independent firms. Cultural differences may also affect entry mode choices (Schneider & DeMeyer, 1991). For example, Japanese managers tend to prefer entry modes that allow higher control over technology (Bartlett & Ghoshal, 1989). Chinese TMTs are very different than their Western equivalents (Zhang, 2007). "Born global" may be a result of managers' experience and more knowledge about world affairs, cultural differences, and international operations in many countries of the world – not only a consequence of technological changes. Research should establish whether MNE managers exhibit greater variance in perceived uncertainty than their counterparts did 50 years ago.

One area of great importance is the ways to avoid inertia given fast changes in the business environment and in technologies. How can an MNE keep its core capabilities dynamic and adjustable in the face of new technologies, different customers, and new suppliers? Behavioral theory is predominantly based on study of individuals and their behavior. Clearly, organizations are composed of individuals. Yet organizations might condition judgment even beyond any individual inefficiency.

The population of MNEs today is much more heterogeneous in a variety of aspects: home countries, their size and their level of development as well as industries, the industry in which they operate; size of the firm as well as years of experience as MNEs. Whether or not the behavior of such a diverse group of firms is the same or alternatively different MNEs behave differently is an important area for future research. Behavioral economists claim that the behavior they unearthed, that is, loss aversion is a universal trait, true in all countries and in all cultures. IB researchers argue that since decision makers in MNEs come from different cultures, they make choices differently. Cultural differences are said to affect MNE strategies (e.g., Benito, 1997; Brouthers & Brouthers, 2001) and performance (e.g., Li & Guisinger, 1992; Park & Ungson, 1997). Furthermore, the role of environmental uncertainty for managers has been explicit in many studies on cultural distance (Barkema & Vermeulen, 1998). Shifting the focus from underlying country-level cultural indicators to indicators of managerial decision making may address some of the recent criticism of cultural distance research (e.g., Shenkar, 2001; Tihanyi, Griffith, & Russell, 2005). *Managerial distance* could capture variations in decision-making heuristics and biases across managers from different cultural traditions. Measuring how managers from different cultures perceive similar decisions could enhance upper-echelon and governance research (see Aharoni, Tihanyi, & Connelly, 2011).

Second, even if the environmental conditions are identical, different decision mechanisms can produce different results. Therefore, one cannot assume that process-independent predictions would hold. In fact, these predictions may turn out to be totally wrong and misleading. Third, some firms attempted to become multinational and failed while other firms in the same industry or home country were very successful in their internationalization efforts. Some MNEs clearly perform better than others. Future research should identify the sources of variability in response to environmental conditions. Fourth, we know very little about the determinants of success in managing an MNE and integrating its activities across the globe or within a region. Ownership advantages eluded as the reason for success are not easy to define. There is no real satisfactory explanation why some firms and industries became global while other firms in the same industry were not. Moreover, early research on the operation of MNEs has seen the primary task of the firm as tangible, repeated, measurable, and defined by the producer. All of these attributes are applicable neither to professional business service firms nor to many networks. Professional firms offer an intangible service, selling expertise that is generally customized, and is based on a close interaction between client and the supplier of the service with little or no economies or scale or of scope, and few possibilities of standardization. Networks are based on trust, not on hierarchy. In this context, research shedding light on what makes an MNE successful by focusing on the inner working of the MNEs is badly needed.

Received IB explanations often ignore not only managerial decision making but also the ability to create a novel strategy and to invent new products. Of course it is hard to avoid noticing that for a large number of MNEs the distinctive competence is based on innovation that *created* new markets – markets that did not exist and thus the costs of conducting market transactions could not be compared to the costs of using internal hierarchies.

Certain managers of firms in small countries decide to make the firm they lead a global firm to avoid the restrictions of growth from a small market base. Small firms sometimes enter international market immediately upon inception producing highly specialized goods for niche markets (Knight & Cavusgil, 1996, 2004). A strategy, after all, must be unique. It "must be predicated on building, maintaining and defending a competitive advantage" (Aharoni, 1993, p. 45). Clearly it is easier to study a large population by mathematical manipulation of a database than to follow trajectories of a unique strategy. Bandwagon behavior explains some foreign investment decisions but certainly not all or even most of them. Outliers adopt more proactive routes toward globalization by the innovation of a new path. Strategies of firms are very heterogeneous and such differences cannot be explained by economic models (or, for that matter, by population ecology explanations; Hannan & Freeman, 1977, 1984). Further, different managers may lead the same firm in similar environmental conditions to different strategies and to different locations around the globe.

Most past research on MNEs from Vernon (1971) to Rugman (2005) concentrated on the giant firms. Yet, there are about 80,000 MNEs most of which are small- and medium-sized. We should learn about these firms at least to find out if they face different problems and obstacles in the path toward globalization of operations. We should also learn about the working of MNEs from small countries – in which the firm is a significant part of the GNP and thus may have much too strong political, not only economic, clout (Aharoni, 2000a). It is true that the largest MNEs account for 90% of the world's FDI stock. Yet IB theory must also be able to explain internationalization of small firms and of firms from small economies, which present different challenges than large economies (Aharoni, 1994). Perhaps one can learn from outliers more than from a study of averages and populations.

Several researchers have demonstrated the existence of a home bias in portfolio selection (French & Poterba, 1991; Tesar & Werner, 1995). Despite the well-documented gains and reduced risk from international diversification, investors overwhelmingly prefer investments in domestic firms and in firms whose headquarters is in their country of residence (Coval & Moskowitz, 1999). Researchers also unearthed home bias in trade – preferring trade with neighbor countries or even states (McCallum, 1995; Wolf, 2000). Several explanations were offered for the home bias, from an emphasis on barriers to international movements to preference of geographic proximity and amplification of information asymmetries between countries. All of the explanations seem quite inadequate given the globalization of capital. Research is badly needed on behavior that causes home bias and to prescribe how a home bias could be eliminated or reduced.

In the specific area of top management, past research has focused on two dimensions of TMT characteristics: TMT demographics and heterogeneity of the team (Tihanyi, Ellstrand, Daily, & Dalton, 2001). TMT heterogeneity refers to the differences among team members in demographics and important cognitive aspects, values, and experiences. Hambrick and Mason (1984) assumed that heterogeneous TMT can obtain information from different sources and different opinions on the problem from team members. This difference in opinions would allow the TMT to make high-quality decisions and obtain a greater capability to solve problems. Diversity provides a TMT with a range of different viewpoints and causes a cohesive team to be more receptive to the need for change (Hambrick & Mason, 1984). On the other hand, diversity reduces team cohesion and increased miscommunications, thereby leading to slower pace of strategic change

(Hambrick & Mason, 1984). However, while greater homogeneity lead to faster decision making, it may also lead to insular thinking, and therefore, to strategic persistence in conditions when strategic change is appropriate. There is a lack of agreement among academicians as to whether heterogeneous or homogeneous TMT is better for firm performance (Amason, 1996; Amason & Sapienza, 1997; Boone & Hendriks, 2009). Moreover, the contexts and dynamics of TMT vary across countries (Glunk et al., 2001). Therefore, the impact on the performance of the firm may be different in different cultures. Cultural differences affect the attitudes, values, and faith of managers (Ronen & Shenkar, 1985), thereby influencing their strategy selection. Further, a study of TMT heterogeneity should take account of the impact of social context in which team members are embedded (Rau, 2008; Zhang, 2007).

CONCLUSIONS

International business research has become more rigorous over the past 50 years, owing to developments in computing technology and statistical software and to broader availability of international databases. Unfortunately, increased mathematical manipulation has often come at the cost of practical relevance. In their search for elegance and rigor, IB researchers ignored the rich evidence on psychological aspects of decision making, the complexity of decision making under uncertainty, and the accumulation of commitments. In most studies, outcomes are deterministic, the firm is treated as a black box and managers – if they are mentioned at all – are assumed to be rational calculators of costs and benefits. To be sure, certain differences among firms originating from different nations (and therefore cultures) are acknowledged.

The study of decision making in MNEs should take into account the many insights from a long line of research in behavioral decision making. It should also determine what is universally applicable and what is specific – to a culture, country, industry, size of firm, or other variables. This chapter presented a large compilation of demonstrations from experimental data showing framing effects, hyperbolic discounting of intertemporal choice, endowment effect, fairness, and other circumstances under which rationality as defined by classical economists does not hold. It is hoped that these demonstrations will motivate and inspire young researchers to look for applications for IB theories.

NOTES

1. The Economist Intelligence Unit shows slightly different figures: US$2.09 trillion in 2007, US$1.73 trillion in 2008, plunging by 44% in 2009 (Kekic, 2009).
2. One exception is the structured experiment carried out by Buckley, Devinney, and Louviere (2007). In this experiment the roles of information, biases, and managerial experience were very different in two phases of an FDI investment decision process. The first ("consider") stage is a choice of potential investment options. The second ("invest") stage is the actual choice of the investment. Managers employed more rational measures, including return ratios, cost measures, and market conditions. In the investment-choice phase, however, managers focused more on FDI experience and host country specific factors, such as the political environment and language.
3. Langlois and Csontos (1993, p. 118) argue that behaviorists portray agents as hard headed rule followers or preprogrammed satisficers. These agents act in a deterministic way.
4. The number of airlines alliances has risen markedly from around 20 in the early 1990s to a total of 1,221 by 2001 (UNCTAD, 2004).

REFERENCES

Agnew, J., Balduzzi, P., & Sundén, A. (2003). Portfolio choice and trading in a large 401(k) plan. *American Economic Review*, *93*, 193–205.

Aharoni, Y. (1993). In search of the unique. *Journal of Management Studies*, *30*(1), 31–49.

Aharoni, Y. (1994). How small firms can achieve competitive advantages in an interdependent world. In: T. E. Agmon & R. Drobbnick (Eds), *Small firms in global competition* (pp. 9–18). New York: Oxford University Press.

Aharoni, Y. (1966a). *The foreign investment decision process.* Boston: Harvard Business School.

Aharoni, Y. (1966b). How to market a country. *Columbia Journal of World Business*, *1*(2), 41–49.

Aharoni, Y. (2000a). Globalization and the small, open economy. In: T. Almor & N. Hashai (Eds), *FDI, international trade and the economics of peacemaking.* Rishon Le'Zion, Israel: Academic Studies Division, The College of Management.

Aharoni, Y. (2000b). The role of reputation in global professional business services. In: Y. Aharoni & L. Nahum (Eds), *Globalization of services: Some implications for theory and practice* (pp. 125–141). London: Routledge.

Aharoni, Y. (2002). *European air transportation: Integration, globalization and structural changes.* Swedish network for European studies in economics and business (May). Mölle, Sweden.

Aharoni, Y. (2004). The race for FDI in services – The case of the airline industry. In: L. Oxelheim & P. Ghauri (Eds), *European Union and the race for foreign direct investment in Europe* (pp. 381–406). Amsterdam: Elsevier.

Aharoni, Y., & Ramamurti, R. (2008). The internationalization of multinationals. In: J. J. Boddewyn (Ed), *The evolution of IB scholarship: AIB fellows on the first 50 years and beyond* (Vol. 14, pp. 177–201). Emerald Research in Global Strategic Management.

Aharoni, Y., Tihanyi, L., & Connelly, B. L. (2011). Managerial decision making in international business: A forty-five year retrospective. *Journal of World Business*, *46*(2), 135–142.

Akerlof, G. A., & Dickens, W. T. (1982). The economic consequences of cognitive dissonance. *American Economic Review*, *72*(3), 307–319.

Amason, A., & Sapienza, H. (1997). The effects of top management team size and interaction norms on cognitive and affective conflict. *Journal of Management*, *23*(4), 495–516.

Amason, A. C. (1996). Distinguishing the effects of functional and dysfunctional conflict on strategic decision making: Resolving a paradox for top management teams. *Academy of Management Journal*, *39*, 123–148.

Anderson, E., & Gatignon, H. (1986). Models of foreign entry: A transaction cost analysis and propositions. *Journal of International Business Studies*, *17*, 1–26.

Ansoff, I., & McDonnel, E. (1990). *Implanting strategic management*. Hemel Hempstead: Prentice Hall Europe.

Argote, L. (1999). *Organizational learning: Creating, retaining and transferring knowledge*. Norwell, MA: Kluwer Academic Publishers.

Argote, L., & Greve, H. R. (2007). A behavioral theory of the firm – 40 years and counting: Introduction and impact. *Organization Science*, *18*(3), 337–349.

Arieli, D. (2008). *Predictably irrational*. New York: HarperCollins Publishers.

Arieli, D., Loewenstein, G., & Prelec, D. (2003). "Coherent arbitrariness": Stable demand curves without stable preferences. *Quarterly Journal of Economics*, *118*(1), 73–105.

Arrow, K. J. (1987). Rationality of self and others in an economic system. In: R. M. Hogarth & M. W. Reder (Eds), *Rational choice: The contrast between economics and psychology* (pp. 201–216). Chicago: University of Chicago Press.

Augier, M., & Teece, D. (2007). Dynamic capabilities and multinational enterprise: Penrosean insights and omission. *Management International Review*, *47*(2), 175–192.

Barkema, H. G., Shenkar, O., Vermeulen, F., & Bell, J. H. J. (1997). Working abroad, working with others: How firms learn to operate international joint ventures. *Academy of Management Journal*, *40*, 426–442.

Barkema, H. G., & Vermeulen, F. (1998). International expansion through start-up or acquisition: A learning perspective. *Academy of Management Journal*, *41*, 7–26.

Barnes, J. H. (1984). Cognitive biases and their impact on strategic planning. *Strategic Management Journal*, *5*(2), 129–137.

Barney, J. B. (1991). Firm resources and sustained competitive advantage. *Journal of Management*, *17*, 99–120.

Barnet, R. J., & Müller, R. E. (1974). *Global reach: The power of the multinational corporations*. New York: Simon and Schuster.

Bartlett, C., & Ghoshal, S. (1989). *Managing across borders*. Boston: Harvard Business School Press.

Benito, G. R. G. (1997). Divestment of foreign production operations. *Applied Economics*, *29*, 1365–1377.

Biais, B., Hilton, D., Mazurier, K., & Puget, S. (2005). Judgmental overconfidence, self-monitoring and trading performance in an experimental financial market. *Review of Economic Studies*, *72*, 287–312.

Boone, C., & Hendriks, W. (2009). Top management team diversity and firm performance: Moderators of functional-background and locus-of-control diversity. *Management Science*, *55*(2), 118–165.

Brouthers, K., & Hennart, J. F. (2007). Boundaries of the firm: Insights from international entry mode research. *Journal of Management, 33*(3), 395–425.

Brouthers, K. D., & Brouthers, L. E. (2001). Explaining the national cultural distance paradox. *Journal of International Business Studies, 32,* 177–189.

Buckley, P., & Casson, M. (1976). *The future of the multinational enterprise.* London: Macmillan.

Buckley, P., & Casson, M. C. (2009). The internalization theory of the multinational enterprise: A review of the progress of a research agenda after 30 years. *Journal of International Business Studies, 40*(9), 1563–1580.

Buckley, P. J., Devinney, T. M., & Louviere, J. J. (2007). Do managers behave the way theory suggests? A choice-theoretic examination of foreign direct investment location decision-making. *Journal of International Business Studies, 38*(7), 1069–1094.

Camerer, C. (2000). Prospect theory in the wild. In: D. Kahneman & A. Tversky (Eds), *Choices, values and frames.* New York: Russell Sage.

Camerer, C. F., Babcock, L., Loewenstein, G., & Thaler, R. (1997). Labor supply of New York City cabdrivers: One day at a time. *Quarterly Journal of Economics, 112*(May), 407–441.

Camerer, C. F., George Loewenstein, G., & Prelec, D. (2004). Neuroeconomics: Why economics needs brains. *Scandinavian Journal of Economics, 106*(3), 555–579.

Camerer, C. F., Loewenstein, G., & Rabin, M. (Eds). (2003). *Advances in behavioral economics.* New York: Russel Sage Foundation.

Camerer, C., Loewenstein, G., & Prelec, D. (2005). Neuroeconomics: How neuroscience can inform economics. *Journal of Economic Literature, 43,* 9–64.

Cantwell, J. (1995). The globalization of technology: What remains of the product cycle model? *Cambridge Journal of Economics, 19,* 155–174.

Carpenter, M. A., Geletkanycz, M. A., & Sanders, W. G. (2004). Upper echelons research revisited: Antecedents, elements, and consequences of top management team composition. *Journal of Management, 30,* 749–778.

Casson, M. (Ed.) (2000). *The economics of international business.* Cheltenham, UK: Edward Elgar.

Chandler, A. (1962). *Strategy and structure: Chapters in the history of the industrial enterprise.* Cambridge, MA: MIT Press.

Christensen, C. M. (1997). *The innovator's dilemma when new technologies cause great firms to fail.* Boston: Harvard Business School Press.

Clapham, S. E., & Schwenk, C. R. (1991). Self-serving attributions, managerial cognition, and company performance. *Strategic Management Journal, 12*(3), 219–229.

Coase, R. (1937). The nature of the firm. *Economica, 4*(3), 386–405.

Coff, R. W. (1999). How buyers cope with uncertainty when acquiring firms in knowledge-intensive industries: Caveat emptor. *Organization Science, 10*(2), 144–161.

Cotula, L. (2009). Land grab or development opportunity? International farm land deals in Africa. *Columbia FDI Perspectives,* No. 8, June 22.

Coval, J. D., & Moskowitz, T. J. (1999). Home bias at home: Local equity preference in domestic portfolios. *Journal of Finance, 54*(6), 2045–2074.

Cyert, R. M., & DeGroot, M. H. (1974). Rational expectations and Bayesian analysis. *Journal of Political Economy, 82,* 521–536.

Cyert, R. M., & March, J. G. (1963). *A behavioral theory of the firm.* Cambridge, MA: Blackwell Publishers.

Das, T. K., & Teng, B. S. (1999). Cognitive biases and strategic decision processes: An integrative perspective. *Journal of Management Studies, 36*(6), 757–778.

DellaVigna, S. (2009). Psychology and economics: Evidence from the field. *Journal of Economic Literature, 47*(2), 315–372.

Doz, Y., Santos, J., & Williamson, P. (2001). *From global to metanational: How companies win in the knowledge economy*. Boston: Harvard Business School Press.

Dunning, J. H. (1980). Towards an eclectic theory of international production: Some empirical test. *Journal of International Business Studies, 11*(1), 9–31.

Dunning, J. H. (1994). *Globalization, economic restructuring and development*. Geneva: UNCTAD.

Dunning, J. H., & Lundan, S. (2008). *Multinational enterprises and the global economy* (2nd ed.). Cheltenham, UK: Edward Elgar.

Eckbo, P. (1976). *The future of world oil*. Cambridge, MA: Ballimger.

Einhorn, H. J., & Hogarth, R. M. (1981). Behavioral decision theory: Processes of judgment and choice. *Annual Review of Psychology, 32*, 53–88.

Foster, R., & Kaplan, S. (2001). *Creative destruction – Why companies that are built to last underperform the market and how to successfully transform them*. New York: Doubleday.

French, K., & Poterba, J. (1991). Investor diversification and international equity markets. *American Economic Review, 81*(2), 222–226.

Friedman, T. L. (2005). *The world is flat: A brief history of the twenty-first century*. New York: Farrar, Straus & Giroux.

Fudenberg, D. (2006). Advancing beyond advances in behavioral economics. *Journal of Economic Literature, XLIV*(September), 694–711.

Ghoshal, S., & Moran, P. (1996). Bad for practice: A critique of the transaction cost theory. *Academy of Management Review, 21*(1), 13–47.

Gilovich, T., Griffin, D., & Kahneman, D. (2002). *The psychology of judgment: Heuristics and biases*. New York: Cambridge University Press.

Gilpin, R. (1975). *U.S. power and the multinational corporation*. New York: Basic Books.

Glunk, U., Heijltjes, M. G., & Olie, R. (2001). Design characteristics and functioning of top management teams in Europe. *European Management Journal, 19*(3), 291–300.

Gneezy, U., & Rustichini, A. (2000a). A fine is a price. *Journal of Legal Studies, 29*(1, part 1), 1–17.

Gneezy, U., & Rustichini, A. (2000b). Pay enough or don't pay at all. *Quarterly Journal of Economics, 115*(3), 791–810.

Gupta, A. K., & Govindarajan, V. (2000). Knowledge flows within multinational corporations. *Strategic Management Journal, 21*(4), 473–496.

Hambrick, D. C., & Mason, P. A. (1984). Upper echelons: The organization as a reflection of its top managers. *Academy of Management Review, 9*(2), 193–206.

Hannan, M. T., & Freeman, J. (1977). The population ecology of organizations. *American Journal of Sociology, 82*, 929–964.

Hannan, M. T., & Freeman, J. (1984). Structural inertia and organizational change. *American Sociological Review, 49*(2), 149–164.

Harrison, D. A., Price, K. H., & Bell, M. P. (1998). Beyond relational demography: Time and the effects of surface- and deep-level diversity on work group cohesion. *Academy of Management Journal, 41*, 96–107.

Hayward, M. L., & Hambrick, D. C. (1997). Explaining premium paid for large acquisitions: Evidence of CEO hubris. *Administrative Science Quarterly, 42*(1), 103–127.

Hennart, J. F. (1982). *A theory of multinational enterprise*. Ann Arbor, MI: University of Michigan Press.

Hennart, J. F. (2009). Down with MNE-centric theories! Market entry and expansion as the bundling of MNWE and local assets. *Journal of International Business Studies, 40*, 1432–1454.

Herrmann, P., & Datta, D. K. (2005). Relationships between top management team characteristics and international diversification: An empirical investigation. *British Journal of Management, 16*(1), 69–78.

Huston, L., & Sakkab, N. (2006). Inside Procter & Gamble's new model for innovation. *Harvard Business Review, 84*(3), 58–66.

Hutzschenreuter, T., Pederson, T., & Volberda, H. W. (2007). The role of path dependency and, managerial intentionality: A perspective on international business research. *Journal of International Business Studies, 38*(7), 1055–1068.

Jacoby, N. H. (1974). *Multinational Oil: A study of industrial dynamics*. New York: Macmillan.

Jensen, M. C., & Meckling, W. H. (1976). Theory of the firm: Managerial behavior, agency costs and ownership structure. *Journal of Financial Economics, 3*(3), 305–360.

Johanson, J., & Vahlne, J. E. (1977). The internationalization process of the firm – A model of knowledge development and increasing foreign market commitments. *Journal of International Business Studies, 8*, 23–32.

Johanson, J., & Vahlne, J. E. (1990). The mechanisms of internationalization. *International Marketing Review, 7*, 11–24.

Johanson, J., & Vahlne, J. E. (2009). The Uppsala internationalization process model revisited: From liability of foreignness to liability of outsidership. *Journal of International Business Studies, 40*, 1411–1431.

Jones, G. (2005). *Renewing Unilever: Transformation and tradition*. Oxford: Oxford University Press.

Jones, G., & Khenna, T. (2006). Bring history (back) into international business. *Journal of International Business Studies, 37*, 453–468.

Kahneman, D. (2003). A perspective on judgment and choice: Mapping bounded rationality. *American Psychologist, 58*, 697–720.

Kahneman, D., Knetsch, J. L., & Thaler, R. H. (1990). Experimental tests of the endowment effect and the Coase theorem. *The Journal of Political Economy, 96*(6), 1325–1348.

Kahneman, D., Knetsch, J., & Thaler, R. (1986). Fairness as a constraint on profit seeking: Entitlements in the market. *American Economic Review, 76*(4), 728–741.

Kahneman, D., & Tversky, A. (1979). Prospect theory: An analysis of decision under risk. *Econometrica, 47*(March), 263–291.

Kahneman, D., & Tversky, A. (1982). On the study of statistical intuitions. In: D. Kahneman, P. Slovic & A. Tversky (Eds), *Judgment under uncertainty: Heuristics and biases*. Cambridge: Cambridge University Press.

Katzenstein, P. J. (1984). *Corporatism and change: Austria, Switzerland and the politics of industry*. NY: Cornell University Press.

Kaufman, G. G., Krueger, T. H., & Hunter, W. C. (1999). *The Asian financial crisis: Origins, implications and solutions*. Springer.

Kekic, L. (2009). The global economic crisis and FDI flows to emerging markets. *Columbia FDI Perspectives*, No. 15, October 8. Available at www.vcc.Columbia.edu

Kilduff, M., Angelmar, R., & Mehra, A. (2000). Top management-team diversity and firm performance: Examining the role of cognitions. *Organization Science, 11*, 21–34.

Kindlebeger, C. (1969). *American business abroad.* New Haven, CT: Yale University Press.
Knetsch, J. L. (1989). The endowment effect and evidence of nonreversible indifference curves. *The American Economic Review, 79,* 1277–1284.
Knetsch, J. L., & Sinden, J. A. (1984). Willingness to pay and compensation demanded: Experimental evidence of an unexpected disparity in measures of value, the endowment effect and evidence of nonreversible indifference curves. *The Quarterly Journal of Economics, 99,* 507–521.
Knight, G. A., & Cavusgil, S. T. (1996). The born global firm: A challenge to traditional internationalization theory. In: L. Lindmark, P. R. Christensen, H. Eskelinen, B. Forsstrom, O. J. Sorenson, & E. Vatn (Eds), *Advances in international marketing* (Vol. 8, pp. 11–26). Bingley, UK: JAI.
Knight, G., & Cavusgil, S. T. (2004). Innovation, organizational capabilities, and the born-global firm. *Journal of International Business Studies, 35*(2), 124–141.
Kogut, B. (2003). *The global internet economy.* Cambridge, MA: MIT Press.
Kogut, B., Walker, G., & Anand, J. (2002). Agency and institutions: National divergences in diversification behavior. *Organization Science, 13,* 162–178.
Kogut, B., & Zander, U. (1993). Knowledge of the firm and the evolutionary theory of the multinational corporation. *Journal of International Business Studies, 24,* 625–645.
Kőszegi, B. (2006). Ego utility, overconfidence, and task choice. *Journal of the European Economic Association, 4*(4), 673–707.
Kunreuther, H., Ginsberg, R., Miller, L., Sagi, P., Slovic, P., Borkin, B., & Katz, N. (1978). *Disaster insurance protection: Public policy lessons.* New York: Wiley.
Laibson, D. (1997). Golden eggs and hyperbolic discounting. *Quarterly Journal of Economics, 112,* 443–478.
Langlois, R. N., & Csontos, L. (1993). Optimization, rule following, and the methodology of situational analysis. In: U. Mäki, B. Gustafsson & C. Knudsen (Eds), *Rationality, institutions, and economic methodology.* London: Routledge.
Lawrence, B. S. (1997). The black box of organizational demography. *Organization Science, 8,* 1–22.
Levitt, K. (1970). *Silent surrender: The multinational corporation in Canada.* New York: St. Martin's Press.
Levitt, B., & March, J. G. (1988). Organizational learning. *Annual Review of Sociology, 14,* 319–340.
Li, J., & Guisinger, S. (1992). The globalization of service multinationals in the triad regions: Japan, Western Europe and North America. *Journal of International Business Studies, 23,* 675–696.
March, J. G. (2006). Ideas as art (interview by Diane Coutu). *Harvard Business Review, 84*(10), 82–89.
March, J. G., & Shapira, Z. (1987). Managerial perspectives on risk and risk taking. *Management Science, 33,* 1404–1418.
March, J. G., & Simon, H. A. (1958). *Organizations.* New York: Wiley.
Markóczy, L. (1997). Measuring beliefs: Accept no substitutes. *Academy of Management Journal, 40,* 1228–1242.
Martin, J. A., & Eisenhardt, K. M. (2004). Coping with decline in dynamic markets. Corporate entrepreneurship and the recombinative organizational form. *Advances in Strategic Management* (pp. 357–382). Bingley, UK: JAI.
McCallum, J. T. (1995). National borders matter: Canada–U.S. regional trade patterns. *American Economic Review, 85,* 615–623.

Miller, K. D., & Chen, W. R. (2004). Variable organizational risk preferences: Tests of the March–Shapira model. *Academy of Management Journal, 47*, 105–115.

Moran, T. H. (1987). Managing an oligopoly of would-be sovereign: The dynamics of joint control and self-control in the international oil industry: Past, present and future. *Industrial Organization, 41*(4), 575–608.

Morck, R., Wolfenzon, D., & Yeung, B. (2005). Corporate governance, economic entrenchment and growth. *Journal of Economic Literature, XLIII*(September), 655–720.

Morisset, J., & Andrews-Johnson, K. (2003). *The effectiveness of promotion agencies at attracting foreign direct investment.* FIAS Occasional Paper no. 16. Foreign Investment Advisory Service, Washington, DC.

Mytelka, L. K., & Delapierre, M. (1999). Strategic partnerships, knowledge-based networked oligopolies and the state. In: C. Cutler, V. Haufler & T. Porter (Eds), *Private authority and international affairs* (pp. 129–148). Binghamton, NY: Suny University Press.

Nelson, R., & Winter, S. (1982). *An evolutionary theory of economic change.* Cambridge, MA: Harvard University Press.

Nelson, R. R., & Winter, S. (1973). Toward an evolutionary theory of economic capabilities. *American Economic Review, 63*, 440–449.

Newell, A., & Simon, H. A. (1972). *Human problem solving.* Englewood Cliffs, NJ: Prentice Hall.

North, D. C. (2005). Introduction to understanding the process of economic change. In: *Understanding the process of economic change.* Princeton, NJ: Princeton University Press.

Organization Science. (2007). Special issue on Cyert and March's a behavioral theory of the firm. *Organization Science, 18*(3), 337–542.

Oxelheim, L., & Ghauri, P. (Eds). (2004). *European Union and the race for foreign direct investment in Europe.* Oxford: Elsevier.

Park, S. H., & Ungson, G. R. (1997). The effect of national culture, organizational complementarity, and economic motivation on joint venture dissolution. *Academy of Management Journal, 40*, 279–307.

Parkhe, A. (1991). Interfirm diversity, organizational learning, and longevity in global strategic alliances. *Journal of International Business Studies, 22*, 579–601.

Penrose, E. T. (1968). *The large international firm in developing country: The international petroleum industry.* Westport, CT: Greenwod Press.

Pitelis, C. (2007). Edith Penrose and a learning-based perspective on the MNE and OLI. *Management International Review, 47*(2), 207–220.

Porter, M. E. (1979). The structure within industries and companies' performance. *Review of Economics and Statistics, 61*(May), 215–227.

Porter, M. E. (1980). *Competitive strategy: Techniques for analyzing industries and competition.* New York: Free Press.

Porter, M. E. (1985). *Competitive advantage.* New York: Free Press.

Prahalad, C. K., & Bettis, R. (1986). The dominant logic: A new linkage between diversity and performance. *Strategic Management Journal, 7*(6), 485–502.

Priem, R. L., Lyon, D. W., & Dess, G. D. (1999). Inherent limitations of demographic proxies in top management team heterogeneity research. *Journal of Management, 25*, 935–953.

Rabin, M. (1993). Incorporating fairness into game theory and economics. *American Economic Review, 83*(December), 1281–1302.

Rabin, M. (1998). Psychology and economics. *Journal of Economic Literature, 36*(March), 11–46.

Rabin, M. (2002). A perspective on psychology and economics. *European Economic Review, 46,* 657–685.

Rangan, S., & Sengal, M. (2009). Information technology and transnational integration: Theory and evidence on the evolution of the modern multinational enterprise. *Journal of International Business Studies, 40*(9), 1496–1514.

Rau, D. (2008). Top management team social processes and changes in organizational strategy. *Journal of Business and Management, 14,* 1.

Ronen, S., & Shenkar, O. (1985). Clustering countries on attitudinal dimensions: A review and synthesis. *Academy of Management Review* (10), 435–454.

Rubinstein, A. (2008). Comments on neuroeconomics. *Economics and Philosophy, 24,* 485–494.

Rugman, A. (2005). *The regional multinationals.* Cambridge, UK: Cambridge University Press.

Saari, D. J. (1999). *Global corporations and sovereign nations: Collision or cooperation?* Westport, CT: Quorum Books.

Samuelson, W., & Zeckhauser, R. J. (1988). Status quo bias in decision making. *Journal of Risk and Uncertainty, 1*(March), 7–59.

Schneider, S., & DeMeyer, A. (1991). Interpreting and responding to strategic issues: The impact of national culture. *Strategic Management Journal, 12,* 307–320.

Schwenk, C. R. (1984). Cognitive simplification processes in strategic decision-making. *Strategic Management Journal, 5*(2), 111–128.

Schwenk, C. R. (1986). Information, cognitive biases, and commitment to a course of action. *Academy of Management Review, 11,* 298–310.

Schwenk, C. R. (1995). Strategic decision making. *Journal of Management, 21,* 471–493.

Shefrin, H. M., & Thaler, R. H. (1988). The behavioral life-cycle hypothesis. *Economic Inquiry, 26*(October), 609–643.

Shenkar, O. (2001). Cultural distance revisited: Towards a more rigorous conceptualization and measurement of cultural differences. *Journal of International Business Studies, 32,* 519–535.

Shoham, A., & Fiegenbaum, A. (2002). Competitive determinants of organizational risk-taking attitude: The role of strategic reference points. *Management Decision, 40,* 127–141.

Simon, H. A. (1947). *Administrative behavior.* New York: Macmillan.

Simon, H. A. (1955). A behavioral model of rational choice. *Quarterly Journal of Economics, 69*(1), 99–118.

Simon, H. A. (1985). Human nature in politics: The dialogue of psychology with political science. *The American Political Science Review, 79*(2), 293–304.

Slovic, P., Fischhoff, B., & Lichtenstein, S. (1977). Behavioral decision theory. *Annual Review of Psychology, 28,* 1–39.

Staw, B. M., & Ross, J. (1987). Behaviors in escalation situations: Antecedents, prototypes, and solutions. In: L. G. Cummings & B. Staw (Eds), *Research in organizational behavior* (pp. 39–78). Greenwich: JAI Press.

Stopford, J., & Strange, S. (with Henley, J. S.). (1991). *Rival states, rival firms: Competition for world market shares.* Cambridge: Cambridge University Press.

Stulz, R. (1988). Managerial control of voting rights: Financing policies and the market for corporate control. *Journal of Financial Economics, 20,* 25–54.

Sunstein, C., & Thaler, R. H. (2008). *Nudge: Improving decisions about health, wealth, and happiness.* New Haven, CT: Yale University Press.

Taleb, N. N. (2007). *The black swan: The impact of the highly improbable.* New York: Random House.

Teece, D. (1986). Profiting from technological innovation: Implications for integration, collaboration and public policy. *Research Policy, 15*(6), 285–305.

Teece, D., & Pisano, G. (1994). The dynamic capabilities of firms: An introduction. *Industrial and Corporate Change, 3*(3), 537–556.

Teece, D. J., Pisano, G., & Shuen, A. (1997). Dynamic capabilities and strategic management. *Strategic Management Journal, 18*(7), 509–553.

Tesar, L., & Werner, I. (1995). Home bias and high turnover. *Journal of International Money and Finance, 14*(4), 467–492.

Thaler, R. (1999). Mental accounting matters. *Journal of Behavioral Decision Making, 12,* 183–206.

Thaler, R., & Benartzi, S. (2004). Save more tomorrow: Using behavioral economics to increase employee savings. *Journal of Political Economy, 112*(1), 164–187.

Thaler, R. H., & Shefrin, H. M. (1981). An economic theory of self-control. *Journal of Political Economy, 89*(2), 392–406.

Tihanyi, L., Ellstrand, A. E., Daily, C. M., & Dalton, D. R. (2001). Composition of the top management team and firm international diversification. *Journal of Management, 26*(6), 1157–1177.

Tihanyi, L., Griffith, D. A., & Russell, C. J. (2005). The effect of cultural distance on entry mode choice, international diversification, and MNE performance: A meta-analysis. *Journal of International Business Studies, 36,* 270–283.

Trispas, M., & Gavetti, G. (2000). Capabilities, cognition, and inertia: Evidence from digital imaging. *Strategic Management Journal, 21,* 1147–1161.

Tversky, A., & Kahneman, D. (1974). Judgment under uncertainty: Heuristics and biases. *Science, 185*(4157), 1124–1131.

Tversky, A., & Kahneman, D. (1981). The framing of decisions and the psychology of choice. *Science, 211,* 453–458.

Tversky, A., & Kahneman, D. (1991). Loss aversion in riskless choice: A reference-dependent model. *Quarterly Journal of Economics, 106,* 1039–1061.

Vernon, R. (1966). International investment and international trade in the product cycle. *Quarterly Journal of Economics, 80,* 190–207.

Vernon, R. (1971). *Sovereignty at Bay.* Cambridge, MA: Harvard University Press.

Vernon, R. (1979). The product cycle hypothesis in a new international environment. *Oxford Bulletin of Economics and Statistics, 41,* 255–267.

Von Braun, J., & Meinzen-Dick, R. (2009). *Land grabbing by foreign investors in developing countries: Risks and opportunities* (Available at www.ifpri.org/bp/bp013.asp). Washington, DC: International Food Policy Research Institute.

United Nations Department of Economic and Social Affairs. (1973). *Multinational corporations in world development.* New York: United Nations.

UNCTAD. (different years). *World Investment Report.* Geneva: U.N.

Wells, L., & Mint, A. (1990). *Marketing a country.* FIAS Occasional Paper no. 1. Foreign Investment Advisory Service, Washington, DC.

Wells, L., & Mint, A. (2000). *Marketing a country: Promotion as a tool for attracting foreign investment* (revised edition). FIAS Occasional Papers no. 13. Foreign Investment Advisory Service, Washington, DC.

Werner, S. (2002). Recent developments in international management research: A review of 20 top management journals. *Journal of Management, 28,* 277–305.

Williamson, O. E. (1975). *Markets and hierarchies: Analysis and antitrust implications.* New York: The Free Press.

Williamson, O. E. (1985). *The economic institutions of capitalism*. New York: The Free Press.

Wolf, H. C. (2000). Intranational home bias in trade. *Review of Economics and Statistics, 82*(4), 555–563.

Wolf, M. (2004). *Why globalization works*. New Haven, CT: Yale University Press.

Yoffie, D. B., & Milner, H. V. (1989). An alternative to free trade or protectionism: Why corporations seek strategic trade policy. *California Management Review, 3*(4), 113–131.

Zhang, P. (2007). Top management team heterogeneity and firm performance: An empirical research on Chinese listed companies. *Frontiers in Business Research in China, 1*(1), 123–134.

Zollo, M., & Winter, S. G. (2002). Deliberate learning and the evolution of dynamic capabilities. *Organization Science, 13*, 339–351.

BRINGING MANAGERS' DECISION MODELS INTO FDI RESEARCH

Timothy M. Devinney

ABSTRACT

This chapter presents a structure within which to think about incorporating managerial decision models and managers' decisions into management research in general and foreign direct investment research more specifically. The thinking builds on Aharoni's initial research in The Foreign Investment Decision Process *(1966) while incorporating his most recent call to action around the behavioral models of managers in "Behavioral Elements in Foreign Direct Investment" (2010).*

Keywords: Decision models; foreign direct investment; managers

INTRODUCTION

Foreign direct investment (FDI) is at the core of nearly all aspects of international business (IB) research. Without firms engaging in overseas investment, the notion of the multinational enterprise (MNE) loses it meaning and discussions as far ranging as cultural distance and the returns to multinationality fade into irrelevance. Yet, despite this, our understanding

The Future of Foreign Direct Investment and the Multinational Enterprise
Research in Global Strategic Management, Volume 15, 61–83
Copyright © 2011 by Emerald Group Publishing Limited
All rights of reproduction in any form reserved
ISSN: 1064-4857/doi:10.1108/S1064-4857(2011)0000015009

of the processes underlying the firm's FDI decisions is still limited, normally battled over through two competing traditions.

On the one side is the rationalist formulations derived from economic modeling approaches (e.g., Hymer, 1960; Dunning, 1981; Buckley & Casson, 1976) with their emphasis on the firm's making optimal or quasi-optimal choices in an environment with limited information. In this tradition, firms concentrate on the profitability and rent generation facets of FDI. On the other side resides the quasi-psychological process model, with its emphasis on a mixture of loosely concatenated theoretical precepts drawn from a variety of disciplines (e.g., Johanson & Vahlne, 1977). In this tradition, risk-averse managers make iterative decisions in a world of limited information. For internationalization process theorists, "learning to internationalize" is part and parcel of act of FDI undertaken by firms with risk-averse managers.

Despite their different points of emphasis, neither the internationalization process nor the rationalist approaches to FDI do a very good job of getting at the actual process by which FDI decisions are made by managers *in* firms and those with a more practical bent pick and choose aspects of each when discussing FDI decisions more practically. As noted by Buckley, Devinney, and Louviere (2007), part of the problem is that neither approach attempts to directly model the decision-making structure utilized by managers when making FDI decisions, nor do they utilize methodologies that are easily comparable. They also abstract from the organizational structures within which managers are operating, although the internationalization process approach gives this a bit more consideration. The rationalist approaches make extremely strong assumptions – which are never validated directly – about what managers are seeking to achieve and the constraints under which they operate and invariably validate their models using econometric analyses of secondary or survey data. Those applying internationalization process approaches make quite simplistic assumptions about what managers are doing – again without any direct validation – but never expand their theorizing to cover the broader aspects of the firm's FDI strategy or apply empirical methods that would subject their theorizing to any degree of falsification.

It is my argument in this chapter that we need to look beyond these approaches by: (a) being more *deliberative* in our understanding of the decision-making processes of *managers* operating *within firms and markets* and (b) more demanding of the *linkages between our theoretical structures and our empirical modeling.* In other words, we need to go back to first principles. Rather than struggling to force our theories onto phenomena and worrying about what our data hints to us about the relevance and validity of those theories, we need to go back to the basics and examine how managers are making the decisions they are making and what it is that they are attempting to achieve in making those decisions.

The motivation behind this logic is Yair Aharoni's earliest (1966) and latest (2010) streams of research. Following Aharoni (1966), when I speak of being more deliberative this implies that we take into account the processes by which FDI and firm strategies are defined, options are selected, and ultimate choices made. To paraphrase Aharoni (1966, p. ix):

> Simplifying assumptions ... represent [...] so gross a departure from reality that ... theory [is] an extremely inefficient frame of reference from which to observe, project and prescribe on the subject of capital investment.

We should be prepared to accept that the process is complex and, at times, very messy. Again, quoting Aharoni (1966, p. ix):

> What is needed ... [is] to look for the elements in the baffling complexity ... that could explain behavior and make the variables interrelated and sensible. Instead of basing [our] analysis on the ceteris paribus assumptions, [we should] grapple with the problem as a whole and identify the ceteris.

We should also be prepared to examine the degree to which rationality is irrational or seeming irrationality is rational – that is, there are circumstances when the decisions do not fit models based on optimality alone and may be operating to satisfy less clearly articulated goals. The importance of the process is captured by Aharoni (1966) when he notes in his own investigation of FDI in Israel that: "It became apparent that the process [of FDI] as I observed it had almost nothing in common with the classical theory of capital investment" (p. ix).

In the end, we have a simple issue: Do managers matter for FDI decisions to a degree that we need to account for their influence on FDI outcomes? And if so, do they bring with them all the behavioral baggage of human decision making as well as the complexity and randomness of their organizations? And how do we account for their importance in our models? In asking these questions, I am bookending my discussion with Aharoni's (2010) call for more emphasis on behavioral research in IB. If managers do matter, then methodologically they are a "source of variance" that needs to taken into account, irrespective of the empirical modeling approach we use.

In this chapter, I am not seeking to answer these questions in any definitive way. What I am doing is building on Aharoni's initial research (1966) – which emphasized the FDI process at the level of the firm – and his latest call to intellectual arms (2010) – where he attempts to bring in the cognitively flawed manager – in asking the question of whether we are missing something critical in IB and management research; that is, the relevance of managerial decision making and the context in which those decisions are made. In some sense this call is not unlike John Dunning's challenge to scholars in the 1950s (Dunning, 1958). Dunning asked how one could discuss international trade without recourse to the vehicle of that trade; that is, the MNE (Devinney, 2004). I am asking a similar question. How is it that we can discuss the actions of firms without recourse to the vehicle by which those actions are decided; that is, the manager. If we can, the onus is on us to prove that the manager is irrelevant, not to assume that s/he is so.

I will do this in two ways. First, I will ask some very simple questions about the nature of management research and what implicit assumptions we are making about what managers do and how that influences the scientific and practical relevance of our scholarship. It will be shown that very simple questions lead to some very complex possible implications. At this point, the discussion will not, in-and-of-itself, be concentrating on issues with implications for IB or FDI research alone. This is where we will go next. I will then utilize this thinking to build on the work of Yair Aharoni to ask some more specific questions about FDI research. I will use this discussion to put forth a series of potential questions that will hopefully guide us forward in building more parsimonious and practically predictive theories of FDI.

THE RELEVANCE OF MANAGERIAL CHOICE

It might appear silly to ask the question of whether managers matter to our theories, but the vast majority of management theories – and certainly all of those that would be characterized as "macro" theories – assume that the managers do not matter in any material sense or, if they do, they matter as a "type" rather than as individuals. Another way to think about this is that if the managers truly mattered to our theorizing we would be accounting for them as a source of variance in our studies and modeling them directly. We normally assume that the actions that firms take are the result of "firm" decisions that can be abstracted from the individual managers and the organizational processes that filter those decisions – again as neither of these are effectively modeled in any direct way and at best assumed to be idiosyncratic. However, the reality is that "firms" do not make decisions.

Managers make choices – either as a group or individually – nested in the environments and organizations in which they operate.

What are the implications of this?

Take as a very simple starting point the structure shown in Fig. 1.[1] This is a very straightforward way of thinking about decision making within a firm, but its beauty is its simplicity and what it reveals. We can think of the environment as influencing the manager who must make a choice (we will assume that there is just one manager making the decision). The manager has to account for the firm both as to its direct relevance to the decision and also in terms of the structures and routines that operate that will filter and influence that decision. Once a choice is made by the manager and implemented through the firms systems that choice has outcomes (e.g., profitability and market share).

There are several important implications that derive from this simple structure. First, there are 10 sources of variance as outlined in Table 1. For ease of exposition, I have labeled these sources of *direct variance* and sources of *process variance*. The four sources of direct variance are just the variability that exists with respect to the node in the process – environment, manager, firm, and outcome. It is either the variance in how a node is operationalized if it is a construct[2] – for example, the environment might be measured using surveys of experts or secondary data and outcomes as mixtures of accounting returns – or whether there is an inherent idiosyncrasy that cannot be modeled[3] – for example, the individual heterogeneity of the manager's decision process or firm level differences that cannot be attributed to anything observable about the firm or its industry. Mathematically, what this would imply is that there are error terms subscripted for the specific environments and specific outcomes. In the case of the manager and the firm, the direct variance will be represented by processes that are firm or manager dependent and hence subscripted as

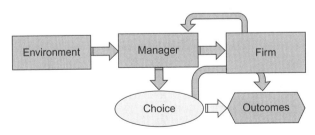

Fig. 1. A Simple Managerial Choice Process.

Table 1. Direct and Process Variance in Managerial Decision Making.

	An Example of a Characterization	Definition and Sources of Bias
Direct variance		
Environment (E)	$\tilde{E}_i = \bar{E}_i + \tilde{\eta}_i$; $\hat{E}_i = \bar{E}_i + \tilde{\varepsilon}_i$. $\tilde{\eta}_i$ is random error in the environment i; $\tilde{\varepsilon}_i$ is the error related to measurement of environment i.	Characterization of the environment. Environmental randomness/complexity; measurement error.
Manager (M)	Each manager's (M) decision models may be different. Manager level heterogeneity.	Managers may apply different decision models, utilize different information, be subject to more or less cognitive bias.
Firm (F)	Each firm's (F) mediation of the decision process may be different. Firm level heterogeneity.	Firms possess idiosyncratic routines and systems, operate with different incentives, utilize different performance metrics and evaluate options differently.
Outcomes (O)	$\tilde{O}_{jF} = \bar{O}_{jF} + \tilde{\mu}_j$; $\hat{O}_{jF} = \bar{O}_{jF} + \tilde{\theta}_{jF}$. $\tilde{\mu}_j$ is random error in outcome j; $\tilde{\theta}_{jF}$ is error related to how outcome j is measured by firm F.	Performance or outcomes that arise. Outcome randomness/complexity; measurement error.
Process variance		
Environment → Manager	$E'_{iM} = e_M(\hat{E}_i, \tilde{\eta}_i)$ Managers perceive an environment based on its measured structure plus how "variable" it is.	Managers' perception of the environment. Managers may not perceive environments in the same way – they may have different models, $e_M(\bullet)$, that lead to different perceptions, E'_{iM}.
Firm → Manager	$\tilde{R}_{kF} = \bar{R}_{kF} + \tilde{\rho}_k$; $\hat{R}_{kF} = \bar{R}_{kF} + \tilde{\nu}_{kF}$ $\tilde{\rho}_k$ is randomness in resource of type k (independent of the firm); $\tilde{\nu}_{kF}$ is randomness related to measurement of the resource k possessed by firm F.	Managers' perceptions of the internal aspects of the firm that are relevant to the decision. Managers must determine interaction between external factors and internal resources and capabilities; resources and capabilities are different and may also be subject to variance.

	Managers create a "resources portfolio" that they believe are available and relevant $$\{R_{1F}, R_{2F}, R_{3F}, \ldots, R_{PF}\} \in \underline{R}_F$$ $$\underline{R}_F = r_{MF}(\hat{\underline{R}}_F | E'_{iM}) + \tilde{\tau}_{MF}$$ $\tilde{\tau}_{MF}$ is randomness related to the inclusion of resources in the set by manager M in firm F.	Managers options must be filtered through firm's organizational routines and approval processes.
Manager→Firm	Managers create a "consideration set" of potential options, $\{C_{1F}, C_{2F}, C_{3F}, \ldots, C_{NF}\} \in \underline{C}_F$, that meet a criteria set up by the firm, $f_F(\bullet)$. $$\underline{C}_F = f_F(E'_{iM}, \hat{\underline{R}}_F) + \tilde{\kappa}_F$$ where $\tilde{\kappa}_F$ is the random component of firm F's process of narrowing down choices.[a]	These routines do not necessarily lead to a set of options that are optimal or even close to optimal.
		Managers choose what they perceive to be the "best" option based upon their decision model.
Manager→Choice	$$C'_{MFi} \in \underline{C}_F = m_M(E'_{iM}, \hat{\underline{R}}_F) + \tilde{\zeta}_M$$ $m_M(E'_{iM}, \hat{\underline{R}}_F)$ represents the manager's systematic decision model.	The manager's decision is based on a structured systematic component and a random idiosyncratic component.
	$\tilde{\zeta}_M$ represents the idiosyncratic random component of the decision attributable to manager M.	Managers may erroneously weigh components of the options, be subject to overconfidence, or be intransitive in their choices.
Choice→Firm→Outcome	$$\hat{O}'_{jF} = o_F(C'_{MFi} | \tilde{\mu}_j, \tilde{\theta}_{jF}) + \tilde{\gamma}_{jF}$$ $o_F(C'_{MFi} | \tilde{\mu}_j, \tilde{\theta}_{jF})$ is the systematic link between the outcome and the choice C'_{MFi} when implemented by firm F, conditional on the measurement and structural characteristics of outcome type j. $\tilde{\gamma}_{jF}$ represents the random component of the implementation on outcome j by firm F.	Firms differ in terms of implementation capabilities.
Choice→Outcome	$$O^*_j = \max_X [\hat{O}'_{jX} = o_X(C'_{MFi} | \tilde{\mu}_j, \tilde{\theta}_{jX}) + \tilde{\gamma}_{jX}]$$ where x is all firms. If all other firms chose C'_{MFi}, how would they have performed?	What the outcome should have achieved or was expected to achieve, independent of the firm?

[a] Note that this stage of the process is not subscripted by M since it is assumed that the "firm" makes this choice independent of the individual manager. This need not be the case but is done in this manner here just to show that the firm could have a process intermediating that is independent of the manager.

such. Note that there is no source of variance in the choice as this is endogenous.[4] Via this logic, it is not the outcomes that are most relevant, but the choices.

The arrows in Fig. 1 show the six sources of process variance. Process variance is the variability that must be modeled as a functional form in the usage of the information and options available and will generally include a systematic and predictable component and an unsystematic random aspect. For example, the manager's choice can have an idiosyncratic manager-by-manager component to it where some factors matter more to some managers and less to others, but do so rationally; that is, some might emphasize the importance of market growth more strongly and others consider return on investment more important, neither of which is "better." Some managers might be more risk averse, exhibit greater overconfidence (e.g., Camerer & Lovallo, 1999; Kahneman & Lovallo, 1993), or be subject more or less to prospect theory biases (e.g., Kahneman & Tversky, 1979). Some managers may simply be better at utilizing the information that is being presented to them (Gary & Wood, 2011). The same sorts of issues arise with respect to the firm. Organizational routines may add noise into the system and be structured in a manner that overweighs specific components of a decision. For example, it was long held that Japanese firms put market share over profitability when entering new markets (Doyle, 1994).

What Fig. 1 and this discussion imply is that we have a considerable number of sources of variation, heterogeneity, and uncertainty when examining even the simplest of managerial decisions. What is also apparent are the assumptions that we make about the nature of the structure that can have a critical impact on whether or not we are truly getting at the essence of what we believe we are examining. Table 1 gives an indication of how we might characterize the components of Fig. 1 and what biases might arise (note, again, that this is just one possible formulation). Although this is not meant to be a definitive list, working through the logic is instructive.

We can think of a manager in a firm scanning the environment within which their choice is going to be embedded. The environment is complex but some aspects can be subjected to analysis, although imperfect analysis (the $\hat{E}_i = \tilde{E}_i + \tilde{\varepsilon}_i$). The manager scans this environment and gets a perception (E'_{im}) of what the environment means to the decision. However, this perception is incomplete and might be significantly biased; that is, $e_M(\hat{E}_i, \hat{\eta}_i)$ need not be "rational." Examining his/her firm they also get a picture of their organization's resources ($\hat{\underline{R}}_F$) and their relevance to the decision. However, this perception is again incomplete and has some error embedded

within it in much the same way that the environment does. In other words, some resources are less certain, as given by $\tilde{\rho}_k$, and how they are measured is imperfect, as given by $\tilde{v}_{kF}$. The manager can pull this "best guess" information together and come up with a set of options that (a) meet some minimum beliefs about what might be good options and (b) fit with the conflicting criteria and routines that operate in their firm ($\underline{C}_F$). This "consideration set" is not necessarily optimal and could include some erroneous options. Finally, from this the manager must make a final choice based upon his or her own decision model (C'_{MFi}). However, the choice is complex and may include criteria that are not clearly or cleanly specified, may also be subject to cognitive bias and can be influenced or skewed by organizational routines and culture and the individual firm's goals. The choice must be implemented by the manager's firm and the choice, together with the extent to which it is implemented effectively, along with many other firm-specific decisions and external factors leads to some performance outcome ($\hat{O}'_{jF}$). However, because that outcome is based on many uncontrolled factors, it, too, will have a random component, as given by $\tilde{\gamma}_{jF}$. Ultimately, the quality of the decision and its implementation has to be measured on some criteria. In this example, the question I have asked is how well this outcome compares to what would have been achieved if that decision had been taken by any other firm, denoted x, or
$$O_j^* = \max_{\forall x}[\hat{O}'_{jx} = o_x(C'_{MFi}|\tilde{\mu}_j, \tilde{\theta}_{jx}) + \tilde{\gamma}_{jx}].^5$$

This example and Table 1 reveal four important issues. First, the factors of relevance to the phenomena we are investigating will have fundamentally unmeasurable variance, as given in Table 1 by $\tilde{\eta}_i$, $\tilde{\mu}_i$, and $\tilde{\rho}_i$. Note that this is different from the measurement error – represented by $\tilde{\varepsilon}_i$, $\tilde{v}_{kF}$, $\tilde{\theta}_{jF}$ – which conceivably can be reduced with better measurement methodologies – and the idiosyncratic error associated with the manager's and firm's decisions. Second, the decision process is "nested." In the example presented by Fig. 1, the decision-making process is nested within the firm, a fact that we conceptualize mathematically in Table 1 by having the consideration set determined via firm-based criteria, $f_F(E'_{iM}, \hat{\underline{R}}_F)$, where the error in the formation of that set is firm centric, $\tilde{\kappa}_F$. Third, the decision-making process has a series of stages that generate intermediate decisions that serve as inputs later in the process. In the example, these intermediate decisions are the perception of the environment, $E'_{iM} = e_M(\hat{E}_i, \tilde{\eta}_i)$ and the consideration set, $\underline{C}_F = f_F(E'_{iM}, \hat{\underline{R}}_F) + \tilde{\kappa}_F$. Finally, the decisions made by the firm and the managers have both systematic – as represented by $f_F(\bullet)$, $r_{MF}(\bullet)$, $m_M(\bullet)$, and $o_F(\bullet)$ – and nonsystematic components – as represented by $\tilde{\kappa}_F$, $\tilde{\tau}_{MF}$, $\tilde{\xi}_M$, and $\tilde{\gamma}_{jF}.^6$ Both are important. The systematic components tell us what the managers and firms are doing when making decisions. The nonsystematic components reveal the certainty with which they are doing so.

Table 1 represents only one of many possible formulations and is not meant to present a definitive decision-making model. My purpose is to hint at what Aharoni calls the "baffling complexity" but also highlights the theoretical and conceptual issues that arise by not accounting for this complexity.

First, whether a researcher recognizes it or not, every study that measures an outcome implies a model whereby some decision maker (or makers) makes a choice (or choices). Yet few management researchers go through the effort to structure their research methodology in a manner that accounts for process and the associated sources of variance. Aharoni (1966, 2010) puts his emphasis on the potential biases and unaccounted for cognitive limitations of the decision makers. What my discussion also reveals is that this is just one part of an even greater degree of baffling complexity driven by the sources of variance and heterogeneity.

Second, few studies ask what the implications are of not accounting for aspects of the process and what is explicitly being presupposed by their assumptions. Take for example, Fig. 2. Fig. 2 is Fig. 1 adjusted for the implications of a "strategic fit model" (e.g., Miles & Snow, 1978) (the dimmed out sections are meant to indicate they are not considered formally in the model). Basically this model discusses the alignment of the firm with the environment and how that implies better performance outcomes. However, it makes very strong assumptions about the role of the manager and the choices that the manager makes. The manager's job is to somehow make the decisions that achieve alignment, yet what this means in terms of managerial actions, what these actions and decisions entail, and whether or not managers who attempt to achieve alignment actually do so are never investigated in any systematic manner. Empirically, managers and their

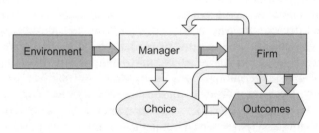

Fig. 2. A Simple Managerial Choice Process.

choices are irrelevant to the outcomes as long as the alignment is achieved. Although the strategic fit model is perhaps one of the most promoted models in management –certainly to MBA students – it leaves out some of the most important elements. Why do managers believe that fit alignment is the correct approach? Is it because they were taught it as MBA students? Because it was part of their organizational culture to be "in alignment"? Because their competitors do it? Because their consultants promote it and justify it with "best practice" cases? Or because it went through a process of trial and error and was found to work the best? Is it possible that managers are making many other complex decisions that just happen to look like a strategic fit model? Or is it because it is simple and easy to understand so that, while imperfect, it reduces implementation errors? This list of such questions could go on for pages.

Within the IB literature, the ownership-location-internalization (OLI) framework of Dunning (1981) and the global integration–local responsiveness approach of Bartlett and Ghoshal (1989) both suffer from this problem. Both assume that the role of the manager is to achieve some aspect of alignment – between internal capabilities and location advantages in the case of the OLI framework or between the degree of integration/responsiveness and market options in the Bartlett and Ghoshal approach. Within the OLI framework, there is no role for the manager at all and very little for the firm to do other than to behave with a singular rationality. Bartlett and Ghoshal appeared to recognize that they had a missing element and they attempted to address it by adding the organization's administrative heritage into the mix. However, they still missed the managerial dimension, which, as it turns out is absolutely critical to the validity and usefulness of their logic. Devinney, Midgley, and Venaik (2000) demonstrated that the failure to account for differences in managerial preferences implies that one can make no statement at all about a firm's location in the global integration–local responsiveness space, rendering what is meant to be a normative framework significantly less functionally prescriptive for managers.

Up to this point, my goal has been to try and articulate how a very simple managerial decision-making process can imply immense complexity when its many components are laid out systematically. What this logic shows is that we need to be very diligent in how we parse up research problems that involve managerial decisions, even when we simplify the problem enormously. Decision makers bring to the process human virtues and vices that show up as both sources of managerial and firm heterogeneity and potential errors and bias whenever information and decisions flow from one point to the next in the process. Note, however, that this does not imply that

I am promoting a realist philosophical stance. I am not advocating, nor do I believe is Aharoni, that one must model the entire decision-making process as it exists in reality, but to recognize more carefully what the implications are of the missing elements. As he notes:

> Our ability to propose and facilitate better courses of action depends on our ability first to understand how people and institutions behave, and why they behave as they do... . (Aharoni, 1966, p. 314)

However, such facilitation involves knowing what components of the process are expendable and which are not; and this cannot be achieved by assuming away the complexity. Nowhere is this more important than in the FDI process, which is one of the most complex, noise riddled, decisions managers must make. It is to this that I turn next.

CONSIDERING FOREIGN DIRECT INVESTMENT IN A DECISION-MAKING STRUCTURE

On the one hand an FDI decision would be expected to differ little from the sort of managerial decisions that have just been discussed. However, FDI by definition implies an even more complex set of potential choices taken by examining more environments with greater sources of variance and greater potentiality for errors in judgment. Aharoni (1966) goes into this in detail highlighting how the process involves many different managers making many intermediate decisions while in consultation with policy makers and advisors. He also points out quite sagely that the initial decision to "look abroad" is itself less than rational in most cases, invariably triggered by any number of initiating forces that might exhibit aspects of serendipity. However, for the purposes of the discussion here I want to abstract from the firm's investment process somewhat and focus more on a singular manager, such as the CEO, who owns the ultimate fiduciary responsibility associated with the decision to be made. In addition, I want to stick to my simple formulation as given in Fig. 1, but now put into the context of the FDI choice. Although one can make the discussion even more complex by bringing in the organization and decision-making process issues that Aharoni (1966) emphasizes, my efforts here are concentrated on the specific decision-making aspects we have been discussing up to this point.

The additional complexity associated with FDI can be seen by relating the elements of Table 1 specifically to the FDI decision. Some of the questions are presented in Table 2 and can be summarized into three basic facets that make FDI decision different from a normal domestic capital investment.

First, FDI decisions will generally operate in a *context of higher complexity*, particularly when compared to domestic-based investment decisions. This applies not only to the environment, a point well made by Aharoni (1966) and many others, but also to the other inputs to the decision – the resources applied, the expected payoffs, the nature of the market competition, the evaluating components of the decision to be made, how the decision is operationalized and implemented, and so on. All of this implies

Table 2. Direct and Process Variance – The FDI Decision Context.

	Some Implications in the FDI Decision Context
Direct variance	
Environment (E)	Many environments are now in play.
Manager (M)	How much more of the manager's decision model is idiosyncratic now that the elements are more uncertain?
Firm (F)	Does the firm have standardized routines and procedures for FDI investments? To what extent does the firm utilize inappropriate models that may add more variance into the decision?
Outcomes (O)	How does one use standard return measures in different tax regimes with different accounting and regulatory requirements? Or when the return is to a portfolio of decisions rather than a single decision alone? Do different firms emphasize the same outcomes, so that decisions compared across firms are comparable?
Process variance	
Environment → Manager	How does a manager perceive multiple environments? What cognitive biases might be operating?
Firm → Manager	When making FDI choices among alternative does the same resource mix apply? What cognitive biases might be operating in the evaluation of the resources?
Manager → Firm	Does the consideration set now include more erroneous inclusions and exclusions now that there is more variance in the potential options? What cognitive biases might be operating?
Manager → Choice	Does the manager have enough experience to know what a good decision model is? Do those with less experience have more bias or a more unsystematic decision component?
Choice → Firm → Outcome	Outcomes are not influenced by one single FDI decision but the portfolio of FDI decisions. How does one link one decision to the right outcome measures?
Choice → Outcome	How does one determine when one FDI option is better when it contains idiosyncratic aspects that reduce comparability and is part of a larger portfolio of decisions

that the potential for error is greater, ceteris paribus, and the opportunities for biases to be revealed will be enhanced.

Second, the decisions invariably involve managers with different perspectives and different abilities. Even in the case of mature MNEs, managers will vary significantly with respect to their international experience and degree of global mindset. This is made even more critical when the FDI decision involves other companies in other cultures – as would be the case with alliances and acquisitions – where each new manager in the process brings with them their own organizational and cultural biases as well as their individual idiosyncrasies. This implies that the *random and idiosyncratic components of the parts of the decision-making process and the final choice will be exacerbated.*

Third, *evaluating the outcomes of any decision is more complex* and potentially subject to distinctive firm effects. The individual preferences of the managers making decisions will, therefore, become more important as there is less likelihood that there is a singular measure of "success." This serves to further exacerbate the seemingly random nature of the decisions being made by managers and increases the potential for managerial intentionality overriding firm-specific aspects of the decision being made (e.g., Hutzschenreuter, Han, & Kleindienst, 2010).

There are a number of both theoretical and practical implications from this. But before getting to these, it is critical in my estimation to argue for a parsimonious and simple model of decision making that captures the logical heart of our discussion and puts Aharoni's work in a broader perspective and allows us to capture the essence of the two prevalent approaches to thinking about FDI. Examining Table 1 the reader will note that most of the structures I have outlined have a consistency in that they break constructs and decisions into two components: a systematic and nonsystemic dimension. This is not arbitrary and follows directly from random utility theoretic (RUT) thinking. According to RUT, choices can be decomposed into a deterministic aspect and a random aspect, the form of which can be derived from basic utility maximization assumptions. What this allows us to do is develop a cascading logic that starts with examination of the basic choice being made by the manager. Hence, when we characterize the manager's choice as $C'_{MFi} \in \underline{C}_F = m_M(E'_{iM}, \hat{\underline{R}}_F) + \tilde{\xi}_M$ we are positing (a) a structure that we can, in theory, model (even if it has idiosyncrasies) – that is, $m_M(E', \hat{R}_F)$ – and (b) a component that is outside our ability to characterize – that is, $\tilde{\xi}_M$. The same is true for the other structures discussed – the choice of resources – $r_{MF}(\bullet)$ and $\tilde{\tau}_{MF}$ – the consideration set – $f_F(\bullet)$ and $\tilde{\kappa}_F$ – and implementation – $o_F(\bullet)$ and $\tilde{\gamma}_{jF}$.

To date, Buckley et al. (2007) are the only scholars to have attempted to estimate a RUT model based on managers' FDI decisions. What they show in their research is that managers can be seen to be operating with a two-stage decision model that includes the formation of a consideration set based on very logical "rationalist" precepts – so that issues like return on investment, market size, and market growth matter a lot – followed by a second-stage decision that is significantly more idiosyncratic as evidenced by the higher variability in the choices made. However, they also show that managers with more FDI experience have more "stable" models for both their consideration set formation and their final choices – as revealed by a better fitting model and one that has more consistent and logical parameters. This latter fact is consistent with the logic of internationalization process thinking and Aharoni (1966).

Hopefully, one should now be seeing a picture that is consistent with Aharoni's seminal thinking about FDI decision making. Although he initially put most of his efforts into examining the nature of the process as a social system with all its flaws, we have brought this around to structured thinking in decision making where we can characterize decisions as having systematic and unpredictable components. This is more than theoretical legerdemain and is where the theoretical, empirical, and practical dimensions come in.

Let us first begin with the random aspects of the FDI decision. Rationalist theory abhors, and/or ignores, the random aspects of the FDI decision, while the process theorists argue that this is what we should emphasize. The RUT logic I am espousing implies that the internationalization process theorists are right metaphorically, but for the wrong reasons. The random component of a decision model is not necessarily the idiosyncratic component. Managers can be rational and logical and consistent in their own minds but idiosyncratic in the choices they make and why they make them. In other works, manager 1's decision model is not manager 2's but they each use a model that is measurable, at least in theory; that is, $m_1(E', \hat{R}_F) \neq m_2(E', \hat{R}_F)$ but both $m_1(\bullet)$ and $m_2(\bullet)$ exist and can be estimated empirically. When they are unpredictable what this means is that their choices are not "systematic." In other words, the choice is not being driven by $m_M(\bullet)$ but by $\tilde{\xi}_M$. What is also relevant here is that although $\tilde{\xi}_M$ represents the random component of the decision, this does not imply that we cannot also characterize and hypothesize it based upon that characterization; we just cannot predict it at any point in time. For example, Buckley et al. (2007) show that certain managers – that is, those with less experience and those working for smaller MNEs – have larger error variances, something that is consistent with internationalization process theory. They also show that this is related to their "overweighting" of political instability in their decision models. In other words, knowing something about the fact that the manager's have greater variance in their choices reveals something about their choices.

From a practical perspective, this can imply that these managers are potentially more susceptible to outside influences – a fact highlighted by Aharoni (1966) – and also potentially subject to or revealing that they are subject to certain types of "random" cognitive biases. In other words, when we see a manager with a less consistent decision model – that is, one where $m_M(\bullet)$ does not explain a lot of the variance in choice – we need to understand that this can imply many different things as to the source of that random aspect of choice.

Second, the systematic aspect of choice will always be idiosyncratic. The more important question is: "whether or not this idiosyncratic aspect of decision making sufficiently material for us to have to account for it?" My point here is that nearly all of our models of FDI choice assume a singular model for which the variance is at the firm and/or locational level. For example, the variance in the OLI model is around the variance of firm-specific and location-specific factors, not around the decision maker making the choice. Similarly, in the internationalization process model, it is assumed that any differences are determinable based on the firm's internationalization maturity. However, what RUT theory allows for the fact that each decision maker will have his or her own model. Empirically, the issue is whether we can discern this model at the individual level or not; that is, can we capture the idiosyncrasies empirically and incorporate them into the model. If we can, then the question becomes whether or not we need to account for the individual manager, groups of managers, or can simply treat all managers as the same. Unfortunately, Buckley et al. (2007) did not attempt to determine the importance of this aspect of decision making, and to date no one has attempted to do this in the case of FDI. However, Perm-Ajchariyawong, Devinney, and Holcomb (2010) show that a manager's decision model associated with the choice to outsource or not outsource an activity is a mixture of two different base models; in other words any manager X's decision model can be structured as $m_x(\bullet) = \omega_{1x}m_1(\bullet) + \omega_{1x}m_2(\bullet)$, where the ω's represent what are known as the mixture weights and can be estimated using Bayesian approaches. What they discovered that is intriguing is that these models are not firm, industry, or country based. All the heterogeneity is at the level of the individual manager, independent of where that manager works.

From a practical standpoint, this last point suggests that much of the variance in what firms choose might be driven by what the individual managers do. Whether we call this managerial intentionality (Hutzschenreuter, Han, & Kleindienst, 2010) or simply managerial heterogeneity does not matter empirically, but certainly is relevant theoretically and practically, as intentional managerial choices are different from simply varied choices that can be modeled. However, it does imply that managerial heterogeneity matters and that to understand these choices we must either attempt to model that heterogeneity or prove that it does not matter materially for the cases we are examining.

Coming back to Aharoni's (2010) call for more consideration of managerial bias, we have the added issue that even $m_M(\bullet)$ may be subject to bias. However, unlike the error component $\tilde{\xi}_M$, the bias here will be systematic. For example, we noted that Buckley, et al. (2007) showed that managers with less experience and in smaller MNEs had different decision models when compared to managers with more experience in larger MNEs. The structure of their choices revealed that they were slightly more risk averse. What they could not answer was whether this was due to rational factors or a source of bias being masked as risk aversion. Similarly, we could flip this around and wonder whether the more experienced managers were themselves biased; perhaps they suffered from a degree of overconfidence bias that was being masked in their apparent higher risk tolerance. My point here is that the decision models are what they are and not only can bias show up in inconsistent decisions but consistent decisions as well.

Third, and finally, the structure of the process as given here provides inputs into the decision calculus of managers and determines their rewards from those decisions. It is important that we examine the parts of this system more thoroughly. It is not uncommon for quantitative research on FDI to discuss mediating and moderating influences and specific effects relating to the firm, industry, and home or host countries and qualitative research to emphasize the longitudinal characteristic of a series of overseas investments as well as aspects of organizational routines. However, even in the case of Aharoni (1966) with his detailed investigation of the process, we see that formally decomposing these components to identify the factors of influence and sources of variance is difficult. This implies, theoretically and empirically, a need not just to study (a) the structure of the process such as given in Fig. 1 and Table 1 and (b) the nature of the specific decision as just discussed, but also (c) to examine the parts of the process in a manner that allows for the determination of specific forms and functions. For example, the first link in the chain represented by Fig. 1 is the manager's perception of the environment, which is represented by me as $\hat{E}_{iM} = e_M(\hat{E}_{i}, \tilde{\eta}_i)$. All that is being given by this is a supposition that managers have perceptions of environments that are based on the data that they have available (the $\hat{E}_i$) and a feeling about the uncertainty surrounding that environment (the $\tilde{\eta}_i$). One can speculate about alternative forms for what is being represented but the important question that has, to my knowledge, never been investigated is what is the form of $e_M(\bullet)$. Although no doubt hundreds, if not thousands, of papers exist that create "environmental" constructs (the $\hat{E}_i$) where pages are devoted in each discussing the properties of the construct, I know of no single paper that has attempted to ask how the managers form the mental models of the environment(s) that they input into their decisions (although we have many theories about what they should do). Similarly, although there are many papers that pay homage to the resource-based view of the firm and devote considerable energy to discussing firm-specific and location-specific assets, exactly what those assets amount to and how they influence FDI location choice is only investigated indirectly. What is interesting is that while a lot of this theorizing discusses the importance of the asset-exploiting and asset-seeking characteristics of FDI, when Buckley et al. (2007) examined this from the standpoint of its influence on top management team FDI decisions, asset exploitation was a middling issue for managers and asset seeking was one of the least considered factors influencing FDI location choices.

More practically it may be that the decisions made by managers at the later stages of the process are quite good. They may be very well thought out and rationally verified through the fiduciary processes of the firm. However, it is possible that error and bias enter in the process not in the final decision calculus but in the inputs to that calculus. For example, how managers perceive the environment may be subject to bias, ultimately all cognitive but induced by any combination of human frailty, cultural bias, and organizational routines and norms. But this need not be materially important. It may be that what really matters is not cognitive bias but measurement bias. Maybe managers are robotic in their ability to make these decisions but simply don't know how to statistically extract the right measures of the environment or resources. Perhaps managers are flawed but firms have become good at weeding out flaw of managerial decision models, such as is done with the pooling of forecasts to come up with a better guess on some future estimate. Although I have no doubt Aharoni would disagree with these last two points of speculation, the proof of the relative importance of the sources and influences of bias is an empirical one.

I will conclude by noting that while others might disagree with the structure I have outlined, it is important not to ignore the elements that make up that structure and assume away their importance. In thinking about FDI we should remember the elements Aharoni (1966) identified as critical to any investigation. First, the FDI investment process is a *system* that is nested. Second, the process takes *time*; in my example as represented by a sequence of *stages*. Third, the decisions are made in a world of *uncertainty*. My formulation argues for this being considered as composed of two types: the native variance of the focal phenomena or construct and the measurement error associated with the information being used by the manager. Fourth, the organization has *goals* to which FDI choice is attempting to contribute. I go beyond this by also giving the manager a direct decision-making responsibility adding the additional complexity of the manager's goals. Finally, the decision is subject to *constraints*, which is embedded in the organizational routines that limit the options considered. Ultimately, managerial decisions such as the FDI capital location decision are made up of many parts, all of which we have to recognize could be relevant to the study of those decisions.

A WORD ON METHODOLOGY

Aharoni (2010, p. 101) calls for IB scholars to focus more on the "studying of decision making in MNEs ... tak[ing] into account the many insights from a long line of research in behavioral decision making." His argument is predicated on a belief that:

> increased mathematical manipulation has often come at the cost of practical relevance. In their search for elegance and rigor, IB researchers ignore the rich evidence on psychological aspects of decision making under uncertainty ...

Where I differ from Aharoni is that I do not believe that elegance and rigor need to be sacrificed for practical relevance. Although he might say that my Table 1 is an exercise in "mathematical manipulation," I would argue that it is an attempt at working through a logical structure that guides us to where sources of variance, error, bias, and rationality potentially reside. Indeed, it is exactly this precision that led to the discovery of nearly all the cognitive biases that he cites.

In addition, what Aharoni does not discuss, and what I consider to be absolutely critical if we are to take up his call, is that we need to rethink out methodologies. To date, empirical IB research has been locked into a three methodology paradigmatic dance. On the one side of the dance floor is the qualitative researcher peering deeply into the eyes of one partner for what seems like forever. In the middle are the survey researchers who attempt to get as many partners as possible to answer their psychometrically sophisticated questions. At the other extreme are the econometric models of secondary data. They have no partners but study the dance floor and the dancers from afar.

Buckley et al. (2007) argue that part of the problem with FDI research has been that theory and methodology have been nested. Those proposing theory A invariably apply a methodology that is different from those that are promoting theory B without recognizing that the test of their theory is biased by the fact that the theory and method are linked. In my example above, all three methodologists would describe a dance so different that one would be hard pressed to believe they were at the same event. However, even accounting for this there are problems in the nature of the empirical studies.

To address the sorts of issues Aharoni discusses and I have outlined here requires experimental and quasi-experimental testing. However, none of the methods used to date in examining FDI amount even to a reasonably well-structured natural experiment. For example, suppose that firm A was trying to decide where to invest next and narrowed its choices down to Burma, Laos, and Pakistan. Also suppose that firm B, in the same industry but acting independently, was also considering where to invest had narrowed its choices down to Pakistan, Indonesia, and Vietnam. Let's assume that firm A decided to go to Laos and firm B to Pakistan. Would we be able to determine their decision model from our database? The answer is a clear no. First, we only know what the firms chose, not what they considered. An econometric database made up of these two firms would now automatically have firm A considering Pakistan (which it actually did) and firm B considering Laos (which it did not). Second, the database would not include any factors that determined the actual decision. As shown by Buckley et al. (2007), the most important factors influencing FDI location choice are exactly the factors absent from our databases – for example, return on investment. Third, the database tells us nothing about the process à la Aharoni (1966) it is possible that firm A chose Laos because the headquarters is in Houston, which has a large Lao community. Fourth, it is possible that both decisions are biased. Firm A may be biased because it believes it understands Lao people and might be able to hire local Lao-Americans to deal with its operations. Firm B might be a company that believes it can deal with risky environments and is willing to run the risk of operating in Pakistan since the returns are large.

My point in this is that when attempting to understand the decision-making process, one must focus on the appropriate methodological approaches. Aharoni calls for more field research. I am calling for more structured experimentation of both the parts and the whole. Both, no doubt, are important but if we are to begin understanding managers and their decisions better we not only need to study them in rerum natura but also in facticius.

THE LAST WORD

Forty-five years ago Aharoni gave us perhaps the most farsighted and insightful examinations of the FDI processes ever written. Yet 44 years later he lamented that many of his "ideas seem[ed] to have been ignored by IB scholars." But perhaps by not all, as the discussion here hopefully indicates. Although I have attempted to provide something of a structure to Yair Aharoni's basic ideas about the managers' decision-making role in the FDI process, my goal has only been to open up the conversation. I believe that this is an important conversation not only for IB researchers but also for researchers in management and business more generally. In some ways, it appears that we have reached the limits of what our macro and micro theories help us to explain and what our methodologies can extract. While empirical modeling and case-based research gotten us to a basic under-standing of firms and industries, and psychometric-based management research has revealed more about people and cultures, we have been woeful in our ignorance of managerial decision making. As managers are ultimately the vector by which decisions that we attribute to firms are made and implemented it would be remiss if we did not begin to dig deeper into the organization and attempt to understand this missing link.

NOTES

1. I should emphasize that Fig. 1 is only one possible formulation. For example, one could argue that the firm precedes the manager as well and serves as a filter both for the information from the environment and choice alternatives.

2. We can think of this in two ways that are relevant. One is that the focal node can be broken into a part that is "systematic" and "predictable" and a part that is random. For example, any environment E_i could be modeled with two component: $\tilde{E}_i = \bar{E}_i + \tilde{\eta}_i$ and $\hat{E}_i = \tilde{E}_i + \tilde{\varepsilon}_i$ (see Table 1). $\bar{E}_i$ represents the environment as it would exist without any noise (by definition we cannot nor will we ever be able to

observe $\bar{E}_i$). The data that we see includes the "true" environment plus noise, $\tilde{\eta}_i$. From our data, $\check{E}_i$, we can extract a model that includes, $\hat{E}_i$, the predictable or systematic component of the environment that can be modeled or characterized as a construct of some form, and the error from the measurement model, $\tilde{\varepsilon}_i$. In the case of the environment or the outcomes, both sources of variance are relevant.

3. In the case of the manager or the firm, where we have no "construct" as such the variance is due to the individual nature of the firm or the manager. Hence, it is not variance in the same sense as discussed in the case of the environment. It is differences between managers and across firms that imply that the models being used are potentially very different. In the statistics literature, this would be considered as individual level or firm level heterogeneity that may or may not have predictable components. This will be discussed further and be clearer when process variance is discussed.

4. This does not mean that the choice does not have variance that is unexplained, as will be discussed in the paragraphs that follow.

5. This is identical to the performance efficiency approach discussed by Devinney, Yip, and Johnson (2010).

6. This last point is important if one wants to apply random utility theoretic decision-making theories and methodological approaches (Train, 2003). Random utility theory models decisions are composed of a measurable model and a random component. If that random component meets certain properties, the decisions can be estimated econometrically using a logit or probit structure.

REFERENCES

Aharoni, Y. (1966). *The foreign direct investment process.* Boston: Harvard Business School.

Aharoni, Y. (2010). Behavioral elements in foreign direct investment. In: T. M. Devinney, T. Pedersen & L. Tihanyi (Eds), *The past present and future of international business and management* (pp. 73–111). Bingley, UK: Emerald.

Bartlett, C., & Ghoshal, S. (1989). *Managing across borders.* Boston: Harvard Business School Press.

Buckley, P. J., & Casson, M. C. (1976). *The future of the multinational enterprise.* London: Macmillan.

Buckley, P. J., Devinney, T. M., & Louviere, J. J. (2007). Do managers behave the way theory suggests? A choice theoretic examination of the foreign direct investment location decision. *Journal of International Business Studies, 38*(7), 1069–1094.

Camerer, C., & Lovallo, D. (1999). Overconfidence and excess entry: An experimental approach. *American Economic Review, 89*(1), 306–318.

Devinney, T. M. (2004). The eclectic paradigm: The developmental years as a mirror on the evolution of the field of international business. In: J. L. C. Cheng & M. A. Hitt (Eds), *Managing multinationals in a knowledge economy: Economics, culture and human resources* (pp. 29–42). New York: Elsevier.

Devinney, T. M., Midgley, D. F., & Venaik, S. (2000). The optimal performance of the global firm: Formalizing and extending the integration-responsiveness framework. *Organization Science, 11*(6), 674–698.

Devinney, T. M., Yip, G. S., & Johnson, G. (2010). Using frontier analysis to evaluate company performance. *British Journal of Management, 21*(4), 921–938.

Doyle, P. (1994). Setting business objectives and measuring performance. *European Management Journal, 12*(2), 123–132.

Dunning, J. H. (1958). *American investment in British manufacturing industry.* London: Allen & Unwin.

Dunning, J. H. (1981). *International production and the multinational enterprise.* London: Allen & Unwin.

Gary, S., & Wood, R. E. (2011). Mental models, decision rules, strategies, and performance heterogeneity. *Strategic Management Journal* (Forthcoming).

Hutzschenreuter, T., Han, U.-S., & Kleindienst, I. (2010). Exploring the role of managerial intentionality in international business. In: T. M. Devinney, T. Pedersen & L. Tihanyi (Eds), *The past present and future of international business and management* (pp. 113–136). Bingley, UK: Emerald.

Hymer, S. (1960). *The international operations of national firms: A study of direct investment.* Ph.D. thesis, MIT, Cambridge, MA.

Johanson, J., & Vahlne, J. E. (1977). The internationalization process of the firm – A model of knowledge development and increasing foreign market commitments. *Journal of International Business Studies, 8*(1), 12–24.

Kahneman, D., & Lovallo, D. (1993). Timid choices and bold forecasts: A cognitive perspective on risk taking. *Management Science, 39*(1), 17–31.

Kahneman, D., & Tversky, A. (1979). Prospect theory: An analysis of decision under risk. *Econometrica, 47*, 263–291.

Miles, R. E., & Snow, C. C. (1978). *Organizational strategy, structure, and process.* New York: McGraw-Hill.

Perm-Ajchariyawong, N., Devinney, T. M., & Holcomb, T. R. (2010). Differentiators of managerial preferences for outsourcing: Experimental evidence of the moderating role of value appropriation. Unpublished manuscript. Available at http://ssrn.com/abstract=1579841

Train, K. (2003). *Discrete choice methods with simulation.* Cambridge: Cambridge University Press.

FDI AND THE ROLE OF FINANCIAL MARKET QUALITY

Jens Forssbaeck and Lars Oxelheim

ABSTRACT

In this chapter we analyze the role of financial factors in the undertaking of cross-border acquisitions. We discuss financial firm-specific advantages as drivers of these acquisitions as well as the role of the development of the home financial market in exploiting these advantages. Based on a sample of 1,447 European firms' cross-border acquisitions amounting to a total of 566 acquisitions spanning from 0 to 18 for individual firms, we find strong evidence in favor of a cost-of-equity effect on the occurrence of FDI, whereas the stand-alone effect of debt costs is indeterminate. However, allowing firm-specific financial characteristics to be conditioned by home-country financial development, both equity costs and debt costs are found highly significant explanatory factors for cross-border acquisitions undertaken by the sample firms.

Keywords: FDI; cost of equity; cost of debt; cost of capital; financial market quality; cross-border acquisitions; firm-specific advantage

The Future of Foreign Direct Investment and the Multinational Enterprise
Research in Global Strategic Management, Volume 15, 85–109
Copyright © 2011 by Emerald Group Publishing Limited
ISSN: 1064-4857/doi:10.1108/S1064-4857(2011)0000015010

INTRODUCTION

Whether the emphasis is on a firm's *ownership advantages* (e.g., Dunning, 1977), its *knowledge capital* (Markusen, 1984), or its potential for gaining economies of scale and scope by *internalizing* transactions (Buckley & Casson, 1976; Rugman, 1981), the focus in mainstream foreign direct investment (FDI) literature is on "real" determinants of firms' international investments. A firm's financial position, by contrast, is typically underplayed as a potential FDI determinant. Financing is treated as a passive function, which smoothly and efficiently responds to firms' needs and demands. Historically, this can be attributed to the fact that mainstream FDI theory has made the (implicit) simplifying assumptions of frictionless financial markets and perfect international financial integration (with some exceptions, see, e.g., Aliber, 1970).

We argue in this chapter that a firm's financial position is not merely a by-product of traditional FDI determinants, such as general economies of scale or investment opportunities, but that information asymmetries in financial markets and (partial) capital market segmentation between countries may give rise to a distinct cost-of-capital effect on cross-border direct investment. If financial markets are to some degree inefficient and/or (partially) segmented internationally, a cost-of-capital effect on FDI can occur through "reactive" or "proactive" firm behavior in response to those inefficiencies. We further argue that these mechanisms will be more important for firms resident in countries with relatively illiquid and/or segmented domestic capital markets. Whereas the importance of target-market location factors is long-since recognized (see, e.g., Dunning, 1977), the potential effect of *home*-country characteristics on firms' propensity to undertake foreign investment has attracted less attention in the FDI literature.

We have in previous work argued for a more prominent role for financial explanations of FDI (see Oxelheim, Randøy, & Stonehill, 2001), and empirically shown that firm-level financial characteristics have a strong effect on the *probability* of undertaking cross-border investments which is robust to the inclusion of traditional FDI determinants (including ownership advantages, target-market location factors and internalization factors; see Forssbæck & Oxelheim, 2008). This chapter develops this previous work in two ways. First, we focus on the *occurrence* of FDI – that is, we are interested in firm-level financial characteristics as explanations for repeated investment. Second, rather than target-market location factors, we focus on the acquiring firm's home-country financial development as a potential conditioning factor for the finance-FDI effect.

We test the effect of financial factors and home-country financial development on the occurrence of FDI in a series of count (Poisson and negative binomial) regressions using a sample of 1,447 European non-financial firms' cross-border acquisitions in a total of 44 target markets. The results reveal a consistently significant explanatory power of cost of equity over a number of different specifications. The stand-alone effect of debt costs, on the other hand, is indeterminate. However, when conditioned by home-country financial development, both cost-of-equity and cost-of-debt matter. In line with our hypothesis, the cost-of-capital effect on FDI proves to be significantly stronger for firms originating in countries that are relatively less financially developed.

Our results strengthen the case for a more prominent role for financial explanations of cross-border direct investment, and press for further work exploring the link between financing and FDI. The results point to the importance of eliminating a "financial disadvantage" for an internationalizing firm.

The chapter is organized in the following way. The second section outlines a number of mechanisms whereby financial factors can be identified as independent drivers of FDI. The ensuing section presents the empirical methodology. The fourth section presents the variables and the dataset. Results are presented and discussed in the fifth section, followed by a conclusion.

FINANCE AND FDI: THEORY, EVIDENCE, AND HYPOTHESES

Finance and FDI: Theory

Existing theories of FDI and of multinationals' cross-border operations emphasize that a firm's ownership of intangible assets can be exploited by FDI. Because foreign firms are generally at a cost disadvantage relative to local firms when entering a new geographical market, it must have some compensating advantage – often termed an "ownership advantage" – which is transferable abroad and of such magnitude that it may compensate for the extra costs that are associated with doing business abroad. Such assets, or advantages, may include various economies of scale and scope,[1] a superior technology, or other types of proprietary knowledge, such as managerial and marketing expertise (Caves, 1971).

Internalization theory (Buckley & Casson, 1976; Hymer, 1976; Rugman, 1981) views these intangible assets as a firm-specific "public good," which is transferable within the firm at a lower transaction cost than would be achieved were the asset to be transferred in any other way between different markets. Markusen (1984) and Horstmann and Markusen (1989) argue that this strongly suggests that multinationality (and hence FDI) is more prevalent in industries where knowledge-based assets are important, because the services of such assets are more easily transported internationally, and they can be supplied to additional production sites at virtually zero marginal cost. Within the industrial organization literature, these insights form the basis of what is often called the "knowledge capital" model of a multinational corporation (MNC), whereas in the international business field, ownership advantages and internalization factors often join hands with "location" factors (such as local market size, wage costs, taxes, etc.) to form the so-called "OLI" framework for explaining why a particular firm undertakes direct investment in a particular destination country (Dunning, 1977, 1988).

While FDI theory thus largely builds on assumptions of market imperfections, these assumptions have rarely been extended to explicitly include financial markets.[2] Allowing for (partial) segmentation, one can distinguish between two main groups of mechanisms whereby financial factors could matter for FDI: *reactive* and *proactive* firm behavior (Oxelheim et al., 2001).

The first group refers to firms' responses to financial market imperfections (and international capital market segmentation). Assuming permanent capital market segmentation implies that risk-adjusted capital costs differ across countries, which would – in turn – imply a financing effect on FDI in simple discount-factor terms: some countries' firms will find foreign investment projects profitable that are forgone by local firms because in net present value terms, local and foreign firms *value* the project differently.

However, we do not have to assume permanent segmentation to find valuation effects. The combination of temporary mispricing of company fundamentals by the market and opportunistic managers has been suggested as explanation for "excessive" stock market effects on investment (both capital expenditure and acquisitions) *domestically* (see, e.g., Morck, Shleifer, & Vishny, 1990; Baker, Stein, & Wurgler, 2003; Shleifer & Vishny, 2003; Gilchrist, Himmelberg, & Huberman, 2005). The international analogy would be to issue stock locally and invest internationally. As noted by Shleifer and Vishny (2003), mispricing may be idiosyncratic or attributable to some specific industry, group of firms, or geographic area. Assuming some degree of correlation between the mispricing of stocks within a country, cost of capital may drive not only investment and acquisitions domestically, but may represent a *particular* (temporary) advantage – or disadvantage, in the case of undervaluation – for undertaking foreign investment projects.

Discount-factor-type motivations for a financing effect on FDI are similar to traditional motivations for FDI in that they assume some firms have an advantage which makes them value foreign investment projects differently than local firms. In fact, a financial influence on FDI may occur even without such valuation effects, in the presence of both financial constraints and capital market segmentation along the lines of leading theories of the exchange-rate effect on FDI.

Froot and Stein (1991) is the first widely quoted paper to impose a financial market imperfection as the source of an unequivocal exchange-rate effect. They assume that some, particularly information-intensive, investments cannot be 100 percent externally financed. In this situation, a real depreciation of the "domestic" currency will enable a "foreign" bidder to bring more net wealth to the investment at equal cost, thereby outbidding the domestic bidder. The effect occurs despite perfect international financial integration and despite equal valuations of the acquired asset/investment by the domestic and the foreign firm (Klein & Rosengren, 1994). Froot and Stein's (1991) wealth effect presumes a financing constraint akin to the one underpinning "pecking-order" theories of capital structure (Myers & Majluf, 1984; Fazzari, Hubbard, & Petersen, 1988). But they assume that financing constraints are equal across countries, and that the wealth effect occurs through real exchange-rate changes. This follows from the maintained assumption of perfect international capital mobility. Relaxing this assumption, the wealth effect could simply be the effect of differences in financial constraints. There is ample evidence in favor of such differences, not least from the finance-growth literature.[3]

There are thus several conceivable mechanisms by which firms' *"reactive"* behavior to financial market inefficiencies may drive foreign investment. The second group refers to *proactive* motivations for a financing-FDI effect. Here, Oxelheim et al. (2001) also make imperfect financial integration and remaining home bias in world capital markets their point of departure. They assume a two-tier world capital market with partial segmentation between national capital markets, where a local firm can choose to stay in its home market and face the local cost of capital, or invest in "proactive financial strategies" to internationalize its cost of capital and reap the benefits of the economies of scale and scope attributable to a multinational firm. Such financial strategies may include cross-listing its stock in a more liquid stock market (Sundaram & Logue, 1996; Foerster & Karolyi, 1999; Miller, 1999; Pagano, Röell, & Zechner, 2002), foreign issues of equity and/or debt (Modén & Oxelheim, 1997), and "bonding" strategies to reduce information asymmetries (Oxelheim & Randøy, 2003). These types of strategy, they suggest, may foment ownership advantages – or, rather, eliminate a financial disadvantage – and such firms are considerably more likely to continue the internationalization process by undertaking FDI.

If financial constraints are more binding and mispricing is more prevalent in financially less developed markets, the "cheap finance" explanation for FDI should be more important in these markets. Similarly, the proactive-financial-strategy story of a firm breaking out of a segmented and illiquid home market to rid itself of a financial disadvantage and "internationalize" its cost of capital suggests that financial factor explanations for FDI are more important for firms originating in countries with less developed financial markets.

Finance and FDI: Empirical Evidence

General support of a role for financial development in FDI is provided by di Giovanni (2005), who finds countries' gross M&A flows to be significantly linked with credit and – particularly – equity market depth.

Tolmunen and Torstila (2005) find that European firms that have cross-listed their stock in the US market are significantly more likely to make acquisitions in the United States. They interpret the results in terms of the European firms' need for a viable "M&A currency," their need to reduce information asymmetries, and overcoming home bias. This is just another way of wording the need to reduce a financial ownership disadvantage.

Forssbæck and Oxelheim (2008) test the hypothesis that financial strength generates advantages that can be exploited through cross-border investment activity in a series of binary-response models, using a sample of European nonfinancial firms' international acquisitions. Controlling for traditional firm- and target-country-specific FDI determinants, they find strong evidence that financial factors play a significant role in explaining cross-border investment.

Baker, Foley, and Wurgler (2009) discuss the possibility of an effect on FDI through a "cheap finance" channel (source-country overvaluation) and/or a "cheap assets" channel (host-country undervaluation). Testing for these effects on aggregate annual data on inward and outward US FDI over the 1974–2001 period, they find strong evidence in favor of a "cheap finance" effect on FDI.

Hypotheses

We develop the existing literature on finance and FDI in two ways. First, we focus on the *occurrence* of FDI, that is, on the *number* of investments undertaken by a firm within a specified sample period. Both "reactive" and "proactive" explanations for a finance-FDI effect suggest that a financial advantage can be exploited by repeated investment. Second, we focus on the acquiring firm's home-country financial development as a conditioning factor for the cost-of-capital effect on finance, in line with arguments advanced in section "Finance and FDI: Theory". Based on these two main ideas, we test the following hypotheses.

Hypothesis 1. A firm's cost of capital (cost of equity and cost of debt) negatively influences the number of cross-border acquisitions undertaken.

Hypothesis 2. The cost-of-capital effect is more pronounced for firms resident in countries with a lower level of financial development.

METHODOLOGY

Our data set allows us to identify how many foreign acquisitions each of the firms in the sample made. We make use of this information to formulate a "baseline" model specification, which allows us to test Hypothesis 1. The basic regression equation takes the form:

$$Y_i = \alpha + \beta' F_i + \delta' X_i + \gamma' C_i + \varepsilon_i \qquad (1)$$

where Y_i is the number of acquisitions made by firm i, F_i a vector of finance-related variables for firm i, X_i a vector of nonfinancial firm-level determinants of FDI, and C_i a set of control variables. This constitutes our "baseline regression" model.

To test Hypothesis 2, we interact our financial variables with various measures of source-country financial development, and add the interaction variables to the basic model specification. Specifically, we interact variables related to equity costs with indicators of home-country equity market development, and variables related to debt costs to indicators of home-country debt market development. We expect that the interaction terms should enter with opposite-sign coefficients to reflect the hypothesis that lower financial market development strengthens the finance-FDI effect.

We start by estimating the equations using the Poisson regression model, which is the point of departure for analysis of integer count data (Cameron & Trivedi, 2003). A common problem with this model, however, is that it assumes mean–variance equivalence in the dependent (count) variable, whereas count data is typically overdispersed (the variance exceeds the mean). The consequence is akin to that of heteroskedasticity in ordinary linear regression models – misestimation of standard errors and increased risk of Type I errors. To test for overdispersion, we use the following test suggested by Cameron & Trivedi (2003):

$$\frac{(Y_i - \hat{Y}_i)^2 - Y_i}{\hat{Y}_i} = \alpha \frac{\hat{Y}_i^2}{\hat{Y}_i} + u_i \tag{2}$$

where $\hat{Y}_i$ is the fitted value of Y_i from the Poisson regression, and the null hypothesis of no overdispersion is rejected if α is significantly different from zero. If overdispersion is found (in effect, this proves to be the case in all of our specifications), we estimate our specifications using the negative binomial regression model, which is less restrictive than the Poisson model.

For all of our specifications, we also report the result of a likelihood ratio (LR) test for the joint significance of the included finance-related regressors. This test is analogous to a simple F-test for linear models, and shows if an unrestricted specification (including the finance-related variables) has a significantly better fit than a restricted specification that explains the occurrence of FDI only in terms of traditional FDI determinants and control variables.

DEFINITIONS AND DATA SET

In this section we describe the variables we use (for a detailed listing, see the data appendix) and their sources, and provide some summary sample statistics.

Variable Definitions and Data Sources

The methodology described in the previous section was applied to a sample of 1,447 firms from countries having adopted the euro (countries constituting the Eurozone), and most of the variables we use are based on financial statement items for these firms from between 1996 and 2000 as reported in the COMPUSTAT Global Industrial Database. Using Eurozone firms presents a particular advantage because it minimizes the risk of mixing up the financial-variable effect with a possible exchange-rate effect (which is easy enough to control for with country-level data, but considerably more cumbersome with firm-level data), but still permits us to explore the effect of variation in source-country characteristics.

The dependent variable (the number of foreign acquisitions) is constructed using information from the Thomson Mergers and Acquisitions Database, which contains data on acquisitions worldwide. The COMPU-STAT firm-level data were matched with the Thomson data, which had previously been filtered to contain only *cross-border* deals completed in 2000, where the acquirer was a firm with EMU-country origin. COMPU-STAT firms that appeared in the filtered Thomson data were flagged for the dependent variable, and the number of acquisitions for each firm added up to form the dependent variable.

The financial variables used are proxies for the cost of equity, cost of debt, credit rating, internal financing, and a cross-listing dummy variable. The proxy for the cost of equity capital is the sales/price ratio. We chose to relate price to sales rather than to earnings – since negative p/e or e/p ratios have no sensible interpretation – and to put sales in the numerator rather than in the denominator in order to avoid the skewness and outlier problem that occurs when some firms in the sample have very low sales (see, e.g., Smart & Zutter, 2003).

The cross-listing dummy takes on unit value for firms that cross-listed their stocks on the NYSE, on NASDAQ, or on the London Stock Exchange during 1996–2000. The variable was constructed using information in factbooks and reports from each of these three stock exchanges.

The cost of debt is simply the firm's actual interest expenditure divided by its total liabilities, as reported in financial statements. The expected effect of the cost of debt on the dependent variable is, however, ambiguous. On the one hand, a reduction in the overall cost of capital through reduced cost of debt would, *ceteris paribus*, increase the level of investment in general, indicating a negative relationship. On the other hand, increased leverage may be a way to finance acquisitions, but will also in general tend to push up the credit risk premium inherent in the cost of debt, indicating a potential positive relationship between the number of acquisition and cost of debt.

As a proxy for firms' credit rating we use Altman's Z''-score, which is a continuous variable constructed from a number of balance-sheet items to reveal the firm's credit risk (see Altman, 2002). In the absence of consistent and comparable series of actual ratings from international credit rating agencies, this provides us with a second-best solution. The basic conjecture is that a higher credit rating should be positively related to the occurrence of cross-border acquisitions. As a final finance-related variable, we include free cash flow over total assets to proxy for internal financing (Stein, 1997; Harford, 1999).

Variables for "traditional" FDI determinants are chosen on the basis of the results of earlier empirical studies, or of surveys thereof (see, e.g., Cantwell & Narula, 2003; Blonigen, 2005). They include firm size, proxies for the importance of knowledge and capital intensity (intangible assets as a share of total assets, the share of fixed capital, and the log of sales per employee), and profitability (return on assets). As a final set of firm-level control variables, we use industry dummies.

Source-country-specific variables are primarily various measures of financial development. We use three measures suggested by Rajan and Zingales (2003): stock market capitalization over GDP, net equity issues over gross fixed capital formation, and private sector credit over GDP. Sources for these variables were IMF *International Financial Statistics* (GDP, investment, and credit) and Eurostat (stock market capitalization). Net equity issues are proxied as the year-on-year change in stock market capitalization, corrected for the change in stock prices as measured by Datastream's overall market price index for each country. The data were collected and the variables calculated for each of the years 1996–2000, and then averaged. In addition to the above-mentioned three financial development variables, we use the shareholder rights and creditor rights indices of La Porta et al. (1998). Finally, we include source-country dummies as control variables in some of the baseline specifications.

Descriptive Statistics

The distribution of the dependent variable – the number of acquisitions undertaken within the sample period – is shown in Table 1. It shows that roughly 80 percent of the sample firms did not undertake any foreign acquisitions during the sample period, 10 percent of the firms made one foreign acquisition, and the frequency decreased gradually for increasingly higher numbers of acquisitions, with the highest number of acquisitions observed for a single firm being 18 (this is the Spanish telephone carrier Telefonica).

Table 1. Frequency Distribution of the Dependent Variable.

Number of Acquisitions	Observations
0	1,177
1	148
2	62
3	22
4	9
5	10
6	7
7	8
8	2
9	1
18	1
Full sample	1,447

Note: The table shows the number of observations for each value taken by the integer count variable "Number of foreign acquisitions". The mean and standard deviation for the full sample were 0.39 and 1.16, respectively.

Descriptive statistics for the independent variables appear in Table 2. As evident from the table, all variables were not available for all firms. Several variables appear to have a skewed distribution; this is less of a problem in the type of nonlinear regression models used in our analysis. The cross-listing indicator is not included in the table since it is a dummy variable. The number of nonzero observations on this variable was 38.

Table 3 shows that correlations between finance-related and other firm-specific variables are often statistically significant but typically very low (with the exception of free cash flow and the return on assets, where the correlation is 64 percent).

RESULTS

Baseline Regression Results

Table 4 reports results from the baseline regressions (Eq. (1)). Models 1 and 3 include the finance-specific variables and the full set of firm-level control variables, including all industry dummies. In specifications 2 and 4, source-country dummies are substituted for the industry dummies as control

Table 2.   Descriptive Statistics, Firm-level Independent Variables.

	Mean	Standard Deviation	Median	Minimum	Maximum	Observations
Financial variables						
Sales/price	2.98	3.52	1.84	0.00	30.7	1,389
Cost of debt	0.027	0.015	0.026	0.000	0.125	1,447
Internal financing	0.004	0.073	0.012	−0.918	0.594	1,421
Credit rating	4.07	3.81	3.16	−16.0	31.6	1,373
Other variables						
Size	5.88	1.88	5.68	1.34	11.7	1,447
Intangibles	0.070	0.10	0.027	−0.002	0.84	1,447
Capital intensity	0.31	0.19	0.27	0.00	0.97	1,447
Sales/employee	5.24	0.71	5.19	0.65	7.79	1,418
ROA	0.079	0.079	0.079	−0.71	0.60	1,447

Note: The table reports summary statistics for the included firm-level variables.

Table 3.   Pearson Correlations, Firm-level Independent Variables.

	Cost of Debt	Internal Financing	Z''-score	Size	Intangibles	Capital Intensity	Sales/ Employee	ROA
Sales/price	0.06**	−0.09**	−0.36***	−0.02	−0.13***	−0.06**	0.10***	−0.24***
Cost of debt		−0.08***	−0.16***	−0.09***	0.01	0.17***	−0.02	−0.04
Internal financing			0.28***	0.07***	0.01	−0.18***	0.02	0.64***
Credit rating				−0.19***	0.01	−0.26***	−0.03	0.49***
Size					0.13***	0.14***	0.08***	0.06**
Intangibles						−0.27***	−0.08***	0.02
Capital intensity							0.00	−0.02
Sales/ employee								0.04

Note: The table reports pairwise Pearson correlation coefficients for the included firm-level variables.
** and *** indicate rejection of the null hypothesis of no correlation at the 5% and 1% significance level (two-tailed), respectively.

variables. In specification 5, finally, insignificant control variables (of which most are industry dummies) were left out. This last specification will be the basis for the subsequent tests including interaction terms between finance-specific variables and source-country financial development.

Specifications 1 and 2 were estimated using the Poisson regression model. The result of the overdispersion test (Eq. (2)) is reported as the *t*-statistic of the α coefficient. As is evident from the table, the null hypothesis of no overdispersion is clearly rejected for both specifications; consequently, the negative binomial regression model is used for the remaining specifications.

The negative binomial regression model in Table 4 shows for all specifications (3–5) the cost-of-equity variable to be strongly significant with the expected negative sign. No other finance variables are found significant in any of the three specifications.

As regards traditional FDI determinants, firm size and high knowledge intensity (as proxied by the share of intangible assets) are positively associated with the occurrence of foreign investment, as expected. The coefficients are economically and statistically significant and highly stable over the different specifications. Especially firm size – for obvious reasons – is strongly related to the number of foreign acquisitions undertaken. Both capital intensity and sales per employee tend to be negatively related with foreign investment activity, although capital intensity is usually insignificant. Also profitability proves to be insignificant as a determinant of the occurrence of cross-border acquisitions. Coefficients for industry dummies, finally, reinforce the impression that firms in sectors with higher knowledge intensity (such as durables, electronics, and services) more often invest abroad.

Specifications 4 and 5, which include source-country dummies, indicate that firms from smaller countries have a higher incentive to invest abroad. The five significant country dummies in specification 5 are those of France, Germany, Italy, Spain, and Portugal (not shown in the table). The first four of these are the largest member countries of the Eurozone and they all enter with negative coefficients. Thus, firms from these countries invest less abroad than they should, given firms' characteristics. This result is consistent with – although no direct evidence of – our Hypothesis 2 that financial advantages are more important for firms resident in smaller, more segmented markets.

LR tests of specifications with and without the included financial variables indicate a very strong incremental explanatory power of these variables. We infer from these results that financial factors clearly are of first-order importance for the occurrence of cross-border acquisitions, and conclude that the results verify Hypothesis 1 – at least as regards equity costs.

Table 4. Determinants of the Occurrence of Foreign Acquisitions, Baseline Cross-sectional Regressions.

	1 (Poisson)	2 (Poisson)	3 (Neg. Binom.)	4 (Neg. Binom.)	5 (Neg. Binom.)
Intercept	−5.03	−2.69	−4.81	−2.86	−3.39
	(−6.62)***	(−5.41)***	(−5.18)***	(−4.06)***	(−4.99)***
Financial variables					
Sales/price	−0.09	−0.10	−0.09	−0.10	−0.10
	(−3.55)***	(−3.93)***	(−2.90)***	(−3.16)***	(−3.20)***
Cross-listing	0.30	0.39	0.39	0.41	0.38
	(2.02)**	(2.58)***	(1.25)	(1.30)	(1.27)
Cost of debt	0.07	0.05	0.03	0.01	0.02
	(2.15)**	(1.36)	(0.51)	(0.24)	(0.39)
Internal financing	0.06	−0.45	−1.21	−1.56	−1.29
	(0.06)	(−0.48)	(−0.84)	(−1.12)	(−1.20)
Credit rating	0.03	0.03	0.04	0.04	0.02
	(1.67)*	(1.87)*	(1.52)	(1.34)	(0.98)
Nonfinancial FDI determinants					
Size	0.57	0.57	0.58	0.56	0.58
	(20.1)***	(20.8)***	(13.6)***	(13.9)***	(14.2)***
Intangibles	1.36	1.92	1.23	2.46	2.32
	(3.12)***	(5.19)***	(1.69)*	(3.49)***	(3.37)***
Capital intensity	−0.29	−0.47	−0.72	−1.02	−0.76
	(−0.83)	(−1.41)	(−1.38)	(−2.01)**	(−1.58)
Sales/employee	−0.19	−0.29	−0.18	−0.22	−0.19
	(−2.22)**	(−3.73)***	(−1.49)	(−1.99)**	(−1.73)*
ROA	−0.63	0.11	−0.45	0.18	
	(−0.55)	(0.09)	(−0.32)	(0.12)	
Control variables[a]					
Industry dummies (# sign.)	All (7)	No	All (2)	No	2 (2)
Source-country dummies (# sign.)	No	All (6)	No	All (5)	5 (5)
Summary					
Observations	1,301	1,301	1,301	1,301	1,301
Adj. R^2	0.35	0.34	0.27	0.22	0.28
Overdispersion test[b]	3.15***	2.35**			

Table 4. (*Continued*)

	1 (Poisson)	2 (Poisson)	3 (Neg. Binom.)	4 (Neg. Binom.)	5 (Neg. Binom.)
LR test of exclusion restrictions[c]	33.3***	43.2***	20.2***	24.2***	22.3***

Note: The table shows coefficient estimates from count regressions of the number of foreign acquisitions on firm-specific characteristics. Definitions of the included variables appear in Table A1 of the appendix. All coefficients are reported with *t*-stats in parentheses.
*, **, and *** indicate rejection of the null hypothesis that the coefficient is equal to zero at the 10%, 5%, and 1% significance level, respectively.
[a]The figures in parentheses refer to the number of dummy control variables that are significant at least at the 5% confidence level.
[b]Test for overdispersion in the Poisson regressions, as specified in Eq. (2). The reported statistic is the *t*-ratio of the α coefficient. Significance indicates rejection of the null hypothesis of no overdispersion.
[c]Likelihood ratio test (χ^2) for the exclusion of the included finance-related variables. Significance indicates rejection of the null hypothesis that coefficients for the included finance-related variables are jointly zero.

The Effect of Source-Country Financial Development

The results of interacting financial FDI determinants with home-country financial development are reported in Table 5. The results strongly confirm the arguments advanced in the second section – which are, in turn, broadly in line with the wealth effect/arbitrage explanation for the financing effect on FDI (Froot & Stein, 1991; Blanchard, Rhee, & Summers, 1993; Baker et al., 2009), as well as with the financial-internationalization effect (Oxelheim et al., 2001) – that financing matters more for firms from financially less developed economies.

When we interact our firm-level financial variables with variables expressing quality of the markets, we find strong support for Hypothesis 2 in the sense that the quality of domestic financial markets matters; both cost of equity and cost of debt interact significantly with measures of financial development. However, low quality of domestic financial markets does not unanimously imply higher cross-border acquisitions.

A significantly positive value for cost of equity and market capitalization indicates that firms benefiting from a firm-specific cost-of-equity advantage have higher probability to undertake a foreign acquisition if domiciled in smaller (thinner) capital market. On the other hand, a firm with such an

Table 5. Determinants of the Occurrence of Foreign Acquisitions, Cross-Sectional Regressions with Financial Development/Finance Interaction Variables.

	1 (Neg. Binom.)	2 (Neg. Binom.)	3 (Neg. Binom.)	4 (Neg. Binom.)
Intercept	−3.90	−5.23	−3.84	−3.93
	(−5.65)***	(−13.5)***	(−5.66)***	(−5.78)***
Financial variables				
Sales/price	0.05	−0.07	−0.08	−0.08
	(0.85)	(−2.51)**	(−2.75)***	(−2.60)***
Cross-listing	0.37	0.96	0.40	0.35
	(1.19)	(0.98)	(1.28)	(1.13)
Cost of debt	0.05	0.04	−0.28	−0.02
	(0.91)	(0.77)	(−2.12)**	(−0.23)
Internal financing	−1.35	−1.64	−1.28	−1.28
	(−1.24)	(−1.62)	(−1.20)	(−1.18)
Credit rating	0.04	0.06	0.03	−0.05
	(1.43)	(2.47)**	(0.93)	(−0.82)
Nonfinancial FDI determinants				
Size	0.56	0.55	0.56	0.56
	(13.6)***	(13.8)***	(13.8)***	(13.8)***
Intangibles	1.82	2.22	2.08	1.93
	(2.68)***	(3.71)***	(3.07)***	(2.86)***
Capital intensity	−0.53		−0.55	−0.41
	(−1.13)		(−1.16)	(−0.88)
Sales/employee	−0.20		−0.20	−0.19
	(−1.69)*		(−1.79)*	(−1.70)*
Interaction variables				
Stock market cap × Sales/price	0.25			
	(2.28)**			
Equity issues × Sales/price	−1.06			
	(−2.45)**			
Shareholder rights × Sales/price	−0.04			
	(−1.75)*			
Stock market cap × Cross-listing		0.68		
		(0.52)		
Equity issues × Cross-listing		−3.31		
		(−1.13)		
Shareholder rights × Cross-listing		−0.10		
		(−0.30)		
Private credit × Cost of debt			0.21	
			(1.89)*	

Table 5. (*Continued*)

	1 (Neg. Binom.)	2 (Neg. Binom.)	3 (Neg. Binom.)	4 (Neg. Binom.)
Creditor rights × Cost of debt			0.06 (2.58)***	
Private credit × Credit rating				0.09 (1.60)
Creditor rights × Credit rating				0.01 (0.80)
Cost of debt × Credit rating			0.01 (0.86)	0.01 (0.87)
Control variables[a]				
Industry dummies (# sign.)	2 (2)	2 (2)	2 (2)	2 (2)
Summary				
Observations	1,241	1,256	1,296	1,296
Adj. R^2	0.30	0.28	0.29	0.28
LR test of exclusion restrictions[b]	31.5***	23.5***	30.3***	25.1***

Note: The table shows coefficient estimates from count regressions of the number of foreign acquisitions on firm-specific characteristics, allowing for interactivity between firms' financial characteristics and their home-country financial development. Definitions of the included variables appear in Table A1 of the appendix. All coefficients are reported with *t*-stats in parentheses.
*, **, and *** indicate rejection of the null hypothesis that the coefficient is equal to zero at the 10%, 5%, and 1% significance level, respectively.
[a]The figures in parentheses refer to the number of industry dummies that are significant at least at the 5% confidence level.
[b]Likelihood ratio test (χ^2) for the exclusion of the included finance-related variables (including interaction terms). Significance indicates rejection of the null hypothesis that coefficients for the included finance-related variables are jointly zero.

advantage will be less inclined to make a foreign acquisition, the higher the issuance activity in the domestic financial market. The investor protection variable indicates that a firm with a cost-of-equity advantage is less inclined to get involved in cross-border acquisitions if home-country investor protection is poor. This may also make sense, however, since undertaking the foreign acquisition may still mean increased exposure to the inferior investor protection at home.

For cost of debt, which was previously insignificant when entered individually, we observe – after the conditioning on source-country financial development – a significant effect. Individually, the cost-of-debt variable now enters with a significantly negative coefficient, suggesting a higher occurrence of foreign investment for a firm with a cost-of-debt advantage, as expected. In addition, a cost-of-debt advantage (the lower the cost the better) together with weaker creditor rights at home, indicates an increased propensity to undertake foreign acquisitions. This observation is also valid for the credit market size; the thinner the home market, the higher the occurrence of cross-border acquisitions.

For the credit-rating variable, we find no significant effect of the interaction with financial development on the number of foreign acquisitions. Finally, source-country financial development variables are not entered individually in the regressions to avoid multicollinearity problems due to high correlation with interaction terms.

A somewhat unexpected result of the count regressions is the relatively weak results for the cross-listing variable. This is unexpected given previous results in the literature (Forssbæck & Oxelheim, 2008; Tolmunen & Torstila, 2005), where preparatory cross-listings have proven to be a strong determinant of cross-border acquisitions. However, since we here analyze repeated cross-border acquisitions, the insignificance may reflect a diminishing return on cross-listing (Modén & Oxelheim, 1997).

To investigate the insignificance of the cross-listing variable further, we run a final round of tests, where the cross-listing dummy is the dependent variable, and other firm characteristics (including finance-related variables) and home-country financial development are the independent variables. We are thus interested in finding out what type of firms are more likely to cross-list their stock on a large foreign stock exchange. Since the dependent variable is now a dummy variable, the appropriate model is a binary-response regression. We thus run a probit regression of the following form:

$$\text{Prob}(D_{\text{CL},i} = 1) = \Phi(\alpha + \beta_1' F_i + \beta_2' X_i + \beta_3' Z_j) \qquad (3)$$

where $D_{\text{CL},i}$ denotes the cross-listing dummy, and Φ is the normal probability distribution function over the closed interval [0,1]. F_i is now the set of finance-related variables for firm i except the cross-listing dummy, X_i is defined as before, and Z_j is the set of financial development indicators for country j (Table 6).

The results show that the probability of being cross-listed is negatively related to the cost of equity, and positively related to credit rating, firm size, and net equity issues. Furthermore, it is negatively related to the home-country's relative equity market capitalization, although this variable is (marginally) insignificant. Thus, larger firms, with better credit rating and lower cost of capital, from countries with a more active (but possibly smaller) stock market are the firms that cross-list their shares. However, as

Table 6.   Determinants of the Probability of Cross-listing.

	Probit Coefficient Estimates
Intercept	−4.26
	(−3.89)***
Financial variables	
Sales/price	−0.21
	(−1.92)*
Cost of debt	0.02
	(0.20)
Internal financing	−0.83
	(−0.48)
Credit rating	0.06
	(2.10)**
Nonfinancial firm characteristics	
Size	0.36
	(5.88)***
Intangibles	0.65
	(0.68)
Capital intensity	0.18
	(0.28)
Sales/employee	−0.13
	(−0.72)
Equity market development	
Stock market cap	−0.62
	(−1.34)
Equity issues	3.14
	(2.44)**
Shareholder rights	−0.01
	(−0.06)
Summary	
Observations	1,241
McFadden pseudo-R^2	0.31
Log likelihood	−89.2

Note: The table shows coefficient estimates from a probit regression of the cross-listing dummy variable on firm-specific characteristics and home-country equity market development. Coefficients are reported with *t*-stats in parentheses.
** and *** indicate rejection of the null hypothesis that the coefficient is equal to zero at the 5% and 1% significance level, respectively.

for the association between cross-listing and the other finance-related firm characteristics, it is not possible to observe the direction of causality: do firms have financial advantages because they have cross-listed, or do they cross-list because they have a financial advantage? In addition, cross-listing is apparently associated with an active domestic market with a higher relative rate of equity issues. This may make sense since it may indicate an increased propensity to tap also other markets for capital and thereby a need to cross-list. These results suggest that we may not be able to unequivocally interpret our cross-listing dummy as an indicator of a firm's need to get rid of a financial disadvantage.

SUMMARY AND CONCLUDING REMARKS

In this chapter we argue that the assumption of (at least partial) international capital market segmentation opens up a number of possible mechanisms for a direct cost-of-capital effect on firms' incentives to undertake foreign investment projects. This "finance-FDI" effect has previously been largely neglected at the firm level in the FDI literature.

Based on count regressions on a sample of European nonfinancial firms and their foreign acquisitions, we find strong evidence in favor of an independent equity-valuation effect on the occurrence of acquisition FDI. Equity-related financial variables turn out to be equally important as, or more important than, most traditional firm-level non-financial determinants of foreign investment. Specifically, our results show that firms with more highly valued equity undertake a higher number of foreign acquisitions, given other relevant firms' characteristics. The effects on the occurrence of foreign acquisitions of financial characteristics not directly related to equity, however, are more complex. The *stand-alone* effect of debt costs is indeterminate, and statistically insignificant. Our proxy for credit worthiness, on the other hand, is sometimes statistically significant, but typically small in economic terms.

Moreover, we find that financial determinants are more important for firms originating in countries that are relatively less financially developed – a finding consistent with our hypotheses. Given the cost-of-equity incentive, firms' inclination to undertake cross-border acquisitions increase with decreasing capitalization of their domestic stock market (but also increase with increasing issuance activity of that market and with increasing investor protection). The two last-mentioned results indicate the market development as a "pull" factor – the firm has an advantage that it cannot waste, whereas in the first case the financial development is to be seen rather as a "push" factor. Similarly, given a cost-of-debt advantage, firms' inclination to undertake cross-border acquisitions increase with decreasing capitalization of their domestic credit market.

Our conclusion is that an explicit consideration of firms' financial positions is necessary to explain cross-border investment. But more work is needed on identifying the exact mechanism whereby the financing-FDI effect occurs. We note in the chapter the difficulty of pinpointing that mechanism, and our results are consistent with several candidate rationalizations for the effect that have appeared in, or can be derived from, the literature. These include a wealth/arbitrage effect (Froot & Stein, 1991; Baker et al., 2009), and a proactive-financial-strategy effect (Oxelheim et al., 2001).

By relying on these rationalizations, over results implicitly point to the maintained importance of (some degree of) international financial market segmentation. The ongoing integration of capital markets, and their increased interdependence and vulnerability to common shocks and crises, therefore urge for further research exploring the link between the changing financial landscape and multinational firms' guest for missing pieces in their production puzzles.

ACKNOWLEDGMENT

The authors would like to thank Yair Aharoni – who in his own seminal work has analyzed the role of managers in FDI decisions – for his very valuable comments on this chapter's economics-oriented approach to this decision. We would also like to thank Cynthia Campbell, Andrew Delios, Ram Mudambi, Clas Wihlborg, and participants at Financial Management Association and European International Business Academy conferences for useful comments on earlier versions of this chapter. Financial support from the NASDAQ OMX Nordic Foundation for Lars Oxelheim is gratefully acknowledged.

NOTES

1. Such as size, monopoly power, better resource capability and usage (Bain, 1956); economies of multiplant structures and common ownership (Caves, 1980); and advantages of multinationality that enable MNCs to capitalize on differences in factor endowments and other local market conditions (Kogut, 1985).

2. With some exceptions; for example, Aliber (1970) suggests that capital market segmentation implies that a multinational firm has an advantage over local firms in that its multinationality enables it to raise capital with a lower exchange-rate risk premium, and thus a lower overall cost. Another example is Dunning (1993), who considers financial market imperfections and recognizes that firms' propensity to own foreign income-generating assets may be influenced by financial and

exchange-rate variables. He also discusses a "financial asset advantage" which refers to "firms' superior knowledge of, and access to foreign sources of capital," but essentially finds this advantage to be a by-product of the size, efficiency, and knowledge capital of the firm.

3. For instance, in Rajan and Zingales (1998), financial development reduces the cost of external finance, which causes industries that are particularly dependent on external finance to grow faster in countries with well-developed financial markets; in a similar vein, Svaleryd and Vlachos (2005) find that finance can be treated as a comparative advantage, and is a robust determinant of industrial specialization between different countries.

REFERENCES

Aliber, R. Z. (1970). A theory of foreign direct investment. In: P. C. (Ed.), *The International Corporation*. Cambridge, MA: MIT Press.

Altman, E. I. (2002). Revisiting credit scoring models in a Basel II environment. In: M. Ong (Ed.), *Credit ratings: Methodologies, rationale and default risk*. London: Risk Books.

Bain, J. S. (1956). *Barriers to new competition*. Cambridge, MA: Harvard University Press.

Baker, M., Foley, C. F., & Wurgler, J. (2009). Multinationals as arbitrageurs: The effect of stock market valuations on foreign direct investment. *Review of Financial Studies, 22*, 337–370.

Baker, M., Stein, J. C., & Wurgler, J. (2003). When does the market matter? Stock prices and the investment of equity-dependent firms. *Quarterly Journal of Economics, 118*, 969–1006.

Blanchard, O., Rhee, C., & Summers, L. (1993). The stock market, profit, and investment. *Quarterly Journal of Economics, 108*, 115–136.

Blonigen, B. A. (2005). A review of the empirical literature on FDI determinants. *Atlantic Economic Journal, 33*, 383–403.

Buckley, P. J., & Casson, M. (1976). *The future of the multinational enterprise*. London: Homes & Meier.

Cameron, A. C., & Trivedi, P. K. (2003). Essentials of count data regression. In: H. B. Baltagi (Ed.), *A companion to theoretical econometrics*. London: Blackwell.

Cantwell, J., & Narula, R. (2003). *International business and the eclectic paradigm*. London: Routledge.

Caves, R. E. (1971). International corporations: The industrial economics of foreign investment. *Economica, 56*, 279–293.

Caves, R. E. (1980). Investment and location policies of multinational companies. *Schweizerische Zeitschrift für Volkswirtschaft und Statistik, 116*, 321–327.

Di Giovanni, J. (2005). What drives capital flows? The case of cross-border M&A activity and financial deepening. *Journal of International Economics, 65*, 127–149.

Dunning, J. H. (1977). Trade, location of economic activity and the MNE: A search for an eclectic approach. In: B. Ohlin, P.-O. Hesselborn & P. M. Wijkman (Eds), *The international allocation of economic activity*. London: Macmillan.

Dunning, J. H. (1988). *Explaining international production*. London: Unwin Hyman.

Dunning, J. H. (1993). *Multinational enterprises in the global economy*. Wokingham Berks: Addison Wesley.

Fazzari, S. M., Hubbard, R. G., & Petersen, B. C. (1988). Financing constraints and corporate investment. *Brookings Papers on Economic Activity, 1*, 141–206.

Foerster, S. R., & Karolyi, G. A. (1999). The effects of market segmentation and investor recognition on asset prices: Evidence from foreign stock listing in the United States. *Journal of Finance, 54*, 981–1013.

Forssbaeck, J., & Oxelheim, L. (2008). Finance-specific factors as drivers of cross-border investment – An empirical investigation. *International Business Review, 17*, 630–641.

Froot, K. A., & Stein, J. C. (1991). Exchange rates and foreign direct investment: An imperfect capital markets approach. *Quarterly Journal of Economics, 106*, 1191–1217.

Gilchrist, S., Himmelberg, C. P., & Huberman, G. (2005). Do stock price bubbles influence corporate investment? *Journal of Monetary Economics, 52*, 805–827.

Harford, J. (1999). Corporate cash reserves and acquisitions. *Journal of Finance, 54*, 1969–1997.

Horstmann, I. J., & Markusen, J. R. (1989). Firm-specific assets and the gains from direct foreign investment. *Economica, 56*, 41–48.

Hymer, S. H. (1976). *The international operations of national firms: A study of foreign direct investment*. Cambridge, MA: MIT Press.

Klein, M. W., & Rosengren, E. S. (1994). The real exchange rate and foreign direct investment in the United States: Relative wealth vs. relative wage effects. *Journal of International Economics, 36*, 373–389.

Kogut, B. (1985). Designing global strategies: Profiting from operational flexibility. *Sloan Management Review, 27*, 27–38.

La Porta, R., López-de-Silanes, F., Shleifer, A., & Vishny, R. W. (1998). Law and finance. *Journal of Political Economy, 106*, 1113–1155.

Markusen, J. R. (1984). Multinationals, multi-plant economies, and the gains from trade. *Journal of International Economics, 16*, 205–226.

Miller, D. P. (1999). The market reaction to international cross-listings: Evidence from depositary receipts. *Journal of Financial Economics, 51*, 103–123.

Modén, K.-M., & Oxelheim, L. (1997). Why issue equity abroad? – Corporate efforts and stock markets responses. *Management International Review, 37*, 223–241.

Morck, R., Shleifer, A., & Vishny, R. W. (1990). The stock market and investment: Is the market a sideshow? *Brookings Papers on Economic Activity, 2*, 157–215.

Myers, S. C., & Majluf, N. S. (1984). Corporate financing and investment decisions when firms have information that investors do not have. *Journal of Financial Economics, 13*, 187–221.

Oxelheim, L., Randøy, T., & Stonehill, A. (2001). On the treatment of finance-specific factors within the OLI paradigm. *International Business Review, 10*, 381–398.

Oxelheim, L., & Randøy, T. (2003). The impact of foreign board membership on firm value. *Journal of Banking and Finance, 27*, 2369–2392.

Pagano, M., Röell, A., & Zechner, J. (2002). The geography of equity listing: Why do companies list abroad? *Journal of Finance, 57*, 2651–2694.

Rajan, R. G., & Zingales, L. (1998). Financial dependence and growth. *American Economic Review, 88*, 559–586.

Rajan, R. G., & Zingales, L. (2003). The great reversals: The politics of financial development in the 20th century. *Journal of Financial Economics, 69*, 5–50.

Rugman, A. M. (1981). *Inside the multinationals: The economics of internal markets*. New York, NY: Columbia University Press.

Shleifer, A., & Vishny, R. W. (2003). Stock market driven acquisitions. *Journal of Financial Economics, 70*, 295–311.

Smart, S. B., & Zutter, C. J. (2003). Control as a motivation for underpricing: A comparison of dual and single-class IPOs. *Journal of Financial Economics, 69*, 85–110.

Stein, J. C. (1997). Internal capital markets and the competition for corporate resources. *Journal of Finance, 52*, 111–133.

Sundaram, A. K., & Logue, D. E. (1996). Valuation effects of foreign company listings on U.S. exchanges. *Journal of International Business Studies, 27*, 66–88.

Svaleryd, H., & Vlachos, J. (2005). Financial markets, the pattern of specialization, and comparative advantage: Evidence from OECD countries. *European Economic Review, 49*, 113–144.

Tolmunen, P., & Torstila, S. (2005). Cross-listings and M&A activity: Transatlantic evidence. *Financial Management, 34*, 123–142.

APPENDIX. VARIABLE DEFINITIONS

Tables A.1, A.2

Table A.1.   Variable Definitions.

Variable	Description	Source
Dependent variable		
Number of acquisitions (integer count variable)	Number of foreign acquisitions undertaken in 2000	Thomson M&A database
Financial variables		
Sales/price ratio	Total sales divided by market value[a]	COMPUSTAT Global Industrials Database
Cross-listing	Dummy variable taking on unit value if the firm cross-listed on NYSE, NASDAQ, or LSE in any of the years 1996–2000, zero otherwise	Annual reports and factbooks from each stock exchange
Cost of debt	Average cost of debt: natural logarithm of $(1 + \text{interest expenditure over total liabilities})$[a]	COMPUSTAT Global Industrial Database
Credit rating	Average Z''-score[a,b]	As above
Internal financing	Free cash flow divided by total assets[a]	As above
Nonfinancial firm-level FDI determinants		
Size	Natural logarithm of total assets in thousands of USD[a]	As above
Intangibles	Intangible assets over total assets[a]	As above
Capital intensity	Plants, property, and equipment (total, net) divided by total assets[a]	As above

Table A.1. (*Continued*)

Variable	Description	Source
Sales/employee	Natural logarithm of the ratio of total sales (in thousands of USD) to number of employees[a]	As above
ROA	Return on assets: EBIT divided by total assets[a]	As above
Financial development variables		
Stock market cap	Stock market capitalization divided by GDP[a]	Eurostat, IFS
Equity issues	Net equity issues divided by gross fixed capital formation[a]	Eurostat, Datastream, IFS
Private credit	Credit to the private sector divided by GDP[a]	IFS
Shareholder rights	Index of anti-director rights; higher value indicates better shareholder protection	La Porta, López-de-Silanes, Shleifer, and Vishny (1998)
Creditor rights	Index of creditor rights; higher value indicates better creditor protection	As above

[a]These variables are observed for the years 1996–2000, and used in the cross-sectional regressions as the average of these yearly observations.
[b]$Z'' = 6.56 \times$ (working capital/total assets) $+ 3.26 \times$ (retained earnings/total assets) $+ 6.72 \times$ (EBIT/total assets) $+ 1.05 \times$ (market value of equity/book value of total liabilities); see Altman (2002).

Table A.2. Descriptive Statistics, Source Country Variables.

	Observations	Mean	Standard Deviation	Minimum	Maximum
Stock market cap.	12	0.64	0.30	0.16	1.33
Equity issues	12	0.23	0.09	0.04	0.65
Private credit	12	0.74	0.23	0.42	1.19
Shareholder rights	12	2.08	1.13	0.00	4.00
Creditor rights	12	1.67	1.18	0.00	3.00

PART II
NEW MULTINATIONALS

THE EVOLUTION OF MULTINATIONALS [☆]

Yair Aharoni and Ravi Ramamurti

ABSTRACT

As an institution, the multinational enterprise has evolved in complexity. From having roots in just a few Western nations, it now has roots in dozens of nations, including many developing countries. Its scope has likewise expanded from natural resource-based industries and manufacturing to a variety of services. And firms are becoming multinational earlier in their lives and at smaller sizes than in the past. This chapter analyzes the evolution of multinationals over the last century, the forces driving that evolution, and distinctive characteristics of the latest wave of multinationals coming out of developing countries. It also explores the risk of a backlash against globalization and multinationals in Western societies, even as these trends gain in popularity in developing countries. It concludes with questions that international business scholars might want to pursue in their future research.

Keywords: MNE evolution; origin of MNEs; emerging-market MNEs; backlash against MNEs; future research questions

[☆]This is an updated and revised version of Aharoni, Y., & Ramamurti, R. (2008). The Internationalization of Multinationals. In: J. Boddewyn (Ed.), *International Business Scholarship: AIB Fellows on the First 50 Years and Beyond* (pp. 177–201). Bingley, UK: Emerald.

The Future of Foreign Direct Investment and the Multinational Enterprise
Research in Global Strategic Management, Volume 15, 113–135
ISSN: 1064-4857/doi:10.1108/S1064-4857(2011)0000015011

INTRODUCTION

The importance, diversity, and scope of MNEs in the global economy have grown exponentially in the post-World War II period, despite short-term ups and downs. From merely a few billion dollars per year in the 1950s, global FDI outflows grew to $51.5 billion in 1980, $239.1 billion in 1990, and $1.231.6 billion in 2000, before falling off sharply as a result of the dot-com bust (Economist Intelligence Unit, 2007). The outflows recovered after 2004, reaching an all-time high in 2007 of $2,146.5 billion, before the global financial crisis caused flows to collapse again in 2008 and 2009. A slow recovery in 2010 was expected to be followed by more robust growth in 2011.

The sales of foreign affiliates of multinational of all nationalities stood at about one-half of world exports in 1960, but by 1982 the two were about equal (US$2.7 trillion and $2.4 trillion, respectively), and by 2007 the former was almost double the latter ($31 trillion vs. $17 trillion, respectively; see UNCTAD, 2008, p. 10). In 1982, the ratio of outward FDI to worldwide gross fixed capital formation was just 1%, but by 1999 it had risen to about 14% (UNCTAD, 2000, p. 4) and by 2007 to 16.2% (UNCTAD, 2008, p. 10). In 2008, there were 82,000 MNEs with 810,000 foreign affiliates, which was 11.3 times the number in 1969 (UNCTAD, 2009). Outward FDI from developed countries consisted of 81% of the world total in 2008, compared to 90% between 1995 and 2000 – the rest of outward FDI originated from developing countries and from transition economies, which, together, are referred to now as emerging markets. The global financial crisis changed the investment landscape, at least temporarily, raising the share of emerging economies in global FDI flows to 43% in 2008 and almost one-half in 2009 (UNCTAD, 2009).

Thus, the growth in FDI has come about not only because existing MNEs have spread their tentacles globally but because wholly new MNEs have emerged in different countries at different times. Indeed, the first survey of MNEs carried out by the United Nations in 1973 identified 16 countries as having outward FDI in 1969 (United Nations, 1973). By 2007, the number of MNE home countries had grown to 135, including 89 developing countries and 9 members of the Commonwealth of Independent States and South-East Europe (UNCTAD, 2008, p. 211).

All in all, a large percent of international economic transactions are accounted for by MNEs, which weave a network of economic linkages across many economies. Since Hymer's pioneering doctoral thesis in 1960, researchers have attempted to understand how is it possible for foreign firms to compete against domestic competitors when they face the extra costs of learning how to operate in a foreign market. The answer proposed was that these firms enjoy some monopolistic advantages, for example, from superior technology, brand recognition, or management skills. Another question was why the MNE makes products abroad rather than export from home or resort to options such as licensing. Instead, different plants in different countries are brought under common control. The answer was the prevalence of transaction costs and their reduction by internalizing transactions within the firm (Buckley & Casson, 1985; Dunning, 1979). This explanation begs another question: why was the United States dominant in creating MNEs when its vast market could sustain multiplant operations. Internalization arguments alone would lead one to expect that MNEs will be based in small countries where multiplant internalization could be achieved only by moving to other countries. At any rate, one interesting unresolved question is why certain countries became home to many MNEs and others did not. The main point of this chapter is that MNEs today are a very diverse species, originating from a very large number of home countries, spawned in many industries, starting at earlier stages of the firm's evolution than before, and including firms of all sizes. This broadening of the origins of MNEs in the last few decades is the result of major shifts in the global economic and political environment, such as the emergence of new technologies, new attitude toward MNEs, and new government policies.

We begin by identifying four major stages in the evolution of MNEs.

FOUR STAGES OF MNE EVOLUTION

In the first phase, MNEs followed the flag of a colonial power. One of the oldest MNEs was the Dutch East India Company, which was granted a monopoly in 1602 for 21 years to carry out colonial activities in Asia. It operated for almost two centuries and was formally dissolved in 1800. The British East India Company – a private enterprise backed by the British crown – operated in the East Indies from 1608 until its dissolution in 1858. French, Portuguese, and Spanish firms also invested in their respective nations' colonies. At this time, the major motivation for internationalization was to extract, transport, and process natural resources, which usually flowed from the colonies to the colonial center, with manufactured goods flowing in the reverse direction. The major force enabling the creation of these firms was the political power of the home government. A few US firms

were also starting to globalize: Around 1900, Rockefeller's Standard Oil
ventured abroad in search of oil reserves (Wilkins, 1974), followed by still
other US oil companies (Yergin, 1991). Between 1870 and 1913 – the golden
age of rapid growth – a few US manufacturing firms pioneered foreign
operations in search of markets, led by Singer Sewing Machine, and
followed later by others, such as Ford Motor Company. Yet, MNEs from
Europe dominated the world stage, accounting for 93% of worldwide FDI
stock, having built international networks on the backs of their home
governments' colonialism (see Table 1). The United States' share at this time
was estimated at only 6% (Buckley & Casson, 1985, p. 200).

Technological advantage, built on the industrial revolution, which began
in Europe, not only gave European firms ownership advantages over foreign

Table 1. Share of Worldwide Stock of Outward FDI (OFDI),
Various Years.

Region/Country	1914	1969	1980	1990	2006
Europe[a]	93%	43.2%	41.1%	49.5%[a]	57.0%[a]
UK	50%	16.2%	14.1%	12.8%	11.9%
France	43%	n.a.	4.2%	6.1%	8.7%
Germany		n.a.	7.5%	8.5%	8.1%
Netherlands		n.a.	7.4%	6.0%	5.2%
United States	6%	55%	37.7%	24.3%	19.1%
Japan	0%	1.3%	3.4%	11.2%	3.6%
Emerging markets	0%	0%	12.7%	8.3%	12.8
Worldwide OFDI stock (US $ bill.)	n.a.	n.a.	571	1,791	12,474
No. of countries required to account for 93% of global OFDI stock[b]	4[b]	9[b]			24[b]

Sources: Data for 1914 from Buckley and Casson (1985, p. 200); for 1969, from UN (1973, p. 139);
for remaining years from http://www.unctad.org/Templates/Page.asp?intItemID=3277&lang=1
Table on "Outward FDI stock by Host Region and Economy (1980–2005), World Investment
Report 2006, 16/10/06."
[a]Europe's share fell secularly from 1914 to 1980 but then began to reverse course, possibly
because of growth in intra-EU FDI, following the Single European Act (1986) and the creation
of the euro.
[b]The countries involved were as follows: in 1914, UK, France, Germany, and Netherlands; in
1969, the previous four plus USA, Canada, Switzerland, Sweden, and Italy; and in 2005, the
previous nine countries plus Australia, and nine EU nations (Belgium, Spain, Norway, Italy,
Denmark, Ireland, Finland, Austria, and Luxembourg) and five emerging economies (Hong
Kong, Russia, Singapore, Taiwan, and Brazil).

rivals but also enabled their home governments to establish military superiority and build global empires. One outlier was Switzerland (Agmon & Kindleberger, 1977).

The two World Wars and the collapse of empires devastated the European MNEs, as foreign subsidiaries were seized by rival powers or nationalized by newly independent countries. In the postwar period, European leaders were determined to foster policies that would prevent a third World War. They initiated a series of market integrating programs that stimulated intra-European FDI as well as FDI from countries outside the bloc, principally the United States, to take advantage of the new opportunities. American firms, which already operated multidivisional and multiregional organizations in the United States, transferred those capabilities relatively easily to the fledgling common market in western Europe.

For approximately two decades, between 1949 and 1971, the economies of the developed nations grew rapidly: reconstruction raised European GDP growth to 5% per year, while Japan galloped along at 10% per year. The US economy grew at 3.8% per year. In the same period, growth in international trade outstripped growth in world output. FDI grew at twice the rate of GNP. European multinationals, mainly those from the United Kingdom, rebuilt their global presence, but the vast majority of new FDI came out of the United States, based on the technological and managerial superiority of its giant firms. The stock of outward FDI by US MNEs rose sharply from $7.2 billion in 1946 to $74.4 billion in 1970.

One of the first systematic efforts at data gathering by the United Nations found that of the 7,276 parent MNEs in the world in 1969, as many as 33.9% were from the United States, 23.3% were from the United Kingdom, and most of the rest were from other western European countries (UN, 1973, p. 138). The same report also showed the book value of global FDI stock at US$ 108.2 billion, of which 55.0% was from the United States, 16.2% from the United Kingdom, and only 1.3% was from Japan (UN, 1973, p. 139). The report also noted "a further central characteristic of multinational corporations is that they are in general the product of developed countries. Eight of the 10 largest multinational corporations are based in the United States" (UN, 1973, p. 7). Note, however, that 3,357 out of the 7,276 firms – nearly half the total – had affiliates in only one foreign country. (Vernon (1971) required a firm to have subsidiaries in at least six countries to be considered an MNE.) Research on MNEs was mainly on US multinationals, with some attention paid to UK multinationals.

Meanwhile, Japan was successfully rebuilding its shattered economy. When the US occupation of Japan ended in 1952, the government launched an ambitious program to create comparative advantage. For two decades, Japan was the best modern example of a "miracle economy," and her prowess in manufacturing skill- and capital-intensive products was established in these years. Between 1950 and 1990, Japan's real income per capita in constant 1990 prices grew by 7.7% per annum to reach US$ 23,970 (Economist, 1993). Japan's exports grew at 15% per year, even faster than her GDP, as firms took advantage of access to markets in the United States and Europe that were opening up as a result of successive rounds of GATT negotiations. The favorable trade balance enabled Japan to increase overseas investments. But it wasn't until the 1985 Plaza Accord that dictated a very strong yen that Japanese firms began to shift production from Japan to assembly plants in export markets (rich countries) and component factories in low-cost Asian neighbors (developing countries).

FDI outflows from Japan rose from a mere US$5 billion in 1980 to a peak of US$ 89 billion in 1989. In this decade, FDI grew at rates of 20–30% per annum, more than four times as fast as world GNP, but the United States was no longer the dominant source; quite the contrary, it became the largest recipient of FDI inflows, including several large investments from Japan. By the late 1980s, the third generation of MNEs had emerged and the multinational firm was very much a Triad phenomenon (see Table 1).

The fourth generation of multinational firms took off in the 1990s, as economic liberalization measures in many countries forced firms even in developing countries to experience global competition for the first time in the postwar period (Amsden, 2001). At the same time, new IT technologies facilitated the creation of "born globals." Both these trends convinced many entrepreneurs that to be successful they had to invest abroad and become internationally competitive.

In China, economic liberalization began as early as 1978, albeit on an experimental basis. Initially, China received FDI mainly from overseas Chinese based in places like Hong Kong, Singapore, and Taiwan. By the 1990s, inward FDI flooded in from other countries, and following China's accession to the WTO on December 11, 2001, FDI skyrocketed to US$ 72.4 billion in 2005. In the 1990s, Chinese firms, including several that were partly or wholly state-owned, began to invest overseas, in search of raw materials or markets, and in the 2000s those investments included acquisitions in Europe and the United States.

When the Berlin Wall crumbled in November 1989, the former Soviet Empire disaggregated and its different components moved toward liberal economic policies. At about the same time, several Latin American econo-mies began to cut government spending and subsidies, privatize state-owned firms, and deregulate industry. They pushed their economies into export-oriented free market strategies. So did other long-time bastions of protectionism, such as Ireland, Israel, or India, all of which opened their market in the 1990s to more competition, foreign trade, and inward FDI.

In India, for instance, this forced many old-time firms to upgrade their products and services, trim costs, benchmark themselves against best-in-class global competitors, and buttress their positions in the home market against foreign competitors that were entering India. Several of these firms then also ventured abroad, in search of markets and resources (Ramamurti & Singh, 2009). At the same time, a new breed of postliberalization firms competed globally from the beginning (Pradhan & Sahoo, 2005). Many of the India's leading firms were not in labor-intensive manufactures, as in East Asia, but in skill-intensive products and services, such as IT services, pharmaceuticals, and engineered products and services (Kapur & Ramamurti, 2001; Boston Consulting Group, 2009).

From being a Triad-dominated phenomenon, the fourth generation of MNEs saw the multinational firm become a much broader phenomenon – in terms of the geographical distribution of home countries, the explosion of FDI in service industries, and the size of individual MNEs. Although developing countries remained net importers of FDI, several of them become important outward investors. At its peak, total FDI outflows from firms in emerging markets reached $304.3billion in 2007 – thirty times that in 1990. This represented about 15% of world outward flows in 2007; in 1990 that share was only 5%. In terms of outward FDI stock, with $1.3 trillion in 2005, emerging markets accounted for 12% of the world total (see Table 1). Three-quarters of the top 100 MNEs from developing countries hailed from Asia.

Another striking trend was the growing number of small- and medium-sized enterprises that were multinationals. In the 1970s, multinationals were regarded as giants, with sales that dwarfed the GNPs of many countries. Although this is still true of the largest MNEs, the vast majority of firms counted by UNCTAD as MNEs in the 2000s were small in size.

CHANGING DRIVERS OF MULTINATIONALIZATION

Dunning's (1979) OLI framework highlights the need for a firm to have ownership advantages that offset the search and transaction costs and the "liability of foreignness" (Hymer, 1976; Zaheer, 1995), which refers to the costs borne by firms operating outside their home country. The timing of when firms in a country multinationalize may therefore be explained partly by when those firms acquire sufficient international competitive advantages to offset the cost of multinationalization. That, in turn, may depend on when a country's firms are exposed to international competition and opportunities. UNCTAD (1998) identified three sets of determinants of FDIs: the economic situation, the regulatory framework for FDI, and investment promotion. These theories and others do not consider explicitly neither they anticipated the role of general technological change, which has reduced the cost of overcoming distance and time-zone separation and expanded the range of goods and services that could be traded internationally. The railroad, the refrigerator, the steamship, the telegraph, and the laying out of the first transatlantic cable in 1866 expanded the scope for trade and investment at the end of the 19th century. In the 20th century came the radio, transcontinental telephones, giant tankers and airliners, and later satellites, computers, and the Internet. Technological change reduced significantly the cost of international transport and communication, and that of computing, as well as the liability of foreignness, all of which promote the multinationalization of firms. New technologies also allowed firms to outsource more activities to the lowest-cost location.

Aside from economic liberalization and technological change, another factor that has helped certain firms become multinationals is improved access to capital. High savings in Asia, coupled with high raw material prices (which boosted the current account surpluses of resource-rich countries) and low interest rates, combined to fuel the internationalization of local firms. The globalization of capital markets improved access to capital for firms in many parts of the world.

Another important factor was the availability of a large number of overseas nationals who could be approached for help to gain access to foreign markets. There were about 50 million Chinese living outside China, mostly in other parts of Asia. When China opened up, it was these overseas Chinese that helped China ramp up its exports of manufactured goods, by transferring their technical expertise, capital, and marketing know-how to small assembly operations in China's special economic zones. Likewise, overseas Indians, many of whom were knowledge workers based in the United States, helped India ramp up its exports of knowledge- and skill-intensive services (Kapur & Ramamurti, 2001). Today, skilled professionals from both countries circulate between Silicon Valley and their home countries, helping to close the knowledge gap between developed and developing countries (Saxenian, 2002).

Technological change and economic liberalization also promoted the growth of "micro-multinationals" (Copeland, 2006). For instance, the popular website, Craigslist.com, was a US company with estimated sales of $100 million that reached customers online in a few dozen countries but employed only 20 people. In fact, technological development and better knowledge of management methods allowed the rise of "born global" small- and medium-sized firms, whose competitive advantage was based on the ability to divide the value-chain activities and disperse it across different countries (Knight & Cavusgil, 1996). In this sense, we now live in a "Lego world" of value-chain building blocks. Even a relatively small firm headquartered in country A, can manufacture components in countries B and C, assemble them in D and E, perform R&D in F and G – and sell the finished products in still other countries. In the post-dot.com bubble era, venture capitalists expect start-ups to tap into the best locations worldwide for every task from the very beginning. This business model has become feasible because of the rise of specialized intermediary firms to which many steps of the value chain can be outsourced and offshored. A sharp decline in IT and communication costs have put the IT systems necessary to coordinate complex supply chains within the reach of even small firms.

Further, domestic firms in many small countries, Switzerland, but also, for example, Finland, Norway, Denmark and Israel, have become multi-nationals in growing numbers in the last two decades (Aharoni, 2006). Most MNEs from these countries were small compared to giants like General Electric (GE), and depended much more on international business (IB) for survival. Nokia, to cite one example, derived 97% of its sales from outside Finland. These firms developed competitive strengths unrelated to the location advantage of their home countries. They achieved scale economies by using the world as their oyster. Most important, they gained world competitiveness by acquiring a "portfolio of locational assets" (UNCTAD, 1995), thereby reaping the benefits of an international division of labor, with each part of the value chain produced in the most efficient location. They also raised capital in foreign markets, while retaining corporate headquarters and the top management in the home country. In the future, MNEs from many more economies are likely to join their ranks, as firms realize that focusing operations exclusively in the home country may deprive them of major efficiency gains and hurt competitiveness (Dunning, 1996). The MNE will become an even more important institution in the global economy.

The United States and the European Union still account for major shares of the world's GDP and therefore also global FDI flows. It is well known that the world's largest three or four hundred MNEs account for about 90% of the world stock of FDI. Since the larger MNEs dominate international business, IB scholars sometimes dismiss the value of studying small MNEs. In our view, IB theory should explain not only the obvious dominance of giant firms and countries but also the flourishing of MNEs from many countries, the growth of born-global MNEs, and the emergence of MNEs from emerging markets.

The MNE is best explained as an interconnected network of business and other relationships with crucial ties to a complex international business environment (IBE). Organizations are not unitary hierarchies but looser linked coalitions of shifting interest groups. The MNE today does not internalize production with all other transactions based in the market. Rather it governs a global network of loosely coupled units with different capabilities (for more on this idea, see Buckley's chapter in this volume). It enjoys command of a specific – as opposed to universal – knowledge and minimizes the risk of its proprietary knowledge being dissipated. It specializes in specific knowledge creation and is a vehicle for knowledge sharing across distance and differentiated contexts. To achieve its business goals, it may compete with rivals, but it also cooperates with its suppliers. By its very nature it can influence nations, competing for inward FDI in a world of mobile productive activities, capital, technology and labor, emphasizing its needs of political and economic stability. IBE is an aggregate of several elements that differ along geographical, social, political, and economic dimensions. Changes in IBE transform the way MNEs operate. In the world of the 21st century, any country can become the home base of MNEs.

THE NEWEST BREED: MNEs FROM DEVELOPING COUNTRIES

Although MNEs from developing countries have appeared on a significant scale only since the 1990s, there was in fact a spurt in the number of such firms in the 1960s and 1970s. That spurt involved annual FDI outflows from developing countries in the hundreds of millions of dollars, not billions of dollars, although by 1980 it had risen to $3 billion. The next spurt did not occur until the 1990s, and accelerated thereafter, peaking in 2000 at $147 billion, followed by a slump until 2002, and a recovery since 2003.

By 2007, as stated earlier, outward FDI from developing and transition economies had risen to $304.3 billion (UNCTAD, 2008, p. 2).

The latest wave of MNEs from developing countries raises several interesting questions. In what ways was the second spurt of outward FDI from developing and transition economies similar to or different from the first spurt? In what ways is their outward FDI similar to or different from that which took place from developed countries (e.g., Mathews, 2002)? Specifically, how do the competitive advantages and strategies of MNEs from developing countries compare with those from developed countries? And how consistent is this phenomenon with predictions of the investment development path (IDP) model (Dunning, 1981)? We offer some facts and a few educated guesses on these questions.

One obvious difference between the first and the second spurts in outward FDI from developing countries is that the second one has involved substantially larger flows, even if one excludes countries that serve as way stations for FDI flows from other countries ("overseas financial centers," such as Bermuda, the British Virgin Islands, the Cayman Islands, and to some extent, Hong Kong). Netting out overseas financial centers, FDI outflows from developing countries reached $292.7 billion in 2008, compared to $3 billion in 1980 and $13 billion in 1990. With a faster increase from China and India (UNCTAD, 2009), outward FDI from emerging markets has grown faster than inward FDI into those countries.

South-South FDI is entirely consistent with the expectation that capital would flow from richer to poorer countries – inasmuch as most of these flows occur from a handful of the more prosperous and advanced developing countries (Hong Kong, Taiwan, Singapore, Malaysia, Brazil, Mexico, and so on) to dozens of less prosperous developing countries. This kind of flow is qualitatively similar to that observed by Wells (1983), and is based on emerging market firms having products, and using processes, that are better suited to developing countries than those possessed by Western MNEs. It is also consistent with the expectation that firms will first invest in their own regions before venturing farther away (Johanson & Vahlne, 1977). Perhaps as Rugman (2005) has argued, many firm-specific advantages are more readily transferred to countries in the same region.

Another similarity in the outward FDI of developing countries in the 1970s and the 2000s was the high degree of concentration: in both periods, the top 10 countries accounted for 80% or more of outward FDI. However, the relative importance of different regions changed; for example, Latin America lost its place as the leading source of outward FDI. Taking their place were several Asian economies.

One surprising development in the 2000s was that about one-fourth of the outward FDI from developing countries went to developed countries; in some years, that share was as high as one-third. This is unprecedented, and such substantial flows from poor to rich countries run counter to the argument that firms in poor countries cannot possess technologies or applications of value compared to developed countries. Most of these investments are in services, including those that support trade. With the increase in outward FDI flows, there has been a rise in the number of multinational firms from developing economies. UNCTAD (2009) counted more than 21,000 such firms – 3,500 of which were from China and 815 from India.

The rapid increase in outward FDI from low-income countries, such as China and India, or even middle-income countries, such as Malaysia and Mexico, does not fit the predictions of the "investment development path" IDP model (UNCTAD, 2006, p. 141). Outward FDI from developing economies has occurred sooner than IDP theory would predict. The relationship between level of development (measured by, say, per capita income) and outward FDI, or that between inward and outward FDI, is more complex than IDP theory suggests. For instance, the recent surge in outward FDI by developing countries has come not from the countries that received the most inward FDI in the past – namely, those in Latin America – but rather from countries in Asia, some of which were quite closed to FDI earlier (e.g., India). Such mismatches are also evident in the experience of industrialized countries: Spain, for instance, though quite advanced relative to developing countries, did not become a major source of outward FDI until it joined the European Union in 1986 (Guillen, 2005, p. 68), and Japan emerged as a major supplier of outward FDI after the mid-1980s without ever being open to inward FDI. (Navaretti and Venables (2004), note that "Japan's economy is virtually closed to foreign MNEs, which account for less than 1% of manufacturing employment," p. 5.)

The important determinant of outward FDI may not be level of development per se, but home country economic policies toward trade and FDI and natural endowments such as the supply of local entrepreneurs (e.g., see discussion in Thomas & Meuller, 2000, pp. 289–291). If a government exposes the economy to greater competition from domestic and multi-national firms, its firms are more likely to become internationally competitive. Once these firms develop ownership-specific advantages, they will exploit them overseas or augment them by acquiring complementary or knowledge-based assets abroad.

Government policies allowing or encouraging outward FDI are also important. In the past, many governments viewed outward FDI as an undesirable transfer of capital and jobs to other countries, but in the 2000s they have viewed it as a way to build globally competitive firms. Sovereign wealth funds are also a new player – albeit a negligible one. More important are state-owned enterprises, mainly from China. Thus, the Chinese government reportedly encouraged state-controlled firms to build global organizations (Buckley, Clegg, Cross, Voss, & Rhodes, 2006), as did the Singaporean government. India (UNCTAD, 2004, pp. 8–10), South Africa (Goldstein & Pritchard, 2006, p. 11), and many other governments simplified procedures and increased the size of overseas investments that their companies could make. Firms in transition economies experienced a radical change in national policies for FDI, compared to the years before 1989, when their economies were closed to FDI from outside the Soviet Bloc. There are a myriad of other examples.

In 2011, EM–MNEs were to be found in many industries. Some were resource seekers, looking for oil, gas, or minerals, often in competition with developed-country counterparts; others operated in knowledge-intensive businesses, financial services, infrastructure services, or products not easily traded, such as cement (Cantwell & Barnard, 2006). Still others operated in industries highly exposed to global competition, such as automotives, fast-moving consumer goods, white goods, or pharmaceuticals (for more on this, see Ramamurti & Singh, 2009).

There is surely more room for growth of such firms. For one thing, significant parts of the world are still outside the domain of free markets. Countries like Cuba, North Korea, and parts of sub-Saharan Africa are not integrated into the global economy, nor are poor peasants in rural China or India as integrated into it as counterparts in prosperous urban areas. As pointed out by Stiglitz (2006), poor countries that don't have the roads or other infrastructure to move products cannot enjoy the fruits of open markets, nor do they have the skills to maximize their interests in complex international negotiations. Moreover, despite deregulation and major reductions in tariffs and government intervention, many economic activities are still highly protected in all countries; for example, farmers are subsidized in most developed countries, and airlines still operate in a regime that does not allow foreign ownership of national carriers (Aharoni, 2002).

Another pocket of underglobalized firms involves state-owned enterprises, many of which were created by governments as instruments of national policy and still enjoy preferential access to public resources and contracts. Many are already involved in international production in industries such as in aerospace, armaments, energy, and consumer durables (see Aharoni, 1980; Anastassopoulos, George, & Pierre, 1987; Vernon & Aharoni, 1981).

Others have already been privatized. However, over time, many more will be placed squarely in private hands, as a result of which they are likely to become more aggressive players in international markets (Vernon, 1979). In China, one can see such aggressive behavior even among state-owned enterprises that have been partly privatized or that have entered into joint ventures with foreign firms (Park, Li, & Tse, 2006).

One indicator of the status of MNEs from any country is a comparison of its share of worldwide FDI outflows and worldwide GDP. By this yardstick, emerging markets are still underrepresented in global FDI outflows: in 2009, at official exchange rates, they accounted for 25% of world GDP but only 17% of world FDI outflows. Using purchasing power parity (PPP), the gap was much bigger because developing countries accounted for 44% of the world's GDP in real terms. However, the gap was closing, and in another decade or two the shares at official exchange rates are likely to be closely matched. In other words, globalization still has a long way to go in emerging markets, and as it advances, the national origin of MNEs is likely to diversify even further, the size distribution of MNEs will become more skewed, and the number of industries in which MNEs operate will increase.

BACKLASH AGAINST DEVELOPING COUNTRY MNEs?

MNEs have not always been seen as a positive force in society. In the 1960s and 1970s, anxiety about the growing power of American MNEs was high around the world, including in Europe, while in the developing world that anxiety applied to foreign MNEs of all stripes. The proliferation of MNEs in the subsequent three decades should not be misunderstood to mean that the old fears about MNEs in host countries have dissipated. Quite the contrary, many of the old fears still persist, but with one key difference: today, those fears are high not only in emerging economies but also in the developed world, including the United States.

In the 1970s, the rallying cause was the fear that MNEs would dominate the weaker and less sophisticated nation-state. Their ability to move resources across borders or to use transfer pricing to minimize tax liabilities was resented. Servan-Schreiber (1967), in his best-selling book, *Le Défi Américain,* warned that US MNEs would take over the French economy. Latin American economists railed against *dependencia* (e.g., Evans, 1979), and others feared the MNE's control of the commanding heights – or the strategic sectors – of the economy.

Since the 1980s, new views of the MNE took hold as governments substituted regulation and intervention with greater scope for free markets and competition. Deregulation, privatization, and competition became the major slogans everywhere. The collapse of communist regimes and the breakup of the Soviet Empire silenced any remaining skeptics of free markets and competition. Transition economies moved as quickly as they could to a market economy and integration with the world economy.

Accordingly, governments all over the world chose to ignore tensions with MNEs and instead to court them to invest within their territories (Ramamurti, 2001). The advantages of additional jobs, technology transfers, exports, and knowledge creation were perceived as outweighing the risks, such as loss of national sovereignty, tax evasion through transfer pricing, "crowding out" of local private enterprise, suboptimal technology choices, or other negative spillovers in the host economy. UNCTAD documented in its annual *World Investment Report* the proliferation of investment promotion agencies, the mushrooming of bilateral investment treaties, and the tendency to create a more hospitable environment for MNEs through regulatory changes. The share of FDI laws that made the investment climate less welcoming to MNEs was 6% during 1992–2002, 12% in 2003–2004, as high as 21% in 2005–2007, and hit a record 30% in 2009 (UNCTAD, 2010, pp. 76–77).

At the dawn of the 21st century, there was considerable anxiety about globalization in the developed economies at least as much as in the developing economies. This reversal of the traditional roles – in which the rich countries championed free markets and international openness, and the poor countries resisted it – occurred over the previous two decades. Going forward, there may well be a serious backlash against globalization in the European Union and the United States. If that were to happen, the expansion of MNEs from emerging markets into developed countries may get slowed down.

FDIs from countries such as China or India are already viewed with some suspicion in the West, and arguments of national security may be advanced to limit the acquisition of developed-economy firms by MNEs from developing countries. This was seen, for instance, in Lenovo (China)'s acquisition of IBM's global PC business in December 2004, where the risk of China acquiring dual use technologies or obtaining a US platform for industrial espionage was among the concerns of the Committee on Foreign Investment in the United States (CFIUS), a multiagency federal panel. Dubai Ports World, a firm owned by the UAE government, got quick CFIUS approval for its indirect acquisition of US ports when it purchased the British firm P&O Steam Navigation Co. but later ran into a storm of protests from Congress and had to abandon its quest. Firms being acquired are declared as a part of a "strategic sector" particularly when the acquirer is a state-owned enterprise or sovereign wealth fund.

Wolf (2004) and others identify several grounds on which acquisitions by emerging-market firms in developed countries might be opposed. The foreign owner might be accused of competing unfairly, spoiling the environment, of shifting jobs from the United States or Europe to low-wage workers back home, or of being unqualified to run the acquired operations. But the most common worry is that the acquisition would threaten national security, and these concerns are amplified if a foreign government owns the MNE. Three-quarters of the Chinese firms in Boston Consulting Group's list of the top 100 MNEs in emerging markets were partly or wholly owned by the state (Boston Consulting Group, 2009).

The potential loss of jobs to emerging economies is yet another source of anxiety for rich countries. In the 19th century, people moved freely across borders in search of jobs and better opportunities. During the 1890s, the inflow of immigrants to the United States equaled 9% of the initial population, in Argentina 26%, and in Australia 17% (Baldwin & Martin, 1999, p. 19). In the century following 1815, around 60 million people left Europe to find better lives in America, South and East Africa, and Oceania (Hirst & Thompson, 1999, p. 23). In the 20th century, on the other hand, products, technology, and capital began to move freely across borders, but the movement of people became more restricted. In such a world, workers couldn't move to where the jobs were, but it became easier for jobs to move to where the workers were. In rich countries, this boosted fears that jobs would move to places where they could be performed at the least cost, thereby hollowing out industries in the rich countries. Digitization and improvements in communications and computing technology made many services, including knowledge-intensive activities and even R&D, susceptible to the same kind of global optimization, striking fear in the hearts of not just blue-collar workers but white-collar workers as well.

Indeed, in one developed country after another, protectionism has raised its head more in the investment area than on the trade front. Both US and European governments have sought to check takeover bids, citing security reasons. Predictions of the demise of the nation-state and the creation of a borderless world have not been realized (Ohmae, 1995). Expectations that national business systems would converge to form a seamless global system have not materialized. According to Doremus, Keller, Pauly, and Reich (1999), multinationals continue to be shaped by the policies and cultures of their home countries even though they globalize their assets and liabilities. It is thus highly likely that developed countries would attempt to restrict what they would perceive as the takeover of their precious assets by foreign firms (Hitt, 2007). In this sense, we may encounter a selective globalization, wherein some areas of economic activity are governed by market forces, while others are restricted on grounds of "fair trade," market failure, or national security considerations.

CONCLUSION AND RESEARCH QUESTIONS

Multinationals have proliferated since they first appeared, in numbers, areas of operations, and national origin. They have changed considerably in response to four major shifts in the environment:

Government policy, which has become increasingly more welcoming of FDI, especially in emerging markets, not just in manufacturing but also in services;

Improvements in information and communication technologies, which have vastly reduced the cost of managing and integrating a globally dispersed value chain;

Bigger and more efficient capital markets, which have broadened access to capital for small- and medium-sized firms, including those in developing countries; and

The strengthening of cross-border social networks among locals and overseas nationals (sometimes referred to as Diaspora), which has accelerated the cross-border flow of information and tacit knowledge and helped firms internationalize.

As a result of these trends, MNEs are being spawned in more countries, in more industries, and at earlier stages of a firm's evolution than before. The vast majority of the world's MNEs are small, and in the extreme some are "born global" firms. These changes have also transformed the well-established Triad-based MNE. As the industrial world has given way to a knowledge- and information-driven world, established MNEs have learned how to manage across national borders, and how to adapt to different markets and cultures. They have also learned how to collaborate in strategic alliances rather than seeking to be stand-alone superstars. More important, from a start as raw-material seekers and tariff-jumpers, they have become efficiency-seekers and innovation-seekers. Today, Western MNEs seek knowledge and ideas as keenly as they once sought natural resources or access to closed markets. They have learned to scan the world for new ideas, acquire start-ups, absorb knowledge from foreign subsidiaries, and to integrate knowledge acquired in all parts of the firm. Their competitive advantages are based less and less on hard assets – such as factories, inventories, or production skills – and more on intangibles, such as knowledge, intellectual property, and relationships.

These developments raise several questions that future research must address. A necessary condition for becoming an MNE is that the firm possesses firm-specific advantages relative to competitors. Precisely what ownership advantages do the newer MNEs from emerging markets enjoy and how did they develop those advantages in a relatively short period of time? What enables emerging market firms to invest "up-market," that is, in countries richer and more advanced than their home countries, as opposed to "down-market," as the product cycle theory would predict? And, how do the strategies of these firms resemble or differ from those of European, Japanese, or American MNEs (Johanson & Vahlne, 2000)? What is in fact the impact of an MNE's country of origin on its strategy? We have educated guesses on these issues (e.g., Khanna & Palepu, 2006; Ramamurti & Singh, 2009) but more research is needed to provide definitive answers.

Existing theory is not very clear on why some countries spawn MNEs and others do not, and precisely why the number of countries spawning MNEs has proliferated in the last two decades. Aliber (1970) suggested that the home country's advantage is related to the strength of its currency. Other explanations are related to the supply of local entrepreneurial talent, the behavior of managers, the ability of the firm to innovate, the impact of governmental policies, as well as the impact of technological changes.

Another intriguing issue is whether the world will be dominated by a handful of megacorporations, as Larry Bossidy, former vice chairman of GE, predicted in 1989: "By the latter part of the 1990s, there may well be fewer than 25 megacorporations in the world, about equally divided among United States, European and Far Eastern companies ... The medium-to-large-size-generalists, serving a limited geographic market and without a specific niche, won't be around anymore" (p. 10). Yet, as discussed, the number of multinationals in the world increased more than 10-fold after 1969. In contrast to Porter's (1986) prediction, giant firms do not dominate many economic fields, even in global industries, which are sometimes populated by a large number of domestic players. One example is the accounting industry, but this is also true of some other service industries (Aharoni, 1999).

Rugman (2005) would recommend that scholars focus only on giant firms since other firms are unimportant in the overall picture of world MNEs. We strongly argue that the emergence of new born globals, the expansion of home countries to many more nation-states, and the emergence of MNEs from developing economies may not be earthshaking in size but must have a place in IB theory. Such a theory should guide managers and policy makers in small firms and states as well as in the large ones.

We thus suggest other questions for future research: How and why do small firms survive and thrive in a global world? When are they doomed to be acquired by industry giants and when can they quickly develop and sustain competitive advantages that allow them to remain independent? How does the behavior of large and small MNEs differ? What are the implications for IB theory as firms become MNEs not necessarily to seek resources but also to gain markets, increase efficiency, absorb new knowledge, or be service-centered MNEs?

More research is also needed on the relationship between MNEs and politics, including their impact on national sovereignty. As early as 1969, Charles Kindleberger claimed "the nation-state is just about through as an economic unit" (Kindleberger, 1969). The expansion of globalization since the end of the Cold War was seen by some scholars as making the nation-state obsolete. Yet, the last century has seen, on the one hand, the amalgamation of states into larger blocs, such as the European Union, and on the other hand, the fragmentation of states into smaller countries. The number of countries has more than doubled in the last three decades of the 20th century, rising from 96 in 1960 to 192 in 1998. The number of countries with less than 1 million people has almost tripled – from 15 to 43. Contrary to expectations, the MNE does not dominate over host countries, and globalization has not made states impotent. Why did earlier predictions prove incorrect? The relationship between globalization and the importance of the nation-state thus deserves more research.

Most economists seem to agree that the benefits of FDI exceed its costs (Oxelheim & Ghauri, 2004, p. 10), and that both inward and outward foreign investments are beneficial, contributing to growth that might otherwise not occur (Moran, Graham, & Blomström, 2005; Kokko, 2006). Others have argued for putting limits on foreign investments, for example, restricting outward FDI that impinges on national security, although defining the national security interest is often controversial, or restricting inward FDI in the "commanding heights of the economy," although this seems to have lost much of its former appeal. Underlying these policy choices is the assumption that a firm's nationality matters, but this too deserves more study. For instance, what changes when an American firm (such as Ford or General Motors) acquires a Swedish firm (such as Saab or Volvo)? Robert Reich (1990) claimed that what really matters is *where* economic activities are carried out, rather than *who* carries them out because at the end of the day the outcome of interest is employment and job creation. For him, a Japanese firm producing in the United States is more beneficial to the US economy than a US firm producing (and thus creating employment) in Asia. Yet, an American-owned Intel may be readier than an Israeli-owned firm to close a factory in Israel. These, however, are hypotheses that need to be thought through carefully and tested in future studies (for a deeper discussion of these ideas, see Seev Hirsch's chapter in this volume).

There are also a host of questions about the welfare implications and political fallout from globalization.[1] How and why is globalization affecting income inequality across countries and within countries? Is globalization sustainable if income inequality within countries increases as globalization intensifies? The sustainability of globalization depends on finding satisfactory answers to policy questions of this sort.

Hopefully, researchers of these and other related topics will be careful in defining the population they study, remembering that MNEs are now quite heterogeneous – in terms of their national origin, size, reasons for overseas investments, industries in which those investments are made, and perhaps also their strategy and structure.

NOTE

1. We are grateful to Nakiye Boyacigiller for bringing this set of issues to our attention.

REFERENCES

Agmon, T., & Kindleberger, C. P. (1977). *Multinationals from small countries*. Cambridge, MA: MIT Press.
Aharoni, Y. (1980). The state-owned enterprise as a competitor in international markets. *Columbia Journal of World Business, XV*(1), 14–22.
Aharoni, Y. (1999). Internationalization of professional services: Implications for accounting firms. In: D. Brock, M. Powell & C. R. (Bob) Hinings (Eds), *Restructuring the professional organization* (pp. 20–40). London: Routledge.

Aharoni, Y. (2002). The globalizer that cannot globalize – The airline transportation industry European International Business Association Annual conference, Athens, December. Available at http://64.233.169.104/search?q = cache:DUe51KvA1xcJ:www.aueb.gr/deos/ EIBA2002.files/PAPERS/C214.pdf+%22the+globalizer+that+cannot+globalize% 22&hl=en&ct=clnk&cd=1&gl=us

Aharoni, Y. (2006). Debunking management myth. *CIIM Management Review, 2*(2), 10–16.

Aliber, R. Z. (1970). A theory of foreign direct investment. In: C. F. Kindleberger (Ed.), *The international corporation.* Cambridge, MA: The MIT Press.

Amsden, A. H. (2001). *The rise of "the rest": Challenges to the west from late-industrializing economies.* New York: Oxford University Press.

Anastassopoulos, J. P., George, B., & Pierre, D. (1987). *State-owned multinationals.* Chichester, UK: Wiley.

Baldwin, R., & Martin, P. (1999). *Two waves of globalization: Superficial similarities, fundamental differences.* National Bureau of Economic Research Working Paper no. 6904 (January). Available at www.nber.org

Boston Consulting Group. (2009). *The 2009 BCG 100 new global challengers: How companies from rapidly developing economies are contending for global leadership.* Boston: Boston Consulting Group.

Buckley, P., & Casson, M. (1985). *The economic theory of the multinational enterprise.* New York: St. Martin's Press.

Buckley, P., Clegg, J., Cross, A., Voss, H., Rhodes, M., & Zheng, P. (2006). Explaining China's outward FDI: An institutional perspective. Paper presented at the International Conference on "The rise of transnational corporations from emerging markets: threat or opportunity?" Columbia University, New York (October 24–25).

Cantwell, J., & Barnard, H. (2006). Do firms from developing countries have to invest abroad? Outward FDI and the competitiveness of firms. Paper presented at the International Conference on "The rise of transnational corporations from emerging markets: threat or opportunity?" Columbia University, New York (October 24–25).

Copeland, M. V. (2006). The mighty micro-multinational. *Business 2.0,* July 28. Available at http://money.cnn.com/magazines/business2/business2_archive/2006/07/01/8380230/ index.htm

Doremus, P., Keller, W. W., Pauly, L. W., & Reich, S. (1999). *The myth of the global corporation.* Princeton, NJ: Princeton University Press.

Dunning, J. H. (1979). Explaining changing patterns of international production: In defense of the eclectic theory. *Oxford Bulletin of Economics and Statistics, 45,* 269–295.

Dunning, J. H. (1981). Explaining the international direct investment position of countries: Towards a dynamic or developmental approach. *Weltwirtschaftliches Archiv, 117,* 30–64.

Dunning, J. H. (1996). The geographical sources of the competitiveness of firms: Some results of a new survey. *Transnational Corporations, 5*(3), 1–30.

Economist Intelligence Unit. (2007). *World investment prospect to 2011: Foreign direct investment and the challenge of political risk.* London: Economist Intelligence Unit.

Economist. (1993). Turning point: A survey of Japanese economy. *Economist,* March 6.

Evans, P. (1979). *Dependent development.* Princeton, NJ: Princeton University Press.

Goldstein, A., & Pritchard, W. (2006). South African multinationals: South-South cooperation at its best? Paper prepared for the SAIIA *Doing business in Africa* volume. Mimeo.

Guillen, M. (2005). *The rise of Spanish multinationals: European business in the global economy.* Cambridge, UK: Cambridge University Press.

Hitt, G. (2007). A higher bar for foreign buyers: Security terms in Alcatel's deal for Lucent signals new era. *Wall Street Journal, 5*(January), A6.

Hirst, P., & Thompson, G. (1999). *Globalization in question: The international economy and the possibilities of governance* (2nd ed.). Cambridge: Polity Press.

Hymer, S. H. (1976). *The international operations of national firms: A study of direct foreign investment.* Ph.D. thesis, 1960, The MIT Press, MA.

Johanson, J., & Vahlne, J. E. (1977). The internationalization process of the firm: A model of knowledge development and increasing foreign market commitments. *Journal of International Business Studies, 8*(1), 23–32.

Johanson, J., & Vahlne, J. E. (2000). New technology, new companies and new internationalization processes? A critical review of the internationalization process model. Paper for the Marcus Wallenberg Symposium on Internationalization, January 10–11, Uppsala, Sweden.

Kapur, D., & Ramamurti, R. (2001). India's emerging competitive advantage in services. *Academy of Management Executive, 15*(2), 20–33.

Khanna, T., & Palepu, K. (2006). Emerging giants. *Harvard Business Review*, October–November.

Kindleberger, C. P. (1969). *American business abroad: Six lectures on direct investment.* New Haven, CT: Yale University Press.

Knight, G. A., & Cavusgil, S. T. (1996). The born global firm: A challenge to traditional internationalization theory. In: L. Lindmark, P.R. Christensen, H. Eskelinen, B. Forsstrom, O.J. Sorenson, & E. Vatn (Eds), *Advances in international marketing* (Vol. 8, pp. 11–26). Greenwich, CT: JAI Press.

Kokko, A. (2006). *The home country effects of FDI in developing economies.* Mimeo. The European Institute of Japanese Studies, Stockholm.

Mathews, J. A. (2002). *Dragon multinationals: A new model for global growth.* Oxford, UK: Oxford University Press.

Moran, T. H., Graham, E. M., & Blomström, M. (Eds). (2005). *Does foreign direct investment promote development?* Washington, DC: The Institute for International Economics.

Navaretti, G. B., & Venables, A. J. (2004). *Multinational firms in the world economy.* Princeton, NJ: Princeton University Press.

Ohmae, K. (1995). *The end of the nation state.* New York: Simon and Schuster.

Oxelheim, L., & Ghauri, P. (Eds). (2004). *European Union and the race for foreign direct investment in Europe.* Oxford: Elsevier.

Park, S. H., Li, S., & Tse, D. K. (2006). Market liberalization and firm performance during China's economic transition. *Journal of International Business Studies, 37,* 127–147.

Pradhan, J. P., & Sahoo, M. K. (2005). *Case study on outward foreign direct investment by Indian small- and medium-sized enterprises.* New York: UNCTAD.

Porter, M. E. (1986). *Competition in global industries.* Boston: Harvard Business School Press.

Ramamurti, R. (2001). The obsolescing 'bargaining model': MNC-host developing country relations revisited. *Journal of International Business Studies, 32*(1), 23–39.

Ramamurti, R., & Singh, J. V. (Eds). (2009). *Emerging multinationals from emerging markets.* Cambridge, UK: Cambridge University Press.

Reich, R. B. (1990). Who is us? (The changing American corporation). *Harvard Business Review, 68,* pp. 53–64.

Rugman, A. (2005). *The regional multinationals: MNEs and 'global' strategic management.* Cambridge, UK: Cambridge University Press.

Saxenian, A. (2002). *Local and global networks of immigrant professionals in Silicon Valley*. San Francisco: Public Policy Institute of California.

Servan-Schreiber, J. J. (1967). In: R. Steel (Trans.), *Le Défi Américain Paris: Denoel*. [*The American challenge*]. New York: Atheneum Press.

Stiglitz, J. E. (2006). *Making globalization work*. New York: W.W. Norton.

Thomas, A. S., & Meuller, S. L. (2000). A case for comparative entrepreneurship: Assessing the relevance of culture. *Journal of International Business Studies, 31*(2), 287–301.

UNCTAD. (1995). *World investment report: Transnational corporations and competitiveness*. New York: United Nations.

UNCTAD. (1998). *World investment report: Trends and determinants*. New York: United Nations.

UNCTAD. (2000). *World investment report: Cross-border M&A and development*. New York: United Nations.

UNCTAD. (2004). *India's outward FDI: A giant awakening?* Paper no. UNCTAD/DITE/IIAB/2004/1, October 20, 2004. Available at http://www.unctad.org/sections/dite_iiab/docs/diteiiab20041_en.pdf

UNCTAD. (2006). *World investment report: FDI from developing and transition economies: Implications for development*. New York: United Nations.

UNCTAD. (2008). *World investment report: Transnational corporations and the infrastructure challenge*. New York: United Nations.

UNCTAD. (2009). *World investment report: Transnational corporations, agricultural production, and development*. New York: United Nations.

UNCTAD. (2010). *World investment report: Investing in a low carbon economy*. New York: United Nations.

United Nations Department of Economic and Social Affairs. (1973). *Multinational corporations in world development*. New York: United Nations.

Vernon, R. (1971). *Sovereignty at bay: The multinational spread of U.S. enterprise*. New York: Basic Books.

Vernon, R. (1979). International aspects of state-owned enterprises. *Journal of International Business Studies, 10*(3), 7–15.

Vernon, R., & Aharoni, Y. (Eds). (1981). *State-owned enterprises in Western economies*. London: Croom Helm.

Wells, L. T., Jr. (1983). *Third world multinationals*. Cambridge, MA: MIT Press.

Wilkins, M. (1974). *The maturing of multinational enterprise: American business abroad from 1914 to 1970*. Cambridge, MA: Harvard University Press.

Wolf, M. (2004). *Why globalization works*. New Haven, CT: Yale University Press.

Yergin, D. (1991). *The prize: The epic quest for oil, money, and power*. New York: Simon and Schuster.

Zaheer, S. (1995). Overcoming the liability of foreignness. *Academy of Management Journal, 38*(2), 341–363.

NEW PLAYERS IN FDI: SOVEREIGN WEALTH FUNDS, PRIVATE EQUITY, AND EMERGING-MARKET MULTINATIONALS ☆

Ravi Ramamurti

ABSTRACT

As FDI flows grew in volume and complexity in the 1990s and early 2000s, three new players appeared on the global stage: sovereign wealth funds (SWFs), which were government-controlled entities with the authority to take significant equity stakes in foreign firms; private equity (PE) firms, which resorted increasingly to cross-border acquisitions, and emerging-market multinational enterprises (EMNEs), which ratcheted up their overseas acquisitions and investments. While none of these players was entirely new, each became more visible in the 2000s. Looking ahead, we anticipate that SWFs will continue to be marginal FDI players, with a few exceptions, despite their high visibility; that PEs will play a highly volatile role, varying from marginal at times to important at

☆ An earlier version of this paper titled "Impact of the Crisis on New Players: The Past, Present, and Future of SWFs, PEs, and EMNEs" was presented at the Vale Columbia Center conference at Columbia University in November 2009 and is to appear in *Transnational Corporations* (April 2010).

The Future of Foreign Direct Investment and the Multinational Enterprise
Research in Global Strategic Management, Volume 15, 137–165
ISSN: 1064-4857/doi:10.1108/S1064-4857(2011)0000015012

others; and that only EMNEs were already quite important in 2009 and likely to gain in importance, as emerging economies become prime movers of the global economy. The global financial crisis of 2008–2009 may thus only have speeded up the inevitable rise of emerging economies as both sources and destinations for FDI. We further conclude that EMNEs will contribute significantly to sustainable development because of their distinctive capabilities in making and selling products for low-income customers, and their emerging competence in "green" technologies.

Keywords: Emerging-market multinational enterprises (EMNEs); sovereign wealth funds (SWFs); private equity (PE); future outlook for FDI; sustainable development; global financial crisis

A recurring theme in Yair Aharoni's contributions to international business has been the view that mainstream research, often led by scholars in the United States, overlooks important international players from other parts of the world. Thus, for instance, he pioneered research on the internationalization of state-owned enterprises (Aharoni, 1980), the challenges of attracting FDI into small countries (Aharoni, 1966), or the prospects for spawning multinationals in small or poor economies (Aharoni & Ramamurti, 2008).

In keeping with that tradition, this chapter analyzes how global FDI flows have changed in the last two decades from one propelled largely by Western multinational firms to one involving a more diverse set of players. In the 1980s, most FDI originated in multinational enterprises (MNEs) from developed countries and flowed to other developed countries; developing countries were only important as hosts of FDI. In the mid-1980s, for instance, only 2% of global outward FDI originated in developing countries, with 98 percent coming from countries such as the United Kingdom, France, Germany, the United States, and, most recently, Japan.[1] There is little information on the destination of the 2–3 percent of outward FDI originating in developing countries, but Wells (1983) estimates that in the 1970s about two-thirds probably went to other developing countries.

Fast forward to 2007, when FDI flows reached their all-time peak of $1.98 trillion, and the picture becomes more complex. Now, there were several new players on the FDI scene. First, there was growing FDI from emerging markets, most of it flowing to other emerging markets, but a significant share also going to developed countries.[2] The share of emerging markets in FDI outflows rose from 3 percent in 1990 to 16 percent in 2008. Another new player with very deep pockets and mixed motives was the sovereign wealth fund (SWF), which as a group had $3.9 trillion in assets, compared to the world's total FDI stock of $16 trillion. After 2005, SWFs began to make FDI-style investments, that is, to take equity positions of 10 percent or more in individual foreign companies. This created anxiety in G-7 countries, resulting in a quick tightening of their FDI rules. A third new player was the private equity (PE) firm, which engaged in many cross-border deals during the M&A boom of the 2000s. PE firms devoted almost 70 percent of their funds to leveraged buyouts, much of it within the developed world.

This chapter surveys the new players on the global FDI stage, how they were affected by the global financial crisis of 2008–2009, and what role they are likely to play in the future. In the short run, there was the question of whether investors from emerging economies, sitting on huge foreign exchange reserves, might take advantage of the crisis to buy companies cheaply or to acquire assets that would otherwise be off-limits for national security reasons.[3] In the long run, there was the question of whether the crisis threatened to dislodge developed-country MNEs as the dominant source of global FDI flows. Finally, the question of whether the new players will facilitate or hinder sustainable economic development is explored.

SOVEREIGN WEALTH FUNDS

SWFs are "special purpose investment funds or arrangements, owned by the general government." SWFs hold or manage assets to achieve their goals, including investing in foreign assets and companies (Banque de France, 2008, p. 1). By definition, therefore, governments, or their appointed agents, call the shots in these organizations. Most SWFs funds had assets under $50 billion, and the eight funds with assets over $150 billion accounted for 70 percent of the assets of all SWFs (see Table 1). The top-15 SWFs included only two from developed countries – Norway's Government Pension Fund and Australia's Queensland Investment Corporation. The rest were either from oil and gas exporting countries (UAE, Saudi Arabia, Kuwait, Russia, Libya, and Qatar) or from Asian exporters with large current account surpluses (China, Singapore, and Hong Kong). SWFs came into prominence in the 2000s as their assets swelled with the rise in commodity prices and current account surpluses in Asia. In countries like China, only 10% of the country's foreign exchange reserves were assigned to an SWF, while in other countries that share could be as high as 75 or 80 percent.

SWFs are by no means new actors – the one in Hong Kong was created in 1935, and half of the top-50 SWFs were created before 1990. But their visibility and importance grew in the 2000s, because the number of SWFs

Table 1.   The World's Fifteen Largest Sovereign Wealth Funds,
October 2009.

Country	Fund Name	Assets ($ Billion)	Inception	Origin	Ratio of SWF to FX Reserve
UAE-Abu Dhabi	Abu Dhabi Investment Authority	627	1976	Oil	13.9
Norway	Government Pension Fund – Global	445	1990	Oil	8.8
Saudi Arabia	SAMA Foreign Holdings	431	n/a	Oil	1.1
China	SAFE Inv. Co.	347.1[b]		N-C	0.2
China	China Investment Corporation	288.8	2007	N-C	0.1
Singapore	Govt. of Singapore Investment Corp.	247.5	1981	N-C	1.4
Kuwait	Kuwait Investment Authority	202.8	1953	Oil	10.6
Russia	National Welfare Fund	178.5[a]	2008	Oil	0.4
China	National Social Security Fund	146.5	2000	N-C	Nil
China–Hong Kong	Hong Kong Monetary Auth. Inv. Portfolio	139.7	1993	N-C	1.0
Singapore	Temasek Holdings	122	1974	N-C	0.7
UAE-Dubai	Investment Corp. of Dubai	82	2006	Oil	1.8
Libya	Libyan Investment Authority	65	2006	Oil	0.8
Qatar	Qatar Investment Authority	65	2003	Oil	8.6
Australia	Australian Future Fund	49.3	2004	N-C	1.8

Source: Sovereign Wealth Funds Institute (http://www.swfinstitute.org/funds.php).
Note: All figures quoted are from official sources, or, where the institutions concerned do not issue statistics of their assets, from other publicly available sources. Some of these figures are best estimates as market values change day to day. Updated October 2009. N-C, noncommodity.
[a]This includes the oil stabilization fund of Russia.
[b]This number is a best-guess estimation.

nearly doubled by 2008 to 53 and, more relevant to this paper, FDI-type investments by SWFs swelled, especially after 2005. In that sense, SWFs can be regarded as new players on the FDI stage. However, over the period from 1987 to 2007, the cumulative FDI of SWFs was about $70 billion, representing only 1.7 percent of their assets and less than 1 percent in terms of global FDI flows. Thus, although SWFs had enormous resources, and despite significant increases in their FDI-type investments from 2005 to 2008, they were marginal FDI players in the overall scheme of things.

Why, then, have SWFs received so much coverage in the Western press? The reason is that their assets are enormous, and they are controlled by governments. Therefore, their every move is watched carefully, especially by policymakers, politicians, and the media in the G-7 countries, particularly when the governments in question were nondemocratic, as was generally the case with SWFs, and when government was Communist, as in China. SWFs' lack of transparency accentuated these fears.

Furthermore, after 2005, SWFs made a series of high-visibility investments in quick succession, most of them involving Western financial institutions, such as investment banks, PE firms, and commercial banks, giving the impression that SWFs were taking advantage of the crisis to snap up shares in institutions that were at the foundation of Western capitalism (see Table 2). One of the early deals involved China Investment Corporation (CIC) taking a 9.99 percent stake in the Blackstone Group for $3 billion just before the firm's IPO. By staying just under the 10 percent threshold that defines the deal as "direct investment," CIC appeared to be deliberately avoiding scrutiny.[4] More broadly, from July 2007 to October 2008, SWFs from Singapore, China, Abu Dhabi, Qatar, and Kuwait invested $76.8 billion in seven large Western banks: Barclays, Citigroup, Credit Suisse, Merrill Lynch, Morgan Stanley, UBS, and Unicredit. Although the stakes held by SWFs in some of these cases were 10 percent or more, they did not seek control rights; yet, the symbolism of government-controlled entities swooping down on the West's financial crown jewels at a time of crisis was threatening, even though the financial institutions had themselves sought SWF investments to tide over the crisis. Former treasury secretary Lawrence Summers observed: "The logic of the capitalist system depends on shareholders causing companies to act so as to maximize the value of their shares. It is far from obvious that this will over time be the only motivation of government as shareholders" (quoted in Cohen, 2008, p. 6). The SWFs themselves claimed they were only being responsible investors, helping to save the global economy from further collapse, and that their motivations were long-run returns and nothing else.

Nonetheless, in 2007 and 2008, a flurry of new policies came out of Japan, Canada, Australia, and Germany that tightened foreign investment rules, especially by state-controlled entities.[5] At the June 2007 G-8 meeting, the leaders declared that SWF investments should not be restricted except when national security was involved, but they also expressed the hope that all parties would cooperate to arrive at a new understanding of how to regulate SWF investments. Out of this emerged a two-track strategy of getting the IMF to work with SWFs to develop new principles on transparency and governance, and getting the OECD to work with the developed nations on regulations of foreign investment by SWFs and SOEs (Cohen, 2008).

Table 2. Bank Investments by Sovereign Wealth Funds, 2007–2008.

Bank	Bank Nat.	SWF	SWF Nat.	Date	Amount (Billions)	Currency	Amount (USD Billions)
Barclays	United Kingdom	Temasek	Singapore	25/07/2007	1	GBP	2.05
Barclays	United Kingdom	China Development Bank	China	25/07/2007	1.5	GBP	3.08
Barclays	United Kingdom	QIA, Challenger	Qatar	31/10/2008	4.3	GBP	6.94
Barclays	United Kingdom	QIA	Qatar	31/10/2008	3	GBP	4.84
Citigroup	United States	Abu Dhabi Investment Authority	Abu Dhabi	26/11/2007	7.5	USD	7.5
Citigroup	United States	GIC	Singapore	15/01/2008	6.9	USD	6.9
Citigroup	United States	KIA, Alwaleed bin Talal	Kuwait	15/01/2008	5.6	USD	5.6
Credit Suisse	Switzerland	QIA and others	Qatar	16/10/2008	6.5	EUR	8.71
Merrill Lynch	United States	Temasek	Singapore	24/12/2007	4.4	USD	4.4
Merrill Lynch	United States	KIC, KIA	Korea, Kuwait	15/01/2008	6.6	USD	6.6
Merrill Lynch	United States	Temasek	Singapore	24/02/2008	0.6	USD	0.6
Merrill Lynch	United States	Temasek	Singapore	28/07/2008	0.9	USD	0.8
Morgan Stanley	United States	China Investment Corporation	China	19/12/2007	5.58	USD	5.58
UBS	Switzerland	GIC	Singapore	10/12/2007	11	CHF	9.75
UBS	Switzerland	Unidentified fund	Middle East	10/12/2007	2	CHF	1.77
Unicredit	Italy	Central Bank of Libya, Libyan Inv. Auth. Libyan For. Bank	Libya	17/10/2008	1.2	EUR	1.61

Source: Banque de France (2008, Appendix 6, p. 12).

So, what is the future outlook for SWFs as FDI players? There are conflicting forces at play, and it is hard to be sure how each will evolve in the future. One near certainty is that the amount of resources controlled by SWFs will continue to grow, but at slower rates than once thought. The financial crisis adversely affected their portfolios in 2008 and 2009, but fresh inflows offset the losses, according to McKinsey & Co. (Roxburgh, Lund, Lippert, White, & Zhao, 2009). Estimates of their assets under management in 2013 range from a low of $5 trillion to a high of $10 trillion, compared to $3.9 trillion in 2008. Working with the lower end of the range, which seems more realistic today, and assuming that SWFs raise their share of assets in FDI-type investments from less than 2 percent to as much as 10 percent by 2013, they would have to make annual FDI-type investments of $80 billion per year for the next few years, representing fully 20–25 percent of all outward FDI from emerging economies. Thus, in theory at least, SWFs could become important new sources of FDI. Whether that will actually happen depends on two important questions: How likely are host countries to permit FDI-type investments by SWFs, and how likely are SWFs to build the capabilities necessary to make and manage FDI-type investments? I am pessimistic on both grounds.

On the first question, the evidence to date has been surprisingly high. The United States in particular has accepted SWF investments in financial services that would have been unthinkable only 2–3 years earlier. No doubt, this was driven by expediency, but even as the crisis eased there was recognition on both sides that they needed each other. This led the SWFs to come together as the International Working Group (IWG), under IMF auspices, to negotiate a set of principles and practices to govern their operations. The aim was to reassure developed countries that they would become more transparent and embrace sound governance principles. After a year of negotiations, they subscribed to the IMF's Santiago Principles, a voluntary code that aimed to:

- Establish a transparent and sound governance structure that provides for adequate operational controls, risk management, and accountability;
- Ensure compliance with applicable regulatory and disclosure requirements in the countries in which SWFs invest;
- Ensure SWFs invest on the basis of economic and financial risk and return-related considerations;
- Help maintain a stable global financial system and free flow of capital and investment.

The IWG's co-chairman told a news conference in October 2008 that "through the implementation of the Santiago Principles we seek to ensure that the international investment environment will remain open" (Wilson, 2008). Early evidence also suggested that Asian SWFs were following through on their commitment to Santiago Principles. Singapore's Government Investment Corporation (GIC) published its first public management report on its portfolio and reported the size of its losses in 2008. The other Singaporean SWF, Temasek, also issued a more detailed annual report after signing the IWG's declaration. Even the Chinese SWF, CIC, issued a more detailed annual report than before, including 2008 performance results and a detailed report on its organization structure and staffing (CIC Annual Report, 2008).

The OECD countries made less progress at their end on clarifying important aspects of their policy, such as the definition of "national security" interests or what constituted a "strategic" industry. SWFs feared that OECD countries would use these issues as excuses for disguised FDI protectionism targeted specifically at SWFs, and that concern remains unresolved at the time of writing. I am not sanguine that as the crisis passes, OECD countries will really welcome direct investments by SWFs, especially in the United States, where direct investment even by state-owned enterprises has been viewed with suspicion. If the United States does not believe that SOEs, including those listed on stock exchanges, pursue commercial goals, how likely is it that they will believe this of SWFs, which are even more under the government's thumb? Moreover, the US Congress will be even more guarded about SWF investments than the executive branch. It was after all pressure from Congress that killed the China National Overseas Oil Company's plans to buy China National Overseas Oil Company or Huawei's plan to co-invest in 3Com.

I am equally skeptical that SWFs will build the capabilities required to make and manage FDI-type investments. For one thing, the main purpose of many SWFs is to help stabilize the economy when foreign exchange earnings nosedive (e.g., because of falling energy prices); illiquid FDI-type investments do not belong in such a portfolio. Norway's SWF is an example of a fund that has eschewed FDI-type investments: its portfolio consists of investments in over 3,500 companies, with holdings of no more than 1 percent in any one company. Seventy percent of SWF assets belong to oil and gas exporting countries for which protection against predictable volatility in energy prices is essential. There are, however, a few SWF's for which a higher risk-return portfolio may be acceptable or even desirable. These include giant SWFs from tiny countries, such as the Abu Dhabi

Investment Authority, or large SWFs from countries with large current account surpluses, such as Singapore's GIC and Temasek, or the CIC. In the last case, with foreign exchange reserves of $2.2 trillion, it makes sense to consider investing a small fraction more aggressively, such as through an SWF.

How likely are these sorts of SWFs to build the capabilities necessary to make FDI-type investments? One inspiring role model for such SWFs is Singapore, whose two funds have an impressive record of long-run performance. Over a 25-year period ending March 2006, Singapore's GIC earned an average return of 9.5% in US dollar terms, and 8.2% in Singapore dollar terms. This was 5.3 percent above global inflation, defined by GIC as the weighted average inflation of the United States, Japan, and the EU. In addition, GIC also claims it has outperformed two benchmark indices for global stocks and bonds (GIC Annual Report, 2008).[6]

Even including the losses suffered in 2008, GIC appears to have earned a long-run return above G-3 inflation or benchmark indices, and Temasek has a similarly impressive record. Other SWFs can therefore be tempted to emulate Singapore's approach in hopes of earning similar returns, especially SWFs from China or Abu Dhabi that have very deep pockets. But will they succeed in replicating the Singaporean model or will they stumble? One view is that Singapore is a special case because its model of state capitalism is supported by an unusually talented and professional civil service of the kind that countries like Abu Dhabi or even China cannot match, and it has deep talent in financial services, being a financial hub. According to Park and Estrada (2009, p. v):

> In principle, FDI represents an attractive means of earning higher returns on FX reserves than traditional reserve assets. In practice, the limited institutional capacity and the political sensitivity of state-led FDI severely constrains the ability of developing Singapore's Government Investment Corporation to undertake FDI on a significant scale. Therefore, the potential for developing Asia's SWFs to become major sources of outward FDI is more apparent than real.

I agree with Park and Estrada's conclusion, but with one important exception – China. I am not sure the Chinese government would concede that it could not put together a professionally and competently run SWF along the lines of Singapore's GIC. After all, China has immense financial talent in Hong Kong and overseas Chinese that it can draw on. Hong Kong itself is a financial center that rivals Singapore. And even though the Chinese civil service is not nearly as professional as Singapore's and is believed to be far more corrupt, it seems to function as a meritocracy, at least in pockets.

So, if the Chinese government made up its mind, it could give CIC sufficient autonomy and protect it from political meddling. By late 2009, there was some evidence that the government was already moving in that direction. For instance, as noted, earlier CIC was showing more openness about its operations, and its 2008 Annual Report described its goals as entirely commercial in nature.[7] Moreover, CIC seems to have used the financial crisis to strengthen its internal talent:

> The global financial crisis has led to the exodus of thousands of professionals from US and European banks and other institutions. In response, Asian sovereign wealth funds are hiring experienced financial talent. For instance, in its most current restructuring, the China Investment Corporation is hiring more than 20 senior professionals from around the globe and has named a former UBS executive to oversee its Special Investments Department, which will take large, long-term positions in publicly traded companies. (Roxburgh et al., 2009, p. 44)

But even if China's SWF imitates its Singaporean counterpart, it will likely proceed cautiously in taking large, long-term positions in publicly traded companies. The 2007–2008 experience of SWFs investing in Western financial service firms has been disappointing; as of October 16, 2008, they had suffered losses of about 20 percent of the initial investment on Credit Suisse, 40 percent on Citigroup, and 60 percent on Morgan Stanley, Merrill Lynch, and UBS. That was one reason why many of them backed off from further investments when the shares of financial institutions were even lower. CIC also had the bad experience and much internal criticism for its ill-timed investment in the Blackstone group. As of end 2008, only 3.2 percent of CIC's portfolio was invested in large positions in individual companies, with 87.4 percent in cash funds![8] It is not easy to build a multibillion dollar portfolio of diversified FDI-type investments; keep in mind that the world's largest MNE, General Electric, has global assets of $420 billion (2007), and the second largest MNE, Vodafone, has global assets of $250 billion – both built over many years (UNCTAD, 2009, Annex. A.1.9, p. 225). It will take time to fully invest a fund with $200–300 billion dollars. Moreover, if CIC really emulates the Singaporean model, I suspect it will look for investment opportunities in other emerging markets, rather than OECD countries, where the chances of earning above-average returns are poorer because of their well-functioning markets.[9] Moreover, investment by the Chinese state raises fewer hackles in emerging markets than it does in the G-7, witness the welcome mat placed for FDI by Chinese firms, including SOEs, in Africa and Latin America.

To sum up, SWFs will find their assets under management growing, and they will be tempted to go for higher returns by making FDI-type investments, but beyond Singapore, only one or two countries will make significant headway in that direction, among them China and possibly Abu Dhabi. Press coverage for any and all such moves will exceed the real economic significance of the deals, and SWFs will probably not make a significant dent on global FDI flows but could add significantly to FDI outflows from emerging economies.

PRIVATE EQUITY FIRMS

PE refers to leveraged buyout funds, venture capital funds, distressed funds, growth funds, and the like that invest in firms whose stock is generally not publicly traded. Seventy percent of the assets managed by PE firms are of the leveraged buyout variety in which nonrecourse debt is leveraged to take existing companies private. PE funds have been around for many years in the United States and they have been an important driver of mergers and acquisitions (M&A). In the 2000s, PE firms had access to abundant cheap funds, from banks, pension funds, insurance funds, wealthy individuals – and SWFs. This led to resurgence in leveraged buyouts, but with a new twist – many were now cross-border buyouts, which helped fuel global FDI flows. However, there is not a straightforward relationship between the value of M&A deals and officially reported FDI flows, because deals may be partly financed locally or from international sources, neither of which shows up as FDI. At the same time, there is no question that heightened cross-border M&A activity is positively correlated with measured FDI flows.[10]

According to a study by McKinsey & Co. (Roxburgh et al., 2009), the total assets under management by leveraged buyout firms rose from $399 billion in 2003 to $1,249 billion in 2008, representing a compound growth rate of 23 percent from 2003–2007 and a 38 percent increase in 2008 alone. Data are only available on the country of origin of funds raised by PE firms, and these indicate that in 2008 North America and Europe accounted for 92 percent of the total, with only 8 percent raised in Asia and the rest of the world. However, in 2003, the share of Asia and the rest of the world was even lower at 2.5 percent (Roxburgh et al., 2009, p. 68). According to UNCTAD, cross-border M&As executed by PE firms and hedge funds accounted for a growing share of the value of all cross-border M&As, rising from 16.6 percent in 1996 to a high of 37.8 percent in the second quarter of 2007, before falling to 11.1 percent in 2008-Q4 and only 9.6 percent in 2009-Q2 (see Table 3).[11] The trend in the value of cross-border M&As by PE firms and hedge funds is even more striking: it rose more than 10-fold from $44 billion in 1996 to $470 billion in 2007 before

Table 3. Cross-Border M&A Purchases by Private Equity Firms and Hedge Funds, 1996–2009 (No. of deals and Value).

Year	Number of Deals		Value	
	Number	Share in Total Cross-border M&As (%)	$ Billion	Share in Total Cross-border M&As (%)
1996	715	12.2	44.0	16.6
1997	782	11.6	55.4	14.9
1998	906	11.3	77.9	11.2
1999	1,147	12.7	86.9	9.6
2000	1,208	12.0	91.6	6.8
2001	1,125	13.9	87.8	12
2002	1,126	17.2	84.7	17.5
2003	1,296	19.6	109.9	26.7
2004	1,626	22.0	173.2	30.5
2005	1,724	19.5	205.8	22.1
2006	1,693	17.7	285.5	25.4
2007	1,890	17.6	469.9	27.6
Q1	451	16.7	73.3	25.3
Q2	520	19.2	183.2	37.8
Q3	439	16.6	115.6	29.5
Q4	480	18.1	97.7	18.3
2008	1,721	17.7	291.0	24.1
Q1	440	17.1	127.1	35.5
Q2	414	16.3	69.9	23.6
Q3	446	18.3	60.4	24.3
Q4	421	19.2	33.5	11.1
2009	711	21.7	43.6	17.2
Q1	362	20.5	34.9	23.1
Q2	349	23.3	8.7	9.6

Source: UNCTAD, *World Investment Report 2008*, p. 26, based on UNCTAD cross-border M&A database.

falling to $291 billion in 2008 and $8.7 billion in the second quarter of 2009 (or the annual equivalent of $34.8 billion, which would be lower than even the 1996 level).

The financial crisis took a heavy toll on PE firms; only hedge funds suffered more severely. The reason was that the cheap funds, leverage, and rising stock markets that made leveraged buyouts (LBOs) possible, unraveled after the financial crisis. Coupled with the global economic slowdown, many PE firms found themselves in crisis, looking for emergency funding from SWFs and others.[12]

These facts lead to the following conclusions about PE firms and FDI flows:

1. PE firms were new players in the FDI space, in the sense that they contributed to FDI flows during the M&A boom of the 2000s, unlike the M&A boom of the late 1980s, when cross-border deals were rarer.[13] In the 2000s M&A boom, PE firms and hedge funds accounted for as much as one-third of the value of cross-border M&As.
2. PE firms were in not in a position to take advantage of the financial crisis to pounce on discounted assets. Quite the contrary, PE firms were unable to go bargain hunting after the crisis, despite large cash holdings, because the credit crunch precluded financial leveraging, which was a crucial part of their business model.
3. Leveraged buyouts depend on a large supply of cheap capital, and as this supply fluctuates, so does the fate of the PE industry. As a result, the contribution of PE firms to global FDI is likely to be highly volatile – periods of large contribution, followed by periods of low contribution.

So, what does all this portend for the future of PE firms? In the near term, the expectation is that they will look for smaller deals, and that they will look for opportunities in emerging markets, where growth is still positive, and firms are smaller and cheaper. If history is any guide, it could take one or two decades before LBOs peak again, given that gap between the last two peaks was 19 years (1988 to 2007). However, I suspect that the next peak could come sooner, because there will be attractive opportunities in emerging markets, and opportunities for LBOs in the developed countries will multiply as internationally competitive emerging-market multinational enterprises (EMNEs) in mature industries force the consolidation of these industries in developed countries. Some of that consolidation will be done by EMNEs themselves, but PE firms may also play a part (see Ramamurti, 2009a) for a discussion of "global consolidators" from emerging markets in steel, cement, aluminum, beverages, food, meat packing, white goods, PCs, and so on).

EMERGING-MARKET MULTINATIONAL ENTERPRISES

EMNEs are perhaps the most important of the new players on the landscape. These are firms in developing or transition economies that have begun to internationalize through exports, foreign sourcing, and direct investment.

Many of these firms are in the early stages of internationalization, that is, they may be more active as exporters than foreign producers of goods and services, and their brands are often not well known outside the domestic market, but in due course their overseas investments are likely to swell and their brands will turn global, as shown in the three-stage model in Table 4 (Ramamurti, 2009a, p. 420). Western MNEs went through a similar process of evolution and deepening of their international activities before eventually having, in some cases, more employees and assets abroad than those at home (Wilkins, 1974). Most EMNEs are still in stage 1 of the three-stage process, many are in stage 2, and very few have reached stage 3.

EMNEs are not new on the FDI stage. The first discernable wave of outward FDI occurred in the 1970s and led to studies by Wells (1983) and Lall (1983), among others. This resulted in the spread of Brazilian and Argentine firms within South America, or Singaporean and Indian firms around Southeast Asia. But that wave quickly died down in the 1980s, as the oil shocks and the debt crisis shut down outward FDI by important outward investors, including Brazil and Argentina, although helping to launch outward FDI from oil exporters such as Kuwait and Saudi Arabia. By the late 1980s, emerging markets accounted for only 8 percent of the

Table 4. Three-Stage Internationalization Model.

	Stage 1: Infant MNE	Stage 2: Adolescent MNE	Stage 3: Mature MNE
Importance of home-country CSAs	High	High to medium, and falling	Medium to low, and falling
Ratio of exports to overseas production	Exports exceed overseas production	Exports and overseas production in balance	Overseas production exceeds exports
Geographic footprint	Few countries in home region, unless EMNE is pursuing the low-cost partner strategy	Several countries, with emphasis on home region	Dozens of countries, in all major regions
Brand	Strong at home, unknown abroad	Strong at home, up-and-coming abroad	Strong global brand
Examples	Most EMNEs	Korean MNEs like Hyundai, LG; China's Lenovo; India's Tata Group	Western and Japanese MNEs, such as IBM, GE, Siemens, Sony, Toyota

Source: Ramamurti (2009a, p. 420).
Note: CSA, country-specific advantage; EMNEs, emerging market multinationals.

world stock of outward FDI (see Table 5) and an even smaller 2–3 percent of outward FDI flows (see Table 6). It wasn't until the mid-1990s that outward FDI from emerging markets began to revive, after Latin America, China, India, and the former centrally planned economies opened up their

Table 5. World FDI Outward Stock and Share of Top 12 Emerging Economies, 1990–2008 (Amounts in US$ Billion and Shares in %).

Region/Economy	1990	2000	2008
World ($bn) of which:	1,785.58	6,069.88	16,205.66
Developed countries ($bn)	1,640.41	5,186.18	13,623.63
Emerging economies[a] ($bn)	145.17	883.70	2,582.03
Share of world outflows			
Developed countries, % share	91.87	85.44	84.07
Emerging economies[a], % share	8.13	14.56	15.93
Top-12 Emerging economies (based on 2008 FDI outward stock)			
Hong Kong ($bn)	11.92	388.38	775.92
% Share of emerging economies	8.21	45.04	32.92
Russia ($bn)	n/a	20.14	202.84
% Share of emerging economies	n/a	2.34	8.61
Singapore ($bn)	7.81	56.76	189.09
% Share of emerging economies	5.38	6.58	8.02
Taiwan ($bn)	30.36	66.66	175.14
% Share of emerging economies	20.91	7.73	7.43
Brazil ($bn)	41.04	51.95	162.22
% Share of emerging economies	28.27	6.02	6.88
China ($bn)	4.46	27.77	147.95
% Share of emerging economies	3.07	3.22	6.28
Korea ($bn)	2.30	26.83	95.54
% Share of emerging economies	1.58	3.11	4.05
Malaysia ($bn)	0.75	15.88	67.58
% Share of emerging economies	0.52	1.84	2.87
South Africa ($bn)	15.00	32.33	62.33
% Share of emerging economies	10.33	3.75	2.64
India ($bn)	0.12	1.86	61.77
% Share of emerging economies	0.08	0.22	2.62
UAE ($bn)	0.01	1.94	50.80
% Share of emerging economies	0.01	0.22	2.16
Mexico ($bn)	2.67	8.27	45.39
% Share of emerging economies	1.84	0.96	1.93

Source: Calculated from UNCTAD (2009, annex B1, p. 251).
[a]Developing countries plus transition economies of Southeast Europe and the Commonwealth of Independent States.

Table 6. World FDI Outflows and Share of Top 12 Emerging
Economies (Amounts in USD Billion and Shares in %).

Region/Economy	2006	2007	2008
World ($bn) of which:	1,396.92	2,146.52	1,857.73
Developed countries ($bn)	1,157.91	1,809.53	1,506.53
Emerging economies[a] ($bn)	239.01	336.99	351.20
Share of world outflows			
Developed countries, % share	82.89	84.30	81.10
Emerging economies[a], % share	17.11	15.70	18.90
Top-12 Emerging economies (based on 2008 FDI outflows)			
Hong Kong	44.98	61.12	59.92
% Share of emerging economies	20.89	21.41	20.47
Russia ($bn)	23.15	45.92	52.39
% Share of emerging economies	10.75	16.08	17.90
China ($bn)	21.16	22.47	52.15
% Share of emerging economies	9.83	7.87	17.82
Brazil ($bn)	28.20	7.07	20.46
% Share of emerging economies	13.10	2.48	6.99
India ($bn)	14.34	17.28	17.69
% Share of emerging economies	6.66	6.05	6.04
UAE ($bn)	10.89	14.57	15.80
% Share of emerging economies	5.06	5.10	5.40
Malaysia ($bn)	6.08	11.09	14.06
% Share of emerging economies	2.82	3.88	4.80
Korea ($bn)	8.13	15.62	12.80
% Share of emerging economies	3.78	5.47	4.37
Taiwan ($bn)	7.40	11.11	10.29
% Share of emerging economies	3.44	3.89	3.52
Singapore ($bn)	13.30	24.46	8.93
% Share of emerging economies	6.18	8.57	3.05
Mexico ($bn)	5.76	8.26	0.69
% Share of emerging economies	2.68	2.89	0.24
South Africa ($bn)	6.07	2.96	−3.53
% Share of emerging economies	2.82	1.04	−1.21

Source: Calculated from UNCTAD (2009, annex B1, p. 247).
[a]Developing countries plus transition economies of Southeast Europe and the Commonwealth of Independent States.

economies and embraced globalization. As shown in Table 5, the outward
FDI stock of emerging economies rose sixfold from $145 billion in 1990 to
$862 billion in 2000, and almost tripled again by 2008 to $2,582 billion. As a
result, their share of outward FDI stock rose from 8 to 16 percent in 2008,

and their share of FDI outflows rose to 19 percent. This is impressive, inasmuch as outward FDI from developed countries grew at annual rates above 20 percent in these years.

At the same time, the origin of outward FDI flows continued to be highly concentrated: in both 1990 and 2008, the top-12 countries accounted for 90 percent or more of FDI outflows and 80% or more of FDI stock of all emerging economies. The following eight developing countries were on the top-12 list in both 1990 and 2008: Brazil, China, Hong Kong, Korea, Mexico, Singapore, South Africa, and Taiwan. Two countries prominent on the 2008 list but missing on the 1990 list were India and Russia, and if there was a noticeable regional shift in those 18 years, it was the relative decline of outward FDI from Latin America and the relative rise of that from Asia.[14]

By 2008, the annual outward FDI flows from emerging economies neared $350 billion. While this was small compared to the $1.506 billion outflow from developed countries, it was comparable to the amounts facilitated by PE firms, which at its peak involved deals worth $470 billion (2007). It is anybody's guess what fraction of the PE deal value shows up in official measures of FDI, given the complex financing and staggered payments that are often involved. As a first approximation it is probably fair to conclude that EMNEs contributed about as much to global FDI flows as PEs did at their zenith, and more than 20 times as much as SWFs ever did.

EMNE contribution to outward FDI was also more stable and less volatile than that of PEs, although it too went through cycles. In 2008, when buyouts engineered by PE firms collapsed, and outward FDI from developed countries fell by 15 percent, it rose by 2 percent for emerging economies as a whole and by 54 percent for the BRICs (see Table 7). All four BRIC countries registered increases, but Indian firms were constrained by tightening credit in international markets, and Russian firms by falling energy prices, while Brazil's 189% increase was from an artificially low base. The really special case here was China, whose FDI grew by 132% to $52 billion, because Chinese companies did not face a credit crunch, "allowing its corporates the financial leeway to continue investing abroad at a time when foreign competitors had to cut back" (OECD, 2009, pp. 6–7).

In 2009, the financial crisis finally had a negative effect on outward FDI from emerging economies – but once again, it was almost certain that this decline would be less than that of developed countries.[15] As a result, emerging economies' share of outward FDI flows was likely to increase again in 2009. Among the BRICs, Russia experienced a 15 percent drop off in 2009-Q1, compared to the same period in 2008, India was projected to

Table 7. BRIC Outward FDI Flows, 2007–Early 2009.

Country	2007 (USD Billion)	2008		2009		Comments
		USD Billion	% Change YoY	USD Billion	2009 Period	
Brazil	7.07	20.46	+189%	0.94	Jan–May	−87% vs. Jan.–May 2008
Russia	45.96	52.39	+14%	13.0	Q1 (15% decline YoY)	Numbers shown are from Bank of Russia, which estimates FDI more reliably and conservatively (Panibratov & Kalotay, 2009). Data from the Russian statistical agency show OFDI commitments for Q1 stood at $38 billion, not all of which may fructify
India	17.28	17.69	+2%	4.65	Jan.–Mar.	Q1 consistent with past two years levels. Bharti Airtel's $23 billion merger deal with MTN of South Africa failed for a second time. Sterlite Industries' $1.7 bid for bankrupt US copper firm, Asarco, still in play

| China | 22.47 | 52.15 | +132% | n/a | Davies (2009) notes: "Anecdotal evidence suggest that China's outward FDI growth continued to accelerate in early 2009. China's direct investments in Australia alone reportedly rose ... to \$13 billion [in Q1] ... Deals made in [2009 Q1] already reportedly exceed China's record FDI outflow in 2008" (p. 1–3). Presumably this is after excluding Chinalco's failed \$19.5 billion bid for a take in mining firm Rio Tinto "In early 2009, outflows from [China] continued to rise. Indeed, significant exchange rate fluctuations and falling asset prices abroad as a result of the crisis have created M&A opportunities for Chinese companies" (UNCAD, 2009, p. 17) |
| Total | 92.78 | 142.69 | +54% | n/a | |

Source: 2007 and 2008 data from UNCTAD (2009, annex B.1, pp. 247–250); Brazil 2009 data from Mortimore and Razo (2009) and Lima and Barros (2009); Russia 2009 data from Panibratov & Kalotay (2009); India 2009 data from Pradhan (2009); and China 2009 data from Davies (2009).

drop off significantly as well, and Brazil was expected to drop to a fraction of the 2008 level (see Table 7). Only China looked likely to buck the trend by increasing its outward FDI in 2009, despite Chinalco's failure to conclude the $19.5 billion bid for a stake in the Australian mining firm Rio Tinto.

To sum up, the financial crisis slowed or even reversed the rate of growth of outward FDI from emerging economies, but these countries still did much better than developed countries and contributed much more to outward FDI flows than either SWFs or PE firms. In 2008, outward FDI flows increased for all four BRIC countries, but the early evidence from 2009 indicated that only Chinese MNEs would see continued growth in outward FDI, helping to fulfill the government's "go global" policy – despite resistance to Chinese investment in many developed countries (Davies, 2009).

EMNE CONTRIBUTION TO SUSTAINABLE DEVELOPMENT

In the longer run, there are at least two important questions about EMNEs that are worth examining: Will the upward trend in FDI by EMNEs continue for another decade or two, and, if it does, would that be good for sustainable economic development? I believe the answer on both counts is yes.

Consider first the sustainability of the EMNE phenomenon. One cannot take this for granted, because in the past outward FDI from developing countries has fizzled out after showing promise, notably after the first wave of the 1970s. There is also no question that EMNE expansion in the 2000s was fueled by unprecedented access to cheap capital, high growth rates in the home market, and export opportunities in developed countries, particularly the United States. It is hard to say when these "perfect storm" conditions will recur in the future. I will however address one aspect of the EMNE phenomenon that bears on the sustainability of their international expansion, and that is whether EMNEs posses real competitive advantages that can be the foundation for lasting and profitable internationalization.

On the surface, EMNEs may not appear to possess real competitive advantages, because, unlike established Western MNEs, they normally do not possess cutting-edge technologies or strong global brands (Mathews, 2002). Their spending on R&D or advertising, for instance, is generally not in the range of 5–10 percent of sales, as is the case for leading Western

MNEs. Other experts have argued that EMNEs are merely exploiting emerging economies' country-specific advantages (CSAs), such as cheap labor (e.g., India), access to raw materials (e.g., Russia or Brazil), or cheap capital (e.g., China), rather than knowledge-based capabilities, which are firm-specific and more sustainable (see, e.g., Rugman, 2009). The implication is that the competitive advantages of EMNEs are imitable and hence ephemeral.

These arguments are flawed, as I have discussed elsewhere (Ramamurti, 2009a, 2009b). First, CSAs are in fact not readily available for exploitation by all firms located in a country, as some assume. For example, China may have a high savings rate but the resulting cheap capital is available only to some Chinese firms (SOEs) and not others (local private firms); and India has inexpensive talent, but exploiting that talent requires skills and local embeddedness not possessed by all firms. More importantly, as discussed in Ramamurti (2009a), EMNEs have succeeded in their home markets because they:

(1) have a really deep understanding of local consumers, who are much poorer than Western consumers and have quite different needs and preferences;
(2) are very low-cost players, whose methods for cost reduction are not easily imitated by Western firms;
(3) are strong in mid-tech industries that are neither so simple that any emerging-market firm can succeed in them nor so sophisticated that they are dominated by Western MNEs; and
(4) know how to operate effectively in environments characterized by weak political and economic institutions (on this point, see Cuervo-Cazurra and Genc, 2008).

These are significant and sustainable advantages that, along with CSAs, enable EMNEs to expand not only into other emerging markets but under certain circumstances also into developed countries (on EMNE internationalization strategies, see Ramamurti, 2009a). Over time, I do anticipate that Western MNEs will acquire some of these capabilities and learn to thrive in emerging markets, but I also anticipate that some EMNEs will build capabilities in technology and branding that will rival those of Western MNEs. In other words, a convergence in capabilities between EMNEs and Western MNEs may occur over two or three decades, as it has, for instance, between Western firms and leading Japanese or Korean MNEs. It is certainly possible that Western MNEs are more likely than EMNEs to emerge eventually as winners, but in the interim, I see EMNEs doing quite well internationally, especially because two-thirds of world GDP growth in the future will occur in emerging markets and it will take Western MNEs time to beat EMNEs at their own game.

On the second question of whether EMNEs will contribute to sustainable development, I think the answer is a definite yes. The contributions that EMNEs have made to sustainable development have been largely overlooked. One aspect of sustainability is inclusive growth, and in that sense EMNEs have contributed far more than Western MNEs to serving the middle class and the poor in emerging markets. Unilever's strategy of serving the poor in developing countries with low-priced single-serve sachets has received much publicity (e.g., Prahalad, 2004), but this strategy was a response to the drubbing it received in India at the hands of local firms like Nirma that captured a large slice of the detergent market with an ultra low-cost branded product. Nokia's low-cost cell phones grew out of the drubbing the firm received in China from local firms such as Ningbo Bird and Amoi. Citibank's or Barclays' embrace of microfinance grew out of the demonstrated success of Bangladesh's Grameen Bank, not the other way around. Pfizer's and Novartis' embrace of generic drugs and new approaches to R&D emerged as a response to competition from EMNEs such as Ranbaxy, Dr. Reddy's, and Teva.

Consider the case of Bharti Airtel, which brought ultra low cost wireless telephone service to more than 110 million users in India. Its average price per minute is 1–2 US cents, compared to 10–20 times as much in developed countries. Bharti Airtel has achieved low costs through a unique business model involving outsourcing and risk partnership with suppliers. While 99 percent of billing is postpaid in developed countries, it is exactly the other way around in Airtel's case, because prepaid service takes out the risk of billing errors and defaults. The company developed original methods to sell minutes in very small increments to far-flung users. Bharti's average revenue per user per month was under US$6 in September 2009, compared to $51 for Verizon in the United States. Yet, Bharti Airtel has been highly profitable and had a market capitalization in 2009 of US$ 25 billion. Had it been up to Western MNEs, such as Vodafone or AT&T, wireless service in India may have been provided at much high prices to a thin slice of the Indian population, compared to the hundreds of millions who enjoy telephone service today.

Local firms and EMNEs have pioneered innovative approaches to serving low-income consumers with low-cost products, appropriate technologies, and novel methods for distribution and marketing. This results in more jobs, more local sourcing, and more suitable technology (and therefore more technological spillovers) than would have been generated by Western

MNEs. For these reasons, EMNEs are better for emerging markets than Western MNEs. The success of EMNEs in other emerging markets is sometimes seen as the result of South–South affinity, but I suspect it has more to do with the fact that EMNEs bring products and processes better suited to these markets.

There is much discussion in the mainstream literature on positive knowledge spillovers in developing countries from Western MNEs to local firms (e.g., Meyer & Sinani, 2009), but hardly any recognition of the "reverse spillovers" from EMNEs and local firms to Western MNEs. EMNEs are spreading their innovations to other emerging markets, directly through FDI, and indirectly by training Western MNEs on how to succeed in emerging markets. Western MNEs are slowly waking up to the fact that they can learn valuable lessons from EMNEs for exploitation not only in emerging markets, but from time to time also in developed markets.[16] This has led to considerable interest among Western MNEs of the concept of reverse innovation, that is, the transfer of innovations from poor to rich countries (Govindarajan & Ramamurti, 2011).

EMNEs are global welfare enhancers for other reasons as well. They are stirring up cozy global oligopolies of Western firms in, for instance, telecom equipment, pharmaceuticals, regional jets, and consumer goods. By serving as low-cost partners in industries such as information technology, software development, knowledge-process outsourcing, toys, and textiles, to name a few, EMNEs like Infosys, TCS, or Li & Fung help keep down costs for consumers everywhere. By investing in mature industries, such as steel, cement, and aluminum, in developed countries, EMNEs such as Tata Steel, Cemex, and Hindalco are helping to restructure and rationalize industries that might otherwise shut down altogether in these countries.

EMNEs are also contributing to sustainable development in another sense – by helping to develop "green" technologies. Three examples will illustrate the point. One of the world's top-5 wind energy firms is Suzlon, an Indian company that came from nowhere to become a global player with unmatched cost structure, because 85 percent of its headcount is in low-cost countries, while the other four leading firms have 70 percent or more of their headcount in high-cost countries (see Ramamurti & Singh 2009). Similarly, in solar energy, Chinese firms like Suntech and Sunergy aspire to become leading players. A third example is Brazilian MNE, Petrobras, which has been the world's largest buyer of ethanol for blending with gasoline and has provided R&D and infrastructural support to local suppliers, as a result of which gasohol accounts for 15.7 percent of Brazil's fuel consumption.

Not all EMNEs are technological laggards simply trying to catch up with Western MNEs: in green technologies, more than a few are shaping up to be "global first-movers" (Ramamurti, 2009a, pp. 411–412).

CONCLUDING REMARKS

We have examined the past, present, and future prospects for three new players on the FDI stage: SWFs, PEs, and EMNEs. Our conclusion on SWFs is that their assets under management will grow, and they will be tempted to go for higher returns by making FDI-type investments, but beyond Singapore, only one or two countries will make significant headway in that direction, among them possibly China and the UAE. Press coverage for any and all such moves will exceed the real economic significance of the deals, and SWFs will probably not make a significant dent on global FDI flows but may add significantly to FDI outflows from emerging economies.

PEs have played a much bigger role in outward FDI in recent years, but their role has shrunk dramatically after the financial crisis. I expect there will be a revival of PEs as credit eases and opportunities for industry consolidation and restructuring present themselves in developed countries, partly as a result of heightened competition in mature industries from EMNEs. At the same time, PE firms will pursue opportunities more vigorously than before in emerging markets.

But the most important new player on the FDI stage is the EMNE. As discussed, EMNEs already account for almost 20 percent of global FDI outflows, and their share has steadily drifted upward, even during this crisis. But more importantly, EMNEs contribute to sustainable development, because their products, processes, pricing, and marketing are all better suited to emerging markets than what Western MNEs typically have to offer. EMNEs also benefit consumers and producers in developed countries by breaking up cozy oligopolies, lowering prices, supplying cheap but good inputs, and helping to restructure rust-belt industries. Finally, a number of "global first-movers" will emerge out of emerging markets in tomorrow's "green" industries. China and India will be among the leading developers and adopters of "green" technologies, because of the size of their markets and the technical and entrepreneurial talent available in these countries.

To be sure, it will take a long time for EMNEs to rival Western MNEs in importance, but their share of world outward FDI flows will slowly edge up, as it has in the last decade. This will also accelerate FDI inflows into emerging economies, because half or more of their direct investments go to other emerging economies. In addition, emerging economies will become magnets for inward FDI from developed countries, because of their high rates of growth and large, low-cost talent pools. Indeed, in 2009, for the first time, emerging markets were expected to attract more inward FDI than developed countries.[17] To be sure, this will change as growth rebounds in the developed world, but what seemed like an aberration in 2009 could soon become the norm.[18] But there are several uncertainties ahead. One is whether the heightened recognition among Western MNEs of the importance of emerging markets will result in their gobbling up fledgling EMNEs via mergers and acquisitions. Another is whether emerging-market governments will prevent that from happening by tightening FDI rules or by applying entirely new tools to the task, as when China used anti-monopoly laws to block Coca-Cola's bid for Huiyan Juice Group. In other words, going forward, both the strategies of Western MNEs and the policy response of host emerging markets are clouded by uncertainty. What is certain, though, is that emerging markets will become far more important as both sources and destinations for FDI, as they become the engines of global growth.

NOTES

1. The inaugural *World Investment Report* of 1991 notes: "During the 1980s, the number of developed countries which became significant outward investors increased, eroding the established positions of the United States and the United Kingdom. The most important of the new outward investors was Japan: investments abroad by Japanese transnational corporations increased at an annual rate of 62 percent from 1985 to 1989" (UNCTAD, 1991, p. 4).

2. Emerging markets refers collectively to developing countries and transition economies, such as China or the former Soviet Union.

3. Referring to emerging-market firms, for instance, the *World Investment Report 2009* notes: "those with abundant cash at their disposal may take advantage of the present low prices of assets to make new acquisitions in order to strengthen their presence in developed-country markets and foster their technological capabilities" (UNCTAD, 2008, p. 24).

4. Subsequently, China Investment Corporation reached an agreement with Blackstone to increase its holding to 12.5 percent, and in October 2008 the firm confirmed having crossed the 10 percent threshold (Xin, 2008).

5. Cohen (2008, p. 9) sums up the developments, "Past legislation has been also been updated in Canada, France, Germany, and Japan – all members, like the United States, of the Group of Seven advanced economies (G-7) – as well as in several other leading OECD countries. As early as December 2005, France issued a new decree mandating prior authorization for foreign investments in eleven sectors that may affect 'national defense interests.' In August 2007, Japan revised its regulation of inward investment to address ... 'the changed security environment

surrounding Japan and trends in international investment activity.' In December 2007 the Canadian government issued 'clarifications' of its rules on foreign investment for state-owned enterprises under the Investment Canada Act. In February 2008, Australia articulated six principles that will now govern reviews of foreign investments by SWFs and other government-linked entities .... And in April 2008 Germany passed new legislation authorizing policy makers to pre-examine selected foreign investments, particularly those coming from SWFs."

6. These are Morgan Stanley's World Equity Index and an enhanced Lehman Brothers World Bond Index.

7. CIC's operating principles are described as follows (China Investment Corporation, 2008):

    a. CIC selects investments based on economic and financial objectives, and an assessment of the commercial return.

    b. CIC allocates capital and assets within the given risk tolerance of the owner to maximize shareholder value.

    c. CIC usually does not seek an active role in the companies in which it invests nor attempts to influence those companies' operations.

    d. CIC seeks long-term, stable, sustainable, and risk-adjusted return.

8. Interestingly, China initially charged its SWF a 4.3% interest on funds provided by the government, but after the financial crisis seeing CIC's portfolio deteriorate, the government turned the initial $200 billion contribution from debt into equity. In 2008, CIC reported a global portfolio return of −2.1 percent (CIC Annual Report 2008, p. 34).

9. According to Desai (2008), the accounting rate of return on inbound FDI to the United States averaged only 4.3 percent, compared to 12.1 percent for outbound FDI from the United States. He concludes that "America is a beautiful country for stock portfolio investors and a very difficult one for direct investors."

10. *World Investment Report 2000*, on the theme of cross-border M&As, wrestled with this problem, noting, "it is not possible to determine precisely the share of cross-border M&As in FDI inflows. M&As can be financed locally or directly from international capital markets; neither is included in FDI data .... Moreover, payments for M&A (including those involving privatizations) can be phased over several years. It is therefore possible for the ratio of the value of cross-border M&As to total FDI flows – for the world as a whole or for individual countries – to be higher than 1" (UNCTAD, 2000, pp. 10–14).

11. The UNCTAD cross-border M&A database does not break down the data for PE firms and hedge funds.

12. McKinsey & Co. summed it this way: "The global financial crisis has thrown into reverse the forces that had fueled the growth and success of leveraged buyout (LBO) funds in recent years. From 2002 through 2007, rising equity markets and cheap credit helped buyout firms generate high returns, while the ensuing flood of investor capital boosted buyout assets under management more than threefold. But now, with credit tight and equity markets far below their peaks, buyout funds are struggling ... Many companies acquired at the top of the market are performing poorly. And new fundraising has dried up as private equity investors assess their

portfolio losses and face large capital commitments to the industry. (Roxburgh et al., 2009, p. 67).

13. Interestingly, there is not a single reference to "private equity" or "buyouts" in the 2000 issue of the *World Investment Report*.

14. Latin American countries that were on the top-12 list in 1990, in terms of outward FDI stock, fell in ranking by 2008 (Brazil and Mexico) or dropped out from the list altogether (Argentina), while India and Malaysia joined the list and other Asian countries like China and Hong Kong gained in rank.

15. OECD data on 2009H1 and "net foreign purchases" data (i.e. M&A activity).

16. See, for example, GE's admission in (Immelt, Govindarajan, and Trimble, 2009) that "success in developing countries is a prerequisite for continued vitality in developed ones" (pp. 3–4), or the recognition that "if GE doesn't come up with innovations in poor countries and take them global, new competitors from the developing world – like Mindray, Suzlon, Goldwind, and Haier – will" (p. 5).

17. "FDI flows to emerging markets have held up better because their overall economic performance has been much better than that of the developed world, which has experienced its worst recession since the Second World War. Much of the superior performance of emerging markets is, of course, due to the continued fast growth of China and India. However, even if China and India are taken out of the equation, most emerging markets will have outperformed the developed world in 2009. Emerging markets have thus to some extent "decoupled" from the developed economies .... Finally, the increased share of emerging markets in outward investment is increasing the share of emerging markets in inward flows because a disproportionate share of outward investment by emerging markets goes to other emerging markets" (Kekic, 2009, p. 3).

18. Kekic (2009) notes that almost 60 percent of companies surveyed by the Economist Intelligence Unit expect to derive more than 20% of their total revenue in emerging markets in five years, compared to 31 percent at present, suggesting that "the shift in the distribution of global FDI flows in 2009 is a longer-term development and not just a transitory phenomenon" (p. 3).

REFERENCES

Aharoni, Y. (1966). *The foreign investment decision process*. Division of Research, Graduate School of Business Administration, Harvard University.

Aharoni, Y. (1980). The state-owned enterprise as a competitor in international markets. *Columbia Journal of World Business, 15*(1), 14–22.

Aharoni, Y., & Ramamurti, R. (2008). The internationalization of multinationals. In: J. Boddewyn (Ed.), *International business scholarship: AIB fellows on the first 50 years and beyond* (pp. 177–202). Bingley, UK: Emerald.

China Investment Corporation. (2008). *Annual Report 2008*. Available at http://www.swfinstitute. org/research/CIC_2008_annualreport_en.pdf.

Cohen, B. C. (2008). *Sovereign wealth funds and national security: The great tradeoff*. Department of Political Science Working Paper, University of Santa Barbara, CA (August). Available at http://www.polsci.ucsb.edu/faculty/cohen/working/pdfs/ SWF_text.pdf

Cuervo-Cazurra, A., & Genc, M. (2008). Transforming disadvantages into advantages: Developing-country MNEs in the least developed countries. *Journal of International Business Studies, 39*(6), 957–979.

Davies, K. (2009). While global FDI falls, China's outward FDI doubles. *Columbia FDI Perspectives 5*, May 26.

Desai, M. (2008). *Why the U.S. should encourage FDI.* Working Knowledge. Boston, MA: Harvard Business School. Available at http://hbswk.hbs.edu/item/5984.html

De France, B. (2008). Assessment and outlook for sovereign wealth funds. *Focus 1*, November 28.

Government Investment Corporation. (2008). GIC Report 2008/2009. Singapore.

Govindarajan, V., & Ramamurti, R. (2011). Reverse innovation, emerging markets, and global strategy. *Global Strategy Journal* (forthcoming).

Immelt, J., Govindarjan, V., & Trimble, C. (2009). How GE is disrupting itself. *Harvard Business Review*, October, 1–11.

Kekic, L. (2009). The global economic crisis and FDI flows to emerging markets. *Columbia FDI Perspectives 15*, October 8.

Lall, S. (1983). *The new multinationals: The spread of third world enterprises.* Chichester, UK: Wiley.

Mathews, J. (2002). *Dragon multinationals.* Oxford, UK: Oxford University Press.

Meyer, K., & Sinani, E. (2009). When and where do foreign direct investment generate positive spillovers: A meta-analysis. *Journal of International Business Studies, 40*(February), 1075–1094.

Mortimore, M., & Razo, C. (2009). Outward investment by trans-Latin enterprises: Reasons for optimism. *Columbia FDI Perspectives 12*, August 17.

Organization for Economic Cooperation and Development (OECD). (2009). International investment flows collapse in 2009. *Investment News 10*, June.

Panibratov, A., & Kalotay, K. (2009). Russian outward FDI and its policy context. *Columbia FDI Perspectives 1*, October 13.

Park, D., & Estrada, G. B. (2009). *Developing Asia's sovereign wealth funds and outward foreign direct investment.* ADB Economics Working Paper Series No. 169. ADB, Manila, Philippines.

Pradhan, J. P. (2009). Indian FDI falls in global economic crisis: Indian multinationals tread cautiously. *Columbia FDI Perspectives 11*, August 17.

Prahalad, C. K. (2004). *Fortune at the bottom of the pyramid: Eradicating poverty through profits.* Upper Saddle River, NJ: Pearson Education Inc. for Wharton School Publishing.

Ramamurti, R. (2009a). What have we learned about emerging-market MNEs? In: R. Ramamurti & J. Singh (Eds), *Emerging multinationals in emerging markets* (Chapter 13, pp. 399–426). Cambridge UK: Cambridge University Press.

Ramamurti, R. (2009b). The theoretical value of studying Indian multinationals. *Indian Journal of Industrial Relations: Special issue on the global Indian firm, 45*(1), 101–114.

Ramamurti, R., & Singh, J. V. (2009). *Emerging multinationals in emerging markets.* Cambridge, UK: Cambridge University Press.

Roxburgh, C., Lund, S., Lippert, M., White, O. L., & Zhao, Y. (2009). *The new power brokers: How oil, Asia, hedge funds, and private equity are faring in the financial crisis.* Report, McKinsey Global Institute, McKinsey & Co., July.

Rugman, A. (2009). Theoretical aspects of MNEs from emerging economies. In: R. Ramamurti & J. V. Singh (Eds), *Emerging multinationals in emerging markets* (pp. 42–63). Cambridge, UK: Cambridge University Press.

UNCTAD. (1991). *World investment report 1991. The triad in foreign direct investment.* New York: United Nations Conference on Trade and Development.

UNCTAD. (2000). *World investment report 2000: Cross-border mergers and acquisitions and development.* New York: United Nations Conference on Trade and Development.

UNCTAD. (2008). Sovereign wealth funds beginning to play major role in foreign direct investment through mergers and acquisitions. Press release, September 24.

UNCTAD. (2009). *World investment report 2009. Transnational corporations, agricultural production and development.* New York: United Nations Conference on Trade and Development.

Wells, L. T., Jr. (1983). *Third world multinationals.* Cambridge, MA: MIT Press.

Wilkins, M. (1974). *The maturing of multinational enterprise: American business abroad from 1914 to 1974.* Cambridge, MA: Harvard University Press.

Wilson, S. (2008). Wealth funds group publishes 24-point voluntary principles. *IMF Survey Magazine*, October 15. Available at http://www.imf.org/external/pubs/ft/survey/so/2008/new101508b.htm

Xin, Z. (2008). CIC raises stake in Blackstone to 12.5 percent. *China Daily*, October 18. Available at http://www.chinadaily.com.cn/bizchina/2008-10/18/content_7118119.htm

REVISITING THE "MODERN" MULTINATIONAL ENTERPRISE THEORY: AN EMERGING-MARKET MULTINATIONAL PERSPECTIVE

Stéphane J. G. Girod and Joshua B. Bellin

ABSTRACT

Using Triad-based multinational enterprises as their empirical setting, influential scholars in international management uncovered key organizational characteristics needed to create globally integrated and locally responsive multinationals. They proposed a "modern" theory of multinationals' organization (Hedlund, 1994). But recently, a new generation of multinationals from emerging markets has appeared. Little is known about their organizational choices and some scholars even doubt that they leverage organizational capabilities altogether. Does the "modern" theory still hold in their case? This exploratory study of three emerging-market multinationals (EMNEs) discloses that for reasons related to their origin in emerging economies and to the competitive specificities of these economies, EMNEs approach the global and local conundrum in ways which are both similar – and vastly different – from recommendations of the "modern" theory. We inductively develop a new theory that accounts for the evolution of organizational capabilities in EMNEs to reconcile

The Future of Foreign Direct Investment and the Multinational Enterprise
Research in Global Strategic Management, Volume 15, 167–210
Copyright © 2011 by Emerald Group Publishing Limited
ISSN: 1064-4857/doi:10.1108/S1064-4857(2011)0000015013

global integration and local responsiveness. We discuss its implications for the executives of both emerging and Triad-based multinationals.

Keywords: Emerging-market multinationals (EMNEs); organizational strategy; harmonization; hierarchical networks

INTRODUCTION: HOW DO EMERGING-MARKET MULTINATIONALS ORGANIZE TO COMPETE GLOBALLY AND LOCALLY?

A rising force in the world economy (Ramamurti & Singh, 2009; Sauvant, 2008), emerging-market multinationals (EMNEs) are altering the international competitive landscape. While they accounted for 5.6 percent of the Global Fortune 500 in 1985, their share reached 19 percent in 2010, tripling since 2003. For example, names such as Mittal, Tata, and Geely have been at the forefront of economic news when they acquired Triad-based institutions such as Arcelor, Corus, and Volvo, respectively.

Together with other EMNEs such as Cemex, Huawei, Infosys, and Embraer, EMNEs are jolting the competitive ecology by threatening the dominant Triad-based species thanks to their business model innovations. Anecdotal evidence indicates that EMNEs "are reinventing systems of production and distribution, and they are experimenting with entirely new business models. All the elements of modern business, from supply chain management to recruitment and retention are being rejigged or reinvented in one emerging market or another" (The Economist, 2010). Empirical research suggests that EMNEs can leapfrog their more established counterparts thanks to "cost innovation," a competitive model that consists of selling highly customized products and services previously available only at premium prices, now at low prices (Zeng & Williamson, 2007).

As they rapidly internationalize, many EMNEs may need to create organizational architectures that can reconcile the seemingly contradictory imperatives of global integration, necessary to benefit from their new scale and maintain their cost advantages, and local responsiveness, necessary to successfully overcome their liability of foreignness across various markets (Bartlett & Ghoshal, 1989). Therefore, one may ask: which organizational choices do EMNEs make to execute on their international strategy and manage the trade-offs entailed by global integration and local responsiveness?

Despite international management researchers' rising interest in EMNEs, we have no answers to this question yet. Indeed, by and large, researchers have mostly focused so far on EMNEs' international strategies. Studies have covered related topics such as the drivers of EMNEs' internationalization (Buckley et al., 2007; Mathews, 2006), EMNEs' business models (Van Agtmael, 2007), their strategic behavior (Luo & Rui, 2009), their ability to create global innovation networks (Prahalad & Krishnan, 2008), and their foreign entry modes, including the spectacular mergers and acquisitions that speed up their internationalization (Kumar, 2009).

However, this paucity of research on EMNEs' choices as they create globally integrated and locally responsive organizations is problematic for theory and practice. According to certain scholars, EMNEs may represent altogether a new generation of organizations that highly reflect the institutional context in which they were born (Guillen & Garcia-Canal, 2009). Therefore, their organizational choices may differ from those predicted by international management theories developed with Triad-based lenses. Westney and Zaheer (2009, p. 358) recently pondered this possibility as follows: "A critically important development has been the internationalization of firms from emerging market countries that are just beginning to wrestle with the organizational challenges of internationaliza-tion. Will these firms follow the trajectories identified by the classic theories of MNE evolution, or will they follow one or more distinctive paths?" The little we know about EMNEs' organizations is so fragmented and contradictory that it makes it difficult to answer this important question.

THE "MODERN" MNE PARADIGM TO BALANCE GLOBAL INTEGRATION AND LOCAL RESPONSIVENESS

The "modern" MNE theory (Hedlund, 1994) is currently the dominant classic theory of MNE organizational evolution to which Westney and Zaheer refer. In the 1980s, several researchers came to realize that across more and more industries, MNEs would have to create organizational architectures that would reconcile two seemingly contradictory imperatives: global integration on the one hand and local responsiveness on the other hand (Bartlett & Ghoshal, 1989; Hedlund, 1986; Prahalad & Doz, 1987). These critics argued that the previous theoretical paradigm of MNEs organization conceptualized as a multidivisional hierarchy (Buckley & Casson, 1976;

Egelhoff, 1982; Hennart, 1982; Rugman, 1981; Stopford & Wells, 1972) was no longer fit for these new strategic imperatives for two reasons. First, the previous paradigm overstated the role of headquarters in allocating resources and centralizing strategic activities, while simultaneously overemphasizing the minimization of transaction and information-processing costs (Galbraith & Nathanson, 1978; Tushman & Nadler, 1978) and underemphasizing the necessity of cross-unit collaboration and trust (Ghoshal & Moran, 1996; Nohria & Ghoshal, 1997).

And, second, this perspective overstated the role of the organizational structure as a coordinating mechanism (Martinez & Jarillo, 1989). According to its critics (Bartlett & Ghoshal, 1990; Prahalad & Doz, 1987), this emphasis would force managers to prioritize either efficiency if they chose global business unit structures *or* responsiveness if they chose geographic unit structures. A matrix structure would neither balance global integration nor local responsiveness since, as the critics argued, the matrix was not a structure but a frame of mind articulated by horizontal and linking processes and a binding common culture enabled by intense cross-country socialization of managers. Consequently, emphasizing or trying to change the organizational structure was irrelevant (Bartlett, 1981).

Based on several in-depth case studies of American, European, and Japanese MNEs (e.g., Procter & Gamble, Matsushita, Philips), these scholars proposed three new organizational paradigms to reconcile global integration and local responsiveness: the "transnational" (Bartlett & Ghoshal, 1989), the "multifocal" (Prahalad & Doz, 1987), and the "heterarchy" (Hedlund, 1986). Hedlund (1994) argued that these three paradigms shared sufficient characteristics to form a "modern" theory of the MNE organization. To reconcile global integration and local responsiveness, the "modern" MNE became a flat organizational network characterized by the "geographical dispersion of strategic assets and leadership roles; upgrading of the role of 'foreign subsidiaries'; horizontal communication across borders; utilization of knowledge from several organizational bases; the impotence of solely formal methods of coordination; new roles for management at headquarters as well as other levels" (Hedlund, 1994, p. 87).

According to Westney (1999, p. 57), these three models of the new multinational "emphasized flexibility and networks, the flattening of the management hierarchy, the pushing of responsibility [from headquarters] to front-line units, and the importance of process rather than formal structure." The diffusion of the "modern" MNE was subsequently verified with more empirical studies across Triad-based MNEs (Birkinshaw & Morrison, 1995; Ghoshal & Nohria, 1993; Harzing, 2000).

DO EMNEs FOLLOW THIS "MODERN" ORGANIZATIONAL PARADIGM?

If EMNEs represent a new generation of organizations (Guillen & Garcia-Canal, 2009), they may approach the global–local conundrum in a different way than the one prescribed by the "modern" theory. Unfortunately, extant research is too limited and even contradictory to provide conclusive answers to this question.

Indeed, on the one hand, certain scholars argue that EMNEs' international success is mainly due to their rich endowment in country-specific advantages such as cheap labor costs, abundant access to natural resources or capital, and state protection, but not to strong firm-specific advantages (FSAs) such as organizational capabilities (Dunning, Changsu, & Park, 2008; Rugman, 2008). In this perspective, EMNEs would be unlikely to properly balance global integration and local responsiveness, let alone confirm or challenge the tenets of the "modern" multinational theory.

On the other hand, other researchers propose that EMNEs have truly developed some firm-specific organizational capabilities (Pillania, 2009). Guillen and Garcia-Canal (2009, p. 34) argue that EMNEs' international expansion "was possible due to some valuable capabilities developed in the home country, including project-execution and political and networking skills." According to Mathews (2006), while EMNEs may be comparatively poor in FSAs such as brands or core technologies and may be resource-seekers because they are latecomers in the international game, they may have developed other sorts of capabilities. He proposes a pull "LLL" theory of EMNEs internationalization that substitutes the well-known push "OLI" model (Dunning, 1981). In the OLI model, MNEs expand by internalizing and exploiting their abundant FSAs. But in the LLL theory, EMNEs thrive internationally by *linking* with partners, *leveraging* incumbents and partners' resources, and *learning* from partners by repeating linking and leveraging processes. Although he falls short of demonstrating it because his emphasis is not on organizational choices, Mathews hints that to support this model of internationalization, EMNEs do compete on unique organizational capabilities, for instance in relationship management. However, none of these studies truly determined how these capabilities were helping EMNEs to address the global–local conundrum and whether their choices were contrasting with the "modern" MNE theory.

PROPOSING A NEW FRAMEWORK TO UNDERSTAND HOW LEADING EMNEs BALANCE GLOBAL INTEGRATION AND LOCAL RESPONSIVENESS

This study seeks to close these gaps by unravelling the enigma of EMNEs. Our research questions aimed to explore which organizational choices allow EMNEs to reconcile global integration and local responsiveness and whether these choices contrast with the "modern" MNE theory. Because these questions were largely underexplored, we adopted an inductive approach based on a qualitative research design involving three EMNEs in two industries (Yin, 1994).

Our theoretical contribution is an original, holistic framework that enriches the field of international organization strategy and provides an organizational explanation to EMNEs' international competitiveness. This framework reflects the three EMNEs' organizational trajectory by articulating how they have created new organizational capabilities around structure, management processes, and management technologies (sources of greater global integration) to enhance their original ones in human and social capital management (sources of local responsiveness).

Our framework confirms a key principle of the "modern" MNE theory: to balance global integration and local responsiveness, EMNEs do aim to create learning networks and therefore emphasize human and social capital FSAs. However, for reasons related to their origin in emerging economies and to the competitive specificities of these economies (and perhaps reflecting a different globalization era and a different degree of maturity), the path, organizational choices, and configuration they choose to build such networks differ substantially from those prescribed by the "modern" MNE theory. Thus, an implication of our theory is to delineate the "modern" MNE model's contextual boundaries in time and in space.

As classic in inductive research, the next section details our research design. We then articulate the core concepts of our inductively developed theory. Next, we engage in a discussion where we contrast our findings with the "modern" EMNE principles, formulate several testable propositions, and conclude with important managerial implications.

METHOD: RESEARCH DESIGN AND SETTING

Because we focused on a relatively unexplored phenomenon for which we needed to obtain sufficient granularity, an inductive research design based on comparative case studies was the most appropriate (Yin, 1994). Multiple cases allow researchers to use each case's findings to confirm or disconfirm inferences drawn from the others in a way that produces more robust and generalizable theory than single-case and ethnographic designs (Eisenhardt & Graebner, 2007).

Our industry and sample selections were intertwined and guided by theoretical considerations. Because the "modern" MNE perspective is based on the study of large Triad-based MNEs, we had to focus on comparably large EMNEs (to control for differences in size that may conflict with our conclusions; arguably, managing a small firm is not as complex as managing a large one). Out of the 41 industry sectors referenced by Dow Jones Industry Classification Benchmark (ICB, 2008), telecommunications (a high-velocity industry) and oil and gas (a more stable industry) were among the few that contained a number of large EMNEs – an important consideration to ascertain that if one or more multinationals did not grant us access, we could still access other sufficiently large EMNEs.

Before sampling from these two industries, we also had to ensure that they would be theoretically suitable, that is, they faced equally strong pressures for local responsiveness and global integration. Unfortunately, past studies documenting levels of transnational exposure by industry were dated (Kobrin, 1991) and incomplete (Nohria & Ghoshal, 1997). Thus we turned to 11 one-hour, semistructured interviews of industry experts in Europe, the United States, and Asia-Pacific (six for telecoms, five for oil and gas).[1] With the exception of one respondent who thought that the telecommunications industry was more prone to local responsiveness than global integration, the experts agreed that industry players faced constraints to be both globally integrated and locally responsive. In the light of such a consensus, we retained these two industries and proceeded to sample.

Using Dow Jones Factiva, we ranked the 20 largest, publicly listed emerging-market telecommunications and oil and gas companies by sales revenues that qualified as multinationals (Stopford, 1992). We focused on publicly listed firms both because of the larger availability of secondary information for triangulation purposes and because state-ownership (common in emerging markets oil and gas) can reduce the pressure for efficiency (Rugman, 2008). We began negotiating access with the largest ones across 17 emerging countries, since it was theoretically important to compare multiple emerging nations. Although we aimed to obtain access to two telecommunications and two oil and gas EMNEs in preferably four countries, we eventually got access to three multinationals that we call "Telco1" based in Asia, as well as "Telco2" and "Enerco1" – both based in the same African country. They were all multibillion dollar EMNEs. Table 1 provides key facts about them.

DATA COLLECTION

We collected data using two main types of sources: semistructured, one-to-one interviews and published, secondary data. We relied on the interviews as the main source of information with the documentary information serving as key material for triangulation.

We conducted 23 one-hour, in-person interviews with the top executive teams. Since top executives are usually directly involved in the choices and decisions related to strategy and organizational alignment to achieve global efficiency and local responsiveness, they were key informants (Kumar, Stern, & Anderson, 1993). Therefore, although we acknowledge that the theory generated in this study only reflects their vision rather than the collective sense-making of various types of organizational members, our approach casts a rare and valuable light on top executive teams' management philosophy in EMNEs. For reasons related to our research question, we sought for positional and geographic variety; we interviewed top executives at headquarters (COO, heads of main functions) and in the operating units (global business units heads, regional heads, local unit heads) to capture different opinions on the global–local tension. The reliance on multiple informants also allowed us to clarify what could appear to us as inconsistencies across respondents (Miller, Cardinal, & Glick, 1997). All interviews were recorded and transcribed. We conducted all interviews between November 2008 and March 2009.

Our interview protocol contained semistructured questions prompting rich descriptions of how senior executives were configuring their organization to balance global integration and local responsiveness, including what organizational capabilities were critical and why; how they were deployed and why; who made key organizational decisions and why; how did these

Table 1. Key Facts about Sampled EMNEs.

Region of origin	Telco1	Telco2	Enerco1
	Asia	Africa	Africa
Transforming events	• Purchased by current owner in 2002 • Two major international acquisitions in 2005 and 2006	• Multibillion dollar acquisition in 2006	• 2000 joint venture with oil major partner in Africa • Major international acquisition in chemicals in 2001
Ownership Strategy	Publicly listed since the early 2000s Wireline voice and data, internet broadband, data services	Publicly listed in the mid-1990s Mobile telecommunications voice and data, business solutions	Publicly listed since the late 1970s Integrated oil, gas, and chemicals company
Leadership positions	• World leader in two industry segments	• Pan-African and Middle-Eastern mobile phone operator	• World no. 2 in one industry segment
Sales revenues in US$ (2008)	>2 bn	>10 bn	>15 bn
Workforce	>5,000	>14,000	>30,000
First internationalized in	2001	1997	1992 but significant take off in 2000
Foreign sales over total sales (2008)	>50%	>50%	>40%
International footprint	>40 countries in developed and emerging markets	>20 countries in Africa and the Middle-East	>30 countries in developed and emerging markets
Compounded annual growth rate of sales revenues (2006–2009)*	30%	29%	19%
Compounded annual growth rate of profit margin (2006–2009)*	42%	27%	13%
Tobin's *q**	1.30	1.40	2.10
No. of interviews	11	5	7

*Data from Capital IQ (Standard & Poors). We sought to compute the compounded annual growth rate of their foreign sales rather than total sales, but the companies did not report this statistic consistently over time.

choices change over time and why; and how they will need to change in the future and why.

Prior to the interviews, we also collected unobtrusive data from various public sources that helped us build a comprehensive company profile for each EMNE. Sources included business press articles, financial analysts' reports, industry reports, annual reports, and material from the companies' websites. We thereby built comprehensive narratives of the companies' internationalization history. We compiled short biographies of the top executive team that we would interview. To assess whether there would be some correlation between organizational choices and performance, we computed the compounded annual growth rates of sales revenues (a proxy of how well companies seize local opportunities to grow) and of the profit margin (a proxy of how well the companies can achieve cross-border synergies) using the Capital IQ database of Standard & Poor. When the primary data collection began, we were already very familiar with each company's external and internal context. This unobtrusive data collection method allowed us to establish trust with our respondents, verify certain declarations during the interviews, and ask clarifying questions if we spotted some inconsistencies (Webb, Campbell, Schwartz, & Sechrest, 1966).

DATA ANALYSIS

We used a multistep analytical strategy. We first analyzed each case through the lens of our research question to identify important theoretical constructs. Within each case, we first identified the initial concepts in the data, grouping them into categories (open coding), using the in-vivo approach recommended by Strauss and Corbin (1990) to remain as close as possible to informants' terminology. Second, we looked for relationships between these categories, which enabled us to aggregate them further. All along, we used tables and graphs to simplify the analysis (Miles & Huberman, 1994). We consistently triangulated the interview answers with published materials. To increase the robustness of our conclusions, each author first coded each case separately before we compared our analyses and consolidated a common coding structure, resolving discrepancies by going back to the data. This recursive process enabled us to refine our coding within the first case, and then by integrating the findings of the second case and of the third case, we obtained the overarching dimensions and the relationships that compose our framework. To establish the validity of our analysis, we wrote a case study for each EMNE that we validated with their top executive teams.

FINDINGS: A HOLISTIC CONFIGURATION OF ORGANIZATIONAL CAPABILITIES TO BALANCE GLOBAL INTEGRATION AND LOCAL RESPONSIVENESS

Our interviews reveal that the three EMNEs have followed a similar, accelerated organizational evolution through which they have crystallized common principles to balance global integration and local responsiveness Their organizational choices strongly reflect their emerging-market heritage and the consciousness that protecting this heritage is essential to outcompete their Triad-based rivals, in particular in emerging economies.

We find that as they were growing internationally and as the industry conditions were changing around them, these EMNEs could not solely rely on the original FSAs in human and social capital management – based on entrepreneurial culture and relationship management capabilities – that guaranteed their successful local responsiveness. Rather, they also had to build more integrating FSAs.

To begin with a high-level summary of our findings which are explained in depth in the following sections, the three EMNEs chose to nurture their original FSAs by supporting them with a hierarchical network organizational structure that helped them enact the "harmonization" of management processes and upgrade the role of management technologies. This approach resulted in a greater balance between global integration and local respon- siveness. Therefore, the three EMNEs used internationalization not just to get new FSAs in structure, management processes, and management technologies, but also to strengthen those that they inherited from their home countries. In this process, organizational structure played a pivotal role. Fig. 1 represents this approach.

ORIGINAL ORGANIZATIONAL FSAs IN HUMAN AND SOCIAL CAPITAL SECURED HIGH LOCAL RESPONSIVENESS AT THE OUTSET OF INTERNATIONALIZATION

Interviewed executives observe that one of the reasons explaining their companies' international success was their light coordinating approach based on FSAs in entrepreneurial culture and interpersonal relationship management. They explain that the ability to listen and adapt to customers

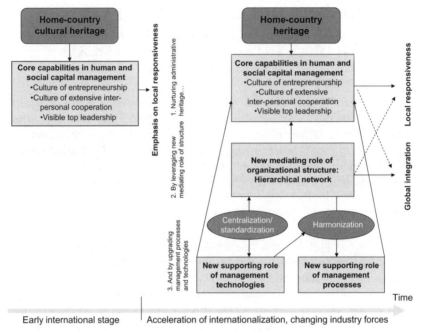

Fig. 1. The Three EMNEs' Organizational Choices to Reconcile Global
Integration and Local Responsiveness.

and/or local stakeholders, strengthened by a propensity of employees to
informally network across borders, were strengths they derived from their
home countries and that home-country expatriates contributed to transfer
abroad. Thus, human and social capital FSAs enhanced local responsiveness and created a minimal level of cross-country integration.

Telco1

Created as a state-owned company for the domestic market, Telco1 was
privatized and acquired by an important Asian business group shortly
before losing its monopoly in 2002. Anticipating fierce competition at home,
it immediately began its internationalization. Before two game-changing
acquisitions in 2005 and 2006, it operated in six Asian and European
countries.

Interviewed executives who supervised this strategic change assessed that the company's relationship management and its totally customer-focused entrepreneurial culture were the main coordinating mechanisms in this pioneering period. As one global business unit head explained, this culture derived from an "audacious, confident and focused" new leadership team that infused an enthusiastic spirit among the workforce thanks to its constant contact with employees through regular traveling and intense communication. This entrepreneurial, relationship-driven approach translated into a force, which, in his words, was bringing "new thinking around the customer experience to completely reinvent [the company's] services and bring a very personalized level of experience."

Besides, the company would extensively rely on an informal network of home-country expatriates who exchanged with one another. These expatriates brought with them this highly customer-responsive culture, which was related to the company's home-country approach to business. Indeed, we heard:

> Typically, managers or leaders in our country are quite flexible in their approach. That's the way business is run here ... [They are] accommodating, flexible, very caring about customers' needs and [about] others' needs ... They go the extra mile to meet the business demands or the customer demands.

Enercol

Enercol is an African MNE and its unique technology makes it one of the world's leaders in the conversion of gas and coal to liquids. Its internationalization took off in 2000. By 2006 when it entered a second internationalization phase in oil and gas, it already had three major operations in three foreign countries (in Africa and the Middle East).

Executives explained that their employees' "can-do" culture translated into an entrepreneurial mindset that was shared at all levels of the organization. It was characterized by a shared determination to rise to all local challenges and by employees helping each other across countries through informal networks, hence maintaining a human-based, light level of cross-border integration. As one functional vice president put it:

> If I want to get things done somewhere in the world, I'll find my buddies. These networks are built when people get promoted to an opportunity on an international project and then have these informal connections back with the home country.

Another Enerco1 functional vice president explained that the home-country cultural heritage largely explained this entrepreneurial culture and propensity to network:

> It is really about [our country]'s pragmatic cultural style ... People in our country don't like to be defeated by anything. So, if there is a problem somewhere, you will soon find people across the company who will start contributing or who will make others available to go and fix it.

This pragmatic approach and "can-do" spirit shared by leaders and employees brought strong flexibility and local responsiveness because it allowed Enerco1 to mobilize powerful interpersonal networks to meet local objectives. It also gave the company a competitive advantage over its powerful Western counterparts: because it could rely on a powerful internal network of dedicated employees who would do whatever it takes to fix problems if they appeared, the company was prepared to accept higher risks in its foreign entry decisions. For example, according to the executive in charge of international operations, this ability to appreciate risks differently was making a commercial difference locally: "As the minister [of oil-producing country X] explained to me 'when I do business with Western companies, they don't come to my country. I have to meet them in countries they consider safer.'" Thanks to Enerco1's different appreciation of country risks, itself based on its confidence in its internal network' entrepreneurial mindset, this host country was more prone to grant Enerco1 licenses to explore.

Telco2

Telco2 came from the same African country. Today one of the world's most successful mobile phone operators, it was still very young when it first internationalized in 1997. Before its second internationalization phase began, following a game-changing acquisition in 2006, it was already operating in eight African countries.

Telco2 executives also saw a link between their home-country heritage and their FSA in strong relationship management, which has been so essential for them to navigate the regulatory and institutional complexities of other emerging markets by establishing trust with foreign parties. For example, a functional senior executive explained how expatriates could establish trust with foreigners and enhance local responsiveness:

> You have never seen how good the [the people of this country] are at mentoring, educating, helping. The Westerners can't do it. We can show empathy for others and see other people's value systems and make sure that our values and theirs match each other.

Direct relationships between top leaders, local unit managers, and local boards were an essential coordinating mechanism. Each top executive would insist on being highly visible in foreign operations. Each top executive would join each quarterly board meeting of one of the local units not because the company did not hold a controlling stake but because cultivating a personalized relationship with local board members and local countries was a guiding principle to enhance local responsiveness. A senior vice president explained that this personalized approach helped reduce political uncertainty and enabled corporate managers to directly sense the markets' evolution since board members were influential and well-informed local stakeholders. He explained, "To work in emerging markets, the needs are completely different. Circumstances change very, very quickly. You need strong local support." For the top executives, it was "really that process of connecting" that made the company successful.

CHANGING INTERNAL AND EXTERNAL CIRCUMSTANCES EXPOSED THE LIMITS OF THESE EARLY FSAs

However, as internal and external pressures to intensify global integration while retaining strong local responsiveness appeared, interviewed executives realized that relying mostly on relationship management and entrepreneurial leadership FSAs was no longer possible.

In 2005 and 2006, Telco1 made two very large acquisitions that increased its international footprint to 40 countries across almost all continents. In just four years, the company was "reborn global." Similarly in 2006, Telco2 took over a very large mobile phone operator, and overnight, it began operating in more than 20 countries in Africa and the Middle-East. Both companies' foreign sales over total sales ratio jumped well above 50 percent. In 2006, following the appointment of a new CEO a year earlier, Enerco1 was decidedly accelerating its internationalization strategy by beginning the negotiation of projects in America, China, India, and Australia. It was becoming important for them to anticipate on the organizational strains that this growth would entail. This new scale also meant that opportunities for synergies, and therefore global integration, could not be ignored. With a growing proportion of foreign employees and conversely a declining proportion of expatriates, the home-based-derived FSAs analyzed above would reach limits.

Some new trends in the market place also meant that the three EMNEs had to address multiple strategic opportunities and challenges that contained some seemingly contradictory global and local imperatives. These trends also meant that their organizational capabilities had to evolve to effectively balance global integration and local responsiveness. Table 2 details how the three EMNEs translated the market trends into new strategic and organizational imperatives.

The three EMNEs were at a crossroads. Their senior executives realized that they needed new capabilities around their organizational structure, their management processes, and management technologies to accelerate their cross-border integration. As one Telco1 regional executive declared, "with only the people focus [i.e. the capabilities based on relationship management, visible and entrepreneurial leadership, informal networking], you will hit the ceiling in terms of how fast and how quickly you can grow or how the organizational performance can kick in." Telco2's COO also recalled that informal networking was reaching its limits since it could exclude recently joined foreign employees: "In some parts of our company, there were a lot of groupings which, if you were not part of, it was difficult to have your views heard or to participate effectively." Becoming more inclusive to new foreign employees and developing standard ways of operating was necessary. A similar analysis emerged at Enerco1.

To increase integration without stifling local responsiveness, executives decided to support their original FSAs in entrepreneurial culture and networking management with new FSAs in organizational structure, management processes, and management technologies. A functional senior executive at Telco1 voiced this principle, underscoring how important to them supporting the company's human and social capital was: "With the best processes in the world, if your people, if your management is not visionary, your best processes will not help you." This principle aimed at cultivating the companies' original competitive advantage by avoiding the mistakes made by some large Triad-based multinationals that, in their view, did not sufficiently invest in their human and social capital and often operated as stifling bureaucracies, which damaged local responsiveness. As the international senior vice president of Telco1's parent business group noted, "We don't want to become a GE or a Unilever." Rather the company wanted to be managed as "a global start-up with [home country] roots," a metaphor highlighting the combination of scale (integration), agility, and entrepreneurship (responsiveness), and also the consciousness of the benefits derived from its origin in a large emerging economy. Similarly, Enerco1 executives were careful to create their distinctive model. As one respondent

Table 2. Market Trends Translated into Strategic and Organizational Implications.

	Market Trends	Strategic and Organizational Implications	
Oil & Gas	Securing license to operate in host countries in context of increasingly competitive battles for exploration blocks.	How do we take a localized approach to partnerships while creating a global methodology to become a partner of choice?	Partnerships
Telecom	Accessing key markets and licenses, roaming agreements, and spectrum allocation, while also securing increasingly costly and knowledge-intensive resources to respond to technological convergence.	How do we take a localized approach to partnerships but coordinate these into our global ecosystem of partners?	
Oil & Gas	Shortage of people combining scientific, managerial, and cross-cultural working skills. Particular shortage of geologists and engineers in developed economies.	How do we develop talent locally but also leverage talent globally?	Talent
Telecom	Shortage of skilled talent, especially with technology skills.	How do we develop talent locally but also leverage talent globally?	
Oil & Gas	International pressure for credible alternative energy sources. Integrated oil companies losing technological leadership, a key competitive advantage.	How do we stimulate innovation locally while strengthening innovation globally?	Innovation
Telecom	Technological convergence and intensifying competition are accelerating the pace of product and technological life cycles, bringing changes across entire business models.	How do we scale innovation and benefit from pockets of local innovation simultaneously?	
Oil & Gas	Rising pressure on cost structures due to threat of energy substitutes, compounded by rising technical challenges of exploration and production activity and by oil prices volatility.	How do we increase cost discipline without stifling local responsiveness and flexibility?	Cost discipline
Telecom	Increasing demand for offering integration but with important variations across countries combined with increasing cost pressures.	How do we increase efficiency globally while improving customer experience locally?	
Telecom	Trend of "empire builders." High acquisition activity across diverse markets underlies a race for scale within and across continents.	How do we preserve the local know-how of our acquisitions but integrate them across borders to leverage our scale?	Integration of acquisitions

observed, "One thing we must be careful is that we don't become a super-major."

This overarching design principle that reflected emerging-market roots and competitive realities showed that the three EMNEs' evolution did not simply mean "catch-up" but also innovation.

We now turn to analyze how the companies developed new FSAs to scale their original ones and increase global integration without stifling local responsiveness.

EMNEs SCALE THEIR SOCIAL AND HUMAN CAPITAL WITH A HIERARCHICAL NETWORK STRUCTURE TO BALANCE GLOBAL INTEGRATION AND LOCAL RESPONSIVENESS

To create cross-country synergies but remain locally responsive, the three EMNEs undertook radical restructurings that scaled their original networking and entrepreneurial culture. Their new semidecentralized structures relied on distributed networks of leadership across units and countries, virtual headquarters, and horizontal *and* top-down relationships. Because these networks combined flat and vertical attributes, we propose the term "hierarchical networks."

Telco1

In 2007, senior executives distributed leadership across hierarchical levels, regions, and functions. Replacing an international-division structure, the new structure was based on global business units, within which the geographic units grouped into six regions were subsumed to enhance local responsiveness. This choice enabled the company to abolish the distinction between home-country and foreign businesses (it also separated home-country headquarters from global headquarters) and therefore to develop a global mindset based on equal attention for all.

The heads of the two main business units were based in different countries. Their global teams, including the heads of the various offering lines, were distributed around the six regions and had authority over local decision-makers. Enhancing the entrepreneurial spirit in the company, the latter were empowered to make real-time decisions without having to wait for the authorization of a superior based in another time zone because the accountability lines were clearly defined. Diversity of employees' origins was also important. Distributed leadership and diversity enhanced local responsiveness. One global business unit head commented:

> If you take the top 50 people in the business, they're distributed across twelve cities ... so we can be as close to our customers and markets as possible. When we look at the top 50 people again, less than one-third of them are [home-country nationals]. It's not necessarily a practice that even some of the other telecommunication companies have managed to pull off. We hold onto this passionately because we believe that the mix of the people and the location of the people need to reflect our thinking ... [about how to best serve customers in each market].

Structural innovations institutionalizing interdependence across countries and business units aimed to overcome the traditional silos inherent to this structure (Galbraith, 2001). Headquarters were playing a direct role in creating these relationships. For instance, the main supporting functions (e.g., HR, finance, IT), organized as shared services, were based in the home country for the whole company to benefit from its low-cost advantage. The functional heads decided who and where the global process owners would be to enhance the accountability of operational execution. One of the shared services was a Global Product Organization that stimulated the cooperation of the three business units to prepare joint offerings (integrating voice, internet, and data solutions) to global multinational customers.

These arrangements coexisted with lateral cooperation between units, without headquarters' involvement. For example, as the head of the home-country region explained, "Regional managing directors meet on a regular basis to set coordinated objectives and to measure and monitor the results."

The global management committee's approach to strategy formulation was inclusive and encouraged risk taking and entrepreneurship further down the hierarchy. According to a second business unit head, when the company reformulated its strategy in 2006, top managers encouraged employees' initiatives even if it could mean failure:

> At the executive committee level we basically said: "We want six services and three are going to fail, and we want buy in from the board." And we communicated to our teams. "We're going to get you on board and we're going to make sure you're putting the best possible effort, but given it's all new for us, there will be services that fail.

But, simultaneously, strategy decisions were the global management committee's responsibility that senior executives often conducted virtually due to the physical distance between them. There were no multiple strategic apexes.

Thus, Telco1's networked structure combined hierarchy and empowerment, to the point where decision-making authority was centrally directed in a "light touch" approach without relying on overbearing central control.

Telco2

Thanks to a combination of influence from headquarters, outright hierarchical intervention, global centers of excellence, and broad empowerment, Telco2's restructuring in 2006 allowed the company to create more cross-country synergies and to retain its local responsiveness. In practical terms, this meant the ability to present a unique face to multimedia service providers or to introduce more cost discipline and leverage its scale vis-à-vis handset makers.

Telco2 also separated its home-country headquarters from its global headquarters and deployed a four-region organizational structure, grouping its country units according to similar languages and cultural traits. Each region was placed under the responsibility of a regional vice president, but country managers retained the profit and loss responsibility and accountability to protect local responsiveness. These regional vice presidents were geographically distributed to stay closer to country units and speed up decision-making. They were not expatriates. They promoted regional initiatives and synergies (horizontal learning), and top-down (initiatives that headquarters wanted to implement) and bottom-up learning (reporting to headquarters).

To avoid excessive bureaucracy and functional duplication, each region received a very limited support staff, largely because the top management team preferred to organize the majority of the regional support from headquarters. But because, as a senior executive put it, "by nature, we hate the fat-cat syndrome and you know there's no worse place to put a fat cat than at the center," this arrangement soon became insufficient due to the company's rapid growth (between 2006 and 2009, the compounded annual growth rate of its sales revenues was 30%). At the time of our interviews, executives were considering an arrangement in which larger foreign units would be entrusted with regional back-office supporting responsibilities, thus keeping the global and regional levels lean and focused on strategic initiatives. Highlighting the company's frugal mindset and desire to avoid repeating Western competitors' mistakes, the chief financial officer explained:

> If you look at large global corporations headquartered in the U.S., as an example ... Within each region you would probably have a regional headquarters. And the regional headquarters would be staffed up by virtually the same number of functions as they have at their headquarters ... But there is a great opportunity for us to say that we go for a sort of hub and cluster organization. So we provide the support services for the

French-based companies, let's say, from a Cote d'Ivoire, for all the English-speaking companies from a Ghana or a Nigeria.

Entrusting local units with activities that would support other units and foster networking would simply extend the principle of centers of excellence already implemented from 2006. As the chief technology officer explained, "I believe in centers of excellence. You identify them across the operating companies. If I talk about satellite compression, Sudan is my center of excellence. If I want to talk outsourcing, Iran would be my role model." Yet, also implying hierarchical characteristics in the network, centers of excellence were spotted, nurtured and approved by headquarters that maintained a hierarchical oversight and attributed global charters. Akin to Telco1, strategy-related decisions were concentrated by the top management team.

Enerco1

In the vein of what was taking place in the two telecom EMNEs, Enerco1 was implementing a hierarchical network based on a mix of vertical and flat organizational characteristics. The structural innovations brought by Enerco1's senior executives aimed to strengthen the interdependencies across operations internationally while scaling the relationship management and entrepreneurship capabilities that had defined the company's success in terms of local responsiveness.

In 2006, senior executives created a coordinating layer of four global business "clusters" that each supervised several divisions while the business divisions kept the profit and loss responsibility to maintain close proximity with their markets. These clusters were thinly staffed to limit bureaucracy. The clusters aimed to enhance synergies across business and geographic units not just to improve efficiency, but also to increase knowledge flows and allow employees to come up with operational innovations and new ideas. According to the chief strategy officer, this light, new structure respected the company's original entrepreneurial spirit:

People actually participate on the basis of "I can make an improvement." So they will work longer hours and whatever. I'm always amazed how many people actually go out of their way and comment. Because if they feel they can improve it, they actually do. And that's the component that needs to be maintained.

Second, the new structure emphasized a clearer determination of individual accountability to foster hierarchical oversight in what was, by now, a much larger organization. As the chief strategy officer also noted, the goal was to "move faster by having somebody who can go down the line and actually be held accountable for something that is not done, or rewarded for something that's been done very well."

Third, senior executives set up shared central functions that straddled and linked the clusters and divisions. These functions included health, safety and environment (human safety was a major concern in this industry), finance, technology, and human resources. Shared services would support the company's international growth plan, for example, by planning where and how to invest in talent.

Finally, the restructuring entailed the creation of foreign-based centers of excellence in training and education to scale the "Company Way" across borders. One executive noted, "We've now got an Academy going with a University in Scotland, so we are creating centers of excellence where we can grow talent exposed to the [Company] Way."

More changes were about to come. Since shared services institutionalized and made the exchange of knowledge more encompassing across the company, when our interviews took place, executives were thinking to add procurement and IT shared services. Top executives were also considering the creation of a global headquarters separated from the home-country headquarters.

EMNEs LEVERAGE THEIR HIERARCHICAL NETWORKS TO "HARMONIZE" MANAGEMENT PROCESSES AND ENHANCE GLOBAL INTEGRATION WHILE PROTECTING LOCAL RESPONSIVENESS

To create organizations that could balance global integration and local responsiveness, in accordance with their overarching design principle, senior executives also aimed to scale and support their companies' original FSAs with stronger FSAs in management processes. By management processes, executives referred to capabilities for directing, linking individuals and groups across the company and coordinating work flows to deliver their offerings to customers (Nadler & Tushman, 1997). Important processes in our interviews were planning, credit, procurement, and talent management processes.

Strengthening capabilities in management processes did not simply mean investing more; it also meant increasing standardization. We uncovered a mechanism by which the three EMNEs were strengthening their FSAs in management processes without overstandardizing. Telco1 executives called this mechanism "harmonization." Because the two other EMNEs did not use this term but used a similar approach, we propose "harmonization" as a common concept.

Harmonization was based on selective standardization decisions taken thanks to the semidecentralized organizational structure that created opportunities for headquarters, business, regional and local units to share authority when deciding how much to standardize management processes. As one Telco1 executive highlighted, "I wouldn't use the word standardize; I would use the word harmonize. It's not a question of force-fitting and saying [to business and local units] 'this is what you've got to do. Period.'" This was echoed by a Telco2 executive who declared: "Leadership here isn't leadership by 'do what I say'." Because force-fitting standards from the top would backfire later on, senior executives preferred adopting a medium-term view by organizing a conversation where internal stakeholders from all around the world commonly decided which processes would have to be local, regional, or global.

A greater amount of standards increased cross-country efficiency and enhanced the consistency of product and service delivery in each foreign market. But because harmonization allowed some local differentiation of management processes, it stimulated local innovation and entrepreneurship. Moreover, it created more inclusive employee networking since it allowed leaders of recently acquired operations to contribute to defining new standards. Thus, harmonized management processes expanded the three EMNEs' original relationship management propensity.

Paradoxically, because headquarters were not imposing all standards but promoted a principle of "meritocracy," that is, retained standards could originate from who held the best practice anywhere in the network, global and local units were more trusting of the standardization proposals from headquarters. Counter-intuitively, because the degree of centralization of the decision authority to deploy management processes was only moderate, the standardization of processes progressed more steadily.

Telco1

Telco1 was using harmonization to strengthen the role of management processes without stifling local responsiveness. For example, in the financial area, the financial vice president explained that all financial managers around the world agreed to develop one common credit management framework in 2007. This framework stipulated how each subsidiary should go about credit access (e.g.,, managers agreed on the percentage beyond which subsidiaries needed central approval). But within this common framework, actual processes for credit management could vary locally:

> I'll give you an example of the credit policy. The framework is standardized and applies to each geographical unit, each geographical sector or country ... And each of the countries uses that framework to develop a policy but that policy again has to be approved by the comptroller who sits in one place ...

One area where harmonization of processes was particularly important was in talent and people development. Harmonization meant that decision-making authority was shared. Headquarters took the lead in standardizing certain processes, while local units could decide whether for all the other processes they would develop a country-based solution or adopt a standard.

For example, headquarters led the process of defining and implementing the structure of talent management. This entailed defining one mission and the common core values that would support it. These values were leadership (engagement, high performance), entrepreneurship (customer-orientation, continuous improvement), and ethics (respect for the individuals and society that reflected the home-country culture).

To ensure that the mission and values were binding employees, headquarters standardized a common performance appraisal structure across all units, which included an assessment of how well each employee lived the company mission and values. Employees' bonus was partially based on their team-work and knowledge-sharing performance to develop their communication and relational capabilities. Moreover, managers' bonuses became linked to employees' engagement and satisfaction measured annually through a worldwide survey. Because senior executives could ascertain that middle and front line managers were sharing these common values across borders, they in turn did not have to impose overly centralized planning processes on them. As a global business unit head remarked, "for our planning process we don't have to give directives. It's subtle."

But local units could choose the processes supporting the content of talent management. For example, local leaders were in charge of setting performance goals for their employees. To ensure the attractiveness of the company locally and comply with local regulations, they would also determine the pay scales and the content of the various incentives and rewards.

Telco2

Telco2's hierarchical network allowed global headquarters, and regional and local units to share responsibility to decide how to strengthen the role of management processes to increase cross-border integration without stifling local responsiveness.

Decisions around harmonization were often a result of planned meetings where two-way feedback could be shared. First, despite a large number of local units, top executives continued sitting on local boards – some sitting on up to six boards. These visits were a first occasion for hearing about new practices in the countries and, if they were successful, to report these practices to other countries. Second, the quarterly meetings – in the home country – of all country and regional managers were another opportunity to discuss which processes should be standardized. Different units would showcase what headquarters thought were best process practices (on the basis of their success at reducing cost or increasing market share) and headquarters would also showcase their own new process initiatives which they had usually piloted beforehand in volunteering local units.

Telco2 was also actively building new capabilities in processes. One of these quarterly meetings resulted in Telco2's overall adoption of the disciplined procurement process created by the company it acquired in 2006. Interestingly, akin to Telco1, we also found a great effort at harmonizing the processes supporting people's development. Headquarters was in charge of standardizing processes to strengthen the original entrepreneurial culture. For example, it launched a process where all employees could nominate colleagues for companywide awards and recognition around four categories: knowledge sharing, customer service, high performance, and living the company values. The four winning employees would be publicly rewarded. As the chief human resource officer discussed, this process is:

> Where you pick up innovations. Recently, Ghana won the customer service award because an employee saved somebody's life. Because of the way they managed the process and carried on, and the innovation they applied in Ghana, the call center agent was able to take a life-saving decision.

If these innovations were transferred elsewhere, they could enhance integration, responsiveness, or both. But local units could decide which processes would support the content of talent management (e.g., which recruitment processes, training processes, etc.) to stay locally responsive.

Enerco1

The company harmonized its management processes to both create one "Company Way" that could be easily applied to new projects and countries and to avoid "cutting back on the 'can-do' culture," as one executive explained. Two convergence programs called "functional" and "operational excellence" were the frameworks within which functional, divisional, country, and top executives engaged in a global conversation and knowledge exchange to determine which processes should be standardized or not.

Enerco1 was using "big rules" to frame these global conversations and determine how the decision authority on processes should be shared between global and local units and headquarters. A first rule, for example, was to select the value-chain activities where more process standardization would need to take place: processes supporting customer-facing and government relationships would need to retain a higher local content. But processes supporting the company's core operational technology and its research and development labs at home, in the UK and in the Netherlands could be more standard. It did not follow that all the standards were flowing from the home country. A senior executive explained, "if you take the UK just as an example... it's certainly a center through which we gain access to knowledge skills capability that leads to certain innovation elsewhere in the globe."

A second rule was to look at the nature of the processes. As the head of one these programs explained:

> Clearly we're looking for opportunities to standardize the highly transactional processes, typically high volume transactions processes such as accounts payable, payroll, accounts receivable, procurement, applications support, etc. which are easily standardized to benefit from economies of scale. But the ones that are not transactional by their nature will be where there will be more difference.

Employee safety was a third rule to differentiate between standard and local processes. An executive noted that processes that could create safety risks if not respected were standardized: "[in a plant or a mine] ... it's very safe it you do it exactly how you're supposed to do it and you don't take chances and you're not creative. You get creative in a plant or a mine, you kill people."

EMNEs LEVERAGE THEIR HIERARCHICAL NETWORKS TO CENTRALLY STANDARDIZE MANAGEMENT TECHNOLOGIES AND ENHANCE GLOBAL INTEGRATION WHILE PROTECTING LOCAL RESPONSIVENESS

In addition to strengthening management processes through harmonization, interviewed executives in the three EMNEs realized that they needed to build new FSAs in management technologies to create an organization that could balance global integration and local responsiveness. Here, respondents referred to supporting communication and information software and tools – such as enterprise-resource-planning (ERP) platforms and intranet applications – that could link people and groups across borders, functions, and divisions.

To create these new capabilities, interestingly, the three EMNEs did not rely on harmonization but rather on top-down, centrally defined standardization – thereby leveraging the more hierarchical dimension of their networked structures. Indeed, executives considered the sheer scale of the investments that were required as well as the complexity of the integration task caused by myriad of technological platforms – a result of excessive local autonomy and multiple acquisitions in their first internationalization phase. For example, an Enerco1 executive declared: "We severely under-invested in certain technologies like connectivity and we acquired disparate technologies across the group ... That's why we ended up with 17 versions of SAP... ." Importantly, executives assessed that it was by centrally creating a common backbone of management technologies that their companies could more flexibly balance global integration and local responsiveness. Standard management technologies would enhance global integration by enabling employees to share and support one another more effectively since they could exchange information on compatible bases. As Telco2's COO explained, "if the systems are different, let's say whether it's a billing system or it's an ERP platform, then people cannot work across, people cannot support each other. So, ideally, you should have one system." This would strengthen the companies' original capabilities in relationship management, and by providing communication tools to share and measure best practices, it would also support harmonization decisions.

Standardizing management technologies would also support local responsiveness by enabling employees to make more timely and well-informed customer decisions. For example, Telco1's headquarters created a common application in the intranet that allowed all employees to access and post information related to customers and partners, which greatly improved the accuracy and timeliness of global account management. Better decisions also justified the broad empowerment and distributed leadership principles contained in the organizational structure. In this sense, global integration enhanced local responsiveness, making the two concepts less antagonistic than what they could seem. As one Telco1 executive concluded, by standardizing these technologies, "our overall model becomes much, much more flexible and scalable. And that makes us able to take our market delivery to the next level."

DISCUSSION: TOWARD A THEORY EXPLAINING HOW LEADING EMNEs BALANCE GLOBAL INTEGRATION AND LOCAL RESPONSIVENESS

When he proposed the concept of "heterarchy," Hedlund (1986, p. 32) wrote: "In terms of geographical and corporate origins, heterarchical MNCs are more likely to evolve from less than gigantic firms, and from contexts with a history of rather autonomous and entrepreneurial subsidiaries... MNCs from newly modernizing nations may stand an even better chance." The patterns of organizational choices across three EMNEs in two industries, analyzed in the previous sections, hint that his prediction is only partially correct. The "modern" theory of multinational organization, developed with Triad-based lenses, only incompletely explains how EMNEs approach the global–local conundrum. We find that the three EMNEs do place a high emphasis on FSAs resulting from their human and social capital as the "modern" theory recommended to Triad-based multinational executives; however, contrary to this theory, human and social capital is an original FSA that the three EMNEs seek to protect to remain locally responsive. Moreover, the organizational choices made to create new organizational FSAs that can deliver superior human and social capital FSAs very much differ from the recommendations of the "modern" MNE theory. Table 3 synthesizes the comparison between the "modern" MNE theory and our EMNE-orientated theory.

Our theoretical contribution is a new, more holistic model, which, by explaining how leading, nonstate owned EMNEs design organization architectures that can reconcile global integration and local responsiveness,

Table 3. Theoretical Framework of EMNEs' Organizational Choices.

	"Modern" MNE Theory	Revised "Modern" Theory for EMNEs
Trajectory: from software to hardware	• From hardware (structure, technologies) to software (leadership, culture, values, people, processes) (Bartlett & Ghoshal, 1993) • Reviving entrepreneurship and creating networks (Hedlund, 1994)	• From hardware to hardware and software • Protecting entrepreneurship and networking
Administrative heritage: from liability to opportunity	• Constituted a form of "organizational inertia" (Doz & Prahalad, 1991)	• Turned upside-down: becomes an opportunity source of organizational innovation to balance integration and responsiveness
Top leaders: from context builders to context builders and visible linking agents	• Focus on context setting (such as creating shared values and creating purpose) but not best placed to ensure cross-unit linkages (Bartlett & Ghoshal, 1993) • Catalysts and facilitators more than resource controllers or performance allocators (Hedlund, 1994)	• Focus on context setting too but are highly visible and interventionist to ensure cross-unit linkages • Differentiated role: top leaders play both roles
Organizational structure: from background to foreground	• Differentiated network where the MNE internalizes the country-specific advantages of certain local units for the benefit of the whole (Hedlund, 1986; Nohria & Ghoshal, 1997) • Geographic dispersion of assets and functions (Hedlund, 1986) • Role of formal organizational structure de-emphasized at the profit of processes and systems (Doz & Prahalad, 1991; Hedlund, 1986)	• Similar • Similar • Organizational structure is at the center of a different hierarchy of capabilities. It scales original networking and entrepreneurial capabilities and facilitates "harmonization" of processes

Table 3. (*Continued*)

	"Modern" MNE Theory	Revised "Modern" Theory for EMNEs
	• Major strategic change can take place without a formal structural change (restructuring seen as unnecessary form of radical change) (Bartlett & Ghoshal, 1998; Prahalad & Doz, 1987); "change of the formal organization will not give rise to heterarchy" (Hedlund, 1986, p. 27)	• Organizational restructuring essential to create new organizational capabilities
	• Nonhierarchical, decentralized model based on accountable microunits where front line managers are empowered (Bartlett & Ghoshal, 1993)	• Front line managers are empowered, moderate centralization effected in harmonization but persistent sense of hierarchy based on centrality of corporate headquarters to ensure integration
	• Lean headquarters and distributed leadership (Bartlett & Ghoshal, 1993)	• Similar but local units do not bypass headquarters
	• Multiple centers: several strategic apexes emerge (Hedlund, 1994)	• Corporate strategy is geographically consultative but under top managers' responsibility; no multiple strategic apexes that shift over time
Coordination by processes: from "radical decentralization" to harmonization	• "Radical decentralization" means emphasis on horizontal coordination processes (internal benchmarking, best-practice identification) (Bartlett & Ghoshal, 1993)	• Horizontal and vertical coordination: shared responsibility for deployment of management processes—"harmonization"
	• Normative coordination (values, culture) to guarantee trust (Hedlund, 1986), rather than hierarchical, calculative control	• Calculative and normative coordination. Calculative control is accepted because local units retain sufficient autonomy, which protects trust
Coordination by technologies: a centralized approach to standardization	• Ambiguity: (i) important for supporting, democratic communication in the transnational but little emphasis on how it can play this supporting role (Bartlett & Ghoshal, 1993) vs. (ii) weak role of technologies in heterarchy	• Headquarters play a centralizing role in the creation of a standard backbone of communication technologies, which fosters global integration and local responsiveness

delineates more accurately the contextual boundaries of the "modern" MNE theory. Moreover, this framework provides us with an organizational explanation of leading EMNE's international competitiveness.

Aware that the small number of EMNEs and emerging countries represented in our sample limits our ability to generalize, we develop below a set of propositions that subsequent research could test, for example, thanks to a large-scale, quantitative design.

Organizational trajectory and priorities have shifted from an emphasis on the "software" to an emphasis on the "software" and the "hardware." In the "modern" theory, multinational executives who needed to create globally integrated and locally responsive organizations were urged to shift their attention from a mechanistic, hierarchical model focused on the organizational hardware (organizational structure and management technologies) to the software based on common values, linking processes, and trust. As Bartlett and Ghoshal (1993, p. 40) put it, "To capture the energy, commitment and creativity of their people, these managers are replacing the hard-edged strategy-structure-systems paradigm of the M-form with a softer, more organic model built around purpose, process and people."

Although our findings clearly highlight that EMNEs aim to tame bureaucracy because it can hamper human and social capital, they also contrast with the "modern" MNE theory in two ways. First, in terms of trajectory, EMNEs do possess FSAs in entrepreneurial culture and relationship management right from the outset of their internationalization. These FSAs are internalized home-country-specific advantages and are extremely important to their local responsiveness. By contrast, the "modern" MNE theory holds that because creating informal coordinating mechanisms such as employee networking and informal communication is costly, it is only when the need for global integration increases that MNEs invest into them (Martinez & Jarillo, 1991).

The second important difference stems from the fact that the three EMNEs do not substitute the hardware with the software, but rather create an organization that accounts for the importance of both. The newly created FSAs in hierarchical network structures and management technologies are highly important supporting and enabling capabilities. We find that management processes are not organic per se, as implied by Bartlett and Ghoshal, since they can only enhance social and human capital if they are enabled by the right type of organizational structure. The new FSAs not only strengthen EMNEs' ability to create cross-border synergies, but also protect their local responsiveness thanks to broad empowerment and networking, both of which reinforce their original entrepreneurial spirit.

These differences lead us to propose:

Proposition 1. EMNEs which seek to support their original FSAs in entrepreneurial culture and relationship management with new FSAs in organizational structure, management processes, and technologies are more likely to successfully balance global integration and local responsiveness.

Administrative heritage: From liability to opportunity: In the "modern" MNE theory, the "institutional heritage" of a firm constrains the development of new capabilities, and constitutes a form of "organizational inertia" (Doz & Prahalad, 1991, p. 158). But the three EMNEs we studied considered their home-country origin and the resulting administrative heritage as an asset to preserve and to extend to accommodate more turbulent market conditions. Again the three EMNEs were turning a Triad-based concept upside down.

Role of top leaders: from context builders to context builders and visible linking agents: In the "modern" MNE theory, top executives focus on context setting, creating shared values and a sense of purpose, but are not best placed to ensure cross-unit linkages. This role is better achieved by middle managers. As Bartlett and Ghoshal (1993, p. 35) wrote, "while the top level context setting and the front line personal networks can provide the enabling conditions for [the] vital horizontal process, it is the middle managers who are best placed to facilitate these cross-unit linkages." For Hedlund (1994, p. 85), top managers are catalyst of knowledge diffusion rather than monitors and resource allocators; in the heterarchy, "there is a need for integration to give direction and consistency to the knowledge development activities. In the N-form, this is top management's primary role. However, it must be exercised in a rather indirect way, lest the effectiveness of the intensive and diffused processes at 'lower' levels is compromised."

Our case studies confirm the high involvement of top executives in the creation of the right context, communicating the vision, creating shared values, and instilling the urgency of a global mindset among employees. Top managers are also catalyst of knowledge, for example, in their leadership in the deployment of management technologies. But a contrasting characteristic of senior leadership in the three companies is its high visibility, as a cornerstone for linking units. For instance, we saw the highly extensive engagement of top leaders in local boards at Telco2 and the implications that these contacts had in the harmonization process. To some extent, this finding may be explained by the nature of emerging-market operations. As a global business unit director of Telco1 explained, in emerging economies, senior executives have to be even more visible because for market, cultural, and institutional reasons a lot of challenges need to be addressed through interpersonal relationships rather than process-based, virtual relationships:

> I would say that emerging markets are more resource driven in the sense that you need to be much more present in the market itself than in developed countries. For example, in the developed countries, in some business you can almost operate remotely in the sense that processes are well established, the market is growing at its normal pace and so on. So it's easier to do the day-to-day activity.

What we imply here is not that top managers were the only cross-unit linking agents, but that they see their role in this domain as more essential and more direct than what the "modern" MNE theory acknowledges.

We also found that in addition to this coordinating role, senior executives played a strong controlling role – they were controlling individuals and units, for example, thanks to the benchmarks comparing how well employees live the corporate values – and held the commands of internal resource allocation. Therefore, senior managers' ability to play multiple roles simultaneously, thanks to tremendous progress in communication technologies, enhanced global integration and strengthened their companies' original local responsiveness. Consequently, we propose:

Proposition 2. EMNEs whose top leaders are able to simultaneously perform multiple roles (context setters, linking agents, top-down controllers) will be more likely to successfully balance global integration and local responsiveness.

Role of the organizational structure: from background to foreground of the organizational architecture: Our findings support important aspects of the "modern" MNE theory. Structurally, the three EMNEs are increasingly working as formal networks. Our observation of centers of excellence, spread out among foreign countries (in company subsidiaries or outsourced through partners) and which play a strategic role for the whole company, supports the differentiated network perspective of the "modern" MNE theory in which the MNE internalizes the country-specific advantages of certain units for the benefit of the whole company (Hedlund, 1986; Nohria & Ghoshal, 1997).

Our conclusions strongly differ with the "modern" MNE theory, though, in that the latter does not recognize the organizational structure as a fundamental coordinating mechanism. Doz and Prahalad (1991, p. 159) noted: "formal structure in an organization (e.g., organization structure) is nothing more than a shorthand way of capturing the underlying subprocesses – managers' mindsets… , a consensus on strategy, and power to allocate resources consistent with strategy." In structure, Hedlund saw division rather than integration; he wrote: "Insisting on combination has important organizational implications. Integrating mechanisms become more important than differentiating ones" (Hedlund, 1994, p. 83). The nature of structure is also different. Dispersed strategic centers could relate to one another unmediated by the corporate center (Hedlund, 1986) and the emphasis was on flat, nonhierarchical networks. Finally, organizational restructuring was at best unnecessary to create a globally integrated and locally responsive organization and at worst counter-productive (Bartlett, 1981). For instance, Doz and Prahalad (1991, p. 160) wrote: "Major strategic redirection can take place without a formal structural change" and Hedlund (1986, p. 27), "Change of the formal organization will not give rise to heterarchy. Subtler changes in management processes are required."

By contrast, structure matters in the three EMNEs, a conclusion that echoes Aharoni's (1996) points in the context of professional service firms. First, *structure works as a bridge* between older and newer, supporting capabilities. Structure enables the entrepreneurial culture and relationship management FSAs to scale more effectively across borders. Structure also allows harmonization to unfold, thanks to the trust created by the decision-sharing mechanisms, thus enabling management processes to become more consistent across borders yet at the same time also more empowering, not stifling. It is intriguing that from a totally different context, in their recent study of Western professional service firms, Segal-Horn and Dean (2008) also conclude that it is the organizational structure that holds the management processes together, not the other way round. Such converging conclusions suggest either an original limitation in the "modern" MNE theory or that, under the effect of very different competitive, technological, and environmental conditions, management practice has had to evolve since that theory was developed.

Second, *structure works as a hierarchical network based on both vertical and horizontal relationships*. Because the aim of structure is not to be stifling, we observe a combination of top-down and lateral relationships in the three EMNEs' structures that are customized according to the companies' needs. While assets are distributed across countries (centers of excellence at Telco2 and Enerco1) or leadership is distributed through virtual headquarters to better suit local market needs and leverage the benefits of multinationality through knowledge transfers (Telco1), the concept of "headquarters" remains and forms the continuing apex of the organizational hierarchy. While strategy is consultative, it is not participative and remains the top team's responsibility. Global charters are not self-determined; headquarters plays an active role in encouraging, supervising, coordinating, and changing them if necessary. As we have seen, the hierarchical dimension in the structure allows headquarters to centralize decisions around management technologies and to standardize them.

But even the most recent works which revisit the "modern" MNE theory do not allow for the possibility that multinationals which rely on multidirectional learning and networks of interdependent units across countries can also rely on hierarchical features. This is the case, for example, with the "cellular" and "instant global network" models of multinationals proposed by Zander and Mathews (2006), which they see as pure heterarchies. Here, there is extensive networking, but it is not as equalitarian as what the "modern" theory holds.

Third, *reorganizations matter*. Organizational restructuring has been essential for the three MNEs to create coherent regional groups to build appropriate synergies across countries (Telco2) and coherent business units to foster more consistent operational processes and integrate product offerings for more local responsiveness (Telco1 and Enerco1). More structural changes were set to come to further refine the hierarchical network. Clearly, their executives do not see structures as permanent (Hedlund, 1994, p. 83). They were proud of their recent structural initiatives. Although these companies cultivate a continuous improvement philosophy thanks to harmonization, they are also aware that breaking up with past routines requires periodic radical restructurings. In this sense, they should be more seen as ambidextrous organizations (Luo & Rui, 2009; Tushman & O'Reilly III, 1996).

Why are structure and hierarchy still important concepts for EMNEs that exhibit other behaviors reminiscent of the "modern" MNE theory? Competing in emerging markets and today's volatile competitive conditions in the two industries may require this sense of subtle hierarchy to make the network more governable (there is less confusion of responsibilities) and agile (distant decision-makers can communicate and make decisions in very little time). As Birkinshaw and Terjesen (2003) noted, Western managers got lost in overly sophisticated linking processes when they strived to implement the principles of the transnational organization. Thus, they created more inward-oriented bureaucracies than the ones they were supposed to replace. As they try to define their models, leading EMNEs seek to avoid these mistakes and appreciate the coordinating force of a simple but well-defined hierarchy.

These arguments lead us to propose:

Proposition 3. EMNEs that seek to nurture their original FSAs in entrepreneurial culture and relationship management will be more likely to create a hierarchical network structure.

Proposition 4. To create a hierarchical network, EMNEs will be more likely to implement a large-scale organizational restructuring.

Proposition 5. EMNEs that deploy a hierarchical network structure will be more likely to successfully balance global integration and local responsiveness.

Coordination by management processes: from "radical decentralization" to harmonization: In the "modern" MNE theory, scholars emphasize the importance of horizontal over vertical integration and coordination. Bartlett and Ghoshal (1993, p. 27) talked of "radical decentralization" when they described ABB's core organizational principle, in stark contrast with the hierarchy. Consequently, they also emphasized that middle managers led the decisions related to the standardization of management processes. They wrote: "This management group spends considerably more time and effort managing activities such as internal benchmarking, best practice identification, and technology transfer – all aimed at linking and leveraging the company's widely distributed resources and capabilities" (Bartlett & Ghoshal, 1993, p. 33). The "modern" MNE theory also holds that integration takes place primarily thanks to normative control (processes for creating common values and culture thanks to intense socialization of employees) and trust than through calculative control which follows a logic of opportunism punishment (Hedlund, 1986, p. 24).

By contrast, in addition to the integrating/coordinating role played by the hierarchical network, our study discloses a coordination mechanism – *harmonization* – that is equally horizontal and vertical, normative and calculative. It is absent from the "modern" MNE theory. Harmonization leverages the principle of distributed leadership contained in the hierarchical network to allow top, functional, regional, business, and geographic unit managers to share responsibility and decide which management processes should be standardized or remain local, and assess where the best standards should come from in the organization. The distributed leadership structure allows some local independence, which is source of local variation. The global conversation that takes place with harmonization provides opportunities to identify the best practices and the best standards from wherever they emerge in the world. Therefore, harmonization stimulates standardization but protects the local sense of entrepreneurship.

Harmonization also scales the original networking propensity in the organization by including all managers, independently of their origin, in a formalized conversation. In contrast to Hedlund (1986, 1994) who emphasizes that internally developed knowledge is critical to the network organization – and therefore "modern" MNEs should limit the recruitment of external top managers and acquisitions – we find that the three EMNEs have grown by successive acquisitions and have been keen to retain their acquired firms' leaders. Harmonization works as a socializing process of knowledge transfer from these acquisitions and as a motor enabling external growth through successful mergers and acquisitions.

But harmonization also reserves to headquarters the ability to define certain standard processes. For example, we saw how active Telco1's and Telco2's headquarters were at deciding the standards underpinning the structure of human resource management, including shared core values. We also found that country managers can retain certain country-specific processes as long as they meet the annual objectives defined by headquarters (with their participation). But as soon as their performance dips, thanks to clear lines of accountability, headquarters can step in, impose a standard or even replace the country manager. Thus, counter-intuitively, calculative control coexists with normative control because harmonization guarantees a sufficient level of trust. Therefore, we propose:

Proposition 6. EMNEs that harmonize their management processes – that is, leverage their hierarchical network to share decision-making authority with global and local units to decide how to standardize management processes – will achieve greater economic integration and local responsiveness.

Coordination by management technologies: A centralized approach to standardization to foster networking: The significance of management technologies is ambiguous in the "modern" MNE theory. As seen above, Bartlett and Ghoshal (1993) on the one hand de-emphasized the role of management systems compared to people-, culture-, and process-related FSAs. But on the other hand, they also highlighted how much the corporate information system helped ABB to create a broad, transparent communication, essential to networking. While they emphasized its democratic nature, they did not explain how this system came into existence in the first place.

Our findings show that EMNEs provide extensive attention to the development of FSAs in management technology to increase global integration while protecting local responsiveness. Moreover, if communication and learning are to become democratic as suggested by Bartlett and Ghoshal, it seems that EMNE headquarters must centralize the decisions related to the consolidation of dispersed technological platforms and standardize them. Here, they directly leverage the hierarchical dimension of their recently created organizational structures but are able, simultaneously, to scale their networking propensity.

It is because technologies are standardized that they allow greater visibility at the center and encourage senior leaders to share or delegate more responsibility at the business, regional, functional, and local levels. Compatible technologies also allow employees and managers to access important knowledge in real time, which helps them make fast and informed decisions for their clients locally and when necessary, to coordinate important decisions across borders for their global accounts. If leaders are distributed around the world, their ability to coordinate their decisions in real time depends on the availability of compatible technological platforms. Besides, standard technologies ease the internal benchmarking of processes and therefore facilitate harmonization. This is why top-down centralization, not harmonization, is a more appropriate mechanism to deploy management technologies. Paradoxically, the centralization and standardization of management technologies facilitate the independence and local responsiveness of local units within a globally integrated architecture. Hence our last proposition:

Proposition 7. EMNE headquarters that leverage their hierarchical authority to centralize and standardize management technologies will more effectively balance global integration and local responsiveness.

To summarize, our findings indicate that the "modern" EMNE theory only partially accounts for the organizational choices made by EMNEs to balance global integration and local responsiveness. Although an important comparable core principle is to value human and social capitals, we note six types of differences that lead us to rethink the relationships and causalities that link the core organizational concepts (soft and hard organizational FSAs) discussed in the "modern" MNE theory. In addition to these firms' origin in emerging economies and to the competitive dynamics of these economies, perhaps these discrepancies also stem from the fact that leading EMNEs have only recently gained strength on the competitive stage. As Ramamurti (2009) explains, even leading EMNEs are still adolescent multinationals compared to their Western, mature counterparts that formed the core of "modern" MNE theory. Therefore, our contribution is to extend rather than reject the "modern" MNE theory (Gammeltoft, Barnard, & Madhok, 2010) by highlighting its contextual boundaries in time and in space.

MANAGERIAL IMPLICATIONS

Our framework suggests the importance for EMNEs to support original entrepreneurial and relationship management FSAs with (i) hierarchical networks, (ii) harmonization of processes, and (iii) standardization of management technologies – all of which are critical if they want to begin balancing global integration and local responsiveness. The strong profitability growth of the three companies since 2006 (see Table 1) indicates that these choices are already enabling them to benefit from cross-border synergies. Moreover, although their impressive top line growth might be partially explained by the sheer growth enjoyed by most emerging economies, even during the recent so-called "global" downturn, they might not have achieved similar results over time if their local responsiveness ability was substantially diminished. The guiding organization design principle contained in this theory has therefore multiple implications for multinational executives in both emerging and developed markets.

For executives of even more recently internationalized emerging companies, the message is clear and they can learn from their leading peers: once they are fully committed to competing in the international market place, they should elevate their attention to organizational structure, management processes, and technologies. But they cannot lose sight of their original strengths in entrepreneurial culture, visible leadership, and relationship management, which are critical drivers of local responsiveness, in particular in other emerging markets.

For executives in developed markets, the first message is to realize that their leading emerging-market competitors might not simply compete on low-cost basis (see, e.g., Dunning et al., 2008; Rugman, 2008). They are also very quickly building new organizational skills and innovating while they do so. Importantly, by deploying hierarchical networks and using harmonization of management processes, they scale and strengthen their original capabilities. This design choice could give them more flexibility and local responsiveness, in particular in rapidly growing emerging markets.

Although Triad-based MNE executives need to deal with different organizational legacies to create "super global and super local" organizations, by remembering that centralization and standardization are distinct concepts, they too could begin benefiting from harmonization. The changes entailed might be more difficult to implement for American MNEs that have traditionally embraced a more global "cut-and-paste" organizational approach centralized from the home country and for Japanese MNEs that still extensively centralize decisions through their expatriates. We also conclude that they might be ill advised to neglect their organizational structures and to focus instead solely on processes, confirming previous recommendations (Birkinshaw & Terjesen, 2003).

CONCLUDING REMARKS

Our aim was to assess how relevant the "modern" MNE theory was to explain EMNEs' organizational choices to balance global integration and local responsiveness. As a result, we sampled larger, more visible, and more successful EMNEs than the average emerging-market firm, and we acknowledge this potential limitation. We also recognize that the number of multinationals and countries represented is small. Therefore, as with all case study research, an issue is to determine the generalizability of our findings. Although this is a question to which future large-scale empirical studies should answer, several factors help alleviate this potential limitation.

Indeed, first, we find similar high-level choices between firms across two very different industries, one mature and the other younger and more dynamic – although what these choices mean in terms of process deployment, for example, are clearly industry-specific. Second, it also appears that these choices were found across EMNEs that belong to a business group (Telco1) and those that do not. Third, two firms in different industries came from the same home-country (Telco2 and Enerco1), which help us determine more confidently the role that the home country plays in original organizational FSA endowments. Finally, although the differences across emerging markets and their firms should not be underestimated, the common patterns identified in this study confirm past research that has explained that EMNEs share some similarities (Gammeltoft et al., 2010; Khanna & Palepu, 2010; Luo, 2002).

Despite these potential limitations, this study represents an original effort to deepen our understanding of the development and functioning of EMNEs' organizational capabilities. It begins accounting for the competitive advantages that EMNEs can derive from their organizational strategy, how these advantages are developed, and how they help EMNEs compete successfully with Triad-based MNEs (Ramamurti, 2009). It highlights the sensitive contextual boundaries of the "modern" MNE. Our revised theory suggests that EMNEs are aiming to innovate and create a new organizational model to avoid replicating the mistakes of some of their Triad-based peers and that they are better characterized by their ability to reconcile hierarchy and network, top-down and lateral leadership, culture structure and processes, and continuous and radical change.

NOTE

1. For example, we interviewed the former chairmen of Shell and BP in oil & gas, and the chairman of the GSM Association for telecoms. In these interviews, we asked to describe whether their industry faced more pressures to be locally responsive, more pressures to be globally efficient or more pressures to be both simultaneously. We do not reproduce the results of these interviews but data are available from the authors.

ACKNOWLEDGMENTS

The authors want to thank Rebecca Piekkari, Saku Mantere, Ingmar Bjorkman, Robin Gustafsson, David Light, Susan Segal-Horn, Carine Peeters, Paul Verdin, Alain Noel, and Ravi Ramamurti for their useful comments on earlier versions of this chapter.

REFERENCES

Aharoni, Y. (1996). The organization of global service MNEs. *International Studies of Management and Organizations*, *26*(2), 6–23.

Bartlett, C. A. (1981). Multinational structural change: Evolution versus reorganization. In: Lars. Otterbeck (Ed.), *The management of headquarters–subsidiary relationships in multinational corporations*. Aldershot: Gower.

Bartlett, C. A., & Ghoshal, S. (1989). *Managing across borders: The transnational solution*. Boston: Harvard Business School Press.

Bartlett, C. A., & Ghoshal, S. (1990). Matrix management: Not a structure, a frame of mind. *Harvard Business Review*, *68*(July–August), 138–145.

Bartlett, C. A., & Ghoshal, S. (1993). Beyond the M-Form: Toward a managerial theory of the firm. *Strategic Management Journal*, *14*(8), 23–46.

Bartlett, C. A., & Ghoshal, S. (1998). *Managing across borders: The transnational solution* (2nd ed.). London: Random House Business Books.

Birkinshaw, J. M., & Morrison, A. (1995). Configuration of strategy and structure in subsidiaries of multinational corporations. *Journal of International Business Studies*, *26*(4), 729–753.

Birkinshaw, J. M., & Terjesen, S. (2003). The customer-focused multinational: Revisiting the Stopford and Wells model in an era of global customers. In: J. M. Birkinshaw, S. Ghoshal, C. Markides, J. M. Stopford & G. Yip (Eds), *The future of the multinational firm*. Chichester, UK: Wiley.

Buckley, P., Clegg, J., Cross, A., Liu, X., Voss, H., & Zheng, P. (2007). The determinants of Chinese outward foreign direct investment. *Journal of International Business Studies, 38*(4), 499–518.
Buckley, P. J., & Casson, M. (1976). *The future of the multinational enterprise.* London: Macmillan.
Doz, Y., & Prahalad, C. K. (1991). Managing DMNCs: A search for a new paradigm. *Strategic Management Journal, 12*(Summer), 145–164.
Dunning, J. H. (1981). *The eclectic theory of the MNC.* London: Allen & Unwin.
Dunning, J. H., Changsu, K., & Park, D. (2008). Old wine in new bottles: A comparison of emerging-market TNCs today and developed-country TNCs thirty years ago. In: K. P. Sauvant (Ed.), *The rise of transnational corporations from emerging markets: Threat or opportunity?.* Cheltenham, UK: Edward Elgar.
Egelhoff, W. G. (1982). Strategy and structure in multinational corporations: An information-processing approach. *Administrative Science Quarterly, 27*(3), 435–458.
Eisenhardt, K. M., & Graebner, M. E. (2007). Theory building from cases: Opportunities and challenges. *Academy of Management Journal, 50*(1), 25–32.
Galbraith, J. R. (2001). *Designing the global corporation.* San Francisco, CA: Jossey-Bass.
Galbraith, J. R., & Nathanson, D. (1978). *Strategy implementation: The role of structure and process.* Saint Paul, MN: West.
Gammeltoft, P., Barnard, H., & Madhok, A. (2010). Emerging multinationals, emerging theory: Macro- and micro-level perspectives. *Journal of International Management, 16*(2), 95–101.
Ghoshal, S., & Moran, P. (1996). Bad for practice: A critique of the transaction cost theory. *Academy of Management Review, 21*(1), 13.
Ghoshal, S., & Nohria, N. (1993). Horses for courses: Organizational forms for multinational corporations. *MIT Sloan Management Review, 34*(2), 23–35.
Guillen, M. F., & Garcia-Canal, E. (2009). The American model of the multinational firm and the 'new' multinationals from emerging economies. *Academy of Management Perspective, 23*(2), 23–35.
Harzing, A. W. (2000). An empirical analysis and extension of the Bartlett and Ghoshal typology of multinational companies. *Journal of International Business Studies, 31*(1), 101–120.
Hedlund, G. (1986). The hypermodern MNC: A heterarchy?. *Human Resource Management, 25*(1), 9–35.
Hedlund, G. (1994). A model of knowledge of management and the N-form corporation. *Strategic Management Journal, 15*(5), 73–90.
Hennart, J. F. (1982). *A theory of multinational enterprise.* Ann Arbor, MI: The University of Michigan Press.
ICB. (2008). Industry Classification Benchmark. Dow Jones.
Khanna, T., & Palepu, K. (2010). *Winning in emerging markets: A roadmap for strategy and execution.* Boston: Harvard Business Press.
Kobrin, S. J. (1991). An empirical analysis of the determinants of global integration. *Strategic Management Journal, 12*(Summer), 17–31.
Kumar, N., Stern, L. W., & Anderson, J. C. (1993). Conducting interorganizational research using key informants. *Academy of Management Journal, 36,* 1633–1651.
Kumar, N. (2009). *India's global powerhouses.* Boston: Harvard Business Press.
Luo, Y. (2002). *Multinational enterprises in emerging markets.* Copenhagen: Copenhagen Business School Press.

Luo, Y., & Rui, H. (2009). An ambidexterity perspective toward multinational enterprises from emerging economies. *Academy of Management Perspective, 23*, 49–70.

Martinez, J. I., & Jarillo, J. C. (1989). The evolution of research on coordination mechanisms in multinational corporations. *Journal of International Business Studies, 20*(3), 489–514.

Martinez, J. I., & Jarillo, J. C. (1991). Coordination demands of international strategies. *Journal of International Business Studies, 22*(3), 429–444.

Mathews, J. A. (2006). Dragon multinationals: New players in 21st century globalization. *Asia Pacific Journal of Management, 23*(1), 5–27.

Miles, M., & Huberman, A. M. (1994). *Qualitative data analysis: An expanded sourcebook*. Thousand Oaks, CA: Sage.

Miller, C. C., Cardinal, L. B., & Glick, W. H. (1997). Retrospective reports in organizational research: A reexamination of recent evidence. *Academy of Management Journal, 40*, 189–204.

Nadler, D. A., & Tushman, M. L. (1997). *Competing by design: The power of organizational architecture*. New York: Oxford University Press.

Nohria, N., & Ghoshal, S. (1997). *The differentiated network: Organizing multinational corporations for value creation*. San Francisco, CA: Jossey-Bass.

Pillania, R. K. (Ed.) (2009). Guest editorial Special Issue on emerging markets and multinational enterprises*Multinational Business Review, 17*(2), 5–10.

Prahalad, C. K., & Doz, Y. (1987). *The multinational mission: Balancing local demands and global vision*. New York: Free Press.

Prahalad, C. K., & Krishnan, M. S. (2008). *The new age of innovation: Driving co-created value through global networks*. New York: McGraw-Hill.

Ramamurti, R. (2009). What have we learned about emerging market MNEs?. In: R. Ramamurti & J. V. Singh (Eds), *Emerging multinationals from emerging markets*. Cambridge, UK: Cambridge University Press.

Ramamurti, R., & Singh, J. V. (2009). *Emerging multinationals in emerging markets*. Cambridge, UK: Cambridge University Press.

Rugman, A. M. (1981). *Inside the multinationals: The economics of internal markets*. London: Croom Helm.

Rugman, A. M. (2008). How global are TNCs from emerging markets?. In: K. P. Sauvant (Ed.), *The rise of transnational corporations from emerging markets: Threat or opportunity?*. Cheltenham, UK: Edward Elgar.

Sauvant, K. P. (2008). *The rise of transnational corporations from emerging markets: Threat or opportunity?*. Cheltenham, UK: Edward Elgar.

Segal-Horn, S., & Dean, A. (2008). Delivering 'effortless experience' across borders: Managing internal consistency in professional service firms. *Journal of World Business, 44*(1), 41–50.

Stopford, J. M. (1992). *Directory of multinationals* (4th ed.). Basingstoke: McMillan.

Stopford, J. M., & Wells, L. T. (1972). *Managing the multinational enterprise: Organization of the firm and ownership of the subsidiaries*. London: Longman.

Strauss, A., & Corbin, J. (1990). *Basics of qualitative research*. Newbury Park, CA: Sage.

The Economist. (2010). The world turned upside down. April 15.

Tushman, M. L., & Nadler, D. A. (1978). Information processing as an integrating concept in organizational design. *Academy of Management Review, 3*, 613–624.

Tushman, M. L., & O'Reilly, C. A. III. (1996). Ambidextrous organizations: Managing evolutionary and revolutionary change. *California Management Review, 38*(4), 8–30.

Van Agtmael, A. (2007). *The emerging markets century*. London: Simon and Schuster UK Ltd.

Webb, E., Campbell, D., Schwartz, R., & Sechrest, L. (1966). *Unobtrusive methods: Non-reactive methods in the social sciences*. Chicago: Rand-McNally.

Westney, E. (1999). Organisational evolution of the multinational enterprise: An organisational sociology perspective. *Management International Review*, *39*(1), 55–75.

Westney, E., & Zaheer, S. (2009). The multinational enterprise as an organization. In: A. M. Rugman (Ed.), *Handbook of International Business* (2nd ed.). Oxford: Oxford University Press.

Yin, R. K. (1994). *Case study research: Design and methods* (2nd ed.). Thousand Oaks, CA: Sage.

Zander, I., & Mathews, J. A. (2006). Beyond heterarchy – Emerging futures of the hypermodern MNC. Paper presented at DRUID Summer Conference, Copenhagen.

Zeng, M., & Williamson, P. J. (2007). *Dragons at your door*. Boston: Harvard Business School Press.

PART III
THE CHANGING ROLE OF
MULTINATIONALS

THE IMPACT OF GLOBALISATION AND THE EMERGENCE OF THE GLOBAL FACTORY

Peter J. Buckley

ABSTRACT

This chapter analyses the rise of the 'global factory' – the globally integrated network centred on a focal multinational enterprise. This is a response to the increased volatility of the global economy and involves the creation of systems that allow flexibility in both the location and the control of increasingly 'fine-sliced' activities, the avoidance of monopoly and the evolution of new management skills. Foreign direct investment is only one strategy amongst several utilised by globally integrated multinationals.

INTRODUCTION

The thesis of this chapter is that foreign direct investment (FDI), once the mainstay and key strategic weapon of multinational enterprises (MNEs), is now in decline.[1] It is being replaced by more flexible, globally integrated networks of the type called here 'the global factory'. This chapter traces the decline of FDI, the fundamental reasons behind its decline and the rationale for the rise of the global factory.

The Future of Foreign Direct Investment and the Multinational Enterprise
Research in Global Strategic Management, Volume 15, 213–249
Copyright © 2011 by Emerald Group Publishing Limited
All rights of reproduction in any form reserved
ISSN: 1064-4857/doi:10.1108/S1064-4857(2011)0000015014

MULTINATIONAL ENTERPRISES IN THE WORLD ECONOMY

Key features of MNE operations in the global economy are

- Uncertainty and market volatility
- Flexibility and the value of options
- Co-operation through joint ventures and business networks
- Entrepreneurship, managerial competence and corporate culture
- Organisational change, including the mandating of subsidiaries and the 'empowerment' of employees

Flexibility may be defined as the ability to reallocate resources quickly and smoothly in response to change. The significance of flexibility is greater, the greater is the amplitude and frequency of change in the environment. As far as MNEs are concerned, the impact of change is captured by the volatility induced in the profit stream. The volatility of profit that would occur if the firm made no response to change summarises the impact on the firm of volatility in its environment.

The international diffusion of modern production technology has increased the number of industrial powers, and hence increased the number of countries in which political and social disturbances can impact significantly on global supplies of manufactured products. The liberalisation of trade and capital markets means that the 'ripple' effects of shock travel farther and wider than before (Casson, 1995, chap. 4). Ripples are transmitted more quickly too: news travels almost instantaneously, thanks to modern telecommunications. Thus speculative bubbles in stock markets spread quickly around the world. Following the breakdown of the Bretton Woods system, exchange rate fluctuations have created a new dimension of financial volatility too.

As a result, any given national market is now affected by a much wider range of disturbances than ever before. Every national subsidiary of an MNE experiences a multiplicity of shocks from around the world. It is no longer the case that a national subsidiary has to respond to shocks originating in its national market alone. The shocks come from new sources of import competition and new competitive threats in export markets too. While most shocks reveal themselves to firms as competitive threats, new opportunities for cooperation may sometimes be presented as well. The awareness of this sustained increase in volatility has led to a search for more flexible forms of organisation.

Increased volatility is not the only reason for greater interest in flexibility. Contemporary culture is very much opposed to building organisations around a single source of monopoly power. The nation state, for example, is under threat from advocates of regional government. The traditional role of the state, to supply defence, can in principle be affected through multilateral defence treaties in which politically independent regions club together for this specific purpose. The demise of the Soviet bloc, and the subsequent political realignment between its member states, may be seen as an example of this kind of cultural change at work. This distrust of monopoly power may be linked to an increase in other forms of distrust, as suggested below.

The aversion to internal monopoly is apparent amongst MNEs as well. This movement began in the early 1980s when the powerful central research laboratories of high-technology MNEs were either closed down, shifted to the divisions, or forced to operate as suppliers to 'internal customers' in competition with outside bodies, such as universities (Casson, Pearce, & Singh, 1991). Headquarters' bureaucracies came under attack shortly afterwards, as 'de-layering' got underway. The favoured form of firm has become a federal structure of operating divisions drawing on a common source of internal expertise, but where each division belonging to the federation is free to out-source expertise if it so desires. As with any trend, there has been a tendency for certain advocates to take it to extremes. Just as the 'golden age' was rife with suggestions that oligopolies of hierarchical MNEs would come to dominate world markets so recent years spawned visions of the 'network firm', the 'virtual firm' and the 'global factory'. A factor common to these visions is a 'fuzzy' boundary of the firm, where the firm fades into the market through joint ventures with declining proportional equity stakes. Fuzzy boundaries can be configured in many different ways. The research agenda outlined in Buckley and Casson (1998) places arguments for fuzzy boundaries on a rigorous basis and predicts the specific form that fuzziness will take in each particular case.

DYNAMIC FOREIGN MARKET ENTRY (AND EXIT)

If we consider the problem of modelling market entry from a dynamic, rather than a static, point of view (Chi & McGuire, 1996), then the most important point to take into account is that the foreign market can decline as well as grow. Divestment or withdrawal must be considered as serious strategies. Clearly, these strategies do not apply until the market has been entered, but once it has been entered they may need to be used. Static models assume that the market will be constant, while very simple dynamic models (such as Buckley & Casson, 1981), only suppose that the market will grow. In a volatile environment, a market may grow to begin with, attracting investment, but then going to decline, requiring divestment instead. Such explicit recognition of adverse scenarios is a characteristic of the new research agenda.

Switching between strategies is costly, and the costs depend on both the strategy the firm is switching from and the strategy the firm is switching to. In some cases, switching costs decompose neatly into a cost of exit from the old strategy and a cost of setting up the new strategy. Detailed modelling of such costs is a key element of the new research agenda.

To preserve flexibility, it is important for the firm to choose at the outset strategies whose exit costs are low. This tends to favour exporting over host-country production and licensing over internalisation. In other words, it reveals FDI as a high-risk strategy. Switching decisions can be mistaken, however, because the information upon which they are based is poor. Expected switching costs are reduced by avoiding unnecessary switches. Different strategies afford different opportunities for capturing information from the host environment and feeding it back to inform subsequent switching decisions.

FDI offers better opportunities for information capture than either licensing or exporting, since ownership of assets confers ownership of information too. This means, for example, that if volatility caused the market to unexpectedly grow, then the foreign investor would recognise this quickly. Since it is often cheaper to expand existing capacity than to build from scratch, the foreign investor also faces lower cost of capacity expansion than does an exporter who decides to switch to foreign production at this stage. While exporting continues to confer more flexibility in response to market decline, therefore, FDI investment confers more flexibility in respect to market growth. Is it possible to find a strategy with a better combination of characteristics than either exporting, licensing or FDI? An international joint venture (IJV) may provide the answer (Kogut, 1991). Investing in a 50:50 partnership with a host-country producer lays off some of the risks associated with wholly owned FDI. At the same time, information capture remains reasonably good. There is an option to expand capacity if there is unexpected market growth, and a further option to increase commitment by buying the partner out. There is also an easy option to withdraw by selling out to the partner. The partner provides a ready market for divested assets than an ordinary direct investor lacks. There is a downside, of course – an obvious problem is that the partners may themselves become a source of volatility. This is why trust is such an important element in an IJV. In this way the emphasis on risk management within the new research agenda leads to the emergence of new 'compromise strategies', which would be dominated by more conventional strategies were it not for the 'option value' they possess within a volatile environment.

IJV options can only be exercised once, of course, unless the investor switches back to an IJV arrangement at a later date, when they can be exercised all over again. This explains IJV instability as a rational response to the role that IJVs fulfil. An IJV in which the options are never exercised is probably inferior to a wholly owned investment, while an IJV in which the options are exercised at the first available opportunity does not last for very long. When IJVs are chosen because of their option value, it is normally inefficient to switch out right away, or to never switch at all. The optimal timing of a switch is one at which uncertainty about future market growth is dispelled for a reasonable period of time. This implies that the duration of IJVs is, on average, fairly short, and relatively variable. This new approach provides a simple means of deriving such hypotheses about the period of time for which a given strategy will be pursued. This argument for flexibility can be extended beyond IJVs. For instance, MNEs often establish 'listening posts'; wholly owned but small investments with built-in capability to expand should conditions dictate growth. Listening posts focus on the collection of (local) strategic information.

INTERACTION BETWEEN NATIONAL MARKETS

The globalisation of markets has been a major factor in the growth of volatility, as explained above. A feature of many global markets is the use of regional production and distribution hubs, where several neighbouring countries are serviced from the same location. The regional hub, like the IJV, can be understood as a strategy that offers superior flexibility. Just as an IJV offers a compromise ownership strategy, a regional hug offers a compromise location strategy. Because the hub is nearer to each market that is the home location, it reduces transport costs, and offers better information capture too. Yet, because it is close to several markets, it avoids exclusive commitment to anyone. If one market declines, production can be switched to other markets instead provided the shocks affecting the national markets are independent (or less than perfectly correlated, at any rate) the hub provides gains from diversification. These are real gains that only the firm can achieve, as opposed to the financial gains from unrelated product diversification, which have proved disappointing in the past because they are best exploited through the diversification of individual share portfolios instead.

The two strategies of IJV and hub can be combined (Fig. 3). Since one (the IJV) is an ownership strategy and the other a location strategy they can, if desired, be combined directly in an IJV production hub. Closer examination of the issues suggests that this is not normally the best approach, however. The model suggests that a combination of a wholly owned production hub supplying IJV distribution facilities in each national market is a better solution. A hub facility is too critical to global strategy to allow a partner to become involved, because the damage they could do is far too great. Even with a wholly owned hub facility, the combination still affords considerable flexibility to divest or withdraw from any single market. The advantage of the combination is that when divesting, the distribution facility can be sold to the partner, while the production capacity can be diverted to markets elsewhere. These options for divestment are combined with useful options for expansion too. This example illustrates the crucial role that the concepts of flexibility and volatility play in analysing foreign market entry in the modern global economy. Without these concepts it is impossible to fully understand the rationale for IJVs and production hubs. It is also impossible to understand why these strategies have emerged at this particular historical juncture and not before.

GLOBAL STRATEGY

In a volatile environment the level of uncertainty is likely to be high. Uncertainty can be reduced, however, by collecting information. Flexibility was defined above in terms of the ability to respond to change. The costs of response tend to be smaller when the period of adjustment is long. One way of 'buying time' to adjust is to forecast change. While no one can foresee the future perfectly, information on the present and the recent past may well improve forecasts by diagnosing underlying long-term trends. Collecting, storing and analysing information therefore enhances flexibility because by improving forecasts, it reduced the costs of change. Another way of buying time is to recognise change as early as possible. In this respect, continuous monitoring of the business environment is better than intermittent monitoring because the potential lag before a change is recognised is eliminated. Continuous monitoring is more expensive than intermittent monitoring, though, because more management time is tied up. Investments in better forecasts and speedier recognition highlight the trade-off between information cost and adjustment cost. This trade-off is particularly crucial when volatility is high. High volatility implies that more information should be collected to improve flexibility, which in turn implies that more managers need to be employed. This is reverse of the usual recommendation to downsize management to reduce overhead costs.

To improve flexibility whilst downsizing management, the trade-off between information cost and adjustment cost must be improved. There are two main ways of doing this. The first is to reduce the cost of information processing through new information technology (IT). The second is to reduce adjustment costs by building flexibility into plant and equipment, both through its design and its location. A combination of IT investment and flexible plant can reconcile greater flexibility with lower management overheads in the manner to which many MNEs aspire.

The information required for strategic decision making is likely to be distributed throughout the organisation. It is no longer reasonable to assume that all the key information can be handled by a single chief executive, or even by the entire headquarters management team. It is difficult to know in advance where the really crucial information is like to be found. Every manager therefore needs to have the competence to process information effectively. Managers need to be able to recognise the significance of strategic information that they acquire by chance and to have the power of access to senior executives in order to pass it on. In other words, ordinary managers need to become internal entrepreneurs.

Few entrepreneurs have sufficient information to make a good decision without consulting other people, however. In a traditional hierarchical firm, the right to consult is the prerogative of top management. If ordinary managers are to have the power to initiate consultation, and act upon the results, then channels of communication within the firm need to be increased. Horizontal communication, as well as vertical communication, must be easy, also that lower level managers can readily consult with their peers.

A natural response is to 'flatten' the organisation and encourage managers to 'network' with each other. This improves the trade-off between local responsiveness and strategic cohesion (Bartlett & Ghoshal, 1987; Hedlund, 1993). Unfortunately, though, there has been some confusion over whether flatter organisations remain hierarchies at all. However, as Casson (1994) shows, the efficient managerial processing of information normally requires a hierarchical structure of some kind. The key point is that the more diverse are the sources of volatility, the greater are the advantages of widespread consultation. The less predictable is the principal source of volatility on any given occasion, the greater is the incentive to allow consultation to be initiated anywhere in the organisation. In practice this means that an increased demand for flexibility is best accommodated by flattening the organisation, whilst maintaining basic elements of hierarchy.

If flexibility were costless, then all organisations could build in unlimited flexibility at the outset. In practice, the greater is flexibility, the higher transactions costs become. For example, the flexibility to switch between different sources of supply and demand (described above) means that relations with customers and suppliers become more transitory than before. Cheating becomes more likely, because the prospect of further transactions between the same two parties is more remote. Direct appeals to the other party's loyalty lose their credibility too.

The same effect occurs when internal entrepreneurship is promoted. Internal entrepreneurs are given more discretion to act upon information that they have collected for themselves, and this increases their opportunity to cheat. Giving managers a direct stake in the business activities they help to build is one solution. The firm incubates new business units in which particular managers, or groups of managers, have equity stakes. An alternative approach is to appeal to the integrity of managers instead. They are treated well, and in return are expected to be open and honest about what they know. Greater flexibility therefore implies greater costs in promoting a corporate culture that reinforces moral values (Buckley & Casson, 2001).

Mass customisation is another important means of reconciling scale and differentiation (efficiency and responsiveness) for example textiles – bespoke garments en masse from offshore sites with rapid delivery. This is associated with 'Lean retailing' where distribution and design centres linked to production centres by electronic means. Electronic ordering and automated distribution centres and inventory management systems linked to customers enable rapid response to customer needs. This combines IT, speed and flexibility with low labour costs. So the custom made versus bulk manufacture divide becomes fine. De-duplication of function becomes possible where electronic links allow single locations to service the whole firm's needs. Rather than a call centre for each division or country, a single one can serve all. There is also a tendency for reintegration of the supply chain from independents back to the major manufactures or in specialist subcontracting firms as e-commerce has matured.

THE DECLINE OF FDI

The traditional MNE was a vertically, as well as horizontally, integrated firm. In consequence, each division of the firm was locked into linkages with other divisions of the same firm. As global competition intensified, there was growing recognition of the costs of integration of this kind. Commitment to a particular source of supply or demand of any product, intermediate good or service is relatively low cost in a high-growth scenario, since it is unlikely that any investment will need to be reversed. It is much more costly in a low-growth scenario, where production may need to be switched to a cheaper source of supply, or sales diverted away from a depressed market. The desire for flexibility therefore discourages vertical integration – whether it is backward integration into production or forward integration into distribution. It is better to subcontract production and to franchise sales instead. The subcontracting of production is similar in principle to a 'putting out' arrangement, but differs in the sense that the subcontractor is now a firm rather than just a single worker.

A network does not have to be built around a single firm, of course. A network may consist of a group of independent firms instead. Sometimes these firms are neighbours, as in the regional industrial clusters described by Best (1990), Porter (1990) and Rugman, D'Cruz and Verbeke (1995). Industrial districts, such as 'Toyota city', have been hailed as an Asian innovation in flexible management, although the practice has been common in Europe for centuries (Marshall, 1919). As tariffs and transport costs have fallen, networks have become more international and 'virtual'. This is demonstrated by the dramatic growth in intermediate product trade under long-term contracts. For example, an international trading company may operate a network of independent suppliers in different countries, substituting different sources of supply in response to both short-term exchange rate movements and long-term shifts in comparative advantage.

By establishing a network of joint ventures covering alternative technological trajectories, the firm can spread its costs whilst retaining a measure of proprietary control over new technologies. The advantage of joint ventures is further reinforced by technological convergence, for example, the integration of computers, telecommunications and photography. This favours the creation of networks of joint ventures based on complementary technologies, rather than on the substitute technologies described above (Cantwell, 1993). Joint ventures are important because they afford a number of real options (Trigeorgis, 1996), which can be taken up or dropped depending on how the project turns out. The early phase of a joint venture provides important information which could not be obtained through investigation before the venture began. It affords an opportunity later on to buy more fully into a successful venture – an opportunity that is not available to those who have not taken any stake. It therefore provides greater flexibility than does either outright ownership or an alternative involving no equity stake. (Buckley, Casson, & Gulamhussen, 2002).

DISINTERMEDIATION AND REINTERMEDIATION

Disintegration was also encouraged by a low-trust atmosphere that developed in many firms. Fear of internal monopoly became rife, as explained above. Production managers faced with falling demand wished that they did not have to sell all their output through a single sales manager. Sales managers resented the fact that had to obtain all their supplies from the same small set of plants. Each manager doubted the competence of the others, and ascribed loss of corporate competitiveness to selfishness and inefficiency elsewhere in the firm. Divisions aspired to be spun off so that they could deal with other business units instead. On the contrary, managers were wary of the risks that would be involved if they severed their links with other divisions altogether. The result is that a much more complex strategy set faces decision makers in multinational firms.

The new value chain is shown in Fig. 1, which illustrates both the impact of 'disintermediation' on the vertically integrated firm and the opportunities for reintermediation. Electronic commerce reduces costs by cutting warehousing costs, improving data exploitation, reducing the necessity to hold stock and diminishing fixed capital requirements. Increased costs arise from the costs of maintaining a reliable web site, logistics and distribution costs (major beneficiaries of e-commerce are delivery firms) and possible reductions in economies of scale and scope.

STRATEGY, E-COMMERCE AND NETWORKS

These changes are challenges for 'old economy' companies including the integration of online functions with existing brand and back office infrastructure. B2B and building online links with suppliers and customers imply the redesign of business processes networks. Smaller companies may find it easier to operate internationally because it is easier to reach

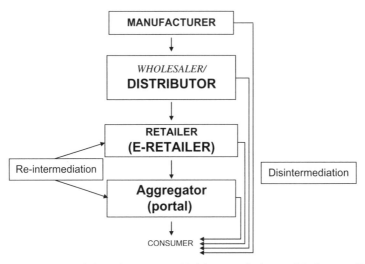

Fig. 1.   New Value Chain: The Impact of Disintermediation and Reintermediation.
Source: Economist e-commerce.

customers, but there are still information problems, logistics and management control. This is not just transport costs, but also regulatory differences between countries, cultural distance, and other factors.

A natural way to cope with these pressures is to allow each division to deal with external business units, as well as internal ones. In terms of internalisation theory, internal markets become 'open' rather than 'closed'. This provides divisional managers with an opportunity to bypass weak or incompetent sections of the company. It also provides a competitive discipline on internal transfer prices, preventing their manipulation for internal political ends, and bringing them more into line with external prices. There are other advantages too. Opening up internal markets severs the link between the capacities operated at adjacent stages of production. The resulting opportunity to supply other firms facilitates the exploitation of scale economies because it permits the capacity of any individual plant to exceed internal demand. Conversely, it encourages the firm to buy in supplies from other firms that have installed capacity in excess of their own needs.

The alignment of internal prices with external prices increases the objectivity of profit measurement at the divisional level. This allows divisional managers to be rewarded by profit-related pay based on divisional profit rather than firm-wide profit. Management may even buy out part of the company. Alternatively the firm may restructure by buying in a part of an independent firm. The net effect is the same in both cases. The firm becomes the hub of a network of inter-locking joint ventures (Buckley, 1988, 1996a). Each joint venture partner is responsible for the day-to-day management of the venture. The headquarters of the firm coordinates the links between the ventures. Internal trade is diverted away from the weaker ventures towards the stronger ones, thereby providing price and profit signals to which the weaker partners need to respond. Unlike a pure external market situation, the partners are able to draw upon expertise at headquarters, which can in turn tap into expertise in other parts of the group.

GLOBAL KNOWLEDGE DIFFUSION

As Buckley and Carter (2002) point out, problems in the global organisation of MNEs are frequently presented as oppositions. Typical are global/local, centralise/decentralise, standardisation versus adaptation, and efficiency versus responsiveness. These issues are not independent of knowledge management. Global/local issues centre on the costs of managing knowledge flows and the combination of general 'company-wide' knowledge and separable, spatially fixed local-specific knowledge. Spatial questions are one part of dealing with knowledge -intensive organisations, but spatial issues are bound up with a whole set of temporal, organisational, strategic and process issues (Buckley & Carter, 2002, p. 46). As Murtha, Lenway, and Bagazzi (1998) show, strategy emerges from mind-sets that are changing over time – global and local issues are capable of synthesis. The role of management knowledge is a crucial and under researched phenomenon of globalisation.

Global management of knowledge does enable the separation of key activities which can be therefore managed in different ways. This has led to strategies of outsourcing, mass customisation and de-duplication of functions which can be spatially separated, bundled and differentiated and consolidated respectively. Murtha, Lenway, and Hart (2001) examine the process of global knowledge creation and dissemination in a fascinating, detailed industry case study of the type that can be replicated and extended.

The goal of a modern sourcing strategy is to obtain the optimum combination of inputs from the variety of opportunities open in the global market. Normally, this will be geographically diverse and the means of procurement will be varied. Thus, both the location factor (where the inputs are acquired) and the internalisation/externalisation choice of means of procurement will vary with circumstances and will change over time. The ability of firms to 'mix and match' their sourcing strategy has been greatly enhanced by the use of the internet for procurement and the increasing use of 'outsourcing' whereby external offers can be compared to internal courses of supply, and the scope of the firm's internal activity adjusted accordingly. These strategies enable increased specialisation and localisation to enhance the division of labour globally and for individual firms to benefit from this in creating a global business network that encompasses many locations for activities with mixed ownership/contracting modes of procurement. The reduced need for co-location locationally diversifies the firm's production base.

Similarly, the market servicing strategy comprises a mix of exporting, licensing/contracting and investment activities, again suggesting a mix of ownership and location strategies in different spatial and temporal circumstances. Here, too, different functions (more housing, distribution, advertising) can be either centrally and globally organised or differentially localised. Ownership too may be fully internal, joint venture/alliance or outsourced.

The interaction of the supply and demand side have yet to be fully studied, but it is safe to assume that large markets exercise a locational pull on inputs, and key input sources encourage local marketing.

MNEs thus seek optimal locations for raw materials, intermediate goods, services 'brain arbitrage' and assembly plants. They also seek entry and exit strategies for markets as they wax and wane over time. This is a suitably complex subject for detailed analysis.

GLOBAL/LOCAL OPERATIONS

There has always been a tension between the pressures to globalise and the need to stay local and to serve individual customers in the strategic decisions of multinational firms. The advantages of global operations are cost based, maximising economies of scale and reducing duplication, thus achieving efficiency. The advantages of localisation are revenue based, allowing differentiation to reach all customer niches and achieving responsiveness. The tension can be summed up in the phrase 'the cost advantages of standardisation versus the revenue advantages of adaptation'.

Much of the strategy of the multinational firm can be explained by the attempts of management to reconcile these pressures (Devinney, Midgley, & Venaik, 2000). Over time, firms (have been advised to) switch their organisation so as to balance these pressures – one example is the 'transnational' type of organisation advocated by (Bartlett & Ghoshal, 1989). However, pressures in different industries push firms towards a strategic imperative (scale in electronics, local demand differences in consumer goods) and different functions require different balances of global/local orientation (finance, production, sales functions). The 'hub and spoke' model below is a key method of attempting to reconcile these conflicts. Cultural differences are of great importance in determining the extent of this balance.

FLEXIBILITY

Flexibility is also needed in R&D. A firm cannot afford to become over-committed to the refinement of any one technology in case innovation elsewhere should render the entire technology obsolete. As technology has diffused in the post-war period, the range of countries with the competence to innovate has significantly increased. The pace of innovation has consequently risen, and the threat of rapid obsolescence is therefore higher as a result. The natural response for firms is to diversify their research portfolios. But the costs of maintaining a range of R&D projects are prohibitive, given the enormous fixed costs involved. The costs of basic R&D have escalated because of the increased range of specialist skills involved, while the costs of applied R&D have risen because of the need to develop global products which meet increasing stringent consumer protection laws. Joint ventures are an appropriate solution once again. By establishing a network of joint ventures covering alternative technological trajectories, the firm can spread its costs whilst retaining a measure of proprietary control over new technologies.

The advantage of joint ventures is further reinforced by technological convergence, for example, the integration of computer, telecommunications and photography. This favours the creation of networks of joint ventures based on complementary technologies, rather than on the substitute technologies described above (Cantwell, 1995).

Joint ventures are important because they afford a number of real options (Trigeorgis, (1996) which can be taken up or dropped depending on how the project turns out. The early phase of a joint venture provides important information that could not be obtained through investigation before the venture began. It affords an opportunity that is not available to those who have not taken any stake. It therefore provides greater flexibility than does either outright ownership or an alternative involving no equity stake.

The desire for flexibility may encourage the firm to produce the same product in several locations so that it can switch production between them as circumstances change. Multiple internal sourcing may therefore be pursued even where some sacrifice of economies of scale is involved. DeMeza and Van Der Ploeg (1987), Capel (1992) and Kogut and Kulatilaka (1994) have all emphasised that firms can switch production between alternative locations in response to real exchange rate shocks. The basic ideas is that MNEs can combine their superior information on foreign cost conditions with their ability, as owners of plants, to plan rather than negotiate output levels, to switch production more quickly than can independent firms.

This strategy requires, however, that the firm should commit in advance to the locations where it believes it will wish to produce. If it is difficult to foresee where the best locations may lie, then flexibility may be enhanced by sub-contracting arrangements instead. Speed of response may be slower, but the range of potential locations is greater. Rangan's (1998) study of production flexibility of manufacturing firms in response to exchange rate changes found that firms did operate flexibly. However the extent of this flexibility was relatively modest and was constrained by past strategies and actions. We can read into this that inertia, possibly from headquarters, was a factor limiting flexibility. Where short-run volatility predominates, multinational integration may well enhance the value of the firm (Allen & Pantzalis, 1996), but long-run volatility may favour the disintegration of the firm instead.

If a firm is seeking flexibility at one stage of production, then it will experience a derived demand for flexibility at adjacent stages of production. This flexibility is conferred by ease of transport to and from all the locations employed at the adjacent stage. Some locations are inherently more flexible in this respect than others, because they are at nodal points on transport networks. They therefore have low transport costs to a wide range of different destinations. For example, if production is dispersed, then warehousing of finished product should be at an appropriate hub. Greater demand for flexibility concentrates demand for warehousing at such hubs – for example, Singapore (for South-East Asia) and Lille (for North-West Europe).

An MNE that is seeking flexibility in its sources of supply will wish to choose a location where government policy is laissez faire, so that there are no import restrictions. It may be seeing flexibility in the range of products if products too. This encourages it to seek out locations with a versatile labour force. Flexibility is also conferred by supplier networks that operate with a high degree of trust. Local production needs to be embedded in an impartial legal system and in strong social networks to ensure that trust is high. An 'invisible infrastructure' of mediating institutions, or equivalently, a large endowment of 'social capital', is therefore a feature of the locations that MNEs committed to flexibility are likely to seek out. Flexibility is not just an element of corporate strategy, but a component of location advantage too. Such location advantage depends crucially on the nature of local institutions and local culture (see Khanna & Palepu, 1999; Ricart, Enright, Ghemawat, Hart, & Khanna, 2004).

Flexibility also has implications for firm-specific competitive advantage. Skill in recruiting imaginative employees becomes a competitive advantage when internal entrepreneurship is required. Charismatic leadership by the chief executive may promote loyalty and integrity amongst key staff. A tradition of informal and consultative management will facilitate the sharing of information amongst employees. One way of expressing this is in terms of the 'capabilities' or 'competencies' of managers, or the human resources controlled by the firm (Richardson, 1960; Loasby, 1999). In a volatile environment where flexibility is crucial, the key resources of the firm are those that promote internal entrepreneurship. The firm consists not of a single autocratic entrepreneur, but a team of entrepreneurs (Wu, 1989) co-ordinated by a leader who promotes high-trust communication between them.

It is worth noting that the need for flexibility does not necessarily support the idea of a 'learning organisation'. To be more exact, flexibility has important implications for what people in a learning organisation actually need to learn. According to Nelson and Winter (1982) learning supports the refinement of existing routines. This is misleading. It suggests that the firm operates in a basically stable environment, and merely learns how to do even better what it already does very well. In a volatile environment, however, much of what has been 'learned' from past experience quickly obsolesces. The truly durable knowledge that needs to be learned in a volatile environment consists of techniques for handling volatility. These techniques include forgetting transitory information about past conditions which are unlikely to recur. But while 'unlearning' or 'forgetting' is important, it is often difficult to do. The difficulty of 'unlearning' helps to explain why so many 'downsizing' and 'de-layering' exercises have identified middle-aged middle managers as targets for redundancy or early retirement. Such people are believed to find it too hard to forget. The 'knowledge' they acquired as junior managers was very relevant during the 'golden age', but has since become obsolete. Some managers have proved sufficiently flexible to be 'retained', but others have not. Those who were too inflexible to benefit from retaining have been required to leave because their 'knowledge' had become a liability instead of an asset in the more volatile situation of today.

HEADQUARTERS AS A SPATIAL MARKET MAKING DECISION TAKER

Fragmentation of the production chain can be accompanied by spatial disaggregation if:

(a) there are technological discontinuities between different stages,
(b) the stages are characterised by different factor intensities, and
(c) the costs of coordination and transport are sufficiently low to make the process economic (Deardorff, 2001).

Each of these elements has a technical, a managerial and a political dimension. Strategies of 'fine-slicing' the production chain have combined with technological change, notably the development of the internet and other communications technologies to allow control at a distance (and without ownership) to become more feasible even for elements of the chain requiring fine control. The opening up of China (and now India) creates access to cheap, well-disciplined labour and the development of logistics practice reduces costs. Products with standard manufacturing interfaces and services with standard processes are ideal for outsourcing. A lack of interaction of the offshored facility with other functions enables a clean interface to be created and a 'fine slicing' cut to be made. Products that should not be outsourced include those where protection of intellectual property is crucial, those with extreme logistics requirements, with high-technology content or performance requirements and those where consumers are highly sensitive to the location of production (Boston Consulting Group, 2004). Issues of corporate responsibility, compliance and adherence to quality standards (especially in view of the 'lead paint in toys' 2007 issue in China) should be added to this list.

THE RISE OF THE GLOBAL FACTORY

The notion of the global factory was introduced in Buckley (2004b) and developed in Buckley and Ghauri (2004) and Buckley (2007, 2009). The basic theory, derived from Buckley and Casson (1976) is that MNEs exploit their intangible knowledge by internalising imperfect international intermediate product markets. The greater the internalisation of such markets across international borders, the more specialisation can occur so that ever finer slices of intangible knowledge can be exploited by the MNE. But now MNEs are becoming much more like differentiated networks. They choose location and ownership policies so as to maximise profits but this does not necessarily involve internalising their activities. Indeed, they have set a trend by outsourcing or offshoring their activities. Outsourcing involves utilising 'buy' rather than 'make' in the Coasean 'externalize or internalize' decision (Coase, 1937). Offshoring involves both the externalisation option together with the 'make abroad' location decision (Buckley & Casson, 1976). MNEs have developed the ability to 'fine slice' their activities on an even more precise calculus and are increasingly able to alter location and internalisation decisions for activities that were previously locationally bound by being tied to other activities and that could only be controlled by internal management fiat.

The development of the global factory has provided new opportunities for new locations to enter international business. Emerging countries such as India and China are subcontracting production and service activities from the brand-owning MNEs. The use of the market by MNEs enables new firms to compete for business against the internalised activities of the MNE. This not only subjects every internalised activity to 'the market test', it also results in a differentiated network (as presented in Fig. 2) which we term 'the global factory'.

The global supply chain is divided into three parts.[2] The Original Equipment Manufacturers (OEMs) control the brand and undertake design, engineering and R&D for the product [although there may be outsourced (see Fig. 2)]. They are customers for contract manufacturers (CMs) who perform manufacturing (and perhaps logistics) services for OEMs. In this so-called modular production network, CMs need to possess capabilities such as mix, product and new product flexibilities while at the same time carrying out manufacturing activities at low costs with mass production processes. Flexibility is necessary to fulfil consumers' product differentiation needs (local requirements) and low cost for global efficiency imperatives (see Wilson & Guzman, 2005). The third part of the chain is warehousing,

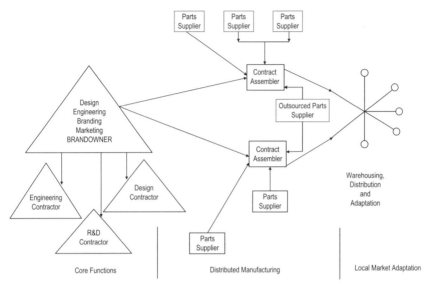

Fig. 2.   Globally Distributed Operations.

distribution and adaptation carried out on a 'hub and spoke' principle to achieve local market adaptation through a mix of ownership and location policies.[3] As Fig. 3 shows, ownership strategies are used to involve local firms with marketing skills and local market intelligence in IJVs whilst location strategies are used to differentiate the wholly owned 'hub' (centrally located) from the jointly owned 'spokes'.

The model analyses a representative MNE that exploits an internationally transferable intangible public good such as knowledge (Buckley & Casson, 1976). It is assumed that this knowledge is embodied in a unique product (or product variety) that is monopolised by the firm usually protected by a brand. Whilst the product has competitors, alternative products are imperfect substitutes (Chamberlin, 1933). The firm therefore faces a downward-sloping demand schedule in each market. The firm defends its intellectual property by internalising the exploitation of this intangible asset. This means that the firm owns its own production facilities – it does not license or subcontract production-and it controls its own marketing – it does not franchise to independent distributors. The firm can, in principle, produce and sell in any part of the world. Any given market may be sourced by local production, or by imports, or a combination of the two. Any

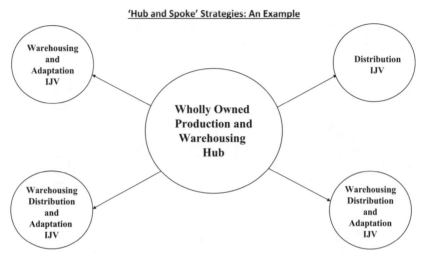

Fig. 3. 'Hub and Spoke' Strategies: An Example.

production plant may serve just the local market, or export markets too; in the limiting case it may become an 'export platform', which produces only for export.

If markets were fully integrated, then MNEs would be obliged to charge the same price for the same product in every country, because if they did not then arbitragers would buy up their product in the cheaper markets and export it to the more expensive ones. Some counties have introduced competition policies to encourage arbitrage of this kind (e.g. Internet retailing of motor car imports). In practice, though, many MNEs retain effective control over the pricing of their products – especially when products are branded, patented, or otherwise unique. It is assumed in this model that whilst the firm's internal market is fully integrated, its home and foreign markets remain sufficiently distinct that it can set a different mark-up on the common internal price in each market.

By contrast, the firm has no power to impose discriminatory process on customers in a given country. It can set different prices in different countries, but must charge the same price to all customers in the same country. This contrasting treatment is designed not to simplify the model but rather to reflect reality. In a typical industry there are normally more customers for the product than suppliers of production sites, and customers are more reluctant to enter into long-term contracts than suppliers. To achieve the same degree of control over a customer that it has over its production site, a firm would normally need to integrate forward through acquisition of its customer's business, which is often completely impractical, and usually uneconomic.

The competitive advantage of interconnected firms (Lavie, 2006) arises from the ability of the focal firm to extract rents from assets that it does not necessarily own. Such assets may be quasi-internalised. This idea can be traced to Penrose's (1959) point that it is not the resources themselves, but the services that they provide, that generate value for the firm (Lavie, 2006, p. 241). Forsgren, Holm, and Johanson (2005) refer to the 'embedded multinational' to reflect the close interconnection between firm and environment.

KEY ELEMENTS OF THE GLOBAL FACTORY

A key attribute of a successful global factory is flexibility. As described above, flexibility is the ability to reallocate resources quickly and smoothly in response to change. This will never be costless, and the costs of flexibility need to be borne in mind (Buckley & Casson, 1998a). Flexibility is a response to increasing volatility arising from globalisation and from opposition to monopoly, including internal monopoly. The idea that global factories avoid internal monopoly, to escape 'hold-up' problems from crucial single activities under-performing, is borne out by the extent of internal (and quasi internal) competition throughout the system leading to dualities and multiplicities of supply sources and to the use of the market to put competitive pressure on internal activities.

A key purpose of flexible structures is to provide resilience. Systems are resilient if they can absorb shocks. Resilient firms can thus survive downturns, crises and panics (like the 'credit crunch' of 2009). In a globalised world, shocks from any part of the global economy are rapidly transmitted around the world (the 'sub-prime' crises of 2008–2009). Competition with the global factory, multiple alternative sources of supply of key inputs, access to many national markets and supply sources, intelligent use of forecasting and internal transfer of knowledge are all sources of built-in resilience of the global factory.

The above review suggests that the manufacturing system of the future will use 'distributed manufacturing' where products are more responsive to customer needs through flexible factories. In flexible factories, all plants within the system can make all the firms' product models and can switch between models very quickly by a combination of software and robots. The global factory will be the very antithesis of 'Any colour as long as it's black'. It will have a single factory design for its distributed global plants and attention to staff training so that replication and perfect substitutability between plants is achieved. Customers will be able to dictate which parts, sub-assemblies or 'add-ons' they require in the final assembly and the distributed manufacturing function will resemble Fig. 3, where production is pushed from the hub into the spoke. Brand owners will control design, engineering and marketing while outsourcing large areas of production to parts suppliers and they may well contract out final assembly. Thus 'built to order' products will be produced close to the final customer. Globalisation implies location near the customer, not a single large-scale plant. It is the high fixed costs of existing factories that compel manufacturers to achieve large scale production, and a reduction of fixed costs means that production can be more easily tailored to final demand.

Two simple illustrations can be given of the power of the global factory to use location and ownership decisions to create a complex, but efficient, response to global economic conditions – and to respond to changes in those conditions. First, a complex offshoring and outsourcing strategy can reduce location and transaction costs. An offshoring decision takes place where (in this example) early stages of processing are relocated to a lower-cost foreign country. Intermediate inputs are exported to this foreign-located facility and serve finished goods transported from it. Local inputs are supplied to the offshore unit thus providing linkage and spillover effects to the local economy (Buckley, Clegg, & Wang, 2002, 2004, 2006, 2007a, 2007b). This *location* decision can be combined with an *ownership/internalisation* decision because the offshore plant can be 'captive' (owned, internalised) or non-captive-controlled through the market by contract. If we envisage the full panoply of such decisions in a global factory, we can see the complexity, sophistication and difficulty of these ever-changing strategies in a volatile world economy.

Multinational firms have to reconcile pressures to be globally efficient with the need to be locally responsive. The efficiency imperative dictates standardisation, economies of scale and uniformity of product and process. The localisation motive mandates adaptation, differentiation and close liaison with customers. Those pressures have to be accommodated and the global factory is the ideal structure with which to do so. A mixed 'glocal' strategy can steer an optimal path between rigid standardisation versus differentiation strategies as in the example of marketing shown in Fig. 3 as a 'hub and spoke' strategy across an economic space. The 'glocal' strategy seeks the best compromise for each element of the marketing strategy as the balance of global and local pressures dictates across different national markets. This glocalised strategy is well suited to being combined with the 'fine-slicing' of activities across the complex set of processes in the whole network of the global factory.

The global factory is, of course, a network (Buckley, 2004b). It is a network held together by control of key assets and flows of knowledge and intermediate products (Buckley, 2007). Networks, like any other form of organisation have both benefits and costs (the latter are often ignored). Global factories are both horizontal and vertical networks. The benefits of the horizontal network arise from learning and the diffusion of knowledge. The benefits of the vertical network arise from the coordination of activities. However, the horizontal network runs the risk of collusion on price whilst vertical integration can be used as a barrier to entry. The degree to which benefits outweigh costs depends on the extent to which the global factory's networks are open and transparent versus being closed and opaque. Public policy towards global factories needs to concentrate on the degree of openness and transparency. Competition policy in particular should be addressed to these ends.

TRANSACTION COSTS MINIMISING CONFIGURATIONS IN THE FIRM

Transaction costs exist in assembling the business processes of firms – collections of activities that are technologically or managerially linked so that they jointly affect value added. The overall costs of organisation are determined by losses due to the imperfect motivation of process members (which result, in part at least, from the incentive structure) and imperfect information and coordination which flow from the architecture of the firm (the allocation of responsibilities amongst individuals and groups and communication between them), together with the resource costs associated with incentives and architecture (Buckley & Carter, 1996). Thus transactional links within the firm enable us to split up the 'black box' and trace costs and benefits of combining activities within intra-firm processes. Furthermore, it is possible to specify losses from imperfections in motivation, information and coordination and to balance these against the costs necessary to correct these imperfections.

Views about the nature of human behaviour and actions will influence how an outsider might feel about the likelihood of these costs being significant; for example, motivation loss (and the cost of correcting it) will be greater, the greater is the degree of opportunism ('self-seeking with guile'). However, if we believe that individuals naturally seek and appreciate teamworking, then motivation costs will be low.

Buckley and Casson (1988) applied internalisation theory to IJVs. IJVs are conceptualised as arising from three key factors: internalisation economies in one or more intermediate goods markets, indivisibilities and barriers to merger. Under certain environmental conditions, IJVs can be an optimal organisational solution (Buckley & Casson, 1996). In joint ventures, mutual trust can be a substitute for expensive legalism. Joint ventures provide an ideal institution for the exercise of mutual forbearance, leading to a commitment to cooperation and to the creation of reputation effects where a reputation for cooperative behaviour can lead to further coordination benefits. These effects can be good substitutes for ownership. Skills in joint venturing and the learning effects that arise can lead to a widespread for non-ownership forms of cooperation as in many global factories.

NEW MANAGEMENT SKILLS

The rise of the global factory has been paralleled by the growth of new management skills. These include the ability of managers to 'fine-slice' activities – to cut the constituent elements of processes into finer and finer slivers. The virtue of this strategy is that is allows each element to be optimally located and controlled. The advantages of the choice of location and the choice of mode of governance can then be forensically applied to each component of the global factory by management.

Together with fine-slicing goes control of information. The information structure of the global factory is a major source of its strength, allowing information to be obtained and to be disseminated to those decision takers best placed to use it. It is the control of this complex flow of information on external conditions and internal competences that is far more important than control of physical assets, the use of which can be increasingly outsourced. The general adage that 'you don't have to own something to control it' applies increasingly to physical assets but emphatically not to intangible assets such as brands and to knowledge.

The use of increasingly complex structures involving both internalised and externalised activities requires that externalised activities be carefully monitored (for quality control reasons for example) and integrated with those activities under the ownership of the global factory. 'Interface competence' – the ability to coordinate external organisations into the strategy of the focal firm, to liaise with external bodies and governments and to cohere these activities into a grand strategy – are at the heart of the skills necessary to organise a successful global factory. This has implications for the style of management that is needed. A new, more subtle cooperative mode of operation is increasingly necessary. Management needs to be 'hard nosed' in requiring adherence to targets (on quality and reliability) but in managing outside the boundaries of the firm, with subcontractors and alliance partners, skills beyond 'command and control' are vital.

Although complex in detail, the key analytical decisions in the global factory are very simple – control and location. The manager of the global factory has to ask two very straightforward questions of each activity in the global network. Where should this activity be located? How should this activity be controlled?

The first question of the optimum location for each activity is of course complicated by managing the interrelationships between activities. The relocation of one piece of the global network will have profound effects on many others as the links in Fig. 1 illustrate but the principles of least cost location are paramount.

The second question concerns the means of control. Should the activity be managed by the market via a contract and price relationship or should it be internalised and controlled by management? There are of course important mixed methods such as joint ventures that have elements of market relationships and elements of management fiat.

It is of course essential to realise that these decisions are taken in a volatile, risky and dynamic situation, that the decision-making process is information intensive, and the environment and competitive pressures are constantly changing. These decisions have to be revisited on a continuing basis. However the principles should never be overwhelmed by detail. As this book goes on to show, the need for flexibility, for judicious collection and use of information and for a knowledge management strategy and complements to the key decisions of location and control.

THE FUTURE GLOBALISED, DISTRIBUTED FIRM

Outsourcing and Logistics

Many input functions are now viably outsourced – even human resources departments and procurement. Digital delivery of product is analogous on the output side. The danger is the loss of core competencies (outsourcing IT 'loses part of company's brain'). This development contributes to volatility and increases the mobility of activities internationally, as a great deal of outsourcing functions are competed for on a global basis. The policy of promoting linkages (forward as well as backward) followed by many agencies of national and local government needs to account for these changing decision-making parameters.

As is always the case, disintegration of established supply chains is followed by reintegration and consolidation. The trend to outsource (disinternalise) manufacturing by major multinationals led initially to subcontracting to independents – many of them located in South East Asia (and Mexico). Contract manufacturing has been growing by 20% per year in the late 90 s and early part of this century. However, CMs are rapidly consolidating, through mergers, and are expected to reach an oligopolistic equilibrium, with around six firms dominating the global market. These firms are becoming supply chain managers, sometimes even organising distribution and repair. These links between customers and suppliers are, of course, facilitated by the use of the Internet. CMs, ensured of future contracts are thus able to achieve economies of scale and to become more capital intensive, replacing unskilled labour by high-tech capital equipment. This trend is accelerated by the competitive imperative becoming speed to market, not cost. A linked supply of available factories in different national locations means that the CMs can switch production lines between these units. Flexibility is achieved by moving these 'shell' factories between principals – entire production lines can be flown in from another location.

Vertical disintegration is thus accompanied by specialisation. The principal concentrates on R&D, design and marketing, while the CM provides a service to the global supplier. Companies with a strong manufacturing culture, and a commitment to a fixed location, may be out competed by more agile 'virtual' firms owning no manufacturing facilities at all.

Coordination

Integration does not equal coordination. Classically, coordination is defined 'as effecting a Pareto-improvement in the allocation of resources such that someone is made better off, and no-one worse off than they would otherwise be' (Buckley & Casson, 1988, p. 32). Despite the fact that coordination sounds as it is always a good thing, there are exceptions.

These are (1) externalities; (2) coordination under duress; (3) empty threats and disappointments; (4) autonomy of preferences.

The first issue refers to people outside the bargain, who may suffer. In the case of the global factory, these may be other organisations that are not part of the network who may lose by being frozen out. Second, where excessive bargaining power or other forms of coercion are used, the beneficial effects of coordination may not appear. Third, expectations may be erroneous on the part of some parties to the bargain or information may be distorted. Finally, the objectives of the parties may change after the bargain by involvement in the global factory. These new objectives may not be satisfied (see Buckley & Casson, 1988, for a fuller exposition in the context of joint ventures).

The externality problem extends to the impact of the global factory beyond the parties involved in being coordinated within the system (suppliers, subcontractors and so on). Those firms and agencies that are not part of a global factory may find themselves excluded from the ability to trade. They may thus be coerced into joining another such network. The control of information within global factories may result in distorted, even coercive, bargains with weaker parties. Entry into global factory system may mean that (new) preferences are not realised.

The presumption that coordination leads to higher welfare for all concerned thus needs to be challenged. However, when examining the myriad of arrangements that lead to the existence and expansion of global factories, coordination of activities in this way leads to many Pareto-improvements that increase world welfare. The analytical challenge is to examine the balance between these beneficial coordinating acts and the negative fallout for those excluded and the negative impact of coercive and damaging arrangements.

THE GLOBAL FACTORY AS A PLANNING UNIT

'The concept of the firm...does not depend on the ramifications of stock ownership or on the mere existence of the power to control, although extensive stock ownership may, and probably should, be on important consideration in any attempt to apply it. On the other hand, long term contracts, leases, and patent licence agreements may give an equally effective control' (Penrose, 1959, pp. 20–21). The true nature of the firm is not a legal entity but as a planning unit (Blois, 1972). The global factory is a system under which effective managerial planning extends across the whole network.

Unfortunately, the extent to this planning system is not evident in either published accounts, which follow legal definitions, or macro-data, which aggregate by artificial industry categories. An important future task is to ensure that data follow reality so that the extent and power of global factories across the international economy can be adequately demonstrated. The quasi-integration of activities within global factories as exemplified by the unitary planning system is often more powerful than the legal or accounting rules that define 'the firm'.

LOCAL VERSUS GLOBAL FACTORS

This leads to Porter's (1998) 'globalisation paradox'. Easier movement of goods, people and capital has increased the importance of *local* advantages and where these are hard to copy this has promoted the geographic concentration of economic activity in 'clusters'. Global factories are increasingly well informed, because of their information system, about the existence of clusters and increasingly base their investment location decisions on this intelligence (Enright, 1998, 2000). This can be reinforced by the argument that many firms – and global factories – are influenced by their home environment (Sorge, 2005). This is also true of emerging country global factories who respond to market imperfections in their home economy. For instance, Chinese outward direct investors have access to capital at favourable rates and this influences their internationalisation strategies (Buckley et al., 2007).

In the network structure embodied in the global factory, it is important not to conflate nodes with country. The importance of cities as nodes is increasingly being recognised with cities competing to attract particularly the high value components of the global factory.

INTEGRATION VERSUS RESPONSIVENESS

The conflicting power relationships and the mixed allegiances of individuals to their nation and their employer provide much of the background to the political economy of the global factory. Hymer (1970) examined the integration – responsiveness trade-off ('an organisation structure to balance the need to coordinate and integrate operations with the need to adapt to a patchwork quilt of languages, laws and customs', p. 48). However, Hymer saw this entirely in terms of nationality. Thus the national subsidiary of an MNE was managed by local nationals and the hierarchy was primarily a national one with the United States as hegemon. Hymer's analysis (1970) led to a geographical analysis based on uneven development at the national level (Hymer, 1971). The spatial division of labour (Hymer, 1971) within the corporation was mirrored by nation states. The cross-cutting of national frontiers and hierarchies by multinational firms was not a feature of Hymer's analysis but the spatial distribution that is the result of global factories cross-cuts national frontiers and national groups and classes.

THE MANAGEMENT OF THE GLOBAL FACTORY

The dynamics of the global factory are a response to the modern global economy. Shocks are the norm. Failure is the norm. Only companies that can build resilience into their systems and their management systems will be able to survive more than one economic cycle. The global factory is rarely in equilibrium – it is constantly responding to exogenous shocks through a series of feedback loops (Buckley & Casson, 1998).

Management is a social technology and so it is subject not only to technological advancement in such issues as communications advances but it is also subject to changes in social conditions. This gives rise to differences in management techniques over time and over space, to psychic distance and to cultural differences and attitudes.

On one level, the goal of MNEs and global factories is to create the flat world beloved of Thomas Friedman (Friedman, 2005). The external world in which global factories operate is decidedly spiky. It is riven with differences in taxes, tariffs, governmental regulations, market imperfections and profound cultural differences across countries and classes. Within the global factory however, the goal is to create a flat world by means of a frictionless operating system.

William Egelhoff (2007) identified four tasks where 'hierarchical structures with a corporate HQ are superior to network structures in providing the necessary coordination' (p. 2).

1. Accountability to shareholders.
2. Designing and implementing tight synchronisation among subsidiaries.
3. Identifying and implementing economies of scale and scope.
4. Identifying and addressing issues involving significant innovation.

The global factory structure achieves these objectives by combining central control with network systems.

Key interfaces in the global factory are between the core activities of the brand owner (△) and the distributed manufacturing and service centres (...) and between the latter and the distribution functions of warehousing, distribution and adaptation (○). Secondary interfaces are between out-sourced core functions (including possibly design, engineering and R&D), between first tier assemblers and parts suppliers and the interface with logistics, transport and distribution contractors.

THE POWER OF THE GLOBAL FACTORY

What then gives the global factory its power? Why should the global factory be able to hire the contract manufactures, sales outlets, design houses, logistics companies, advertising consultants and research laboratories rather than the other way round? How can global factories exercise this power without ownership?

The answer, as always, is a combination of factors. These factors are entrepreneurship, control and selection of information, finance and innovation. They are combined within the enabling institutions of the home country which nurture and foster the exercise of entrepreneurship and encourage risk taking and experimentation. This may be also considered as 'second order entrepreneurship', which allows units within the global factor to exercise their abilities to take entrepreneurial decisions.

One such crucial factor is the role of finance. Access to capital markets is a crucial advantage for (the Headquarters of) global factories (Buckley & Casson, 1976, p. 33). Internal capital markets became less important as access to (more perfect) external markets improves. Thus global factories headquartered in home countries with more perfect finance markets can generate much better leverage than can say a Chinese manufacturer (Aulakh & Mudambi, 2005; Buckley et al., 2007). The external capital market also impinges more strongly on global factories in advanced countries. Until recently the share register of major companies rarely moved. Now (2008) hedge funds, private equity investors and Sovereign Wealth Funds move in and out of ownership of leading companies on a regular basis. This discipline of the market impels better operational management.

The power of the global factory arises not only from its brand and its control of information and finance but also to its decision making skill (entrepreneurship) and its dynamic which derives from R&D in all senses – technical, marketing and process innovation. To be long lasting, brands have to receive constant reinvestment. Quality has to be maintained and improved. Advertising promotion and distribution need to be coordinated so as to reinforce the brand. This process of entrepreneurial direction is referred to by Hymer (1968) as 'encephalisation' – putting a brain on the firm. The brain may be a distributed one – not all its functions will be located at Headquarters. There may well be a transfer over time of brain functions from Headquarters to foreign units. There remains, however, a sense of overall control of the global factory centrally even if not all its activities are owned – 'You don't have to own a facility to control it'.

Control without ownership has been identified as a key feature of modern capitalism by amongst others Nolan, Sutherland, and Zhang (2002), Strange and Newton (2006) and Yamin and Ghauri (2007). Nolan et al. point out the control exercised by 'systems integrators' over first tier suppliers and the extent to which being part of a global factory involves the sacrifice of independence in, for example, production planning, design, R&D and delivery.

There is also severe competition within the global factory. Individual units are often set up to compete for contracts or for resources. Pedersen and Petersen (2007) identify 'centres of excellence' as winners and pure sales subsidiaries as losers. Hatani (2007) highlights the extreme competition within the Toyota global factory. This strengthens the hand of Headquarters and transmits market pressure as well as a 'tournament' philosophy to subsidiary units.

Dynamics: Contracting Costs and Entrepreneurship

Why do entrepreneurs hire assets rather than asset owners hire entrepreneurs? The answer lies in non-contractibility. The key function of the entrepreneur is to exercise judgement in the face of uncertainty (Knight, 1921; Casson, 1982). Incomplete contracts have a positive effect on the exercise of entrepreneurship – they allow sequential adaptation to changing circumstances in an uncertain world. The firm is thus the agency by which the entrepreneur (whose services are the most difficult to measure or evaluate) combines his assets (judgement) with physical assets. The firm enables previously segmented areas of judgement and skills to be blended together and thus individual entrepreneurship becomes collective organisation. Individuals with entrepreneurial judgement can thus coalesce within the organisation and combine their skills. Because of the non-contractibility (or rather the extremely high costs of contracting) of these skills, this coalition becomes embedded in the firm, thus giving a transactions cost rationale for 'competencies' residing for a finite period of time in certain companies. 'Sticky capabilities' thus emerge.

CONCLUDING REMARKS

Yair Aharoni wrote an enduring classic in his book 'The Foreign Investment Decision Process' in 1966. That book examined the first foreign investment decision taken by (mostly) smaller firms. Such firms are a long distance away in time, experience and global reach from today's global factories. However, several features remain important from 1966 to 2011. These include – the importance of information, the role of uncertainty, the skill, scope and honesty of management and the enduring importance of national borders.

This chapter has shown that control of information is still critical to global factories. It is now much more easily accessible (through the internet) than it was in 1966, but it needs to be collated, sifted and graded, and, most importantly, to be directed to the support of key decisions – just as the smaller firms in 1966 faced an information barrier, so global factories face the need to control and direct information.

Small firms facing a first FDI in 1966 were often deterred, as Aharoni shows, by radical uncertainty. The volatility of the 21st century economy still constrains the strategy of global factories causing them to adopt real options positions such as joint ventures or listening posts in particular uncertain environments. Political risk in 2011, like 1966, is cited as a major deterrent to commitments in politically risky countries.

Management skill and availability is just as critical as in earlier times. Global factories wage a war to attract, retain and enthuse managers. The need to extend the management team to cope with the widening demands of global operations. Shortages of managerial talent and the diffusion of their time (and attention span) across many arenas means that mistakes are still made of the types referred to in Aharoni's 1966 work where shortage of managerial time led to incorrect decisions.

Moving across national borders was a major challenge for Aharoni's sample of firms in 1966. It is perhaps too much to say that this remains equally critical for a global factory operating in over a hundred countries, but this piece has shown that national borders remain significant. These borders are often cultural frontiers and play their role in ensuring that local factors remain significant in balancing global similarities.

However, the global economy has seen significant restructuring in particular over the past 15 years. MNEs have ceased to become monolithic and are instead networks integrated across the world. The rise of these global factories is the result of location reconfiguration and control reconfiguration on a global scale.

Locational reconfiguration is easily observable. The transfer of mass production to China and mass service operations to India are merely the tip of the iceberg of smaller scale but highly significant transfers of activities as global factories search for least-cost locations for each of their activities.

Control reconfiguration results from a radical and ongoing reappraisal of the internalisation benefits of FDI versus the cost advantages of out-sourcing. Firms are able to fine-slice activities even down to the level of individual tasks so that 'out-tasking' is now feasible. This not only makes external provision feasible, it immediately puts market pressure on all the activities that the firm carries out internally.

NOTES

1. This chapter draws heavily on my earlier work, notably Buckley (2007, 2009) and joint work with Mark Casson (Buckley, & Casson, 1998), Martin Carter (Buckley & Carter, 1996, 2002) and Pervez Ghauri (Buckley & Ghauri, 2004).

2. The literature on global commodity chains, latterly 'global value chains', has much in common with the analysis of the global factory and has much to offer in furthering the research agenda (Kaplinsky, 2001, 2004; Gereffi, 1999, 2001; Kaplinsky, Memedovic, Morris, & Readman, 2003; Gereffi & Memedovic, 2003; Barnes, Kaplinsky, & Morris, 2004: Gereffi, Humphrey, & Sturgeon, 2005).

3. Much of the work on first 'commodity chains' then 'value chains' is strongly empirically based and provides a well thought out research programme, as exemplified by 'A Handbook for Value Chain Research' (Kaplinsky & Morris, 2001). This research programme has gone beyond the original distinction between 'producer driven' and 'buyer driven' chains (Gereffi, 2001; Bair, 2005).

REFERENCES

Allen, L., & Pantzalis, C. (1996). Valuation of the operating flexibility of multinational corporations. *Journal of International Business Studies*, *27*(4), 633–653.

Aulakh, P. S., & Mudambi, R. (2005). Financial resource flows in multinational enterprises: The role of external capital markets. *Management International Review*, *45*(3), 307–325.

Bair, J. (2005). From commodity chains to value chains and back again? Mimeo, Yale University Department of Sociology.

Barnes, J., Kaplinsky, R., & Morris, M. (2004). Industrial policy in developing economies: Developing dynamic comparative advantage in the South African automobile sector. *Competition and Change*, *8*(2), 153–172.

Bartlett, C. A., & Ghoshal, S. (1987). Managing across borders: New strategic requirements. *Sloan Management Review*, Summer, 6–17.

Bartlett, C. A., & Ghoshal, S. (1989). *Managing across borders: The transnational solution*. Boston, MA: Hutchinson Business Books.

Best, M. H. (1990). *The new competition: Institutions of industrial restructuring*. Oxford: Polity Press.

Blois, K. J. (1972). Vertical quasi-integration. *Journal of Industrial Economics*, *20*, 253–272.

Boston Consulting Group. (2004). *Capturing global advantage*. Boston, MA: Boston Consulting Group.

Buckley, P. J. (1996a). The role of management in international business theory. *Management International Review*, *35*(1.1, Special Issue), 7–54.

Buckley, P. J. (1988). The limits of explanation: Testing the internalisation theory of the multinational enterprise. *Journal of International Business Studies*, *19*(2, Summer), 181–193.

Buckley, P. J. (2004b). Cartography and international business. *International Business Review*, *13*(2), 239–255.

Buckley, P. J. (2007). The strategy of multinational enterprises in the light of the rise of China. *Scandinavian Journal of Management*, *23*(2), 107–126.

Buckley, P. J. (2009). The impact of the global factory on economic development. *Journal of World Business*, *44*(2), 131–143.

Buckley, P. J., & Carter, M. C. (1996). The economics of business process design. *International Journal of the Economics of Business*, *3*(1), 5–25.

Buckley, P. J., & Carter, M. (2002). Process and structure in knowledge management practices of British and US multinational enterprises. *Journal of International Management*, *8*(1), 29–48.

Buckley, P. J., & Casson, M. C. (1976). *The future of the multinational enterprise*. London: Macmillan.

Buckley, P. J., & Casson, M. C. (1981). The optimal timing of a foreign direct investment. *Economic Journal*, *92*(361), 75–87.

Buckley, P. J., & Casson, M. C. (1988). A theory of cooperation in international business. In: F.J. Contractor, et al. (Eds), *Co-operative strategies in international business*. Lexington: Lexington Books.

Buckley, P. J., & Casson, M. (1996). An economic model of international joint ventures. *Journal of International Business Studies*, *27*(5), 849–876.

Buckley, P. J., & Casson, M. (1998a). Analysing foreign market entry strategies: Extending the internalisation approach (co-author Mark Casson). *Journal of International Business Studies*, *29*(3), 539–561.

Buckley, P. J., & Casson, M. (1998). Models of the multinational enterprise. *Journal of International Business Studies*, *29*(1), 21–44.

Buckley, P. J., & Casson, M. (2001). The moral basis of global capitalism: Beyond the eclectic theory. *International Journal of the Economics of Business*, *8*(2), 303–327.

Buckley, P. J., Casson, M. C., & Gulamhussen, M. A. (2002). Internationalisation-real options, knowledge management and the Uppsala approach. In: V. Havila, M. Forsgren & H. Hakansson (Eds), *Critical perspectives on internationalisation*. Oxford: Elsevier.

Buckley, P. J., Clegg, J., Cross, A., Zheng, P., Voss, H., & Liu, X. (2007). The determinants of Chinese outward foreign direct investment. *Journal of International Business Studies, 38*(4), 499–518.

Buckley, P. J., Clegg, J., & Wang, C. (2002). The impact of inward FDI on the performance of Chinese manufacturing firms. *Journal of International Business Studies, 33*(4), 637–655.

Buckley, P. J., Clegg, J., & Wang, C. (2004). The relationship between inward foreign direct investment and the performance of domestically-owned Chinese manufacturing industry. *Multinational Business Review, 12*(3), 23–40.

Buckley, P. J., Clegg, J., & Wang, C. (2006). Inward foreign direct investment and host country productivity: Evidence from China's electronics industry. *Transnational Corporations, 15*(1), 13–37(Special Issue in honour of V. N. Balasubramanyam edited by Peter J. Buckley.).

Buckley, P. J., Clegg, J., & Wang, C. (2007a). Is the relationship between inward FDI and spillover effects linear? An empirical examination of the case of China. *Journal of International Business Studies, 38*(3), 447–459.

Buckley, P. J., Clegg, J., & Wang, C. (2007b). The impact of foreign ownership, local ownership and industry characteristics on spillover benefits from foreign direct investment in China. *International Business Review, 16*(2), 142–158.

Buckley, P. J., & Ghauri, P. N. (2004). Globalisation, economic geography and the strategy of multinational enterprises. *Journal of International Business Studies, 35*(2), 81–98.

Cantwell, J. A. (1993). The internationalisation of technological activity and its implication for competitiveness. In: O. Grandstand, H. Hakanson & S. Sjolander (Eds), *Technological management and international business*. Chichester: Wiley.

Cantwell, J. (Ed.) (1995). *Multinational enterprises and innovatory activities: Towards a new evolutionary approach*. Chur: Harwood Academic Publishers.

Capel, J. (1992). How to service a foreign market under uncertainty: A real option approach. *European Journal of Political Economy, 8*, 455–475.

Casson, M. (1982). *The entrepreneur*. Oxford: Martin Robertson.

Casson, M. C. (1994). Why are firms hierarchical? *International Journal of the Economics of Business, 1*(1), 3–40.

Casson, M. C. (1995). *Organization of international business*. Aldershot: Edward Elgar.

Casson, M., Pearce, R. D., & Singh, S. (1991). A review of recent trends. In: M. Casson (Ed.), *Global research strategy and international competitiveness*. Oxford: Blackwell.

Chamberlin, E. H. (1933). *The theory of monopolistic competition: A reorientation of the theory of value*. Cambridge, MA: Harvard University Press.

Chi, T., & McGuire, D. J. (1996). Collaborative ventures and value of learning: Integrating the transaction cost and strategic option perspectives on the choice of market entry modes. *Journal of International Business Studies, 27*(2), 285–307.

Coase, R. H. (1937). The nature of the firm. *Economica, 4*, 386–405.

Deardorff, A. (2001). Fragmentation across cones. In: S. Ardnt & H. Kierzkowski (Eds), *Fragmentation: New production patterns in the world economy*. Oxford: Oxford University Press.

DeMeza, D., & Van Der Ploeg, F. (1987). Production flexibility as a motive for multi-nationality. *Journal of Industrial Economics, 35*(3), 343–351.

Devinney, T., Midgley, D., & Venaik, S. (2000). The optimal performance of the global firm: Formalising and extending the integration: Responsiveness framework. *Organization Science, 11*(6), 674–695.

Egelhoff, W. G. (2007). Evaluating the role of parent headquarters in a contemporary MNC. Headquarters role in the contemporary MNC. Workshop, Uppsala University, 14th–15th September.

Enright, M. J. (1998). Regional clusters and firm strategy. In: A. Chandler, et al. (Eds), *The dynamic firm: The role of technology, strategy, organization and regions.* Oxford: Oxford University Press.

Enright, M. J. (2000). The globalization of competition and the localization of competitive advantage: policies towards regional clustering. In: N. Hood, et al. (Eds), *The globalization of multinational enterprise activity and economic development.* London: Macmillan.

Forsgren, M., Holm, V., & Johanson, J. (2005). *Managing the embedded multinational – A business network view.* Cheltenham: Edward Elgar.

Friedman, T. (2005). The world is flat: A brief history of the twenty-first century, Farrar, Straus & Giroux.

Gereffi, G. (1999). International trade and upgrading in the apparel commodity chain. *Journal of International Economics, 48,* 37–70.

Gereffi, G. (2001). Beyond the producer driven/buyer driven dichotomy. *IDS Bulletin, 32*(2), 30–40.

Gereffi, G., & Memedovic, O. (2003). *The global apparel value chain: What prospects for upgrading by developing countries?* Vienna: UNIDO.

Gereffi, G., Humphrey, J., & Sturgeon, T. (2005). The governance of global value chains. *Review of International Political Economy, 12*(1), 78–104.

Hatani, F. (2007). Managing network evolution in global competition. In the Academy of International Business (AIB) Conference, Indianapolis, USA.

Hedlund, G. (1993). Assumptions of hierarchy and heterarchy: An application to the multinational corporation. In: S. Ghoshal & E. Westney (Eds), *Organization theory and the multinational corporation.* London: Macmillan.

Hymer, S. H. (1968). The multinational corporation: An analysis of some motives for international business integration. *Revue Economique, XIX*(6), 949–973.

Hymer, S. (1970). The efficiency (contradictions) of multinational corporations. *American Economic Review, 60*(2), 441–448.

Hymer, S. H. (1971). The multinational corporation and the law of uneven development. In: J. Bhagwati (Ed.), *Economics and World Order.* New York: World Law Fund.

Kaplinsky, R. (2001). Is globalization all it is cracked up to be?. *Review of International Political Economy, 8*(1), 45–65.

Kaplinsky, R. (2004). Spreading the gains from globalization? What can be learned from value-chain analysis? *Problems of Economic Transition, 47*(2), 74–115.

Kaplinsky, R., Memedovic, O., Morris, M., & Readman, J. (2003). *The global wood furniture value chain: What prospects for upgrading by developing countries? The case of South Africa.* Vienna: UNIDO.

Kaplinsky, R., & Morris, M. (2001). *A handbook for value chain research.* Brighton: University of Sussex Institute for Development Studies.

Khanna, T., & Palepu, K. (1999). Policy shocks, market intermediaries, and corporate strategy: Evidence from Chile and India. *Journal of Economics and Management Strategy, 8*(2), 271–310.

Knight, F. (1921). *Risk, Uncertainty and Profit* (G. J. Stigler, Ed.). Chicago: University of Chicago Press (1971).

Kogut, B. (1991). Joint ventures and the option to expand and acquire. *Management Science*, *37*(1), 19–33.

Kogut, B., & Kulatilaka, N. (1994). Operating flexibility, global manufacturing and the option value of a multinational network. *Management Science*, *40*(1), 123–139.

Lavie, D. (2006). The competitive advantage of interconnected firms: An extension of the resource-based view. *Academy of Management Review*, *31*(3), 638–658.

Loasby, B. J. (1999). *Knowledge institutions and evolution in economics*. London: Routledge.

Marshall, A. (1919). *Industry and trade*. London: Macmillan.

Murtha, T. P., Lenway, S. A., & Bagazzi, R. P. (1998). Global mind-sets and cognitive shift in a complex multinational corporation. *Strategic Management Journal*, *19*, 97–114.

Murtha, T. P., Lenway, S. A., & Hart, J. A. (2001). *Managing new industry creation*. Palo Alto, CA: Stanford University Press.

Nelson, R. R., & Winter, S. (1982). *An evolutionary theory of economic change*. Cambridge, MA: Harvard University Press.

Nolan, P., Sutherland, D., & Zhang, J. (2002). The challenge of the global business revolution. *Contributions to Political Economy*, *21*, 91–110.

Pedersen, T., & Petersen, B. (2007). Headquarters role in the MNC globalisation process. Headquarters role in the contemporary MNE. Workshop Uppsala University, 14th–15th September.

Penrose, E. (1959). *Theory of the growth of the firm*. Oxford: Blackwell.

Porter, M. E. (1990). *The competitive advantage of nationals*. New York: Free Press.

Porter, M. E. (1998). Clusters and the new economics of competition. *Harvard Business Review*, *76*, 77–90.

Rangan, S. (1998). Do multinationals operate flexibly? Theory and evidence. *Journal of International Business Studies*, *29*, 217–237.

Ricart, J. E., Enright, M. J., Ghemawat, P., Hart, S. L., & Khanna, T. (2004). New frontiers in international strategy. *Journal of International Business Studies*, *35*(3), 175–200.

Richardson, G. B. (1960). *Information and investment*. Oxford: Oxford University Press.

Rugman, A. M., D'Cruz, J. R., & Verbeke, A. (1995). Internalisation and de-internalisation: Will business networks replace multinationals? In: G. Boyd (Ed.), *Competitive and cooperative macromanagement: The challenge of structural interdependence*. Aldershot: Edward Elgar.

Sorge, A. (2005). *The global and the local: Understanding the dialectics of business systems*. Oxford: Oxford University Press.

Strange, R., & Newton, J. (2006). Stephen Hymer and the externalisation of production. *International Business Review*, *15*(2), 180–193.

Trigeorgis, L. (1996). *Real options*. Cambridge, MA: MIT Press.

Wilson, J., & Guzman, G. A. C. (2005). Organisational knowledge transfer in modular production networks: The case of Brazil. Paper presented to AIB World conference, Quebec, July.

Wu, S. Y. (1989). *Production, entrepreneurship and profits*. Oxford: Basil Blackwell.

Yamin, M., & Ghauri, P. N. (2007). The business network theory of MNCs: What do headquarters do? Headquarters role in the contemporary MNC. Workshop Uppsala University, 14th–15th September.

THE BORN GLOBAL ILLUSION AND THE REGIONAL NATURE OF INTERNATIONAL BUSINESS

Alan M. Rugman and Paloma Almodóvar

ABSTRACT

The regional nature of MNEs has become a key aspect of international business thinking, since Rugman demonstrated empirically that MNEs are mainly home-region oriented and studied the impact that the regional phenomenon has on firm performance. The extant international business literature on small- and medium-sized firms of interest to Aharoni is also evolving with the consideration of new aspects such as the "born global illusion," and the necessary balance between firm-specific advantages (FSAs) and the liability of foreignness (LOF) when going abroad. This chapter presents new insights on these topics by examining the regionalization of Spanish manufacturing firms, their export sales orientation and their FDI orientation. Finally, we study the impact of FSAs on the intraregional and foreign sales of Spanish companies.

Keywords: Regionalization; born global illusion; home region; firm-specific advantages; liability of foreignness

The Future of Foreign Direct Investment and the Multinational Enterprise
Research in Global Strategic Management, Volume 15, 251–269
Copyright © 2011 by Emerald Group Publishing Limited
All rights of reproduction in any form reserved
ISSN: 1064-4857/doi:10.1108/S1064-4857(2011)0000015015

INTRODUCTION

One of the important contributions to research in the field of international business made by Yair Aharoni is his focus upon the internationalization process by small and medium enterprises (SMEs). Building upon his pathbreaking book on the process of internationalization, Aharoni (1966), a rich and provocative literature has developed examining the nature and extent of small multinational enterprises (MNEs). Generally the small MNEs originate in "small" economies such as Israel and New Zealand and also include Switzerland and Canada. Indeed, one of the most influential books discussing MNEs from small economies is by Agmon and Kindleberger (1977). This book has been reviewed in a favorable manner by Rugman (1980), and this review is reprinted in Rugman (2009).

The objective of this chapter is to reexamine the focus of Aharoni on small MNEs in light of the greater availability of firm level data today. With the exception of Israel, in which 75 percent of the stock of FDI is accounted for by small MNEs (ISB & VCC, 2009), and possibly a handful of other small economies (but not including Canada and Switzerland) the data show that very large MNEs account for up to 90 percent of the world's stock of FDI (Rugman, 2000, 2005).

In particular, the Fortune Global 500 data set (which includes only firms with over US$10 billion in sales) includes at least 400 MNEs, defined as firms with sales in at least one foreign country and/or with 10 percent or greater foreign (F) to total (T) sales. Across these firms the F/T averages 35 percent (Rugman, 2005). However, there is a strong home-region bias such that these firms average regional to total sales (R/T) of 75 percent over the 2000–2008 period (see Table 1). Large firms in services average home-region sales of 83 percent compared to large manufacturing firms at 64 percent. For assets, the R/T is 77 percent, again with services at 84 percent being more intraregional than manufacturing firms, at 69 percent.

Table 1 is based upon the methodology and definitions outlined in Rugman (2005). The broad triad regions are defined as the EU, NAFTA, and the largest eight Asia-Pacific economies. These definitions are based upon data provided by the 500 firms themselves. Since the late 1990s, revisions to accounting standards require that firms issuing equity in stock markets should report the broad geographic segments for their sales and assets. In chapter two of Rugman (2005), each of the 500 firms is classified according to its broad home region. While there could be many definitions of regions it is sensible to examine international business strategy using the data provided by the firms themselves and according to their own definitions

Table 1. Intra-Regional Sales and Assets of the Top 500 Firms.

Year	Number of Firms	Intraregional Sales (%)		
		All Industries	Manufacturing	Services
Panel A: Intraregional sales				
2000	377	76.5	66.6	84.7
2001	417	76.2	65.1	83.8
2002	419	75.8	64.3	83.7
2003	412	75.9	64.1	84.3
2004	423	75.5	64.4	83.9
2005	425	74.7	64.4	82.5
2006	424	74.3	64.0	82.5
2007	420	73.0	62.1	81.8
2008	388	72.7	63.5	80.9
Weighted average		75.0	64.2	83.1
Panel B: Intraregional assets				
2000	312	78.2	70.2	85.1
2001	338	77.7	69.9	83.4
2002	347	77.5	69.2	83.7
2003	351	77.8	69.6	84.1
2004	365	77.9	69.9	84.3
2005	373	77.0	69.7	83.0
2006	371	76.9	69.0	83.7
2007	363	76.3	67.1	84.2
2008	335	75.1	67.2	82.7
Weighted average		77.2	69.1	83.8

Source: Data that have been gathered and managed by Dr. Chang Hoon Oh at Brock University, Canada. The original sources are annual reports of each company. Sample firms are listed on *Fortune Global 500* during 2000–2008.

of the region in which they operate. Thus, criticism of these definitions by Aharoni (2006) is misplaced and unjustified. Strategies of MNEs must be related to analysis of the location of their sales and assets.

Looking at this issue of the definition of triad regions in a more positive manner, Aharoni is correct to link the internationalization process (and strategy) to analysis of the liability of foreignness (LOF). We would all agree that internationalization takes place when its benefits exceed its costs. The focus of the Reading School upon internalization theory (Buckley and Casson, 1976; Rugman, 1981) and the eclectic paradigm (Dunning, 1977) suggests that firm-specific advantages (FSAs) in tacit knowledge and systems integration can be exploited internationally within the network of an MNE, subject to the LOF. Internalization theory is thereby fully consistent with the Uppsala school of internationalization.

The MNE faces a LOF, so it expands into geographically proximate markets where it can learn about foreign economic regulations, cultures, and other aspects of the LOF. As the MNE develops such location-specific knowledge, it will expand more broadly within its home region. In theory, the MNE could then jump to other broad triad regions, overcoming an interregional LOF. In practice, few large MNEs achieve much global geographic diversification, despite their ability to assess political, country, and cultural risks. Obviously SMEs lack these internal strategic location monitoring processes, so they should be even more home region bound. Yet a huge literature has developed arguing that SMEs can be "born global." Apparently a few cases of rapid internationalization by firms in knowledge intensive, high-technology sectors have led to the rapid development of this born global literature. Somewhat paradoxically, Israel may provide the exception to the rule that SMEs are born local, or at best born regional, rather than born global.

Unfortunately the born global literature misuses the word "global." Globalization is associated with economic integration, modernity, and cultural commonalities (Rugman, 2000). In other words, such pure globalization assumes away the LOF. Yet obviously there remain barriers to economic integration in the form of discriminatory national and regional trade and investment regulations; modernity is largely confined to relatively higher income groups and is denied to poorer people; while cultural and religious differences appear to be robust, especially in the Middle East. Thus, the LOF remains as a basic constraint on globalization.

Ghemawat (2003, 2007) argues that business faces a world of semiglobalization. This is broadly consistent with the theoretical and empirical work of Rugman (2000, 2005), which demonstrates that there are very few truly global MNEs and that the majority of the world's largest 500 firms are home-region based. So why would SMEs be born global?

In this chapter we examine data on the international activities of SMEs from Spain. We find that these firms are born regional. However, we do find that even these Spanish firms suffer from an initial "born global illusion." We argue that the born global illusion is generic to SMEs around the world, including Israeli ones.

Although we do not test Israeli firms specifically, we suggest that instead of assuming them to be born global, it is necessary to find both their F/T and R/T. In terms of R/T Israeli firms face an increasing regional LOF in doing business in Europe due to the pro-Palestinian focus of EU politicians.

Of course, Israel is a country created by noneconomic factors whereby political and religious considerations have led to close ties to the United States and Canada, thereby generating an economic relationship that may mislead analysts into interpreting these special international sales as truly global ones. In other words, while Israeli firms may not operate regionally, neither are they global.

THE REGIONAL SALES OF SPANISH FIRMS

The strong orientation of both large and small business to the home region has been discussed in the literature, and might be explained by the scale and scope economies that can be achieved (Oh, 2009), since FSAs are more easily developed and transferred within the home region because of its similarities and low cultural differences. Spanish companies face lower levels of LOF staying in the EU and they do not have to rely on developing new nonlocation bound FSAs in host economies that are often difficult to achieve because of the interregional LOF (Rugman & Verbeke, 2008). These results are consistent with the seminal work of Rugman (2000) and subsequent research (Rugman, 2001, 2004; Rugman & Verbeke, 2004; Rugman, 2005; Rugman & Collinson, 2005; Collinson & Rugman, 2008; Rugman, 2008; Beleska-Spasova & Glaister, 2009; Cerrato, 2009; Lee & Marvel, 2009; Rugman, Li, & Oh, 2009; Seno-Alday, 2009; Sethi, 2009; Rugman & Oh, 2010).

Here we focus on the foreign sales (mainly exports) of Spanish firms. Data on the international activities of Spanish manufacturing firms are collected from the Survey on Business Strategies (Encuesta Sobre Estrategias Empresariales – ESEE). This information source is an annual questionnaire conducted by the SEPI Foundation with the support of the Ministry of Science and Technology. Our results present information from 2000 to 2008.

Figure 1 graphically presents the domestic and international behavior of Spanish manufacturing firms on average during the period 2000–2008. We can observe the distinction among "HOME" sales generated in the domestic economy (Spain), "ROR" sales achieved in the rest of the home region (the European Union), and "ROW" sales accomplished in the rest of the world. Thus, HOME plus ROR plus ROW will be the total amount of sales by the company (100 percent). Based on this disaggregation of sales, we present two ratios: R/T and F/T.

The first ratio, R/T, represents the regional activity of firms through intraregional sales. On average its value is 94.12 percent. The second ratio,

Total Sales (%)

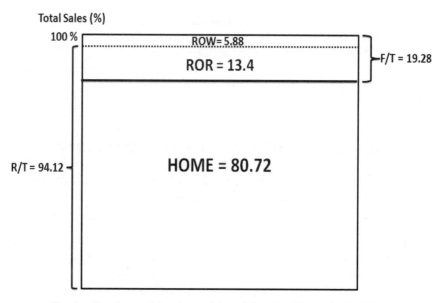

Fig. 1. Foreign and Regional Sales of Spanish Firms (2000–2008).
Notes: Firm-level data. HOME, sales in Spain; ROR, foreign sales in the rest of the
home region; ROW, foreign sales in the rest of the world. F/T, foreign sales over
total sales; R/T, regional to total sales (HOME plus ROR).

F/T, is the most common metric for multinationality (Errunza & Senbet,
1981, 1984; Bello & Williamson, 1985; Bilkey, 1985; Axinn, 1988; Moen,
2002; Kundu & Katz, 2003; Lu & Beamish, 2006; López, Kundu, &
Ciravegna, 2009; Manolova, Manev, & Gyoshev, 2010). On average its
value is 19.28 percent. Both ratios show that Spanish firms are mainly home-
region oriented because 80.72 percent of their sales come from Spain itself
and 13.4 percent come from the EU. There is only a ROW of 5.88 percent.

In order to go into both ratios in depth, Table 2 show the classification of
companies according to their regional/global orientation. Following Rugman and Verbeke (2004) and Rugman (2005), we identify four types of
orientation: (a) home-region, (b) biregional, (c) host-region, and (d) global.
The only distinction from the original metric is related to the definition of
the regions; so in place of the broad triad (EU, NAFTA, and Asia) we will
consider the EU, Latin America, and the rest of the world as the most
representative destinations for Spanish business. It does not make sense to
keep NAFTA as a triad region for Spain because the United States, Canada,

Table 2. Regional Sales of Spanish Firms, by Regional Classification.

	Total[a]	Home Region		Biregional		Host Region		Global	
		Number of firms	%	Number of firms	%	Number of firms	%	Number of firms	%
2000	1,860	1,823	98.01	1	0.05	36	1.94	0	0.00
2001	1,711	1,678	98.07	0	0.00	33	1.93	0	0.00
2002	1,689	1,654	97.93	6	0.36	28	1.66	1	0.06
2003	1,377	1,353	98.26	4	0.29	19	1.38	1	0.07
2004	1,371	1,348	98.32	6	0.44	17	1.24	0	0.00
2005	1,909	1,871	98.01	11	0.58	26	1.36	1	0.05
2006	2,002	1,964	98.10	10	0.50	27	1.35	1	0.05
2007	1,994	1,956	98.09	10	0.50	26	1.30	2	0.10
2008	1,983	1,940	97.83	9	0.45	31	1.56	3	0.15

[a]In order to classify companies according to their regional sales we have 10 missing values in 2000; 13 in 2001; 19 in 2002; 3 in 2003; 3 in 2004; 2 in 2005; 21 in 2006; 19 in 2007; and 26 in 2008 that have been excluded from the sample.

and Mexico are largely irrelevant for Spanish firms. The historical and linguistic bonds that link Spain with Latin America, because of the former colonies that Spain had there, make it a more relevant region. We note that Mexico is not included in Latin America. We will therefore define the regions as the EU, Latin America, and the rest of the world, and, by regional classification, we report regional sales in Table 2; and the export sales orientation in Table 3; and foreign direct investment orientation in Table 4.

Table 2 shows the regional sales of Spanish firms. The R/T ratio is used to identify home-region oriented companies and the disaggregation of F/T for the identification of biregional, host-region, and global oriented companies. We can observe that around 98 percent of Spanish firms during the nine-year period are home-region oriented. Between 1823 and 1940 firms have at least 50 percent of their sales concentrated in the region where the home country is located. This remains stable over time.

We find a small number of biregional oriented firms, meaning by biregional those firms with at least 20 percent of their total sales in each of only two regions, but less than 50 percent in any one region. These firms represent only 0.05 percent of Spanish firms in 2000.

Analyzing the figures for host-region oriented firms, those with more than 50 percent of their total sales concentrated in a region other than the EU, we

Table 3.   The Export Sales Orientation (E_i/TE) of Spanish Firms, by Regional Classification.

	Total	Home Region		Biregional		Host Region		Global	
		Number of firms	%	Number of firms	%	Number of firms	%	Number of firms	%
2000	1,195	898	75.15	26	2.18	269	22.51	2	0.17
2001	1,108	831	75	24	2.17	251	22.65	2	0.18
2002	1,099	851	77.43	29	2.64	195	17.74	24	2.18
2003	899	686	76.31	27	3	164	18.24	22	2.45
2004	896	685	76.45	27	3.01	162	18.08	22	2.46
2005	1,190	916	76.97	42	3.53	204	17.14	28	2.35
2006	1,228	963	78.42	38	3.09	201	16.37	26	2.12
2007	1,232	967	78.49	41	3.33	201	16.31	23	1.87
2008	1,258	988	78.54	44	3.5	201	15.98	25	1.99

Table 4.   The FDI Orientation ($FDI_i/TFDI$) of Spanish Firms, by Regional Classification.

	Total	Home Region		Biregional		Host Region		Global	
		Number of firms	%	Number of firms	%	Number of firms	%	Number of firms	%
2000	216	105	48.61	26	12.04	76	35.19	9	4.17
2001	224	106	47.32	30	13.39	78	34.82	10	4.46
2002	219	97	44.29	34	15.53	75	34.25	13	5.94
2003	183	90	49.18	22	12.02	62	33.88	9	4.92
2004	182	89	48.90	18	9.89	66	36.26	9	4.95
2005	255	130	50.98	33	12.94	80	31.37	12	4.71
2006	273	148	54.21	31	11.36	82	30.04	12	4.40
2007	279	154	55.20	23	8.24	88	31.54	14	5.02
2008	290	157	54.14	28	9.66	91	31.38	14	4.83

can observe that Spanish firms in the host-region decrease from 1.94 percent in 2000 to 1.56 percent in 2008.

And finally, the smallest number of firms belong to the global oriented classification, understanding by global those firms that have at least 20 percent of their total sales in each of the three regions but less than 50 percent in the home or host region. During the years 2000, 2001, and 2004 there were no globally oriented companies and only one company for the years 2002, 2003, 2005, and 2006. In 2008, there were three global companies, but this number only represents 0.15 percent of all Spanish manufacturing firms.

Table 3 displays the Spanish firm classifications according to the export sales orientation. For this purpose, we have created the E_i/TE ratio, where i represents one of the three regions (the EU, Latin America, or rest of the world); E_i is the export sales in region i; and TE is the total amount of exports achieved by the company. The table shows how companies are mainly focused on the home-regional market again (78.54 percent of Spanish firms have at least 50 percent of their exports concentrated in the home region in 2008) and we can observe how this trend has increased 1.045 times since 2000. Table 3 also presents a growing trend of companies that are oriented to two main markets at the same time so, in all, from 2.18 to 3.5 percent of companies have at least 20 percent of their exports in each of only two regions, but less than 50 percent in any of them. But the largest increase in exports is recorded for global companies from only two companies in 2000 with exports among the three regions, to 25 companies in 2008. Spanish firms have increased their global presence 11.7 times during the period 2000–2008 but still fewer than 2 percent of all Spanish firms are "global."

For a deeper understanding of the regional orientation of firms, a third ratio needs to be analyzed, the regional orientation of foreign direct investment. With this purpose we have created the $FDI_i/TFDI$ ratio, where i represents one of the three regions; FDI_i is the number of subsidiaries in region i; and TFDI is the total number of subsidiaries abroad.

Table 4 reports this information about the $FDI_i/TFDI$ ratio. Here we follow the same cutoff points as before, but we measure the subsidiary distribution among regions when the company owns at least 10 percent[1] of the international subsidiary. In general terms, the main destination of FDI is the home region where 54.14 percent of firms in 2008 have at least 50 percent of their subsidiaries concentrated in the European Union. The main orientation for FDI is the home region. The second main orientation is the host region with 31.38 percent of the companies concentrated in a region other than the home region. Fewer than 5 percent of companies are global in 2008 with at least 20 percent of their subsidiaries in each of the three regions but less than 50 percent in the home or host region. When analyzing the trend over time, we discover an increase in the home-region orientation (1.1 times) and in the global orientation (1.2 times); but a decrease in the biregional orientation (−1.2 times) and in the host-region orientation (−1.1 times).

Summing up, when analyzing Table 2, we find that 97.83 percent of companies are focused on the home region in 2008 (they achieve at least 50 percent of their total sales in Spain and/or in the EU). When examining the E_i/TE ratio in Table 3, we observe that 1,258 of 1983 Spanish manufacturing firms (63.44 percent of the companies) carry out exports; and 78.54 percent of them have at least 50 percent of their exports concentrated in the home region (the EU) in 2008. And when studying the FDI_i/TFDI ratio in Table 4, we detect that 290 of 1983 Spanish manufacturing firms in 2008 (14.62 percent of companies) carry out FDI; and 54.14 percent of them are home-region oriented. So, we can conclude that Spanish firms demonstrate a strong home-region orientation.

For deeper analysis of the regional orientation of Spanish manufacturing firms, Table 5 repeats the above analyses but breaks the sample down into 20 manufacturing industries for the year 2008.

We can observe that home-region orientation is not related to manufacturing industries' technological intensity. Following the classification presented by the OECD (2005), we observe how "Food and Tobacco" – a low-technology sector – has a strong home-region orientation according to all the ratios (Regional Sales: 9.33 percent; Export Sales Orientation: 6.52 percent; and FDI Orientation: 5.86 percent); and, in the same way, "Chemical products" – a high-technology sector – depicts the same home region presence (6.30 percent, 6.36 percent, and 5.52 percent, respectively).

According to the regional sales column the only three sectors that appear to be remotely globalized are: "chemical products," a high-technology sector; "metallurgy and metallic products," a medium-low-technology sector; "agricultural machinery," a medium-high-technology sector. According to the export sales orientation ratio (E_i/TE) the most globalized sectors are "chemical products," "nonmetallic products" and "electrical accessories and materials." According to FDI orientation ratio (FDI_i/TFDI), the most globalized sectors are "food and tobacco," "chemical products," "electrical accessories and materials," and "agricultural machinery." Overall, there are no strong industry effects; Spanish manufacturing firms are home-region based across all 20 sectors.

INTERNATIONAL ORIENTATION OF SPANISH FIRMS

This section investigates how FSAs have an impact on the intraregional and foreign sales of Spanish manufacturing firms.

Table 5. Regional Sales, Export Sales Orientation, and FDI Orientation by Manufacturing Sector (2008).

Industry	Regional Sales					Export Sales Orientation					FDI Orientation				
	Total	Home Region	Bi-regional	Host Region	Global	Total	Home Region	Bi-regional	Host Region	Global	Total	Home Region	Bi-regional	Host Region	Global
Meat products	71	3.58	0	0	0	44	3.26	0	0.16	0.08	4	1.38	0	0	0
Food and tobacco	187	9.33	0.05	0.05	0	103	6.52	0.16	1.35	0.16	30	5.86	0	3.45	1.03
Beverages	40	2.02	0	0	0	27	1.35	0.08	0.72	0	7	1.03	0	1.03	0.34
Textiles and clothing	127	6.40	0	0	0	74	4.85	0.24	0.79	0	10	1.72	0.34	1.03	0.34
Leather and footwear	47	2.37	0	0	0	32	2.23	0.08	0.24	0	1	0	0	0.34	0
Wood and wood products	70	3.53	0	0	0	28	1.99	0.08	0.16	0	5	1.38	0.34	0.34	0
Paper and publishing	68	3.43	0	0	0	51	3.74	0.16	0.16	0	12	2.76	0	1.03	0
Edition and graphic arts	105	5.30	0	0	0	46	2.62	0.16	0.72	0	7	1.03	0	1.38	0
Chemical products	131	6.30	0.05	0.20	0.05	110	6.36	0.40	1.67	0.16	28	5.52	1.38	2.07	0.69
Rubber and plastic products	107	5.35	0.05	0	0	79	5.64	0.16	0.48	0	15	2.41	0.34	2.41	0
Nonmetallic products	155	7.77	0	0.05	0	66	3.82	0.16	0.95	0.32	26	4.14	1.38	3.10	0.34
Ferrous and nonferrous metals	71	3.48	0	0.10	0	61	4.13	0.08	0.64	0	12	2.76	0.34	1.03	0
Metallurgy and metallic products	249	12.30	0	0.20	0.05	113	7.55	0	1.19	0.24	24	5.17	1.03	2.07	0
Agricultural machinery	139	6.25	0.20	0.50	0.05	114	6.12	0.48	2.31	0.16	33	5.86	1.72	3.10	0.69
Office products and data processing	25	1.21	0.05	0	0	15	0.72	0.16	0.24	0.08	8	1.03	0.34	1.03	0.34
Electrical accessories and materials	105	5.19	0	0.10	0	82	4.53	0.48	1.19	0.32	27	5.86	0.34	2.41	0.69
Automobiles and motors	99	4.99	0	0	0	88	6.04	0.32	0.64	0	22	3.79	1.03	2.76	0
Transport material	41	1.92	0	0.15	0	33	1.91	0.16	0.56	0	5	1.03	0	0.34	0.34
Furniture products	106	5.19	0	0.15	0	63	3.66	0.08	1.27	0	9	1.03	1.03	1.03	0
Miscellaneous manufacturing	40	1.92	0.05	0.05	0	29	1.51	0.08	0.56	0.16	5	0.34	0	1.38	0
Total	1,983	97.83	0.45	1.56	0.15	1,258	78.54	3.50	15.98	1.99	290	54.14	9.66	31.38	4.83

The *independent variables* (FSAs) are $R\&DIntensity_{it}$, which is measured as R&D expenditure divided by sales for firm i in year t; $AdvIntensity_{it}$, which is measured as advertising expenditure divided by sales for firm j in year t; $LnSize_{it}$, as the natural log of (employees + 1) for firm j in year t; Age_{it} as the number of years from the constitution of firm j to year t; and $Foreign\_ownership_{it}$ as the percentage of ownership that a foreign company has in the company located in Spain.

The *control variable* is $Sector_{it}$ that represents the company's main activity according to CNAE-93 code for 20 manufacturing industries.

Finally, we include two alternative *dependent variables* to proxy the regional orientation of the company: (a) R/T that represents the intraregional sales over total sales; and (b) F/T that is the multinationality ratio, foreign sales over total sales.

Both dependent variables R/T and F/T are restricted to the interval [0,100]. This means they are left- and right-censored. We employ a two-limit Tobit specification to estimate the censored regressions because coefficients from the ordinary least squares (OLS) regression might be biased and inconsistent as they do not account for the difference between censored and noncensored observations, so OLS regression might provide inconsistent estimations of the parameters as the sample size increases (Long, 1997).

In the Tobit model, the behavior of the dependent variable is captured in the index function y_{it}^* with the variable y_{jt} being the observed value for R/T or F/T for firm i in year t. The panel data Tobit structure with random effects is:

$$y_{it}^* = \beta' x_{it} + u_{it}$$

$$u_{it} = v_i + \varepsilon_{it}; \quad [v_i \sim NID(0, \sigma_v^2)] \dots [\varepsilon_{it} \sim NID(0, \sigma_\varepsilon^2)]$$

$$y_{jt} = \begin{cases} y_{it}^*, & \text{if } y_{it}^* \geq d \\ y_{it}^*, & \text{if } y_{it}^* \leq f \quad i = 1, 2, \dots, N \\ 0, & \text{otherwise} \quad \dots \dots t = 1, 2, \dots, T \end{cases}$$

where y_{it} is the dependent variable for firm i and year t; y_{it}^* is the latent dependent variable, d and f are the censoring limits; and u_{it} is the common error term that is split into a time-invariant individual random effect: v_i; and a time-varying idiosyncratic random error: ε_{it}. We report these results in Table 6.

Table 6. Tobit Regression With Panel Data (2000–2008) for
Intraregional Sales (R/T) and Foreign Sales (F/T).

	R/T		F/T	
	Model I	Model II	Model I	Model II
R&DIntensity	0.0015***	0.0016***	−0.0012**	−0.0014**
	(0.0003)	(0.0003)	(0.0005)	(0.0005)
AdvIntensity	0.1329***	0.1181***	−0.3015***	−0.2376***
	(0.0280)	(0.0280)	(0.0334)	(0.0344)
LnSize	−1.7290***	−1.6931***	4.4684***	4.6221***
	(0.0827)	(0.0837)	(0.0888)	(0.0911)
Age	−0.0043	−0.0040	0.0067$^+$	0.0087*
	(0.0027)	(0.0027)	(0.0040)	(0.0040)
Foreign_ownership	−0.0003	0.0019	0.0472***	0.0332***
	(0.0029)	(0.0029)	(0.0043)	(0.0036)
S1. Meat-related products		5.6146***		−10.2145***
		(1.0222)		(1.0994)
S2. Food and tobacco		3.9598***		−9.3815***
		(0.8681)		(0.9518)
S3. Beverage		2.8060*		−6.8827***
		(1.1487)		(1.1693)
S4. Textiles and clothing		2.9278***		−5.2482***
		(0.8876)		(0.9443)
S5. Leather, fur, and footwear		−0.1006		0.2264
		(1.0162)		(1.0649)
S6. Timber		4.1605***		−10.0936***
		(0.9888)		(1.0463)
S7. Paper		3.6977***		−8.5969***
		(1.0056)		(1.0688)
S8. Printing and publishing		4.6055***		−11.0530***
		(0.9303)		(1.0444)
S9. Chemicals		1.1094		−1.1100
		(0.8991)		(0.9614)
S10. Plastic and rubber products		2.8411**		−2.7253**
		(0.9106)		(0.9823)
S11. Nonmetal mineral products		1.8237*		−5.9939***
		(0.8807)		(0.9457)
S12. Basic metal products		1.0386		0.3976
		(0.9943)		(1.2368)
S13. Fabricated metal products		0.5257		0.4809
		(0.8380)		(0.9238)
S14. Industrial and agricultural equipment		−2.8526***		3.5534***
		(0.8627)		(0.9752)

Table 6. (*Continued*)

	R/T		F/T	
	Model I	Model II	Model I	Model II
S15. Office mach., and similar	Dropped		Dropped	
S16. Electric materials and		0.4518		−0.4702
accessories		(0.8757)		(0.9455)
S17. Vehicles and accessories		3.0500***		1.1057
		(0.9352)		(1.0584)
S18. Other transportation		−5.0200***		3.7542**
materials		(1.0763)		(1.4553)
S19. Furniture		2.3875**		−6.8942***
		(0.9216)		(0.9818)
S20. Miscellaneous		−3.9767***		7.2119***
		(1.0681)		(1.1340)
Constant	101.5237***	99.6297***	−0.7400*	2.0752*
	(0.3502)	(0.8611)	(0.3672)	(0.9449)
/sigma_u	11.4540***	11.3214***	22.2184***	21.4182***
	(0.0966)	(0.0833)	(0.2727)	(0.1872)
/sigma_e	5.8760***	5.8577***	8.4897***	8.4770***
	(0.0356)	(0.0354)	(0.0495)	(0.0498)
Rho	0.7917	0.7888	0.8726	0.8646
	(0.0036)	(0.0034)	(0.0031)	(0.0025)
Wald test	544.64***	1017.14***	3435.84***	6092.40***

Standard deviations in parentheses.
$^+p<0.1$; $^*p<0.05$ $^{**}p<0.01$; $^{***}p<0.001$.

We use the Wald test to assess the significance of Models I (which only contain the FSAs variables) and Models II (which include the control dummy variables for sectors – S.1 ... S.20 – as well). The introduction of the control variables *Sectors* does not change the behavior of the independent variables R/T nor F/T, so we may well assert that our regressions are robust and we discuss only the results for Models II.

With regard to $R\&DIntensity_{it}$, we observe how for a one-unit increase in the FSA variable the R/T ratio increases 0.16 percent (with a p value <0.001); while the F/T ratio decreases almost in the same amount (0.14 percent). $AdvIntensity_{it}$ behaves in a similar way because if a company were to increase the advertising intensity 1 percent, the R/T orientation would increase 11.81 percent, while the F/T would diminish 23.76 percent.

These results demonstrate that the R&D and Advertising intensities are region bound. So, the more investment focused on enhancing the R&D and

Advertising endowments of the firm, the higher the penetration in the home region. The company will obtain a higher income from the domestic country (Spain) and the rest of the region (the EU). However, F/T experiences a decrease that might be due to the lower purchasing power of other regions such as Latin America. Higher investment in R&D and Advertising is usually related to differentiation strategies that imply higher added value that frequently means higher prices. So, investment oriented to improve quality or brand perception is typically more successful in developed countries with greater purchasing power. R/T collects information about the domestic economy (Spain); Spain's home region (the EU) fulfills the former requirement; but F/T collects information not only from developed economies such as the EU or countries such as the United States, Canada, or New Zealand but also includes Latin America as a whole region, and developing economies such as China, India, or Morocco.

$LnSize_{it}$ demonstrates the opposite behavior, so a one-unit increase in its $LnSize$ is associated with a 1.6931 unit decrease in the predicted value of R/T, and also with a 4.6221 increase in the predicted value of F/T. With these significant results (p value < 0.001) we can assume that the bigger the company the greater the level of multinationality of the Spanish firm and the greater the capacity for increasing production and achieving scale economies, as well as capacity for customizing production.

Finally, the Age_{it} of the company (that is usually considered a proxy for its experience) and foreign ownership (*Foreign_ownership*$_{it}$) in the firm located in Spain do not play any role in the regional penetration (R/T) of firms; however, both of them are significant in the F/T model. When the company ages one year, the predicted value of F/T increases 0.0087 times. That means that with more experience it is likely to reach new markets outside the home region. If the company were to receive 1 percent more of foreign ownership, the F/T would increase 3.32 percent. Foreign ownership could be seen as a source of financial resources that may allow the company to pursue new international markets, as well as a source of international experience.

When revising the roles that the 20 manufacturing sectors play in regional and foreign penetration, we observe the large impact they exert because 13/14 of the 20 sectors are significant (presenting opposite signs for R/T and F/T). The four most influential sectors (with reference to sector 15: "Office machinery and similar") that are home-region oriented are: (a) "meat and related products," a sector mainly oriented to the home region with a positive coefficient of 5.6146 for the R/T model and a negative one (-10.2145) for the F/T model; (b) "printing and publishing," the predicted value of R/T will be 4.6055 times higher for companies located in this sector than in the "office machinery and similar" one; (c) "timber," which is regional oriented as well with a positive estimation of 4.1605 for the R/T model but a negative estimation of -10.0936 for the F/T model; and (d) "food and tobacco" that presents a coefficient of 3.9598 for the R/T model while its coefficient is -9.3815 for the F/T.

The only three sectors that are not home-region oriented are: (a) "other transportation material" with a negative relationship with R/T of -5.0200 and a positive one with F/T of 3.7542; (b) "miscellaneous" that shows an estimation of -3.9767 with respect to R/T but a positive 7.2119 with respect to F/T; and (c) "Industrial and agricultural equipment" with a negative relationship regarding to R/T of -2.8526 and positive one of 3.5534 regards to F/T.

CONCLUDING REMARKS

Despite a large literature on the possible global nature of new and small business, both theory and empirical evidence suggests that firms perform regionally rather than globally. Both large MNEs and smaller firms experience a LOF in going abroad. This LOF increases across the broad triad regions of North America, Europe, and Asia. If MNEs find it difficult to adapt their business model across these broad regions, then theory indicates that smaller firms must find it even more difficult to operate globally.

Here we examine the regional and global sales of Spanish manufacturing firms. Basically these firms, both large and small, are mostly home-region based. Some firms have activities in Latin America, but they are relatively few in number compared to the vast majority of firms that are home-region based. This empirical work supports recent work by Rugman (2005) and others showing that both large and small firms are regional rather than global in their operations. The relevance of this for this book is that small firms from small economies such as Israel should not suffer from a born global illusion. Expansion abroad is highly likely to be confined to a few key markets, often in the home region of these small firms. Such a finding is consistent with basic international business theory as developed by Aharoni since the choice of entry mode needs to minimize the risk associated with the LOF and allows the firm to gradually learn to expand abroad on the basis of its FSAs.

We conclude that the world is regional, not global. The business models of both large and small firms are usually developed in their home country markets and then taken abroad slowly as they learn about nearby markets in their home region. Of course, some economically isolated countries such as Israel may well have small firms that jump to large markets in North America. However, in general, small firms can forget about global integration and global strategy. International business is about expanding within the firm's home region.

NOTE

1. The cutoff point for defining when a firm carries out FDI is 10 percent because this is the minimum percentage established by OECD (2007).

REFERENCES

Agmon, T., & Kindleberger, C. P. (1977). *Multinationals from small countries.* Cambridge, MA: MIT Press.

Aharoni, Y. (1966). *The foreign investment decision process.* Boston: Harvard University Press.

Aharoni, Y. (2006). Book review: Alan M. Rugman, the Regional Multinationals. MNEs and Global Strategic Management. *International Business Review, 15,* 439–446.

Axinn, C. N. (1988). Export performance: Do managerial perceptions make a difference? *International Marketing Review, 5,* 61–71.

Beleska-Spasova, E., & Glaister, K. W. (2009). The geography of British exports: Country-level versus firm-level evidence. *European Management Journal, 27,* 295–304.

Bello, D. C., & Williamson, N. C. (1985). Contractual arrangement and marketing practices in the indirect export channel. *Journal of International Business Studies, 16,* 65–82.

Bilkey, W. J. (1985). Development of export marketing guidelines. *International Marketing Review, 2,* 31–40.

Buckley, P. J., & Casson, M. C. (1976). *The future of multinational enterprise.* New York: Holmes and Meyer.

Cerrato, D. (2009). Does innovation lead to global orientation? Empirical evidence from a sample of Italian firms. *European Management Journal, 27,* 305–315.

Collinson, S., & Rugman, A. M. (2008). The regional nature of Japanese multinational business. *Journal of International Business Studies, 39,* 215–230.

Dunning, J. H. (1977). Trade, location and economic activity and the multinational enterprise: A search for an eclectic approach. In: B. Ohlin, P. O. Hesselborn & P. M. Wijkman (Eds), *The international allocation of economic activity.* London: MacMillan.

Errunza, V. R., & Senbet, L. W. (1981). The effects of international operations on the market value of the firm: Theory and evidence. *Journal of Finance, 36,* 401–417.

Errunza, V. R., & Senbet, L. W. (1984). International corporate diversification, market valuation, and size-adjusted evidence. *Journal of Finance, 39,* 727–743.

Ghemawat, P. (2003). Semiglobalization and International Business Strategy. *Journal of International Business Studies, 34*, 138–152.

Ghemawat, P. (2007). *Redefining global strategy: Crossing borders in a world where differences still matter*. Boston: Harvard Business School Press.

ISB & VCC. (2009). *The growth story of Indian multinationals*. New York: Indian School of Business and Vale Columbia Center on Sustainable International Investment.

Kundu, S. K., & Katz, J. A. (2003). Born-international SMEs: Bi-level impacts of resources and intentions. *Small Business Economics, 20*, 25–47.

Lee, I. H., & Marvel, M. R. (2009). The moderating effects of home region orientation on R&D investment and international SME performance: Lessons from Korea. *European Management Journal, 27*, 316–326.

Long, J. S. (1997). *Regression models for categorical and limited dependent variables*. Thousand Oaks, CA: Sage Publications.

López, L. E., Kundu, S. K., & Ciravegna, L. (2009). Born global or born regional? Evidence from an exploratory study in the Costa Rican software industry. *Journal of International Business Studies, 40*, 1228–1238.

Lu, J. W., & Beamish, P. W. (2006). Partnering strategies and performance of SMEs' international joint ventures. *Journal of Business Venturing, 21*, 461–486.

Manolova, T. S., Manev, I. M., & Gyoshev, B. S. (2010). In good company: The role of personal and inter-firm networks for new-venture internationalization in a transition economy. *Journal of World Business, 45*, 257–265.

Moen, O. (2002). The born globals – A new generation of small European exporters. *International Marketing Review, 19*, 156–175.

OECD. (2005). *OECD Handbook on Economic Globalisation Indicators*. Paris: OECD Publications.

OECD. (2007). *The OECD Glossary of Statistical Terms*. Available at http://stats.oecd.org/glossary/index.htm. Last accessed on September 9, 2010.

Oh, C. H. (2009). The international scale and scope of European multinationals. *European Management Journal, 27*, 336–343.

Rugman, A. M. (1980). Book review (Agmon, T., & Kindleberger, C. P., (Eds.)) Multinationals from small countries. *Economic Development and Cultural Change, 28*, 871–875.

Rugman, A. M. (1981). *Inside the Multinationals*. New York: Cambridge University Press.

Rugman, A. M. (2000). *The end of globalization: Why global strategy is a myth & how to profit from the realities of regional markets*. London: Random House.

Rugman, A. M. (2001). Viewpoint: The myth of global strategy. *International Marketing Review, 18*, 583–588.

Rugman, A. M. (2004). North American intra-regional trade and foreign direct investment. In: A. M. Rugman (Ed.), *North American economic and financial integration*. Oxford: Elsevier.

Rugman, A. M. (2005). *The regional multinationals. MNEs and global strategic management*. Cambridge: Cambridge University Press.

Rugman, A. M. (2008). Book review of Ghemawat (2007): Redefining global strategy: Crossing borders in a world where differences still matter. *Journal of International Business Studies, 39*, 1091–1093.

Rugman, A. M. (2009). *Rugman reviews international business*. Basingstoke, UK: Palgrave MacMillan.

Rugman, A. M., & Collinson, S. (2005). Multinational enterprises in the New Europe: Are they really global? *Organizational Dynamics, 34*, 258–272.

Rugman, A. M., Li, J., & Oh, C. H. (2009). Are supply chains global or regional?. *International Marketing Review, 26*, 384–395.

Rugman, A. M., & Oh, C. H. (2010). Does the regional nature of multinationals affect the multinationality and performance relationship? *International Business Review, 19*, 479–488.

Rugman, A. M., & Verbeke, A. (2004). A perspective on regional and global strategies of multinational enterprises. *Journal of International Business Studies, 35*, 3–18.

Rugman, A. M., & Verbeke, A. (2008). A new perspective on the regional and global strategies of multinational services firms. *Management International Review, 48*, 397–411.

Seno-Alday, S. (2009). Market characteristics and regionalization patterns. *European Management Journal, 27*, 366–376.

Sethi, D. (2009). Are multinational enterprises from the emerging economies global or regional? *European Management Journal, 27*, 356–365.

UNRAVELING THE RELATIONSHIPS BETWEEN INTERNATIONALIZATION AND PRODUCT DIVERSIFICATION AMONG THE WORLD'S LARGEST FOOD AND BEVERAGE ENTERPRISES

Niron Hashai, Tamar Almor, Marina Papanastassiou, Fragkiskos Filippaios and Ruth Rama

ABSTRACT

This chapter examines the interrelationships between internationalization and product diversification among the world's 135 largest food and beverage enterprises. Based on the argument that food and beverage enterprises enjoy economies of scope when moderately diversifying into new countries and product areas, but encounter resource constraints when extremely diversified and internationalized, we expect to find an inverted U-shaped relationship between the two strategies. Nevertheless, we find that the relationships between the two strategies show both an inverted U-shaped

The Future of Foreign Direct Investment and the Multinational Enterprise
Research in Global Strategic Management, Volume 15, 271–299
Copyright © 2011 by Emerald Group Publishing Limited
All rights of reproduction in any form reserved
ISSN: 1064-4857/doi:10.1108/S1064-4857(2011)0000015016

(when geographic diversification is the dependent variable and product diversification the independent one) and a U-shaped pattern (when product diversification is the dependent variable and geographic diversification the independent one). These results imply that the relationships between internationalization and product diversification among food and beverage enterprises are more complex than currently conceived.

Keywords: Internationalization; product diversification; firm growth; food and beverage

At the beginning of the 21st century, Unilever, one of the leading food and beverage enterprises in the world, decided to launch the "Path to Growth" program, a strategy to transform its business. As a result, Unilever cut its brands from 1,600 to 900, while at the same time extending its international operations and becoming a global company.[1]

Since the beginning of the 21st century, Strauss, an Israel-based food leader and a dairy products company, has acquired a host of South American and East European coffee producers, while at that same period of time expanding its product portfolio by acquiring "Elite" an Israeli sweets and candy firm, as well as various biscuit and cookie bakeries, an apiary and a fresh vegetables company. Lately it has also begun investing in the drinking water business.[2]

Both Unilever and Strauss have made major strategic changes during the last 10 years in their internationalization strategy and their product diversification strategy. Yet, while Unilever decided to prune the breadth of its product diversification while widening its geographical spread, Strauss simultaneously pursued product diversification and internationalization.

The challenges firms face when attempting to make strategic changes has been a recurrent theme in Yair Aharoni's work since his seminal 1966 book. Since both product diversification and internationalization make extensive use of the same resource base possessed by firms, it is very likely that the two strategies are interdependent. Yet, the behavior of Unilever and Strauss seem to contradict one another and question the interdependency of both strategies. The current study aims to unravel the nature of the relationships between internationalization and product diversification at the firm level, while focusing on food and beverage enterprises.

In this chapter, we hypothesize that an inverted U-shaped relationship exists between internationalization and product diversification. We argue in this chapter that a local food and beverage enterprise which tries its hand initially at internationalization and product diversification will enjoy economies of scope. By expanding into foreign markets and in industries simultaneously, the enterprise attains economies of scope which allow it to develop concurrently in two directions. Yet when development along both paths is continued, the limited bundle of fairly fixed resources of such enterprises results in a situation where continued development of one strategy will be at the expense of the other.

In order to explore this proposition, we examine the relationships between internationalization and product diversification of the largest food and beverage enterprises in the world between the years 1996 and 2002 while taking into account their endogeneity (Kumar, 2009) and the level of expansion along each route.[3]

The chapter proceeds as follows: in the next section background literature is presented followed by a conceptual framework which outlines the hypothesized relationship between internationalization and diversification. Subsequently we present our sample, measures, and methods, and then the results of our analyses. We conclude with a discussion and implications of our findings.

BACKGROUND LITERATURE

Many studies suggest that firms have to make an either/or choice between internationalization and product diversification, at least in the short term. Substitution between internationalization and product diversification is assumed as both internationalization and product diversification make use of the same bundle of resources the firm possesses, thereby creating short-run interdependencies between the strategies (Caves & Mehra, 1986; Kumar, 2009). Tallman and Li (1996), who focused on performance, implied in their study that firms with low levels of product diversification can enhance their performance by expanding internationally. Indeed, findings by Pearce (1993) as well as by Davies, Rondi, and Sembenelli (2001) showed a negative relationship between product diversification and internationalization. In a similar vein, Palich, Carini, and Seaman (2000) argued that internationalization decreases the advantages of related product diversification due to international impediments to synergy formation in marketing, production, and technology. Likewise, Meyer (2006) argued that firm growth may be facilitated by "globalfocusing" – increasing internationalization in a narrow set of industries. Studying selected European food chains, Palpacuer and Tozanli (2008) draw a distinction between global strategies characterized by homogeneous market approaches and the search for economies of scale across world macroregions, on the one hand, and home-region strategies by which firms concentrate a large proportion of their activities in the home region and operate a smaller range of activities in extra-regional locations, on the other hand.

This view seems to suggest that firms have a limited resource pool, which can be invested either in product diversification or in furthering internationalization. Indeed, Kumar (2009) recently showed that internationalization and product diversification were negatively associated in the short run, arguably due to limitations in replicating and transferring tacit, causally ambiguous competencies between the two strategies coupled with limitations in absorptive capacity. Kumar (2009) also argued that decisions concerning the extent of development along the two paths were likely to be made *simultaneously and endogenously* by firms after taking into consideration the availability of various resources and not independently as implicitly assumed in past research.

Yet, other studies reported a positive linear relationship between internationalization and product diversification indicating complementarity between the two strategies (Davies et al., 2001; Delios & Beamish, 1999; Hitt, Hoskisson, & Kim, 1997). Davies et al. (2001) argued that for differentiated products, internationalization and product diversification were complementary strategies that enable a firm to maximize its utilization of firm-specific proprietary assets. Their view assumes that specific proprietary assets may foster both internationalization and product diversification simultaneously. Likewise, Delios and Beamish (1999) noted that for highly diversified Japanese firms, internationalization and product diversification complement each other, as the need for assets to enter distant lines of business may be met by the opportunities found to generate or acquire new assets when expanding the firm's geographic scope. This is also supported by Kim, Hwang, and Burgers (1993) who argued that increased internationalization reduces risk and increased returns of product-diversified firms, since additional opportunities are created for such firms. Finally, Hitt et al. (1997) argued that the combination of high levels of internationalization and product diversification create synergies that enable firms to differentiate their products while incurring lower costs than nondiversified firms.

These two streams of contradictory findings are consistent with the anecdotal evidence provided earlier for Unilever and Strauss. In this chapter, we seek to explore the endogenous relationship between internationalization and product diversification by building on the resource-based view (RBV) of the firm. By creating an argument for the existence of nonlinear relationships that allow for complementarity and substitution to coexist at different levels of internationalization and product diversification, we will attempt to shed light on the contradictory findings reported above.

CONCEPTUAL FRAMEWORK

The RBV of the firm views firms as sets of tangible, intangible, and human resources that create capabilities. These capabilities are unique, provided that a given firm's resources are durable and inimitable, hence enabling firms to compete successfully against their rivals (Barney, 1991; Collis, 1991; Peteraf, 1993; Wernerfelt, 1984). We will use the RBV in order to examine the relationship between internationalization and product diversification from different aspects. We will start out by examining the role resources play when arguing the existence of a positive relationship and when arguing the same for a negative relationship between the two strategies. Subsequently, we will build upon these arguments to construct a hypothesis that proposes the existence of a nonlinear relationship between the two strategies.

A Positive Relationship between Internationalization and Product Diversification

Firms possessing unique and inimitable resources are expected to have a greater capability to grow, be it through internationalization through product diversification into different industries (Davies et al., 2001). Internationalization enables firms to develop more diverse resources as they operate in multiple foreign countries with different comparative advantages (Delios & Beamish, 1999) and are exposed to diverse market needs and consumer tastes (Bartlett & Ghoshal, 1989). These resources can be transferred between markets, enabling the firm to continue its internationalization.

Diversification into new product areas enables the exploitation of economies of scope (Teece, 1982; Panzar & Willig, 1981). Tangible and intangible resources which are difficult to transfer in arms length transactions can be effectively transferred between product lines within the firm (Teece, 1982). Thus, it can be argued that if resources are transferable across product and international markets, simultaneous internationalization and product diversification will allow firms to benefit from the synergies created from the combination of greater internationalization and product diversification (Hitt, Hoskisson, & Ireland, 1994; Hitt et al., 1997; Kim, Hwang, & Burgers, 1989).

A Negative Relationship between Internationalization and Product Diversification

Firms usually posses fairly fixed bundles of resources that are costly to change in the short term (Barney, 1991; Penrose, 1959; Montgomery & Wernerfelt, 1988). Thus, firms that expand their international reach and product line breadth simultaneously are likely to encounter problems of trade-offs at a certain point. Such a point is firm specific and reflects managerial and financial resource constraints. When such constraints appear, firms may find themselves dealing with the need to choose between the two strategies. The scarcity of physical and intangible assets, such as finance and management time, is expected to constrain the number and variety of expansion activities a firm can pursue in a given time period (Penrose, 1959; Kumar, 2009). This is likely to lead firms to select the expansion route that matches their resources best (Montgomery & Wernerfelt, 1988) and focus their resources on further expansion along this route.

The costs of realizing synergies for product diversified firms (Palich et al., 2000; Rumelt, 1974, 1982; Simmonds, 1990; Teece, 1982; Varadarajan & Ramanujam, 1987) are expected to be significant and increase rapidly as firms diversify. Such costs result from the need to invest in activity sharing which involves the management of cross-business relationships, sharing of technological development, production, and distribution activities as well as retaining a certain level of reputation for different businesses (Davies et al., 2001). All these may limit the ability to internationalize while diversifying into new product areas. Likewise, internationalization requires firms to direct a significant share of their resources towards their host countries as well as to effectively coordinate their foreign operations (Bartlett & Ghoshal, 1989). Since firms are limited in their managerial and financial resources, when reaching a certain level of internationalization firms will likely face the need to reduce product diversification in order to avoid the exhaustion of these resources.

A Nonlinear Relationship between Internationalization and Product Diversification

Given the potential synergy-led economies of scope that simultaneous internationalization and product diversification drive on the one hand, and the exhaustion of managerial and financial resources they may lead to, on the other, one may expect their relationships to change at different levels of internationalization and product diversification.

At relatively low levels of internationalization firms are likely to have slack resources (Aharoni, 1966; Penrose, 1959; Teece, 1982) that can be used for diversification of their product range. Likewise, as long as firms have not diversified their product range too excessively they are likely to be able to use slack managerial resources and seek for synergies in foreign markets. For instance, as long as a given firm's internationalization is kept mostly within "home-region" markets (Rugman & Verbeke, 2004; Rugman, 2005), it may avoid having to deal with stark cultural and institutional variance between home and foreign markets (Barkema & Drogendijk, 2007; Cuervo-Cazurra, Maloney, & Manrakhan 2007) and employ its managerial resources for further expansion of its product range. Since regional consumer tastes and needs are relatively more homogeneous than global ones, internationalization at the regional level is likely to reduce the need of substantive resource investment in adaptation of products to specific local requirements and retain available resources for introducing a wider range of products while simultaneously internationalizing. Since food products are relatively sensitive to differing consumer tastes (Bartlett & Ghoshal, 1989), food and beverage enterprises may find this particularly appealing as they can leverage their product-specific resources and competencies in relatively similar countries (Filippaios & Rama, 2008). Some authors argue that technology-based durables would be the products least connected to local cultures while food products would be the most connected (Verlegh, 2007).

Thus, we expect internationalization and product diversification to be complementary as long as their managerial and financial resources are not exhausted.

Yet, achieving both high levels of internationalization and product diversification is likely to exhaust such resources and hence outstrip the returns to resources that are applied to a very broad scope, thereby leading to substitution between the two strategies. The combination of both internationalization and product diversification may require firms to possess diverse sets of resources and capabilities and confer upon them costly managerial time and efforts in complex coordination of such resources and capabilities, hence promoting substitution between the two strategies. Taken together we, therefore, hypothesize that:

Hypothesis 1. An inverted U-shaped relationship exists between internationalization and product diversification.

METHOD

The Sample

The hypotheses were tested on a sample of the world's top food and beverage enterprises, which account for one-third of production (Rastoin, Ghersi, Pérez, &Tozanli, 1998) and more than one-half of the technological activities of the world food and beverage industry (Alfranca, Rama, & von Tunzelmann, 2001). Firms in this sample are based in all regions of the world and manufacture not only food and beverages but also nonfood products such as detergents, soaps, and other products. The database includes publicly traded as well as privately held firms which are world renowned from a wide variety of countries, including *Anheuser Busch, Coca-Cola Company, Danone, Heinz, Mars, Nestlé, PepsiCo, Procter & Gamble, Phillip Morris, Sara Lee*, and *Unilever*. The enterprises in the sample hold over 8,000 subsidiaries worldwide, which employ over 3 million workers. These subsidiaries provide us with the industrial and geographical distribution of operations of the analyzed firms. This sample thus allows us to examine a very well-established, internationalized, and diversified industry while controlling for potential industry effects.

The list of firms analyzed was derived from the global AGRODATA database (Institut Mediterraneen de Montpellier, 1990; Padilla, Laval, Allaya, & Allaya, 1983; Rastoin et al., 1998), a database produced by the Institut Agronomique Méditerranéen de Montpellier, France (IAMM). The main sources for compiling the AGRODATA database are Moody's Industrial Manual, the Fortune 500 directory, the "Dossier 5000" published by Le Nouvel Economiste, and the annual reports of the firms.

Since the AGRODATA database requires extensive data collection at the subsidiary level, it does not contain information for every year. The data used in this study pertains to three years: 1996, 2000, and 2002. For each of the three years we examined the 100 world's largest food and beverage enterprises (in terms of sales), 66 of which appeared in all three years. In total this created 265 usable observations[4] pertaining to 135 firms, some of them included in all three years and some only in two of the years. The financial information at the corporate level was compiled from COMPU-STAT, AMADEUS, AGRODATA, and, in some cases, directly from annual reports.

Food and beverage enterprises are considered precursors to other firms in both internationalization and product diversification (Anastassopoulos & Rama, 2005). On average, food and beverage enterprises are older and more internationally experienced (Stopford & Dunning, 1983; Tozanli, 1998) than other firms. The longevity of food and beverage enterprises is often associated with their growth strategies, as leading food and beverage enterprises have sometimes survived for more than a century, among other reasons, thanks to their expansion into a variety of industrial and geographical markets (Anastassopoulos & Rama, 2005; Ding & Caswell, 1995; Gopinath, Pick, & Vasavada, 1999). Food and beverage enterprises often strive to achieve growth since economies of scale and scope are prominent in this industry (Anastassopoulos & Rama, 2005). Growth is certainly not the only motive for internationalization. However, a large size is a very important issue for food and beverage firms since large companies have the opportunity to enter new, profitable markets for foodstuffs (e.g., sauces, precooked dishes, nutraceu-ticals) while keeping oligopolistic control over markets for basic foodstuffs (e.g., sugar, flour), where margins are thinner. Small companies often lack this possibility because they cannot balance thin margins with the enormous volumes of basic foodstuffs marketed by the largest firms (Anastassopoulos & Rama, 2005).

By focusing on the largest food and beverage enterprises in the world, we are able to examine a very well-established, internationalized, and diversified industry at a global level.

Measures of Internationalization and Product Diversification

The absolute number and dispersion of subsidiaries operating in domestic and foreign countries are often used as proxies for internationalization (e.g., Carpenter & Sanders, 2004; Delios & Beamish, 1999, 2005; Lu & Beamish, 2004; Tihanyi, Johnson, Hoskisson, & Hitt, 2003). In this chapter, we build on the geographical distribution of the 8,000 domestic and foreign subsidiaries as measure of internationalization and on the industrial distribution of the subsidiaries as a measure of product diversification. Since both a detailed four-digit level ISIC breakdown and a geographical location are provided for each subsidiary, we can derive proxies of the industrial and geographical distribution of operations of the enterprises.

While we would have liked to compare our subsidiary-level measures with sales-based measures, this data was not available for the firms in our sample as many of them are not publicly traded and do not divulge the data. However, prior research has shown that subsidiary-level data are a reasonable substitute for sales-weighted segment data and they tend to have high correlations with measures based on sales (Sullivan, 1994). Furthermore, since our conceptual framework is rooted in RBV reasoning, referring to subsidiaries as rough proxies of the firm resources can be viewed appropriate in lieu of sales data.

In order to examine the dispersion of activities across markets and industries, we developed country and industry sector entropy measures of subsidiary networks as proxies for internationalization and product diversification respectively. Entropy measures enable researchers to capture both the depth and the breadth of operations (Allen & Pantzalis, 1996) and provide a good indication of the dispersion of firm activities across countries and sectors. For instance, a firm that is operating in n countries, but has most of its subsidiaries concentrated in a single country, should be considered less internationalized than a firm operating in the same number of countries, but with a more uniform distribution of subsidiaries across countries. This is because the latter firm is likely to face higher coordination and control costs for its subsidiary network. Simple absolute number proxies (i.e., number of countries or subsidiaries) cannot fully capture the difference in international dispersion between two such firms, while entropy measures can. Previous studies (e.g., Hitt et al., 1997; Kim et al., 1993; Raghunathan, 1995; Sambharya, 2000) have extensively used entropy measures to capture the degree of internationalization, product diversification, or their combination.

The general formula for the entropy measure is:

$$Entropy\_Measure = \sum_{i=1}^{n} \left[P_i * \ln\left(\frac{1}{P_i}\right) \right]$$

such that $P_i \neq 0$, where P_i is the proportion of subsidiaries operating within segment i. Segment i can represent countries, thereby constructing a "Country Entropy" measure (*country_entropy*), or industrial sectors, thereby constructing a "Sector Entropy" measure (*sector_entropy*). "Country Entropy" measures the dispersion of a network of subsidiaries with respect to the number of countries, whereas "Sector Entropy" does the same with respect to the number of industries.

As previous research has highlighted several problems with entropy measures (e.g., Robins & Wiersema, 2003), we also used a set of "count" measures for internationalization and product diversification. Using multiple measures further enables us to strengthen the robustness of our results (Boyd, Gove, & Hitt, 2005). The *level* of internationalization (*internationalization*) was proxied by the percentage of foreign subsidiaries owned (wholly or partially) by each firm (out of the total number of subsidiaries) while the *level* of product diversification (*diversification*) was proxied by the percentage of noncore subsidiaries (i.e., subsidiaries not in the food and beverage industry) owned out of the total number of subsidiaries.[5]

Finally, an additional set of proxies for internationalization included *regional level* internationalization (Rugman & Verbeke, 2004; Rugman, 2005), measured as the percentage of foreign subsidiaries operating in the home region of the firm (*region_subsidiaries*) out of the total number of subsidiaries, and *global* internationalization, measured as the percentage of subsidiaries outside the home region (*global_subsidiaries*) out of the total number of subsidiaries.[6] The home region of US firms is The Americas; that of European firms, Europe; and that of Japanese firms, Asia. Likewise, we introduced proxies for "related" versus "unrelated" diversification (Rumelt, 1974, 1982). Related diversification (*related_subsidiaries*) was proxied by the percentage of subsidiaries in the food and beverage sector (ISIC 3100) out of the total number of subsidiaries and unrelated diversification (*unrelated_ subsidiaries*) was proxied by the percentage of subsidiaries in nonfood industries out of the total number of subsidiaries. In a similar fashion, we have built entropy measures for global and regional internationalization (*regional_subsidiaries_entropy* and *global_subsidiaries_entropy*) and related and unrelated diversification (*related_sector_entropy* and *unrelated_sector_ entropy*).

Method of Analysis

An important concern when testing our hypothesis is whether internationalization and product diversification are endogenous. The possibility of endogeneity arises from the fact that at any given point a given firm's decision on further product diversification is unlikely to be detached from this firm's level of internationalization and vice versa (Kumar, 2009) due to the fact that both paths make use of the same bundle of fairly fixed resources of the firm.

In order to test the possibility of an endogenous relationship between internationalization and product diversification, we first ran ordinary least squared (OLS) regressions (within-firm fixed effects). The inclusion of within-firm fixed effects suggests that the reported models explain within-firm variation in internationalization or product diversification (i.e., change over time) rather than inter-firm variation. The analysis of within-firm variation seems to be the most appropriate to test our hypothesis, since the logic and reasoning underlying the hypothesis pertains to the impact of *change* in a given level of internationalization or product diversification on subsequent expansion (or contraction) in the alternate path. Fixed effects models further enable us to control for the impact of firm-specific effects which do not change over time on internationalization or product diversification, as well as for industry-specific effects (as industry is fixed per firm).

Subsequently, we employed a system of simultaneous equations taking into account reciprocal causal relationships (Zellner & Theil, 1962). The system employed the following structure:

$$\textit{Internationalization} = f(\textit{diversification, diversification squared, control variables, year effects, firm effects}) \quad (1)$$

$$\textit{Product diversification} = f(\textit{Internationalization, Internationalization squared, control variables, year effects, firm effects}) \quad (2)$$

$$\textit{Internationalization} = f(\textit{related\_subsidiaries, unrelated\_subsidiaries}_t, \textit{control variables, year effects, firm effects}) \quad (3)$$

$$\textit{Product diversification} = f(\textit{region\_subsidiaries}_t, \textit{global\_subsidiaries}_t, \textit{control variables, year effects, firm effects}) \quad (4)$$

As specified in Eqs. (1) and (2), we used regular measures as well as squared measures for product diversification and internationalization. Since we hypothesized a nonlinear relationship between internationalization and product diversification, square terms should enable us to capture possible curvilinear effects (Geringer, Tallman, & Olsen, 2000). In some of the regression models we replace these measures and their square values with measures for related and unrelated product diversification and regional and global internationalization, as specified in Eqs. (3) and (4). The reasoning here is that the related diversification and regional internationalization measures are proxies for relatively moderate levels of internationalization and product diversification (in which case correlation is expected to be positive) while unrelated diversification and global internationalization are proxies for relatively high levels of internationalization and product diversification (in which case correlation is expected to be negative).

The specific system of equations used to test the relationship between internationalization and product diversification was a within-firm fixed effects three-stage least squares (3SLS) regression analysis. This allowed us to avoid a possible bias as a result of correlation between the error term in one equation and the dependent variable in the other (Jaccard & Wan, 1996; Kmenta, 1986; Kumar, 2009). The system included the measures of internationalization and product diversification as dependent and independent variables which enabled us to capture the endogenous relationship in heir respective change between different time periods and also included their square values in order to capture curvilinear effects in such changes. The within-firm fixed effects models further enable us to control for year and firm (corporate) effects and hence compensate for possible firm-specific biases stemming from the fact that we use multiple (up to three) observations per firm.

Control and Instrumental Variables

The relationship between internationalization and product diversification was controlled by variables capturing managerial and financial resources (see Table 1 for a description).

Ln_employees (LAN of the number of employees at the corporate level) controlled for possible firm size effects.[7] This variable measures the company's global number of employees (not its employees in the headquarters). A positive relationship was expected between a firm's size and its level of internationalization and product diversification (Aharoni, 1966; Chandler, 1990; Teece, 1982).

Leverage (measured as the ratio of liabilities to assets) controlled for possible financial leverage effects on internationalization and product diversification. We expected a positive effect of leverage on the ability of

Table 1. Description of the Variables.

Name of Variable	Description	Measurement
Overview of the companies and control variables		
Employees (size of the company)	Total number of employees	Total number of employees
Sales	Global sales	In US $ million
Food sales	Global food sales	In US $ million
Leverage	Liability/assets	Percentage
RD_subsidiaries	Proxy for corporate investments in knowledge creation activities	No. of R&D subsidiaries/total number of subsidiaries (4)
Marketing_subsidiaries	Proxy for corporate investments in marketing activities	No. of marketing subsidiaries/ total no. Of subsidiaries (5)
Measures for product diversification		
Diversification	Level of product diversification	Noncore subsidiaries/total no. of subsidiaries (%)
Related_subsidiaries	Related diversification	Subsidiaries operating in the food and beverages sector (2)/total no. of subsidiaries (%)
Unrelated_subsidiaries	Unrelated diversification	Subsidiaries operating in nonfood industries (3)/total no. of subsidiaries (%)
Core_sales	Instrumental variable for *sector _entropy*	Food and beverages sales/ Total sales (%)
Measures for internationalization		
Internationalization	Level of internationalization	No. of foreign subsidiaries/ total no. of subsidiaries (%)
Region_subsidiaries	Regional level of internationalization	Foreign subsidiaries operating in the home region (1)/total no. of subsidiaries (%)
Global_subsidiaries	Global level internationalization	Foreign subsidiaries operating outside the home region/ total no. of subsidiaries (%)
Home_subsidiaries	Instrumental variable for *country_entropy*	Domestic subsidiaries/total no. of subsidiaries (%)

Notes: (1) Home country excluded. (2) ISIC 3100. (3) Industries other than 3100 (retailing and R&D excluded). (4) These activities correspond to the UN-ISI codes 111024, 312180, 832000 (excluding real estate, marketing and investment counselling services), 832030, 832020, 832021, 932000, and 933000 in the AGRODATA database, plus those affiliates that, included under code 832010 (management and IT services), have the term "research" in the description of their activities. These subsidiaries have an independent status, they are not laboratories attached to production facilities. (5) Indicates involvement of the subsidiary in retailing, supermarkets, hypermarkets, restaurants, and pubs. UN-SIC Codes: 6210, 6220, 6300, 6310.

firms to combine the two strategies as such leverage enables the use of external financial resources.

We further controlled for the impact of corporate-level specific resources on internationalization and product diversification (Delios & Beamish, 1999; Silverman, 1999). For this purpose we used the percentage of different types of subsidiaries out of the total number of subsidiaries as our proxies for R&D and marketing competencies at the corporate level. The share of R&D subsidiaries (*rd_subsidiaries*) functioned as a proxy for corporate investments in knowledge creation activities and controlled for the possible effect of technological knowledge resources; the share of marketing subsidiaries (*marketing_subsidiaries*) out of the total number of subsidiaries was used as a proxy for corporate investments in marketing activities, and controlled for a possible effect of marketing resources.[8] We expected that higher values for *rd_subsidiaries* and *marketing_subsidiaries* would be positively correlated with the levels of internationalization and product diversification (Chatterjee & Wernerfelt, 1991; Silverman, 1999). *EU, Japan* and *USA* were dummy variables which were used to control for specific "country of origin" effects[9] such as institutional differences between the home regions of the corporate, domestic market size, regulatory regime, and economic conditions (Delios & Henisz, 2003; Guillen, 2000; Khanna & Palepu, 2000; Luo, 2004; Rugman & Verbeke, 2004) which may affect internationalization and product diversification levels.

Finally, we included a different control variable in each equation in order to ensure adequate identification of our equation system. A necessary condition for obtaining meaningful parameter estimates in an equations system is that Eq. (1) includes at least one explanatory variable *not* included in Eq. (2) and vice versa[10] (Kmenta, 1986). Such a measure is called "instrumental variable." When measuring internationalization and product diversification by means of the entropy measures (see models 1, 4, 5, and 8 in Table 4) we used *home_subsidiaries*, which measures the percentage of home-country subsidiaries (as an instrumental variable for *country_entropy*) and *core_sales* which measures the percentage of food and beverage sales of each enterprise (as an instrumental variable for *sector_entropy*). These variables captured the size of the enterprise in its home market and its core sector and were expected to be negatively correlated with *country_entropy* and *sector_entropy*, respectively. For the count measures (see models 2, 3, 6, and 7 in Table 4), we used *region_subsidiaries* (percentage of foreign subsidiaries in the home region of the enterprise out of the total number of subsidiaries) and *related_subsidiaries* (percentage of foreign subsidiaries in the food and beverage industry out of the total number of subsidiaries) as different instrumental variables for *internationalization* and *diversification*, respectively. The first variable was expected to be negatively correlated with *internationalization*, while the second one was expected to be negatively correlated with *diversification*.

A key issue when estimating systems of equations is the validity of instruments used. In our case all the available lags of exogenous variables in the system were used as potential instrumental variables. To further test the validity of our instrumental variables we followed Davidson and MacKinnon (1993, p. 532) who have conducted a Hansen/Sargan (Sargan, 1988) test for overidentification of systems. Under the null hypothesis the instrumental variables used are the appropriate ones and are uncorrelated with the disturbances. In this chapter, we reported the Hansen/Sargan test for each equation at the bottom of the respective tables (Hall & Peixe, 2003; Hall, Rudebusch, & Wilcox, 1996). An Akaike information criterion (Akaike, 1974) was used to evaluate the fit of the regression models.[11] The Akaike information criterion complements the *F*-statistics which shows the overall explanatory power of the models.

Descriptive statistics of all measures, depicting our sample characteristics, are presented in Table 2 which shows that the sample is dominated by relatively mature and large firms with sales close to US$7.5 billion and average number of employees approaching 34,000. A correlation table of the variables is also provided in Table 3. It is evident that the corporate size measures (sales and number of employees) are positively correlated. A positive correlation is also found between the percentage of food and beverage sales (out of total sales) and firm size. The table further indicates that the entropy and count measures for internationalization, product diversification, and their combination are, respectively, positively correlated. Overall, the correlation table does not show any evidence of significant correlation between the variables used in the analysis.

RESULTS

We found no significant relationships between the different measures of internationalization and product diversification while using within-firm fixed effects OLS regressions of the two strategies. However, the two strategies did show significant relationships when the within-firm fixed effects system of equations was used, thus supporting the expectation that they are endogenous to each other. Results of the within-firm fixed effects

Table 2. Descriptive Statistics ($n = 135$).

Variable	Obs.	Mean	SD	Min.	Max.
internationalization	265	55.1%	25.7%	3.7%	100.0%
region_subsidiaries	265	22.0%	18.7%	0.0%	100.0%
Diversification	265	40.3%	23.3%	0.0%	100.0%
related_subsidiaries	265	18.2%	17.2%	0.0%	87.5%
unrelated_subsidiaries	265	22.1%	19.2%	0.0%	87.7%
country_entropy	265	0.97	0.43	0.00	1.78
sector_entropy	265	0.71	0.26	0.00	1.29
Global subs entropy	265	0.75	0.50	0.00	1.76
Region subsidiaries entropy	265	0.49	0.40	0.00	1.29
Related sector entropy	265	0.38	0.23	0.00	0.87
Unrelated sector entropy	265	0.37	0.29	0.00	1.14
Employees	265	33960	52548	6500	486000
Sales ($ millions)	265	7543	10243	300	63276
Food sales ($ millions)	265	6991	7689	300	56000
Leverage	265	62.3%	18.1%	4.4%	99.3%
R&D subsidiaries	265	1.6%	3.8%	0.0%	29.2%
Marketing subsidiaries	265	0.1%	0.8%	0.0%	9.5%
Home subsidiaries	265	22.0%	18.7%	0.0%	100.0%
Core subsidiaries	265	35.7%	23.3%	0.0%	95.7%

3SLS regression analysis regarding the level of internationalization and product diversification are presented in Table 4.

Table 4 present several combinations of the explanatory variables in order to verify the robustness of our results. The table includes eight models with the count and entropy measures for internationalization and product diversification. In the first four models (models 1−4), the measures of product diversification serve as the dependent variables, while in the next four models (models 5−8), the measures of internationalization serve as the dependent variables. Each system of equations is represented by the two models appearing in the same column (e.g., 1 and 5, 2 and 6, etc.).

Table 4 shows support for an inverted U-shaped relationship when product diversification is the dependent variable and internationalization serves as the independent one (models 1−4). Results show positive coefficients for the internationalization measures and negative coefficients for their squares (models 1 and 2). This result is further supported in models 3 and 4 where measures for regional and global diversification are used as the independent measures of internationalization. These models suggest that as long as firms internationalize in their home region, they also diversify their products (*region_subsidiaries* and *regional_subsidiaries_entropy* have

Table 3. Correlations.

Variable	(1)	(2)	(3)	(4)	(5)	(6)	(7)	(8)	(9)	(10)	(11)	(12)	(13)	(14)	(15)
(1) internationalization	1.0000														
(2) Region_subsidiaries	0.43*	1.0000													
(3) diversification	-0.08	-0.20*	1.0000												
(4) Related_subsidiaries	-0.18*	-0.11	0.59*	1.0000											
(5) Unrelated_subsidiaries	0.07	-0.15*	0.69*	-0.81*	1.0000										
(6) country entropy	0.73*	0.18*	0.03	-0.18*	0.20*	1.0000									
(7) sector entropy	-0.17*	-0.26*	0.56*	0.21*	0.49*	-0.04	1.0000								
(8) employees	0.23*	-0.04	0.25*	-0.07	0.36*	0.37*	0.25*	1.0000							
(9) Sales	0.26*	-0.08	0.21*	-0.15*	0.38*	0.39*	0.24*	0.80*	1.00						
(10) Food Sales	0.25*	-0.12	0.14*	-0.18*	0.33*	0.40*	0.14*	0.57*	0.82*	1.00					
(11) Leverage	-0.02	-0.15*	0.24*	0.10	0.20*	-0.02	0.26*	0.13*	0.15*	0.05	1.00				
(12) R&D subsidiaries	-0.03	0.08	-0.00	0.08	-0.08	0.02	0.09	-0.04	-0.02	-0.05	-0.04	1.00			
(13) Marketing Subsidiaries	-0.02	-0.08	0.08	-0.04	0.13*	0.05	0.13*	0.02	0.05	0.075	0.10	-0.02	1.00		
(14) Home Subsidiaries	0.43*	1.0000	-0.20*	-0.11	-0.15*	0.18*	-0.26*	-0.04	-0.08	-0.12	-0.09	0.08	-0.08	1.00	
(15) Core Subsidiaries	0.70*	0.41*	-0.67*	-0.48*	-0.37*	0.50*	-0.45*	-0.03	0.00	0.08	-0.10	0.03	-0.04	0.41*	1.00

*Significant at 1%.

Table 4. Level of Internationalization and Product Diversification –
Results of Within-Firm Fixed Effects Three-Stage Least Squares
System of Equations.

Dependent Variable	Sector_entropy Model 1	Diversification Model 2	Diversification Model 3	Sector_entropy Model 4
country_entropy	3.555***			
	(0.581)			
country_entropy ^2	−1.838***			
	(0.327)			
internationalization		3.578**		
		(1.605)		
internationalization^2		−2.280*		
		(1.313)		
Region_subsidiaries			0.338***	
			(0.081)	
Global_subsidiaries			−0.264***	
			(0.057)	
Regional_subsidiaries_entropy				0.229***
				(0.064)
Global_subsidiaries_entropy				−0.231***
				(0.040)
Ln_employees	0.056	0.001	0.023*	0.040*
	(0.042)	(0.039)	(0.012)	(0.022)
Leverage	0.012	−0.402**	−0.032	0.147
	(0.193)	(0.203)	(0.057)	(0.099)
rd_subsidiaries	−0.346	−1.714	−0.860*	1.977**
	(1.559)	(1.355)	(0.447)	(0.779)
Marketing_subsidiaries	0.365	0.832	−1.004	1.737
	(2.220)	(2.010)	(0.651)	(1.153)
Core_subsidiaries	−0.530**			−0.014**
	(0.207)			(0.099)
related_subsidiaries		0.021	−0.965***	
		(0.249)	(0.062)	
Japan	0.776***	1.396**	0.815***	0.491***
	(0.288)	(0.574)	(0.100)	(0.147)
USA	1.252***	1.424**	0.950***	0.588***
	(0.265)	(0.561)	(0.098)	(0.123)
EU	0.106	2.163***	0.865***	0.700***
	(0.366)	(0.705)	(0.080)	(0.122)
year_2000	0.005	0.069**	0.020**	−0.093***
	(0.036)	(0.029)	(0.010)	(0.017)
year_2002	−0.018	0.078**	0.016	−0.152***
	(0.041)	(0.031)	(0.010)	(0.018)
Constant	−1.416**	0.467***	−0.449***	−0.186
	(0.612)	(0.144)	(0.170)	(0.296)

Table 4. (*Continued*)

Dependent Variable	Country entropy Model 5	Internation-alization Model 6	Internation-alization Model 7	Country entropy Model 8
sector_entropy	−12.727***			
	(4.575)			
sector_entropy^2	8.146***			
	(3.118)			
diversification		−1.859***		
		(0.617)		
diversification^2		1.255**		
		(0.574)		
Related subsidiaries			−0.286***	
			(0.098)	
Unrelated_ subsidiaries			0.331***	
			(0.066)	
Related_sector_ entropy				−0.607***
				(0.100)
Unrelated_ sector_ entropy				0.144**
				(0.068)
Ln_employees	−0.191*	0.037	0.024	−0.053*
	(0.111)	(0.026)	(0.018)	(0.029)
leverage	−1.071*	−0.154	−0.204**	−0.227*
	(0.554)	(0.116)	(0.082)	(0.137)
rd_subsidiaries	4.296	−1.689*	−1.452**	1.250
	(3.992)	(0.882)	(0.646)	(1.106)
Marketing_ subsidiaries	18.733**	1.314	1.530	0.518
	(8.452)	(1.296)	(0.947)	(1.585)
Home_ subsidiaries	−0.854**			−0.462***
	(0.371)			(0.090)
region_ subsidiaries		0.235**	0.571***	
		(0.105)	(0.088)	
Japan	−5.452***	1.045***	0.882***	−0.758***
	(1.984)	(0.225)	(0.128)	(0.207)
USA	−5.235***	0.998***	0.838***	−0.536***
	(1.835)	(0.215)	(0.125)	(0.167)
EU	−4.092***	0.540***	0.805***	0.278
	(1.405)	(0.169)	(0.129)	(0.171)
year_2000	0.194**	0.046**	0.073***	0.057**
	(0.088)	(0.023)	(0.013)	(0.023)
year_2002	0.408***	0.055**	0.074***	0.135***
	(0.125)	(0.023)	(0.015)	(0.026)

Table 4. (*Continued*)

Dependent Variable	Country entropy Model 5	Internation- alization Model 6	Internation- alization Model 7	Country entropy Model 8
constant	3.466**	−0.436	−0.636***	1.666***
	(1.429)	(0.317)	(0.235)	(0.349)
N	265	265	265	265
f Eq. (1)	2.79***	15.68***	29.16***	30.36***
f Eq. (2)	6.12***	22.32***	53.95***	21.43***
Hansen/Sargan statistic	3.12	1.13	4.58	3.65
Akaike info. criterion	−456.25	−703.449	−943.512	−465.538
Year effects	$F(2, 170) =$ 5.78***	$F(2, 170) =$ 2.87*	$F(2, 176) =$ 16.57***	$F(2, 176) =$ 13.89***
Firm effects	$F(135, 168) =$ 2.88***	$F(135, 170) =$ 12.42***	$F(135, 176) =$ 22.06***	$F(135, 176) =$ 11.49***

Note: In parentheses – standard errors.
*Statistically significant at 10%.; **Statistically significant at 5%.; ***Statistically significant at 1%.

a positive sign) and that internationalization beyond the home region reduces the level of product diversification (*global_subsidiaries* and *global_ subsidiaries_entropy* have a negative sign), thus supporting our hypothesis regarding nonlinearity.

Table 4 further shows the existence of a U-shaped relationship between internationalization (as dependent variable) and product diversification. Results show negative coefficients for the product diversification measures and positive coefficients for their squares (models 5 and 6). This result is also supported in models 7 and 8 where proxies for related and unrelated diversification are used. The models imply that firms specializing in the production and sale of core products (i.e., food and beverages) find it difficult to internationalize (see the negative signs of *related_subsidiaries* and *related_sector_entropy*), while there is a positive association between *unrelated_subsidiaries* as well as *unrelated_sector_entropy* and the level of internationalization.

Together these results indicate that the relationships between internatio- nalization and product diversification are not only nonlinear, as hypothe- sized, but also asymmetric. It is noteworthy that the revealed asymmetry in our results is feasible in econometric terms since, as noted above, our within-firm fixed effects system of equations adds an additional explanatory variable (the instrumental variable) to either Eq. (1) or (2) that is not included in the other expression. This implies that the concerned relationships are not necessarily portrayed in identical landscapes. When the level of regional or home operations are used as identifying control variables (*home_subsidiaries* or *region_subsidiaries*), the inverted U-shaped between internationalization and product diversification is revealed. On the other hand when core or related operations (*core_sales* or *related_subsidiaries*) are used, the U-shaped relationship between product diversification and internationalization is revealed. We discuss the meaning of the inclusion of these identifying variables in the concluding section below.

The values of the *F*-statistics are high and the Akaike Info Criteria are low, thus further supporting the significance of our results. Moreover, the inflection points in all models are within our sample range of internationalization and product diversification levels, hence also corroborating our findings. Finally, the Hansen/Sargan statistic verifies the null hypothesis of the test, that is, the instrumental variables used are valid and the model is not overidentified.

CONCLUDING REMARKS

The results of the analyses conducted in this chapter shed a new light on results presented in previous studies regarding the relationships between internationalization and product diversification as two important strategic decisions firms make (Aharoni, 1966). Building on the RBV reasoning and basing ourselves on contradictory findings in existing literature, we hypothesized an inverted U-shaped relationship between the two endogenous strategies. Our results, however, paint a more complex picture.

Our results show an inverted U-shaped relationship between product diversification and internationalization when the latter is the dependent variable (and the former the independent one), whereas a U-shaped relationship is found when internationalization is the dependent variable and product diversification is the independent one. The first relationship implies that moderate internationalization is likely to be associated with high levels of product diversification while the second implies that that nondiversified firms, as well as highly diversified ones, are expected to be the most internationalized ones.

While the existence of a U-shaped relationship (in addition to the inverted U-shaped one) is feasible in econometric terms (as explained above), it is not easy to explain in theoretical terms. One compelling explanation to this finding might be the argument that either single business firms or firms with multiple unrelated businesses possess the managerial resources to internationalize their business units; however, the complexity of managing multiple related businesses consumes a considerable amount of resources that prevent such firms from being also highly internationalized (Geringer et al., 2000; Jones & Hill, 1988).

On the other hand, the inverted U-shaped relationship implies that up to certain level, internationalization complements product diversification (e.g., due to synergy creation) but after a certain threshold it becomes a substitute (e.g., due to resource specificity and coordination complexities).

Essentially, the results may imply that food and beverage enterprises which are set to increase their internationalization behave differently than firms deciding to enlarge their product diversification. In the first case internationalization can be conceived as an "independent" variable affecting product diversification, while in the second case product diversification is the "independent" variable affecting internationalization.

Our results may explain why a firm such as the Coca-Cola Company, which was hardly diversified when it started to internationalize in the 1940s, has international sales contributing over 70% to its total sales volume[12] but is still very focused on beverages in its product portfolio. The decision to internationalize when the firm was essentially a single business allowed the firm to continue with this strategy while it also started to diversify. However, at a certain point the firm narrowed its product range and continued internationalizing while maintaining a relatively limited level of product diversification. The results may also explain why Nestlé, which diversified beyond the food and beverage industry already in the 1970s, found it necessary in the 1980s and again in the 1990s to streamline its product portfolio and focus on water, pet food, and ice cream in order to allow the firm to continue growing internationally.[13]

Similarly, our findings may predict that a firm like Strauss, which at first diversified its product line within its home country, and started internationalizing part of its product lines internationally within a few years after initial diversification, will at a certain point in the future need to consider the trade-off between diversification and internationalization. As our results imply, the resources required for coordinating multiple operations, conferred upon firms which become increasingly global in reach (Rugman & Verbeke, 2004; Rugman, 2005), may lead to reduction in ongoing product diversification as the firm decides to increase internationalization (Markides, 1995; Meyer, 2006).

In addition our results suggest that firms choosing to compete with related diversification of geographically bound products (i.e., products that differ substantially in their nature between different foreign regions due to sharply differing consumer tastes) are in need of many resources, which hampers internationalization. Increased diversification may impede the allocation of adequate resources that are required for internationalization of geographically bound products, hence leading to reduction in internationalization as product diversification increases.

In order to cope with this problem, enterprises may decide to focus on products that are likely to be less "geographically bound," either by diversifying into more standardized product areas such as detergents, packing materials, and so forth, or by creating global brands. In this case, internationalization becomes less resource consuming and allows firms to allocate their resources to manage multiple products and gain the organizational capacity to increase internationalization level, as is the case for Unilever for instance, which is actively strengthening its global brands both within and outside the food and beverage industry.[14]

It may further be that the different relationships that we observe are dependent on the initial level of internationalization and product diversification of each firm. Thus, the findings of this study should be generalized with caution. For instance, smaller firms which are constrained by their size and by resources may face different obstacles when choosing to internationalize or to diversify than the firms analyzed in this chapter. In addition there may be specific characteristics of the food and beverage industry (beyond the fact that it is considered relatively geographically bound) that may affect the amount of resources required for joint internationalization and product diversification. Nevertheless, if one accepts the notion that food and beverage firms are precursors to the internationalization and diversification patterns of other large firms producing geographically bound products, our findings might well serve as an indication that the nature of relationships between firms' level of internationalization and product diversification is complex and should be analyzed while taking into account the specific context in which it is conducted.

NOTES

1. Available at http://www.unilever.co.uk/ourcompany/aboutunilever/History/ ?linkid = navigation. Accessed on May 29, 2010. Unilever reported a turnover of € 39.8 billions in 2009.

2. Available at http://www.strauss-group.com/en/MenuItem-AboutUs/History/. Accessed on May 29, 2010. Strauss reported a turnover of NIS 6.3 billions (approx. USD 1.5 billions) in 2009.

3. It is noteworthy that the current study does not aim to analyze the joint impact of internationalization and product diversification on performance and is not concerned with the direct and moderating effects of either strategy on performance.

4. Due to missing data on other items.

5. Affiliates which operate in, respectively, related industries and unrelated industries account for nearly 87% of the total number of affiliates. Most of the rest are primarily active in R&D and retailing; we also take into account such affiliates in our model (rd_subsidiaries, marketing_subsidiaries).

6. Unilever is Dutch/British. In this chapter, however, we consider Unilever to be a Dutch company, following AGRODATA. The company, a conglomerate, has located it Food Division and its main R&D center for food technology and nutrition in The Netherlands (http://www.unilever.comwww.unilever.com). When we calculate its level of regional internationalization we count the percentage of foreign subsidiaries operating in the home region of the firm, that is, Europe (with the exception of The Netherlands, which is considered the home country). It should be noted, therefore, affiliates located in the United Kingdom are considered foreign regional affiliates of the company.

7. An alternative measure of size, Ln_sales (LAN of total sales), was also used yielding similar results.

8. Following Anastassopoulos and Rama (2005), R&D subsidiaries belong to the following industry classifications: 832020, 832021, and 832030. Marketing subsidiaries are those belonging to the 832011 classification.

9. Overall 93% of the firms in our sample originated from these three regions (30% from the United States, 27% from Japan, and 36% from the European Union).

10. The same applies for Eqs. (3) and (4).

11. This measure of fit reports the explanatory power of a model, where lower values of the Akaike information criterion indicate a better fit of the model.

12. Available at http://www.thecoca-colacompany.com/ourcompany/pdf/Company_Fact_Sheet.pdf. Accessed on April 24, 2010.

13. Available at http://www.nestle.com/Resource.axd?Id = CA63136E-CAF5-484B-A97D-4543C6ACED65. Accessed on April 24, 2010.

14. Available at http://www.unilever.com/images/ir_ar08_annual-report_tcm13-163124.pdf. Accessed on April 24, 2010.

REFERENCES

Aharoni, Y. (1966). *The foreign investment decision process.* Boston, MA: Harvard University, Graduate School of Business Administration, Division of Research.

Akaike, H. (1974). A new look at the statistical model identification. *IEEE Transactions on Automatic Control, 19*(6), 716–723.

Allen, L., & Pantzalis, C. (1996). Valuation of the operating flexibility of multinational corporations. *Journal of International Business Studies, 22*(4), 633–653.

Alfranca, O., Rama, R., & von Tunzelmann, N. (2001). A patent analysis of global food and beverage firms: The persistence of innovation. *Agribusiness, 18*(3), 221–238.

Anastassopoulos, G., & Rama, R. (2005). The performance of multinational agribusiness: Effects of product and geographical diversification. In: R. Rama (Ed.), *Multinational agribusinesses*. New York: Food Product Press.

Barkema, H. G., & Drogendijk, R. (2007). Internationalizing in small, incremental or larger steps? *Journal of International Business Studies, 38*(7), 1132–1148.

Barney, J. B. (1991). Firms resources and sustained competitive advantage. *Journal of Management, 17*, 99–120.

Bartlett, C. A., & Ghoshal, S. (1989). *Managing across borders – The transnational solution*. Boston: Harvard Business School Press.

Boyd, K. B., Gove, S., & Hitt, M. A. (2005). Consequences of measurement problems in strategic management research: The case of Amihud and Lev. *Strategic Management Journal, 26*, 367–375.

Carpenter, M. A., & Sanders, W. G. (2004). The effects of top management team pay and firm internationalization on MNC performance. *Journal of Management, 30*, 509–519.

Caves, R. E., & Mehra, S. K. (1986). Entry of foreign multinationals into U.S. manufacturing industries. In: M. E. Porter (Ed.), *Competition in global industries* (pp. 449–481). Boston: Harvard Business School Press.

Chandler, A. (1990). *Scale and scope: The dynamics of industrial capitalism*. Boston: Harvard University Press.

Chatterjee, S., & Wernerfelt, B. (1991). The link between resources and type of diversification: Theory and evidence. *Strategic Management Journal, 12*, 33–48.

Collis, D. J. (1991). A resource-based analysis of global competition: The case of the bearings industry. *Strategic Management Journal, 12*, 49–68.

Cuervo-Cazurra, A., Maloney, M. M., & Manrakhan, S. (2007). Cause of the difficulties in internationalization. *Journal of International Business Studies, 38*, 709–725.

Davidson, R., & MacKinnon, J. G. (1993). *Estimation and inference in econometrics* (2nd ed.). New York: Oxford University Press.

Davies, S. W., Rondi, L., & Sembenelli, A. (2001). Are multinationality and diversification complementary or substitutive strategies? An empirical analysis on European leading firms. *International Journal of Industrial Organization, 19*, 1315–1346.

Delios, A., & Beamish, P. W. (1999). Geographic scope, product diversification, and the corporate performance of Japanese firms. *Strategic Management Journal, 20*, 711–727.

Delios, A., & Beamish, P. W. (2005). Regional and global strategies of Japanese firms. *Management International Review, 45*(1), 19–36.

Delios, A., & Henisz, W. J. (2003). Policy uncertainty and the sequence of entry by Japanese firms 1980–1998. *Journal of International Business Studies, 34*, 227–241.

Ding, J. Y., & Caswell, J. A. (1995). Changes in diversification among very large food manufacturing firms in the 1980s. *Agribusiness, 11*, 553–563.

Filippaios, F., & Rama, R. (2008). Globalization or regionalization? The strategies of the world's largest food and beverages MNEs. *European Management Journal, 26*, 59–72.

Geringer, J. M., Tallman, S., & Olsen, D. M. (2000). Product and international diversification among Japanese multinational firms. *Strategic Management Journal, 21*, 51–80.

Gopinath, M., Pick, D., & Vasavada, U. (1999). The economics of foreign direct investments and trade with an application to the US food processing industry. *American Journal of Agricultural Economics, 81*, 442–452.

Guillen, M. F. (2000). Business groups in emerging economies: A resource based view. *Academy of Management Journal, 43*(3), 362–380.

Hall, A. R., & Peixe, F. P. M. (2003). A consistent method for the selection of relevant instruments. *Econometric Reviews, 22*(5), 269–287.

Hall, A. R., Rudebusch, G. D., & Wilcox, D. W. (1996). Judging instrument relevance in instrumental variables estimation. *International Economic Review, 37*(2), 283–298.

Hitt, M. A., Hoskisson, R. E., & Ireland, R. D. (1994). A mid-range theory of the interactive effects of international and product diversification on innovation and performance. *Journal of Management, 20*(2), 297–326.

Hitt, M. A., Hoskisson, R. E., & Kim, H. (1997). International diversification, effects on innovation and firm performance in product-diversified firms. *Academy of Management Journal, 40*, 767–798.

Institut Mediterraneen de Montpellier (IAMM). (1990). *Les 100 premiers groupes agro-alimentaires mondiaux.* Montpellier, France.

Jaccard, J., & Wan, CK. (1996). *LISREL approaches to interaction effects in multiple regression.* Thousand Oaks, CA: Sage.

Jones, G. R., & Hill, C. W. L. (1988). Transaction cost analysis of strategy-structure choice. *Strategic Management Journal, 9*, 159–172.

Khanna, T., & Palepu, K. (2000). The future of business groups in emerging markets: Long run evidence from Chile. *Academy of Management Journal, 43*(3), 268–285.

Kim, W. C., Hwang, P., & Burgers, W. P. (1989). Global diversification strategy and corporate profit performance. *Strategic Management Journal, 10*(1), 45–58.

Kim, W. C., Hwang, P., & Burgers, W. P. (1993). Multinationals' diversification and the risk-return trade-off. *Strategic Management Journal, 14*(4), 275–286.

Kmenta, J. (1986). *Elements of econometrics* (2nd ed.). New York: Maxwell Macmillan International Editors.

Kumar, S. M. V. (2009). The relationship between product and geographic diversification: The effects of short-run constraints and endogeneity. *Strategic Management Journal, 30*(1), 99–116.

Lu, J. W., & Beamish, P. W. (2004). International diversification an firm performance: The S-curve hypothesis. *Academy of Management Journal, 47*(4), 598–609.

Luo, Y. (2004). Building a strong foothold in an emerging market: A link between resource commitment and environment conditions. *Journal of Management Studies, 41*(5), 749–771.

Markides, C. C. (1995). Diversification, restructuring and economic performance. *Strategic Management Journal, 16*(2), 101–118.

Meyer, K. E. (2006). Globalfocusing: From domestic conglomerates to global specialists. *Journal of Management Studies, 43*(5), 1109–1144.

Montgomery, C. A., & Wernerfelt, B. (1988). Diversification, Ricardian rents, and Tobin's q. *RAND Journal of Economics, 19*, 623–632.

Padilla, M., Laval, G. G., Allaya, M-C., Allaya, M. (1983). *Les cent premiers groupes Agro-Industriels Mondiaux.* Montpellier, France.

Palich, L. E., Carini, G. R., & Seaman, S. L. (2000). The impact of internationalization on the diversification-performance relationship: A replication and extension of prior research. *Journal of Business Research, 48*, 43–54.

Palpacuer, F., & Tozanli, S. (2008). Changing governance patterns in European food chains: The rise of a new divide between global players and regional producers. *Transnational Corporations, 17*(1), 69–100.

Panzar, J. C., & Willig, R. D. (1981). Economies of scope. *American Economic Review*, *71*, 268–272.

Pearce, R. D. (1993). *The growth and evolution of multinational enterprise. Patterns of geographical and industrial diversification*. Aldershot, UK: Edward Elgar.

Penrose, E. T. (1959). *The theory of the growth of the firm*. New York: Wiley.

Peteraf, M. (1993). The cornerstones of competitive advantage: A resource-based view. *Strategic Management Journal*, *14*(3), 179–191.

Raghunathan, S. R. (1995). A refinement of the entropy measure of firm diversification: Toward definitional and computational accuracy. *Journal of Management*, *21*(5), 989–1002.

Rastoin, J. L., Ghersi, G., Pérez, R., & Tozanli, S. (1998). *Structures, performances et stratégies des groupes agro-alimentaires multinationaux*. Montpellier, France: AGRODATA.

Robins, J. A., & Wiersema, M. (2003). The measurement of corporate portfolio strategy: Analysis of the content validity of related diversification indexes. *Strategic Management Journal*, *24*(1), 39–59.

Rugman, A. (2005). *The regional multinationals: MNEs and "global" strategic management*. Cambridge: Cambridge University Press.

Rugman, A., & Verbeke, A. (2004). A perspective on regional and global strategies of multinational enterprises. *Journal of International Business Studies*, *35*, 3–18.

Rumelt, R. P. (1974). *Strategy, structure, and economic performance*. Cambridge, MA: Harvard Business Review Press.

Rumelt, R. P. (1982). Diversification strategy and profitability. *Strategic Management Journal*, *3*, 359–369.

Sambharya, R. S. (2000). Assessing the construct validity of strategic and SIC-based measures of corporate diversification. *British Journal of Management*, *11*, 163–173.

Sargan, J. (1988). Testing for misspecification after estimation using instrumental variables. In: J. D. Sargan & E. Maasoumi (Eds), *Contributions to econometrics* (Vol. 1). Cambridge: Cambridge University Press.

Silverman, B. S. (1999). Technological resources and the direction of corporate diversification: Toward an integration of the resource-based view and transaction cost economics. *Management Science*, *45*(8), 1109–1124.

Simmonds, P. G. (1990). The combined diversification breadth and mode dimensions and the performance of large diversified firms. *Strategic Management Journal*, *11*, 399–410.

Stopford, J. M., & Dunning, J. H. (1983). *Multinationals: Company performance and global trends*. London: McMillan Publishers.

Sullivan, D. (1994). Measuring the degree of internationalization of a firm. *Journal of International Business Studies*, *25*(2), 325–342.

Tallman, S., & Li, J. T. (1996). The effects of international diversity and product diversity on the performance of multinational firms. *Academy of Management Journal*, *39*(1), 179–196.

Teece, D. J. (1982). Towards an economic theory of the multiproduct firm. *Journal of Economic Behavior and Organization*, *3*, 39–63.

Tihanyi, L., Johnson, R. A., Hoskisson, R. E., & Hitt, M. A. (2003). Institutional ownership differences and international diversification: The effects of board of directors and technological opportunity. *Academy of Management Journal*, *46*, 195–205.

Tozanli, S. (1998). Capital concentration among the food multinational enterprises and development of the world's agro-food system. *International Journal of Technology management*, *16*, 695–710.

Varadarajan, P. R., & Ramanujam, V. (1987). Diversification and performance: A reexamination using a new two-dimensional conceptualization of diversity in firms. *Academy of Management Journal, 30*, 380–393.

Verlegh, P. W. J. (2007). Home country bias in product evaluation: The complementary roles of economic and socio-psychological motives. *Journal of International Business Studies, 38*, 361–373.

Wernerfelt, B. (1984). A resource-based view of the firm. *Strategic Management Journal, 5*(2), 171–181.

Zellner, A., & Theil, H. (1962). Three-stage least squares: Simultaneous estimation of simultaneous equations. *Econometrica, 30*, 54–78.

TRADE IN SERVICES: THE GLOBAL SOURCING OF BUSINESS SERVICES

Arie Y. Lewin

ABSTRACT

In the late 1990s, Yair Aharoni was one of the early international business scholars who spearheaded exploration of FDI in services. This chapter reviews a more recent development of trade in business services that involves the demand for and the emergence of a global sourcing industry for business services such as business processes, information technology infrastructure, software development, engineering services, innovation (product development and design, technology and process breakthrough, etc.), marketing and sales (e.g., customer relationships management), human resource management, contact centers, and knowledge process outsourcing. The chapter is based to a large extent on findings from the longitudinal international Offshoring Research Network (ORN) project, which was initiated in 2004 by the Duke University, Fuqua School of Business Center for international Business Education and Research (CIBER).

Keywords: Trade in services, global sourcing, offshoring, offshorability decision, task characteristics, institutional forces, global service providers, location choice; governance mode

The Future of Foreign Direct Investment and the Multinational Enterprise
Research in Global Strategic Management, Volume 15, 301–313
ISSN: 1064-4857/doi:10.1108/S1064-4857(2011)0000015017

INTRODUCTION

In the late 1990s, Yair Aharoni was one of the early international business scholars who spearheaded exploration of FDI in services. The book *Globalization of Services: Some Implications for Theory and Practice*, coedited with Lilach Nachum, was the result of a conference held at Duke University and was perhaps ahead of its time, but did anticipate and focus on the emergent trade in services. The book case studies focused services involving hotels, aircraft maintenance, international package delivery, international franchising, and the internationalization of accounting firms.

This chapter reviews a more recent development of trade in business services that involves the demand for and the emergence of a global outsourcing industry for business services such as business processes, information technology infrastructure, software development, engineering services, innovation (product development and design, technology and process breakthrough, etc.), marketing and sales (e.g., customer relationships management), human resource management, contact centers, and knowledge process outsourcing. The Offshoring Research Network (ORN) project is also unique because it was designed to advance academic international business research as a large-scale multiyear international academic research project that is informed by management practice (decisions to outsource all manner of business processes) and that in turn results in findings that inform management practice.

The chapter is based to a large extent on findings from the longitudinal international ORN project, which was initiated in 2004 by the Duke University, Fuqua School of Business Center for international Business Education and Research (CIBER). Yair Aharoni was the founding director of the CIBER in 1992. I had the honor and privilege to follow Yair as director in 1996 and have been director ever since.

THE INTERNATIONAL OFFSHORING RESEARCH NETWORK PROJECT

The ORN project tracks the adoption of offshoring business processes over time at the level of the specific task or process by launch year, and the adoption of offshoring strategies at the corporate and function level. As of this writing, it includes 1,445 companies that do, do not, or are considering offshoring of processes; it covers all industries (e.g., financial services), all functions (e.g., IT), all locations (e.g., Latin America), and all delivery models (e.g., captive, hybrid). Since 2007 it is complemented by annual ORN Service Provider Survey (SPS; 540 providers worldwide), comprehensive annual reports, practitioner-oriented thought leadership articles, academic peer-reviewed papers, case studies and follow-up focused surveys, and management debriefing workshops and industry-specific roundtables.

ORN involves co-principal investigators in 11 countries. Table 1 lists the ORN academic research partnerships.

The role of the country research partners is to solicit companies in their country to participate in ORN surveys. Where necessary, the survey is made available to respondents in the language of their country (currently German, French, Flemish, Waloon, Spanish, Italian, Japanese, and Korean). Further data consistency is achieved by linking country university web site seamlessly to the central ORN survey server at Duke. All country research partners have access to the entire database. However, accesses to names of companies and of key informants are kept confidential with exception of names from research partner country.

Fig. 1 summarizes the diffusion of business services outsourcing offshore by function and Fig. 2 summarizes diffusion by industry.

Offshoring of business services started prior to 1989 when GE Capital was an early adopter with the establishment of a BPO captive in Bangalore, India in 1982. It is noteworthy that companies began to offshore IT infrastructure activities, which are seen as largely standardized, simultaneously with the innovation work, which is clearly recognized as a high-value-added activity. This was the first indication that growth of offshoring

Table 1. ORN University Research Partners.

Scandinavia: Copenhagen Business School
United Kingdom: Manchester Business School
Netherlands: RSM Erasmus University
Belgium: ULB – Solvay Business School
Germany: WHU Otto Beisheim School of Management
Spain: IESE
Australia: Macquarie University
Japan: University of Tokyo
Korea: Kyung Hee University
Italy: Polytechnic University of Milan, University of Salerno
France: EMLYON Business School
Thirteen Centers for International Business Education and Research

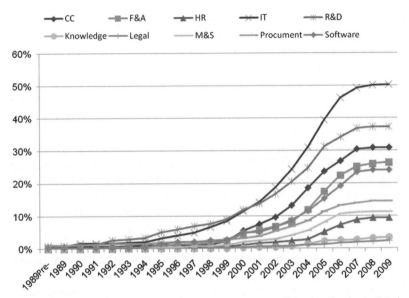

Fig. 1. Cumulative Percentage Growth of Companies Offshoring Business Services by Type of Function. *Source*: Duke University Offshoring Research Network Survey (2005, 2006, 2007/2008, 2009).

business services was not constrained by the conventional wisdom of following an experience value-added value chain. Estimates of the size of the worldwide offshoring market for business services as measured by total value of executed contracts in 2010 ranges from $117 billion (NASSCOM estimate that includes $70 billion just for IT-related outsourcing in India) to $231 billion (OECD) and $281 billion (BCG).

This global sourcing market for business services exceeds the total market value for aircraft maintenance, international package delivery, and accounting and hotel services. ORN data and estimates by various consultancies indicate that the market is still growing rapidly (though it slowed somewhat in 2009), fueled both by the demand side and by the global competition among providers competing on price, quality, and new service offerings. The sections that follow illustrate the range of ORN research by discussing the decision to offshore, the global sourcing of innovation, and the emergence of the global outsourcing industry.

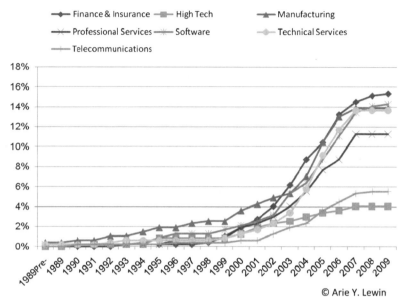

© Arie Y. Lewin

Fig. 2. Cumulative Percentage of Companies Offshoring Business Services by Industry. *Source*: Duke University Offshoring Research Network Survey (2005, 2006, 2007/2008, 2009).

THE OFFSHORABILITY DECISION

Offshore outsourcing has been operationalized by Manning, Lewin, and Massini (2008) to mean that buy-side companies source specific functions and processes that support domestic and global operations from outside their home countries, using third-party service providers in addition to locating such activities offshore in a wholly owned organizational unit usually referred to as a "captive." There is a general agreement (ORN research and other sources) that cost savings are a primary initial reason for why companies choose to outsource offshore business processes or functions (Farrell, 2005; Levy, 2005; Lewin & Couto, 2007). In recent years, however, as companies learn the reality that "labor arbitrage" is a short-term benefit, they increasingly offshore for more strategic reasons, such as to increase organizational flexibility, and to access talent and specialized capabilities

(Lewin & Peeters, 2006a, 2006b; Lewin, Massini, Perm-Ajchariyawong, Sappenfield, & Walker, 2009; Manning et al., 2008; Kenney, Massini, & Murtha, 2009). In other words, firms not only try to cut costs, but also to create value through strategic outsourcing (e.g., Holcomb & Hitt, 2007; Quinn, 1999).

The increased demand for global sourcing has also resulted in a growing global outsourcing industry further fueled by countries aspiring to emulate the Indian miracle by adopting national policies to attract business services outsourcing to their country (e.g., in 2009 China designated 21 cities to become hubs for attracting outsourcing of business services). The resulting growth in number of providers around the world and in industry capacity to provide outsourcing services have increased the rate of commoditization of such services as IT infrastructure, finance and accounting, contact centers, and human resources. In other words, providers compete increasingly on price and find it increasingly difficult to differentiate themselves from other competitors. The resulting global competition has greatly increased the options available to companies for selecting full service as well as specialized providers for specific needs such as knowledge-intensive services (Lewin et al., 2009).

Studies have investigated a range of factors – mainly related to characteristics of a task – assumed to be driving the growth of global sourcing, including information intensity (Apte & Mason, 1995; Mithas & Whitaker, 2007), requisite need for physical presence (Chase, 1981; Apte & Mason, 1995; Blinder, 2007), codifiability (Ancori, Bureth, & Cohendet, 2000; Cohendet & Steinmueller, 2000), standardizability (Davenport, 2005; Mithas & Whitaker, 2007), and modularizability (Mithas & Whitaker, 2007; Gospel & Sako, 2010). However, each of these studies has focused on a single static theoretical lens. The empirical reality suggests that organizations are aware of and are adapting their decisions dynamically to various changes in their environment including technological changes, and comparison with industry peers and with first movers. Virtually all studies on "offshorability"[1] have focused on the demand side to explain which activity can be offshored. For example, Blinder developed an offshorability index by occupation based mainly on the need for physical presence to perform a task. However, so far there has been no attempt to incorporate the role of supply (providers' capabilities and service capacity) in shaping firms' perception of the offshorability of a task (i.e., availability of service providers offering skills and expertise in a particular function and its influence on the decision whether a task can be offshored).

So far, prior studies examine offshorability at an occupation level: whether an occupation is offshorable. However, occupation-level analysis of offshorability provides a rather limited understanding of offshorability because, in practice, an occupation is expressed in the actual execution of several interdependent and independent tasks whose degree of offshorability may differ. To address this gap in the literature, the ORN approach focuses instead on the task-level analysis for gaining insights into the enormous heterogeneity in the managerial decisions of what and when tasks can actually be offshored.

Fig. 3 summarizes the many variables and levels of analysis involved in determining whether a task or process is offshorable. It also distinguishes between arriving at a decision that such tasks or processes are offshorable – offshorability decision – and whether to actually proceed and offshore these activities – offshoring decision. A further analysis is required to determine the geographic location for offshoring and the service delivery model to utilize (e.g., captive, third-party service provider, build–operate–transfer,

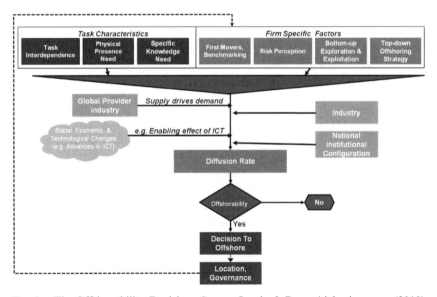

Fig. 3. The Offshorability Decision. *Source*: Lewin & Perm-Ajchariyawong (2010), reproduced with kind permission of the Center for International Business Education and Research, Duke University.

and hybrid). It does rule out establishing a domestic shared services organization (captive or outsource).

In Fig. 3 we note several key variables. First is the role of task characteristics following Blinder (2006, 2009) and other extant studies. An empirical correlation between the prediction of the Blinder (2009) model of which occupations are vulnerable to offshoring and ORN data are not at all correlated (Corr = 0.0012). This is most likely because in the United States occupations are not tightly defined (as, e.g., in Germany) and also because many tasks or processes that make up an occupation can be separated and outsourced on their own. The second group of variables is firm specific. Based on ORN data, early decisions to offshore business processes made prior to 2000 were often made by lower-level managers (local offshoring champions) without the knowledge or approval of corporate management or even business unit or function management. These local decisions could be a reflection of the local rationality of managers as discussed in March and Simon (1958), but it also raises questions about a new phenomenon that Lewin, Manning, Massini, and Peeters (2011) identify as the shifting boundaries of the firm. The advent of Y2K and the offshore outsourcing of large multi-year IT contracts received a big push following the dot-com bust as companies were searching for ways to increase efficiency of their IT infrastructure (e.g., computer centers, networks, server farms, and help desk) and to monetize these activities; in other words, to decrease the working capital and payroll associated with these activities. The model also identifies other drivers such as precedent set by early adopters, and "benchmarking" the weight given to industry comparison groups (Cyert & March, 1963; Massini, Lewin, & Greve, 2005). It also notes that top management could be adopting and articulating a strategy to guide offshoring decisions (Heijmen, Lewin, Manning, Perm-Ajchariyawong, & Russell, 2009; Ocasio, 1997). All else equal, at a macro level, it is clear that growth of offshoring follows traditional diffusion curves and that by 2005 isomorphic pressures may have become the major drivers behind off-shorability decisions. All of these factors can increase the likelihood of a positive decision regarding offshorability as well as oppose it.

The model also notes the need to consider national institutional-level variables. In the United States, the risk of political backlash had the lowest ranking until 2009 when this risk rose slightly in importance from 17% to 22%. In Germany the statutes governing labor rights have the effect of avoiding layoffs, and many companies seem to synchronize the growth of their offshoring decisions to attrition rates (retirements and voluntary turnover) and growth in transaction volume.

So far the discussion has focused on demand side of the decision to offshore. However, the emergence and growth of the global offshoring industry point to the need to incorporate a consideration of the supply of business services outsourcing. How supply drives demand has not received much attention in the literature. The ORN project first launched the SPS in 2007 with follow-up surveys in 2009 and 2010. The newest dynamic observed in the outsourcing industry relates to countries establishing national aspirations for attracting the outsourcing of business services to their shores. Perhaps one explanation is a simple desire to emulate the success of India. The ORN project documents countries that have adopted national policies for attracting the business services outsourcing industry, nurturing the internal capacity for competing for this business, as well as offering tax and other incentives for companies to locate outsourcing or captive operations in their countries. Moreover, several countries (e.g., China, Korea, and Mexico) have announced and implemented various policies with the objective of repatriating their nationals who have earned advanced degrees in science and engineering in developed countries to return to their country (i.e., reversing the brain drain). The consequences are several. First, the competition between providers worldwide has been intensifying resulting in increasing commoditization of services; price competition; eroding margins; and a visible increase in new service offerings such as legal service outsourcing, knowledge and analytical services, and transformational re-engineering of business services. Another example is the emerging shortage of science and engineering talent partly because of the decline in US nationals (but more generally young adults in developed economies) not selecting science and engineering careers as measured by earning advanced degrees in science and engineering.

Estimating the simultaneous effect of demand for outsourcing of business services and the share of supply driving demand represents a complex modeling task. However, the outsourcing offshore of legal services provides an interesting example. The first companies to offshore legal services in 1982 were General Electric Capital and Microsoft. There were almost no followers in the intervening years. By 2009 the ORN project identified 118 legal service providers in India (others can be found in the Philippines and Sri Lanka). Two major events – US Supreme Court decision in April 2006 and an opinion issue by the American Bar Association – give legitimacy to and, hence, fortify the growth of legal services offshoring, especially among American companies. According to the 2009 ORN buy-side survey, legal services are largely offshored to specialized third-party providers and have experienced very high growth rates since 2008.

DISCUSSION

It should be evident that the decision to offshore business processes cannot and should not be explained with single-lens models. The longitudinal ORN data base illustrates that to track and understand this phenomenon it is important to at least adopt a coevolutionary framework for explaining changes in the offshoring phenomenon over time (see, e.g., Lewin et al., 2008). However, a determination that a task or a process is offshorable still needs to be transformed into a decision to offshore. At the very least this requires a choice of location offshore and a choice of service delivery model – captive or outsource. In the early days of offshoring, India and a few cities in India were seen as the most desirable locations. Many of these locations have become high-cost "hot spots" and the ORN data has tracked the emergence of hundreds of cities as destinations. Indeed many companies are developing second- and third-tier city strategies. Also in the early years companies preferred the captive service delivery model over the outsource model. However, by 2009 (according to 2009 ORN survey results) the preference has shifted toward the outsource delivery model regardless of nationality or function (contact center, R&D, engineering services, product design, and product development). Furthermore, the relocation of a delivery model from outsourcing back to a company captive or back to home market is a rare occasion. This phenomenon (choice of location and governance model) needs much further investigation. However, it appears that the initial decision to choose the captive service delivery model is primarily driven by the need to overcome internal resistance to offshoring. As time passes this risk proves to be a nonrisk. To the extent that company selected captive service delivery model as a means for protecting process knowledge or intellectual property over time, many companies discover that managing various tasks and processes offshore is not their core competence and that labor arbitrage effect has diminished. Often this results in rethinking the strategy. The 2009 ORN buy-side survey shows that preference for the captive service delivery model shifts from an 80% preference before 2002 to a 70% preference for the outsource service delivery model in 2009. One explanation could be that as companies grow the scale and scope of processes being offshored, they also discover the inadequacy of their organizational capabilities to coordinate and manage these far-flung activities. They also discover that outsourcing to a provider creates the opportunity to benefit from spillover effect at the provider level whose own survival requires an ongoing effort to learn from many different applications across many clients.

This chapter did not explore the extent to which extant international business research and theories can explain the multidimensional and multilevel offshoring phenomenon. Of course, partial explanations are found in the literature. It could be argued that global sourcing is not a new phenomenon. Manufacturing outsourcing has been growing since the 1960s. The surprising finding from the ORN project is the absence of knowledge transfer from manufacturing practices to the offshoring of business services.

The global sourcing of R&D activities through the location of technology enters offshore is also not a new phenomenon (Cantwell, 1995; Kuemmerle, 1999a, 1999b). However, home country remained the most important single location for R&D (Patel & Pavitt, 1991). Dunning (1993) argued that the strategic motives for FDI include market-seeking (which in the ORN data base is a negligible factor) and efficiency-seeking (labor arbitrage is an important driver for companies in the ORN data base). Other drivers include strategic asset-seeking FDI (Wesson, 1993; Caves, 1998; Dunning, 1993), and companies such as Texas Instruments, GE, and Motorola establishing technology centers in China and India as a way of securing political buy in, and by passing stage model (Delios & Henisz, 2003).

The ORN data does include instances of companies augmenting a firm's knowledge base and home-based R&D capabilities (Dunning & Narula, 1995; Kuemmerle, 1999a; Cantwell, 1991; Dunning 1998; Florida, 1997; Howells, 1990). However, perhaps more surprising, ORN data also reveals instances of companies replacing home-based knowledge and R&D capabilities through outsourcing innovation projects offshore and allowing their engineering and science staffing to decline through attrition without replacing (Lewin, Massini, & Peeters, 2009).

NOTE

1. The term "offshorability" refers to the extent to which a business activity is vulnerable to offshoring (see Blinder 2006, 2009).

REFERENCES

Ancori, B., Bureth, A., & Cohendet, P. (2000). The economics of knowledge: The debate about codification and tacit knowledge. *Industrial and Corporate Change*, 9, 255–287.

Apte, U. M., & Mason, R. O. (1995). Global disaggregation of information-intensive services. *Management Science*, 41, 1250–1263.

Blinder, A. S. (2006). Offshoring: The next industrial revolution? *Foreign Affairs*, 85(2), 113–128.

Blinder, A. S. (2007). *How many U.S. jobs might be offshorable?* CEPS Working Paper No. 142, March. Princeton University, Princeton, NJ.

Blinder, A. S. (2009). How many U.S. jobs might be offshorable. *World Economics, 10*(2), 41–78.

Cantwell, J. (1991). The international agglomeration of R&D. In: M. Casson (Ed.), *Global research strategy and international competitiveness* (pp. 104–132). Oxford: Blackwell.

Cantwell, J. (1995). The globalisation of technology: What remains of the product cycle model. *Cambridge Journal of Economics, 19*(1), 155–174.

Caves, R. E. (1998). Industrial organization and new findings on the turnover and mobility of firms. *Journal of Economic Literature, 36*(4), 1947–1982.

Chase, R. B. (1981). The customer contact approach to services: Theoretical bases and practical extensions. *Operations Management, 29*(4), 698–706.

Cohendet, P., & Steinmueller, W. E. (2000). The codification of knowledge: A conceptual and empirical exploration. *Industrial and Corporate Change, 9*(2), 195–209.

Cyert, R., & March, J. G. (1963). *A behavioral theory of the firm.* Englewood Cliffs, NJ: Prentice-Hall.

Davenport, T. H. (2005). The coming commoditization of processes. *Harvard Business Review, 83*(6), 100–108.

Delios, A., & Henisz, W. J. (2003). Political hazards and the sequence of entry by Japanese firms. *Journal of International Business Studies, 34*(3), 227–241.

Dunning, J. (1993). *Multinational enterprises and the global economy.* Wokingham, UK: Addison-Wesley.

Dunning, J. (1998). Globalization, technological change and the spatial organization of economic activity. In: A. Chandler, Jr., P. Hagström & Ö. Sölvell (Eds), *The dynamic firm* (pp. 289–314). Oxford: Oxford University Press.

Dunning, J., & Narula, R. (1995). The R&D activities of foreign firms in the United States. *International Studies of Management and Organization, 5*(1–2), 39–74.

Farrell, D. (2005). Offshoring: Value creation through economic change. *Journal of Management Studies, 42*(3), 675–683.

Florida, R. (1997). The globalization of R&D: Results of a survey of foreign-affiliated R&D laboratories in the USA. *Research Policy, 26*(1), 85–103.

Gospel, H., & Sako, M. (2010). The unbundling of corporate functions: The evolution of shared services and outsourcing in human resource management. *Industrial and Corporate Change, 19*, 295–325.

Heijmen, T., Lewin, A. Y., Manning, S., Perm-Ajchariyawong, N., & Russell, J. W. (2009). *Offshoring reaches the C-Suite.* 2007/8 ORN Survey Report. Duke University and The Conference Board, New York, NY.

Holcomb, T. R., & Hitt, M. A. (2007). Toward a model of strategic outsourcing. *Journal of Operations Management, 25*(2), 464–481.

Howells, J. (1990). The location and organisation of research and development: New horizons. *Research Policy, 19*(2), 133–146.

Kenney, M., Massini, S., & Murtha, T. P. (2009). Offshoring administrative and technical work: New fields for understanding the global enterprise. *Journal of International Business Studies, 40*(6), 887–900.

Kuemmerle, W. (1999a). Foreign direct investment in industrial research in the pharmaceutical and electronics industries – Results from a survey of multinational firms. *Research Policy, 28*(2–3), 179–193.

Kuemmerle, W. (1999b). The drivers of foreign direct investment into research and development: An empirical investigation. *Journal of International Business Studies, 30*(1), 1.

Levy, D. L. (2005). Offshoring in the new global political economy. *Journal of Management Studies, 42*(3), 685–693.

Lewin, A. Y., & Couto, V. (2007). *Next generation offshoring: The globalization of innovation.* Duke University CIBER/Booz Allen Hamilton Report, Durham.

Lewin, A. Y., Manning, S., Massini, S., & Petters, C. (2011). *The ever changing logic of global outsourcing decisions:* Client strategies, path dependencies, and industry dynamics.

Lewin, A. Y., Massini, S., Perm-Ajchariyawong, N., Sappenfield, D., & Walker, J. (2009). Getting serious about offshoring in a struggling economy. *Shared Services & Outsourcing Network (SSON) Shared Services News,* February, pp. 19–23.

Lewin, A. Y., & Peeters, C. (2006a). The top-line allure of off-shoring. *Harvard Business Review,* March, 22–24.

Lewin, A. Y., & Peeters, C. (2006b). Offshoring administrative and technical work: Business hype or the onset of fundamental strategic and organizational transformation?. *Long Range Planning, 39,* 221–239.

Lewin, A. Y., & Perm-Ajchariyawong, N. (2010). *The offshorability decision: A longitudinal, dynamic multi level view.* Offshoring Research Network Working Paper series, Center for International Business Education and Research.

Lewin, A. Y., Massini, S., & Peeters, C. (2009). Why are companies offshoring innovation? The emerging global race for talent. *Journal of International Business Studies, 40*(6), 902–925.

Lewin, A. Y., Massini, S., & Perm-Ajchariyawong, N. (forthcoming). Role of corporate-wide offshoring strategy on offshoring drivers, risks and performance. *Industry and Innovation, 17,* 337–371.

Manning, S., Lewin, A. Y., & Massini, S. (2008). A dynamic perspective on next-generation offshoring: The global sourcing of science and engineering talent. *Academy of Management Perspectives, 22*(3), 35–54.

March, J. G., & Simon, H. A. (1958). *Organizations.* Cambridge, MA: Wiley.

Massini, S., Lewin, A. Y., & Greve, H. R. (2005). Innovators and imitators: Organizational reference groups and adoption of organizational routines. *Research Policy, 34*(10), 1550–1569.

Mithas, S., & Whitaker, J. (2007). Is the world flat or spiky? Information intensity, skills, and global service disaggregation. *Information Systems Research, 18,* 237–259.

Ocasio, W. (1997). Towards an attention-based view of the firm. *Strategic Management Journal, 18,* 187–206.

Patel, P., & Pavitt, K. (1991). Large firms in the production of the world's technology: An important case of 'non-globalization'. *Journal of International Business Studies, 22*(1), 1–21.

Quinn, J. B. (1999). Strategic outsourcing: Leveraging knowledge capabilities. *Sloan Management Review, 40*(4), 9–21.

Wesson T. (1993). *An alternative motivation for foreign direct investment.* Unpublished Dissertation. Harvard University, Cambridge, MA.

GOVERNANCE OF FOREIGN AFFILIATES AS A DISTINCTIVE CHOICE BETWEEN NETWORKS, MARKET, AND HIERARCHY

Lilach Nachum

ABSTRACT

I argue that distinctive attributes of foreign affiliates, arising from their foreignness and multinationality, affect their choices between networks, market, and hierarchy as alternative modes of governance. Comparative analyses of 193 foreign and local professional services firms in London confirm these theoretical expectations. Market relationships are the preferred mode of foreign affiliates, challenging the view of the MNEs hierarchy as a major source of resources of affiliates. I outline direction for future research that follows from this study, including further inquiry into the distinctiveness of the MNE and the study of international activities of professional services firms.

Keywords: Foreign affiliates' choice of governance modes; market versus hierarchy versus networks; professional services; global cities

Various explanations have been suggested for the choices that firms make between networks, market, and hierarchy as alternative means of organizing

The Future of Foreign Direct Investment and the Multinational Enterprise
Research in Global Strategic Management, Volume 15, 315–334
Copyright © 2011 by Emerald Group Publishing Limited
All rights of reproduction in any form reserved
ISSN: 1064-4857/doi:10.1108/S1064-4857(2011)0000015018

value-creation activities (Geyskens, Steenkamp, & Kumar, 2006). Transaction cost economics explains these choices based on the logic of the cost of transactions (Williamson, 1985, 1991). Networks theories imply that networking provides better access to resources that reside outside the boundaries of the firm than market or hierarchy (Powell, 1990), and it is a particularly appropriate means of organizational learning (Powell, Koput, & Kenneth, 1996). The knowledge-based view of the firm (Kogut & Zander, 1992) assigns these choices to the costs of communication and coordination that firms experience in relation to different types of knowledge.

To what extent do these rationales apply to foreign affiliates? Do they select governance modes based on these same logics? Or do they represent a special case in relation to these choices, one that requires special attention?

Certain unique attributes of foreign affiliates, arising from their foreignness and multinationality, may put to question the validity of knowledge generated in relation to firms in general. Affiliates operate in foreign environments, and are separated from other subunits of their MNEs by time and distance (Roth & Kostova, 2003). Foreignness entails that affiliates experience liabilities (Zaheer, 1995; Zaheer & Mosakowski, 1997) and difficulties in establishing legitimacy (Kostova & Zaheer, 1999) that local firms do not confront. Furthermore, as part of a multinational network (Ghoshal & Bartlett, 1993; Nohria & Ghoshal, 1997), affiliates may have different means of resource acquisitions than those available to local firms. For instance, they may draw on internal resources to a greater extent. Do these attributes of foreign affiliates affect their preferences for alternative means of organizing value-creation activities? And if indeed existing explanations for the choices that firms make do not fully apply to foreign affiliates, what alternative explanations should be offered? In this study I seek to start answering these questions.

In inquiring into these questions, I combine theoretical elements of transaction costs economics, the knowledge-based view of the firm, and networks theory. Knowledge-based theory provides the basis for theorizing that governance choices are related to the knowledge that firms possess internally and vary in relation to the type of knowledge concerned. Based on transaction costs economics, I develop the idea that the nationality of firms affects the costs of transactions, such that these costs vary systematically for local and foreign firms. From network theory I adopt the notion that the characteristics of firms influence their position within networks and their networking behavior. I propose nationality as an additional characteristic and suggest that foreign and local firms are likely to differ in terms of their preferences for networks as an alternative to markets and hierarchy.

By adopting multiple theoretical lenses to the examination of the issues at hand, I am able to reach a level of understanding that each of these on its own would have failed to provide (Johansson, 2004).

Methodologically, the study is based on a comparative analysis of foreign and local firms (Ragin, 1987). The latter were used as a means to isolate those elements of governance choice that characterize all firms from those that are distinctive to foreign firms. The empirical analyses are based on a combination of qualitative and quantitative data (Jick, 1979), based on samples of 193 foreign and local professional services firms in London. This narrow industrial and environmental focus enables me to isolate the impact of nationality from other potential influences that may affect the preferences for governance modes. Studies have shown that a meaningful comparison between foreign and local firms requires reference to narrowly defined industries (Mata & Portugal, 2002). Data collected directly from firms serve to elucidate the divers of choice with considerable vigor and detail.

The analyses show significant differences between foreign and local firms in terms of the choices they make among governance modes. Inconsistent with theory, foreign affiliates exhibit a preference for market arrangements over hierarchy and networks, whereas local firms arrange the majority of their activities via networks. Based on these findings, I maintain that the MNE represents a distinctive context for the examination of the choice of governance modes. This choice is at the center of discussions of the boundaries of firms and the rationale for their existence (Williamson, 1985). The finding that nationality of ownership affects these choices and that foreign firms differ significantly in the choices they make thus has important implications for the understanding of the distinctiveness of the MNE as an organizational form (Sundaram & Black, 1992; Ghoshal & Westney, 1993; Roth & Kostova, 2003). Given the strategic importance of governance modes, such an understanding also bears important lessons for the competitive performance of these firms. The application of theories of organization choices – the knowledge-based view of firms, transaction cost economics, and networking theories – to MNEs enabled me to highlight attributes that remain unnoticed in the non-MNE context, and enriches these theories as well.

THEORY AND HYPOTHESES

Foreign affiliates differ from other firms in that they are foreign in the environments that host them and they are part of a geographically dispersed network (Sundaram & Black, 1992; Ghoshal & Westney, 1993; Caves, 1996;

Roth & Kostova, 2003). Their foreignness raises specific challenges in dealing with the environment (Hymer, 1960; Zaheer, 1995; Zaheer & Mosakowski, 1997), such as those arising from limited local knowledge and higher costs of acquiring local information. Foreign affiliates also have to overcome difficulties of establishing legitimacy in foreign countries (Kostova & Zaheer, 1999), and they confront the challenges of coping with multiple, and often conflicting, sources of external authority and denominations of value (Sundaram & Black, 1992). Being part of a geographically dispersed multiple unit network (Ghoshal & Bartlett, 1993) introduces a level of complexity not experienced by local firms and exposes foreign affiliates to the challenge of coordination and communication over distance, which is further complicated by the cultural, political, and economic diversity of the subunits.

I suggest that these two distinctive attributes of affiliates affect the costs of governance modes, and hence affiliates are likely to exhibit preferences that differ from those of local firms. In the discussion that follows, I draw on the three major theoretical strands developed to explain the choices that firms make between different governance modes – transaction cost economics, networks theory, and the knowledge-based view of the firm – and advance hypotheses that outline the direction of the differences.

Hierarchy versus Market

According to transaction costs (TC) theory, three exchange conditions – environmental uncertainty, frequency of the exchange, and asset specificity, that is, the degree to which the assets involved were developed for specific exchanges – determine the costs of the transaction and the relative efficiency of market versus hierarchy in implementing them (Williamson, 1985). I suggest that as a result of their foreignness and multinationality, foreign affiliates experience these conditions differently, leading to different choices between market and hierarchy than those of comparable local firms.

High uncertainty makes it more difficult for the parties to evaluate each other's actions, favoring hierarchical solutions over the market. Due to difficulties in accessing and interpreting information on the local market (Zaheer, 1995), affiliates are likely to experience greater uncertainty than local firms. Further, affiliates are likely to have less frequent exchanges due to their newness in a country (Hymer, 1960). Low frequency inhibits the establishment of relationships between the parties involved, and therefore favors hierarchical solutions (Williamson, 1991). Differences in the competitive assets possessed by foreign and local firms (Hymer, 1960; Caves, 1996) often entail that the assets of foreign firms are more specific. Furthermore, their weak local roots and knowledge, compared with local firms, may inhibit the ability of foreign affiliates to recognize alternative use for their assets in related activities within a country, further enhancing their specificity. TC theory suggests that transactions with highly specific assets favor hierarchy, whereas the market is the efficient mode for organizing generic assets (Riordan & Williamson, 1985).

Furthermore, due to liabilities of foreignness, affiliates are likely to experience difficulties in writing contracts and guarding their proper execution, and are less likely than local firms to have the ability to specify in a contract the entire conditions for the agreement and anticipate all possible circumstances in the future. To avoid these difficulties, firms turn to hierarchy and internalize the transactions (Williamson, 1985). Affiliates may also be discriminated against by local legal systems and have higher risk of expropriation by host governments compared with local firms (Teece, 1977). This increases the costs of market interactions over hierarchical solutions.

Foreign affiliates may also have less need to rely on the market because they can access via the MNE network many of the resources that local firms acquire on the market. Desai, Foley, and Forbes (2005) show that foreign affiliates rely on internal capital market to a greater extent than local firms do. In some cases, resources provided internally via the MNE hierarchy are of better quality or low costs than those available in the market, creating further incentive for affiliates to prefer hierarchical solutions over market transactions (Desai, Foley, & Hines, 2004). This view is consistent with the conceptualization of the MNE as a vehicle for the internal transfer of proprietary resources and capabilities, primarily knowledge, across borders (Buckley & Casson, 1976; Kogut & Zander, 1992). The critical advantage of the MNE is to perform knowledge combination that markets cannot (Kogut & Zander, 1992, 1993). Almeida, Song, and Grant (2002) show the superiority of hierarchical MNE means of building knowledge across borders over markets (and alliances). Formally:

H1. Compared with local firms, ceteris paribus, foreign affiliates rely on hierarchy more than on markets.

Hierarchy versus Networks

For several reasons, foreign affiliates are likely to prefer hierarchy over networks to a greater extent than comparable local firms. For one, affiliates are likely to experience difficulties in establishing network relationships, raising the costs of these relationships for them and diminishing their benefits. Scholars studying network relationships have acknowledged access to networks as the factor that determines the potential partners available to firms and the intensity of their network relationships (Gulati, Nohria, & Zaheer, 2000). The access of affiliates to local networks in foreign environments is likely to be restricted due to their unfamiliarity with cultural norms and difficulties in apprehending the common values and beliefs that govern network relationships (Zaheer, 1995; Zaheer & Mosakowski, 1997). Their access might be constrained also on the ground of lack of legitimacy (Kostova & Zaheer, 1999) and unwillingness of the members of the network to form relationships with them.

The preference for hierarchy over networks is likely also from the perspective on resource-based theory (Eisenhardt & Schoonhoven, 1996). According to this theory, network relationships are driven by resource needs, and firms possessing extensive resources are less likely to establish them. Foreign affiliates can derive some resources sought in network relationships internally from their MNE network, and therefore they have less need for external relationships for the purpose of resource acquisition. The diversity and richness of the MNE internal network makes a hierarchy solution more attractive for them than for local firms that usually do not have access to such stocks of internal resources. While the type of resources obtained via network and hierarchy may not be the same (Poppo & Zenger, 2002), resources gained via hierarchy may serve affiliates better than those obtained via local network relationships. The wide geographic scope typical of MNE operations often implies that foreign affiliates need interactions that extend beyond the boundaries of the local network to meet their resource needs. For instance, research shows that foreign affiliates tend to serve more multinational clients than local firms do (Jungnickel, 2002). To be able to serve these clients effectively, affiliates need knowledge that matches the geographic scope of their clients, and local relationships may have limits in meetings their needs. Formally:

H2. Compared with local firms, ceteris paribus, foreign affiliates rely on hierarchy more than on networks.

Market versus Networks

Foreign affiliates are likely to exhibit preference for market arrangements over networks more than comparable local firms do. According to TC theory, market transactions are based on exchange between autonomous economic entities managed by the price mechanism (Williamson, 1991), and are administered via contracts and rights that determine opportunities for value creation (Thompson, 2003). Such arrangements are generally preferred when firms do not share a common background with potential partners, and experience difficulties establishing relationships with them (Powell, 1990; Gulati, 1995), which is often the case in relation to foreign affiliates. Market arrangements do not require the social relations necessary for the development of network interactions (Eisenhardt & Schoonhoven, 1996; Uzzi, 1999; McEvily, Perrone, & Zaheer, 2003).

Further, the prospects for continuing interaction (Baker, 1990) are typically less for foreign firms that are less embedded in any given locality, and this encourages the use of market relationships over networks. While unfamiliarity and short duration of operation are likely to impede the ability of foreign affiliates to establish network relationships, these are usually not liabilities when relying on market arrangements. Formally:

H3. Compared with local firms, ceteris paribus, foreign affiliates rely on the market more than on networks.

THE EMPIRICAL SETTING: PROFESSIONAL SERVICES FIRMS IN LONDON

The scope of the study is confined to professional services firms located in London. This enables me to control for environmental and industrial influences that affect the preferences of firms for governance modes, regardless of their nationality.

Professional services represent an interesting setting for the study of the choices that foreign affiliates make among governance modes. Research on this issue has typically focused on high-technology manufacturing industries (e.g., Powell et al., 1996; Eisenhardt & Schoonhoven, 1996; Almeida et al., 2002) and has emphasized the specific nature of innovation in these industries as a major driver of these choices. Much of the theorization of these choices is thus based on the characteristics of such industries, and its applicability to other industries has rarely been tested (Baker, Faulkner, and Fisher (1998) and Uzzi (1999) represent notable exceptions). Professional services provide an opportunity to extend existing theories to a different industrial setting. Further, during the last decade or so there have been considerable changes in the governance modes adopted by professional services firms, notably a surge in various forms of interfirm interactions (Aharoni & Nachumm, 2000), providing a rich setting for studying the choices of firms.

I confine the scope of the study to three professional services industries – management consultancy, legal services, and advertising. Research suggests that a meaningful comparison between foreign and local firms requires reference to narrowly defined industries, such that the impact of nationality of ownership could be isolated from differences associated with industrial affiliations (Mata & Portugal, 2002).

METHODOLOGY

The Data

Data collection proceeded in several phases, and combined quantitative and qualitative methods (Jick, 1979). The first phase involved a series of open-ended, semistructured interviews with selected firms and industry analysts and representatives of industry organizations, supplemented by a variety of secondary sources on professional services firms in London. In this phase I sought to gain a qualitative understanding of the research setting and the issues that drive the choice of governance modes. In total I conducted 17 interviews, each lasting about an hour. I returned to these industry representatives and firms after the completion of the data collection to assist me interpret the results. The interviews helped formulate my thinking and created the ground for the next stage that involved a large-scale survey of a sample of professional services firms and empirical testing.

The sampling frame for this survey was drawn from industry directories and included *Chambers & Partners: A Guide to the Legal Profession* for law firms, *Account List File* for advertising, and *AP's Directory of Management Consultants in the UK* for management consultancy. Industry experts consulted regarded these as the most authoritative and comprehensive sources of information on London's firms in these three industries. To reach a similar representation of local and foreign firms, the sampling procedure was stratified by nationality (i.e., foreign or local) and was random within these categories (Singleton & Strait, 1999).

I approached a total of 600 firms. Telephone interviewing was selected as the method for data collection because it provides many of the benefits of personal interviews, including the provision of direct contact with firms and a first-hand impression of their activities, at lower costs, which enabled me to reach a large number of firms. Another advantage of telephone interviewing is that it often yields higher response rates than alternatives like mailed questionnaires (Pehrsson, 2006). Given the small size of the population I studied, high response rates were particularly important. Firms were guaranteed confidentiality in order to establish confidence that the provision of the data I sought would not undermine the firm's competitive edge. Attempts were made to approach the top management, as it consists of individuals with the broadest knowledge of and responsibility for the strategic issues of interest (CyCyota & Harrison, 2002). However, approaching senior managers often proves difficult and, in some cases, less senior executives were interviewed instead.

After excluding firms that no longer exist, the response rate was 34%, a high response rate when approaching top management. As a yardstick for comparison, in a meta-analysis of response rates from 231 studies that surveyed executives and published in top management journals between 1992 and 2003, CyCyota and Harrison (2006) found an average response rate of 32%. I conducted t-tests and found no significant differences between respondents and nonrespondents in terms of size (number of employees) and growth (changes in number of employees) at the 0.01 and 0.05 levels, respectively. The final sample contains 193 firms, of which 90 are foreign affiliates and 103 local. The industrial breakdown is 88 advertising agencies, 56 law firms, and 49 management consultancies. The differences in sample size mirror closely variations in concentration levels across the three industries.

The telephone interviews were employed for the purpose of collecting data on the choice of governance modes. Other firms data were collected from a variety of secondary sources, including industry publications and directories. Some of these data were verified in the personal interviews. The combination of secondary and direct sources of data removes concerns regarding common method variance problem.

Operation of the Constructs

The attempt to empirically delineate the use of networks, market, and hierarchy as distinctive alternatives of governance is problematic on several grounds. For one, this distinction is ambiguous because the different modes often exist concurrently and are employed simultaneously by the same firm (Bradach & Eccles, 1989; Makadok & Coff, 2009), in some cases for the execution of a same transaction (see Baker (1990) in relation to the employment of banks by car producers). Moreover, it has been argued that many transactions do not correspond neatly to any single modes but rather combine them (Hennart, 1993), making the attempt to distinguish among them empirically most challenging. In addition, the choice between alternatives may not be of a permanent nature, and often changes according to the circumstances and over time.

When designing the questionnaire to firms, I addressed these challenges in several ways. First, I presented firms with a detailed list of activities, and allowed multiple choices, such that the same activity could be implemented via more than a single governance mode. Second, I inquired about the frequency of the various governance modes at a given point in time, and presented the choice between them as a matter of degree rather than as a mutually exclusive choice.

The measurement items were generated through a review of prior literature and consultation with industry analysts and representatives of firms. Based on these preliminary investigations, I constructed a list of activities whereby the choice among varying means of governance is most apparent. My aim was to cover a broad range of activities that provides a rich picture of the choices across multiple types of transactions. After a number of pilot tests and subsequent revisions, I selected the following activities:

- Development of new services
- Improvement of existing services
- Support services outside the firm's line of business
- Implementation of the firm's main line(s) of business
- Recruitment of skilled employees
- HR issues (after recruitment).

Respondents were asked to state, in relation to each of these items, the share of the activity undertaken internally, purchased on the market or implemented via various forms of collaboration in the year preceding the data collection analysis. In the analyses that follow, I present the data as a combined index across all activities, which is calculated as the simple average of the values assigned to each of the three governance modes across all the activities. I do not weigh individual activities because I wish to observe the combined choices of individual firms across all of them.

Control Variables

I include in the analysis a set of firm-specific attributes that according to previous research influence the choice of governance modes. These variables are also likely to vary across foreign and local firms:

1. Size, which affects the choice of governance via its impact on the magnitude of resources available internally, measured by the total number of employees. Employees constitute the most important assets of professional services firms, and their number is an appropriate indicator of their size.
2. Age, as it affects the familiarity with the market and networks and experience in establishing the respective relationships, as well as the costs of governing these relationships. Age is measured by the number of years since the establishment of the London office.
3. Industrial affiliation, two dummies for the three industries studied (advertising, management consulting, and law), to account for possible industrial effects.
4. Governance form, whether partnership or corporation, because it affects the strength of firms' internal relationships, which in turn could affect governance choices (Empson, 2007). This variable is coded as a dummy variable that gets the value 1 for partnership, 0 for corporation.
5. Nationality, because research suggests that the choice of governance modes varies across countries (Shan & Hamilton, 1991; Dyer, 1996). This may introduce variation within the foreign sample that would obscure the differences between foreign and local firms. I introduce a series of dummy variables corresponding to the United States, Japan, the rest of Southeast Asia, Western Europe, and hold "all others" as the base category.

STATISTICAL ANALYSIS

The testing of the hypotheses is based on comparative analyses of the local and foreign samples in terms of their governance mode choices (Ragin, 1987) (Table 1). I employ ANOVA and MANOVA for the test of difference between foreign and local firms and among the governance modes, respectively, using the set of control variables as covariates.

As the comparative analyses in Table 1 show, the choices of foreign affiliates differ significantly from those of local firms in relation to all three

Table 1. Choice of Governance Modes: Foreign and Local
Firms – Sample Averages across Various Activities.

	Market	Hierarchy	Networks	Sig. Test: Governance	N
Foreign	.52	.27	.21	***	90
Local	.34	.20	.46	**	103
Sig. test: foreign/local	***	*	**		

$^{†}p < .10$; $^{*}p < .05$; $^{**}p < .01$; $^{***}p < .001$.

governance modes, but the differences are most apparent in relation to market relationships. These findings suggest that differences associated with nationality of ownership affect firms' choices, providing support for the initial argument underlying this chapter. Foreignness and multinationality presumably affect the costs of the different governance modes, which in turn influence firms' preferences.

Further, market transactions are the preferred governance mode of foreign firms, whereas local firms arrange most of their value-creation activities via networks. This latter mode is the least frequently employed by foreign affiliates. These differences are in agreement with the arguments advanced above in relation to the difficulties that foreign firms experience in embedding themselves in local networks of relationships. The industry analysts and firms interviewed for this study supported this explanation and suggested that in London, relationships are often determined by belonging to the diffused "old boys network," whereby personal contacts are used to identify potential partners and are also critical in client–provider relationships. Referral from former or existing clients was regarded as the most important means of gaining new business. Also recruitment via personal contacts is dominant among local firms, far more common among them than among foreign firms. As the managing director of a local advertising agency puts it: "... how can anyone be certain the degree to which a client's increased sales, market share or profitability is solely due to our advertising campaign, a new marketing strategy or reorganized structure? Referrals and recommendations of people we know overcome some of this ambiguity ...." Another interviewee puts it very succinctly: "People are not buying a commodity, what they're buying is the person they see delivering a particular service, so in that context, it is extremely important ...that they feel confident in the person, and they are prepared to pay for that person. ... Trust is crucial ...."

Foreign firms in contrast appear to base their activities on such relationships to a far lesser extent, most typically not as a deliberate strategy, but rather on an ad-hoc basis. They also seem to be far more concerned about having a very clear idea of the expected benefits before entering into any collaborative arrangements, perhaps due to the need to be accountable for the parent company, and expressed a preference for market-based arrangements: "... I would prefer, for example, to say, fine, we will pay you a commission should you pass the work to us, but I would like to be in control of the situation; but joint ventures – no, not really."

The findings reported in Table 1 fail to support H1 which stated that foreign firms are likely to prefer hierarchy over markets. These findings are inconsistent with knowledge-based view of the MNE as a vehicle for the transfer of knowledge across borders (Buckley & Casson, 1976; Kogut & Zander, 1993). Nor are they in agreement with the findings of Almeida et al. (2002) whereby the MNE internal network was superior to both markets and alliances in cross-border knowledge transfer.

The rationale for the preference for the hierarchy over alternative governance modes lies on the transfer of resources, primarily knowledge, among the MNE subunits (Kogut & Zander, 1993). However, research suggests limits to the internal transferability of MNE resources arising from the context-specificity of the knowledge that provides distinctive competence for sustained competitive advantage, which may lose its value in a different context (Van de Ven, 2004). Further, the type of knowledge of professional services firms may not be suitable for internal MNE transfer. Much of value creation in these industries lies on the creative capabilities of individuals, and in a sense, each time a service is produced it has to be unique (Løwendahl, 2000). This nonstandardized nature of the production constrains the value of internal knowledge sharing. The need for deep knowledge of the client and its environment may further diminish the value of knowledge of remote subunits (Nachum & Keeble, 2001). This type of knowledge often resists transfer and is likely to be costly to transfer over distance (Teece, 1977).

Yet another explanation for the failure to support H1 might be sought in the partnership structure common in professional services industries (Greenwood, Hinings, & Brown, 1990), which lacks the sense of authority and control typical to corporations. Notwithstanding the growing integration of these partnerships (Empson, 2007), local offices tend to enjoy considerable autonomy and may interact with other subunits to a limited extent.

The results of the analyses provide support for H2 and H3, suggesting that, in agreement with theory, foreign affiliates have a preference for hierarchy and market arrangements over networks, probably reflecting the difficulties they experience in creating trust and legitimacy necessary for the formation of network arrangements.

CONCLUDING REMARKS

In this study I compared the choices that foreign and local firms make among market, hierarchy, and networks as alternative governance modes for organizing value-creating activities, in order to examine to what extent and in which ways nationality of ownership affects these choices. The findings show that foreign affiliates exhibit a preference for market transactions over hierarchy and networks, whereas local firms implement most of their transactions via networks followed by the market. These different choices presumably reflect varying costs of governance modes for local and foreign firms.

The study makes several important contributions to the theory of the MNE. For one, it elucidates the distinctive nature of the MNE in terms of the choice of governance modes, an aspect of their behavior that, although has received substantial attention, to the best of my knowledge has not been examined in comparison with local firms. The merits of this comparative approach lie in that it enables me to isolate the factors that are shared by all firms from those that are distinctive to foreign affiliates. The choices that firms make among governance modes determine their boundaries. Deepening the understanding of such critical aspect of the choices they make is thus fundamental for the understanding of the MNE.

Further, the preferences of the affiliates I studied for market arrangements over hierarchy provide important theoretical insights regarding the benefits of the MNE internal networks and their limits as an alternative governance mode to markets and networks. Discussing these findings in light of the type of knowledge of professional services firms, I suggested that the dichotomy between codified and tacit knowledge as determining firms' preferences for different organization modes may not be sufficient to capture the range of knowledge types that affect these choices (Kogut & Zander, 1992). Additional types of knowledge that ought to be considered may include its context-specificity and its sources, whether in individuals or the organization as a whole.

The study also contributes to TC theory, by examining the impact of firm-specific characteristics on the choice of governance modes. The focus of TC theory has been on the characteristics of transactions as the factors that determine the choices that firms make between alternative governance modes (Williamson, 1985, 1991). Variations across firms in terms of the costs of transactions they experience have received only scant attention (see Nickerson & Bergh (1999) for a notable exception). I extend the TC logic and suggest that the costs of alternative governance modes vary not only by the characteristics of the transaction, but also across firms, and hence firms exhibit different preferences for varying alternatives. I illustrate this variation in relation to one characteristic of a firm – nationality of ownership – and show that foreign and local firms make significantly different choices, probably reflecting the varying costs of alternative modes for them.

LOOKING FORWARD: WHERE SHOULD WE GO FROM HERE?

This chapter opens up large areas for future research. For one, there is a need to further the understanding of the distinctiveness of the MNE and extend it to other aspects of their character and behavior. This issue is fundamental for the development of a theory of the MNE as separate from that of firms in general and provides the rationale for the field of international business as a distinct field of inquiry. Only if these firms differ from other firms in some fundamental way is there a need to study them on their own (Ghoshal & Westney, 1993). Otherwise, what is known in relation to firms in general can be applied, with some minimal modifications, to the MNE. Notwithstanding a few notable exceptions (Roth & Kostova, 2003), these issues have received only scant attention, in an academic field that was originated in the attempt to understand why the MNE exists (Hymer, 1960; Caves, 1996), and later on turned to the inquiry of the challenges of managing the MNE (Ghoshal & Bartlett, 1993).

One way to pursue this issue forward is by adopting a finer distinction of the local sample that is used as the benchmark for the comparison with foreign affiliates, notably whether purely domestic or local MNEs. A number of studies have shown that comparisons of foreign firms with these two groups of local firms yield different results (Doms & Jensen, 1998; Jungnickel, 2002). This approach provides a more nuanced way to examine the sources of the differences between foreign and local firms. Comparing foreign affiliates with local MNEs is indicative of differences between MNEs operating in their home country or in foreign countries, that is, differences arising from foreignness but not from multinationality. A comparative analysis that contrasts foreign firms with purely domestic local firms is informative regarding differences that originate in both foreignness and multinationality.

Another important task for future research is to examine the performance and competitive implications of the choices that foreign affiliates make among governance modes. The link with performance would provide normative indications as to whether the preferences of affiliates are appropriate, that is, do they enhance their ability to compete successfully, or rather impede it? The impact of governance choice on performance has not received much empirical verification (see Dyer (1996) for a notable exception), although according to TC theory such an impact should exist via the effect of this choice on efficiency and costs.

There is also a need to deepen the understanding of professional services firms, such that the broader validity of findings based on these firms can be evaluated. Given the growing importance of these industries – on their own, and via their impact on the operation of firms in other industries – additional research in this direction is warranted. With reference to the choice of governance modes, certain characteristics of these industries are likely to affect the preferences of firms for particular governance modes. These may deter generalizations, and would benefit from more research attention. For one, due to the nontradability of professional services and the need for high levels of local adaptation, foreign activity is overwhelmingly in the form of horizontal investment (Nachum, 1999). The choices that affiliates make between alternative governance modes are likely to differ from those made in vertical investment. These two types of investments arise from the internalization of the market for intermediate product markets and for knowledge, respectively, a variation that is likely to lead to varying preferences for governance modes. Furthermore, the relationships of professional services firms with their clients, particularly the rules regarding potential conflicts of interest between different clients (Baker et al., 1998; Haywards, 2003), may restrict the reliance on network arrangements. The need to validate the findings with reference to different industries appears to be most important in relation to the preference I found for market arrangements over hierarchy. I attributed these findings to specific characteristics of these industries, notably the patterns of knowledge creation and diffusion.

More attention is warranted by future research to the impact of context on the choice of governance mode by foreign affiliates. For instance, research shows that firms located in large metropolitan areas exhibit different make or buy preferences and have greater tendency to outsource.

The developed market offering of such locations provide more viable alternative for hierarchy for such firms than for those in rural areas (Greenstein, Forman, & Glodfarb, 2008). The regulatory framework in a country, notably in relation to foreign firms, is also likely to affect the choice of governance mode, and probably accentuates the differences between foreign and local firms in that regard.

More attention to the dynamic nature of the choice of governance mode is also warranted. Governance choices, notably of foreign firms, evolve and change over time (Teece, 1986), as firms become more familiar with the foreign environment. Firms often "experiment" with various modes, and go through a process of trial and error, that is inherently dynamic. Such research should be undertaken with the broader view of developing a dynamic theory of the MNE, which is not fully equipped with means to explain change.

REFERENCES

Aharoni, Y., & Nachumm, L. (Eds). (2000). *Globalization of services: Some implications for theory and practice*. Routledge: London.

Almeida, P., Song, J., & Grant, M. R. (2002). Are firms superior to alliances and markets? An empirical test of cross-border knowledge building. *Organization Science, 13*(2), 147–161.

Baker, W. E. (1990). Market networks and corporate behavior. *American Journal of Sociology, 96*(3), 589–625.

Baker, W. E., Faulkner, R. R., & Fisher, G. A. (1998). Hazards of the market: The continuity and dissolution of interorganizational market relationships. *American Sociological Review, 63*(2), 147–177.

Bradach, J. L., & Eccles, R. G. (1989). Price, authority and trust: From ideal types to plural forms. *Annual Review of Sociology, 15*, 97–118.

Buckley, P., & Casson, M. (1976). *The future of the multinational enterprise*. Houndmills: Palgrave Macmillan.

Caves, R. (1996). *Multinational enterprise and economic analysis* (2nd ed.). Cambridge: Cambridge University Press.

Cycyota, C. S., & Harrison, D. A. (2002). Enhancing survey response rates at the executive level: Are employee- or consumer-level techniques effective? *Journal of Management, 28*(2), 151–176.

Cycyota, C. S., & Harrison, D. A. (2006). What (not) to expect when surveying executives: A meta-analysis of top manager response rates and techniques over time. *Organizational Research Methods, 9*(2), 133–160.

Desai, M. A., Foley, C. F., & Forbes, K. J. (2005). Financial constraints and growth: Multinational and local firm responses to currency depreciations. Mimeo, Harvard University

Desai, M. A., Foley, C. F., & Hines, J. R. (2004). The costs of shared ownership: Evidence from international joint ventures. *Journal of Financial Economics, 73*(2), 323–374.

Doms, M. E., & Jensen, J. B. (1998). Comparing wages, skills, and productivity between domestically and foreign-owned manufacturing establishments in the United States. In: R. E. Baldwin, R. E. Lipsey & J. D. Richardson (Eds), *Geography and ownership as bases for economic accounting* (pp. 235–258). Chicago: University of Chicago Press.

Dyer, J. H. (1996). Does governance matter? Keiretsu alliances and asset specificity as sources of Japanese competitive advantage. *Organization Science, 7*(6), 649–666.

Eisenhardt, K. M., & Schoonhoven, C. B. (1996). Resource-based view of strategic alliance formation: Strategic and social effects in entrepreneurial firms. *Organization Science, 7*(2), 136–150.

Empson, L. (Ed.) (2007). *Managing the modern law firm*. Oxford: Oxford University Press.

Geyskens, I., Steenkamp, J. B., & Kumar, N. (2006). Make, buy, or ally: A transaction cost theory meta-analysis. *Academy of Management Journal, 49*(3), 519–543.

Ghoshal, S., & Bartlett, C. (1993). The multinational corporation as an interorganizational network. In: S. Ghoshal & E. D. Westney (Eds), *Organization theory and the multinational corporation* (pp. 77–104). New York: St. Martin Press.

Ghoshal, S., & Westney, E. D. (1993). Introduction and overview. In: S. Ghoshal & E.D. Westney (Eds), *Organization theory and the multinational corporation* (pp. 1–23). New York: St. Martin Press.

Greenstein, S., Forman, C., & Glodfarb, A. (2008). Understanding the inputs into innovation: Do cities substitute for internal firm resources? *Journal of Economics and Management Strategy, 17*(2), 295–316.

Greenwood, R., Hinings, C. R., & Brown, J. (1990). P^2-form strategic management: Corporate practices in professional partnerships. *Academy of Management Journal, 33*(4), 725–755.

Gulati, R. (1995). Does familiarity breed trust? The implications of repeated ties for contractual choice in alliances. *Academy of Management Journal, 38*, 85–112.

Gulati, R., Nohria, N., & Zaheer, A. (2000). Strategic networks. *Strategic Management Journal, 21*(3), 203–215.

Hayward, M. L. A. (2003). Professional influence: The effect of investment banks on clients' acquisition financing and performance. *Strategic Management Journal, 24*(9), 783–802.

Hennart, J. F. (1993). Explaining the swollen middle: Why most transactions are a mix of "market" and "hierarchy". *Organization Science, 4*(4), 529–547.

Hymer, S. H. (1960). *The international operations of national firms: A study of foreign direct investment*. Cambridge, MA: MIT Press.

Jick, T. D. (1979). Qualitative and quantitative methods: Triangulation in action. *Administrative Science Quarterly, 24*(4), 602–611.

Johansson, F. (2004). *The medici effect: Breakthrough insights at the intersection of ideas, concepts, and cultures*. Boston, MA: Harvard Business School Press.

Jungnickel, R. (Ed.) (2002). *Foreign-owned firms: Are they different?* Houndmills: Palgrave Macmillan.

Kogut, B., & Zander, U. (1992). Knowledge of the firm, combinative capabilities, and the replication of technology. *Organization Science, 3*(3), 383–397.

Kogut, B., & Zander, U. (1993). Knowledge of the firm and the evolutionary theory of the multinational corporation. *Journal of International Business Studies, 24*(4), 625–646.

Kostova, T., & Zaheer, S. (1999). Organizational legitimacy under conditions of complexity: The case of the multinational enterprise. *Academy of Management Review, 24*(1), 64–81.

Løwendahl, B. R. (2000). *Strategic management of professional service firms* (2nd ed.). Copenhagen: Copenhagen Business School Press.

Makadok, R., & Coff, R. (2009). Both market and hierarchy: An incentive-system theory of hybrid governance forms. *Academy of management Review, 34*(2), 297–320.

Mata, J., & Portugal, P. (2002). The survival of new domestic and foreign-owned firms. *Strategic Management Journal, 23*(4), 323–343.

McEvily, B., Perrone, V., & Zaheer, A. (2003). Introduction to the special issue on trust in an organizational context. *Organization Science, 14*(1), 1–4.

Nachum, L. (1999). *The origins of the international competitiveness of firms: The impact of location and ownership in professional service industries.* Aldershot: Edward Elgar.

Nachum, L., & Keeble, D. (2001). MNE linkages in localized clusters: Foreign and local firms in the media cluster of Central London. Best Papers Proceeding, Academy of Management, International Management Division, Washington, DC.

Nickerson, J. A., & Bergh, R. V. (1999). Economizing in the context of strategizing: Governance mode choice in Cournot competition. *Journal of Economic Behavior and Organization, 40,* 1–15.

Nohria, N., & Ghoshal, S. (1997). *The differentiated network: Organizing multinational corporations for value creation.* San Francisco, CA: Jossey-Bass Publishers.

Pehrsson, A. (2006). Business relatedness and performance: A study of managerial perceptions. *Strategic Management Journal, 27*(3), 265–281.

Poppo, L., & Zenger, T. (2002). Do formal contracts and relational governance function as substitutes or complements? *Strategic Management Journal, 23*(8), 707–725.

Powell, W. W. (1990). Neither market nor hierarchy: Network forms of organization. *Research in Organizational Behavior, 12,* 295–336.

Powell, W. W., Koput, K. W., & Kenneth, W. (1996). Interorganizational collaboration and the locus of innovation: Networks of learning in biotechnology. *Administrative Science Quarterly, 41*(1), 116–139.

Ragin, C. C. (1987). *The comparative method: Moving beyond qualitative and quantitative strategies.* Berkeley, CA: University of California Press.

Riordan, M., & Williamson, O. E. (1985). Asset specificity and economic organization. *International Journal of Industrial Organization, 3,* 365–378.

Roth, K., & Kostova, T. (2003). The use of the multinational corporation as a research context. *Journal of Management, 29*(6), 883–902.

Shan, W., & Hamilton, W. (1991). Country-specific advantage and international cooperation. *Strategic Management Journal, 12*(6), 419–432.

Singleton, R. A., & Strait, B. C. (1999). *Approaches to social research* (3rd ed.). Oxford: Oxford University Press.

Sundaram, A. K., & Black, J. S. (1992). The environment and internal organization of multinational enterprises. *Academy of Management Review, 17*(4), 729–757.

Teece, D. J. (1977). Technology transfer by multinational firms: The resource cost of transferring technological know-how. *The Economic Journal, 87*(2), 242–261.

Teece, D. J. (1986). Transaction cost economics and the multinational enterprise. *Journal of Economic Behavior and Organization, 7,* 21–45.

Thompson, G. F. (2003). *Between hierarchies and markets: The logic and limits of networks forms of organization.* Oxford: Oxford University Press.

Uzzi, B. (1999). Embeddedness in the making of financial capital: How social relations and networks benefit firms seeking finance. *American Sociological Review, 64*(4), 481–505.

Van de Ven, A. (2004). The context-specific nature of competence and corporate development. *Asia Pacific Journal of Management, 21,* 123–147.

Williamson, O. (1985). *The economic institutions of capitalism*. New York: Free Press.
Williamson, O. (1991). Comparative economic organizations: The analysis of discrete structural alternatives. *Administrative Science Quarterly, 36*(2), 269–296.
Zaheer, S. (1995). Overcoming the liabilities of foreignness. *Academy of Management Journal, 38*(2), 341–363.
Zaheer, S., & Mosakowski, E. (1997). The dynamics of the liability of foreignness: A global study of survival in financial services. *Strategic Management Journal, 18*(6), 439–464.

GLOBAL SERVICE MULTINATIONALS FROM A SMALL OPEN ECONOMY – THE CASE OF ISRAELI HIGH-TECH SERVICE PROVIDERS

Niron Hashai

ABSTRACT

The chapter investigates the determinants of the extent of foreign services multinationals originating SMOPECs. An inverted U-shaped relationship between the level of technological knowledge and extent of foreign services provision is found, stemming from the facilitating and inhibiting effects of technological knowledge on foreign services provision. Standardization of services and their automation positively moderates this relationship. Overall, the chapter highlights the increased importance of relatively small global service providers from SMOPECs as a new type of multinational that is likely increase in its dominancy in the near future.

The Future of Foreign Direct Investment and the Multinational Enterprise
Research in Global Strategic Management, Volume 15, 335–353
Copyright © 2011 by Emerald Group Publishing Limited
ISSN: 1064-4857/doi:10.1108/S1064-4857(2011)0000015019

INTRODUCTION

Traditionally multinational corporations (MNCs) are conceived as large industrial firms coming from the world's largest countries and exploiting their economies of scale when operating worldwide. Large firms have more resources to establish and coordinate internationally dispersed activities and are well-positioned to develop global brand names and exploit economies of scale and scope globally (Agarwal & Ramasawi, 1992; Aharoni, 1966; Aliber, 1970; Buckley & Casson, 1981; Caves, 1971, 1996; Cavusgil, 1984; Chandler, 1986, 1990; Dunning, 1977, 1988; Porter, 1985).

Yet, in the last few decades more and more firms from small open economies (SMOPECs) such as Sweden, Denmark, Norway, Taiwan, and Israel are becoming part of the global economy (Aharoni, 2000). Many of these firms are small and often also very young when they start out the international operations (Aharoni, 1994; Knight & Cavusgil, 2004; Oviatt & McDougall, 1994) and even more interestingly are not pure manufacturers, but also engage in some kind of service provision (Aharoni & Nachum, 2000; Aharoni, 2004). In many instances, this is because these firms are considered highly technology intensive and provide intangible products which require frequent interaction with their customers (e.g., software) or services such as internet, storage and data centers, cellular services, or telecommunications (Aharoni & Hirsch, 1996; Almor, Hashai, & Hirsch, 2006).

It follows therefore that small, Hi-Tech, service providers from small countries are another type of MNC, yet this type of firms has not received much attention in extant international business research.

Given the increased importance of services in international trade and investments (Aharoni & Nachum, 2000; Kolstad & Villanger, 2008) and the increased importance of intangible inputs such as technological knowledge in the world's economy, this type of firms are likely to become as important (if not more) as large industrial MNCs from large countries where foreign direct investment (FDI) is concerned.

The current chapter aims to aid with the understating of the international characteristics of Hi-Tech global service providers from a small economy by analyzing several factors affecting the extent of internationalization of Israeli Hi-Tech service providers. Israel is a SMOPECs renowned for its Hi-Tech sector and entrepreneurial spirit where many Hi-Tech firms become international almost at birth (Hashai & Almor, 2004). It, therefore, serves as a suitable setting to test questions regarding the linkage between various characteristics of small service providers and their extent of foreign services provision. Of particular interest are the relationships between the level of technological knowledge and the extent of foreign services provision as well as the moderating effect of specific characteristics of the provided services such as level of standardization and automation on the technological knowledge-extent of foreign services provision relationship.

Next, the chapter discusses why technology-intensive service multi-nationals from a SMOPECs face different internationalization challenges than other firms. Then, a conceptual framework leading to a set of hypotheses regarding the associations between the nature of these firms' services and their extent of foreign services provision is presented. These hypotheses are tested on a sample of Israel-based Hi-Tech service providers. Finally, the results are presented and discussed, and their implications for future research on FDI are highlighted.

What Makes Service Multinationals from a Small Open Economy Unique?

Services and Products – Not a Clear-Cut Distinction
Services are distinct from products in the fact that they require some kind of interaction with the firm's customers and cannot be inventoried (Boddewyn, Marsha, Halbrich, & Perry, 1986; Roberts, 1998). It follows from this definition that the production and consumption of services must take place simultaneously (Bhagwati, 1986; Hirsch, 1989; Sampson & Snape, 1985).

This observation implies that in the international context there are three ways of providing a services abroad (Aharoni, 1999): (1) supplying the service from the home country to customers located at foreign countries, (2) supplying the service from operations based in the host country to indigenous customers, and (3) foreign customers receive service at the home country of the service provider (such as in the case of tourism).

Yet, it is noteworthy that the distinction between "services" and "products" is not so obvious. While there are certainly pure services such as banking, accounting, telecommunications, etc., there are hardly products that do not require any accompanied service. Any product requires transportation in order to reach its customers. Other commonly used services include communication, insurance, finance, warehousing, packaging, etc. In other words, there is not always a clear-cut distinction between service and product supplying.

Intangible services can therefore be supplied on their own (in the case of pure services) or must accompany any tangible good before the latter can be used or consumed. An important distinction between supplied services is whether they are "universal" or "firm specific" (Almor, et al., 2006).

Services that are commonly provided by specialized firms can be labeled "universal." Such services usually include: transportation, communication, insurance, finance, or warehousing. These services usually imply for a large set of products and are not specifically related to a particular product or to a specific technological knowledge. In contrast, firm-specific services are those that require some kind of proprietary knowledge of the manufacturer of the associated products (Hirsch, 1989; Almor & Hirsch, 1995) and often tend to be associated with new and complex products. Firm-specific services include various sales promotion activities in order to create awareness of the product, demonstrate its attributes, and when necessary "tailor" the product to specific customer requirements. Firm-specific services further include training, installation, running in, maintenance, and repairs (Almor et al., 2006). Such services must therefore be tightly related to a particular product or to a specific technological knowledge.

Fig. 1 (adopted from Almor et al., 2006) illustrates the concept of service intensity as applied to transactions involving products and associated services. Total service costs are measured by the difference between total costs of the transaction (denoted by C_T) and the manufacturing costs (denoted by C_M). Services costs represent the difference between the two and are measured by (C_T-C_M). Denoting manufacturing cost plus the cost of required firm-specific services by C_{FS} service costs is divided into two parts: the cost of universal services – denoted by (C_T-C_{FS}) and the cost of firm-specific services, denoted by ($C_{FS}-C_M$). Service intensity (S_I) is defined as $S_I = C_{FS}/C_M$, that is, the ratio of firm-specific services costs to unit manufacturing costs. When firm-specific services account for a high proportion of the total transaction costs the product under consideration is labeled service intensive.

Fig. 1 implies that products and services, in fact lie on a single continuum. If the cost of manufacturing is null, one may refer to a "pure" service. On the other hand, any other product has some component of services embedded in its total costs be they universal or firm-specific where the greater the ratio of firm-specific services costs to unit manufacturing costs the greater is a product's service intensity. One would expect high service

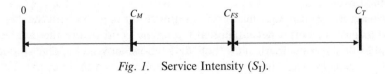

Fig. 1. Service Intensity (S_I).

intensity to imply more frequent and intensive interaction between the firm and its consumers.

The Costs of Distance for Service Multinationals Originating in SMOPEC.
SMOPECs are defined as developed countries that are small in terms of their gross domestic product (GDP) relative to the world's largest economies (Aharoni, 2000). Due to their distance from the world's largest markets service multinationals from SMOPECs are disadvantaged compared to their large country originating service multinationals in several aspects including: the timely supply of services, the cost of supplying services, and perceived reputation (Aharoni, 2000). The greater ability of MNCs from large countries to rely on domestic resources and cater domestic customers allows them to save on cross-border transactions, especially where service-intensive products and pure services are involved.

Service providers from SMOPEC need to engage in extensive intra- and inter-firm interactions. Intra-firm interactions are required to facilitate bilateral information and knowledge flows among R&D, production, sales, and customer support. These flows may include data on product specifications, manufacturing instructions, feedback regarding product design, and so forth (Adler & Hashai, 2007; Almor et al., 2006; Buckley & Hashai, 2004; Casson, 2000). The nature of interaction between the firm and its customers was discussed in detail earlier in connection with the concept of service intensity.

The cost of interaction between the firm's functions is higher when they are located in different countries (Kogut & Zander, 1993; Teece, 1977). The cost of interaction with customers similarly rises with geographic distance and with the time it takes to provide the relevant firm-specific services. This is particularly relevant to international interactions where additional costs associated with distance are incurred. These costs are often labeled "the liability of foreignness" (Hymer, 1976; Zaheer, 1995) and stem from the need to communicate in multiple languages, bridge geographic and cultural distance, and accommodate different legal systems and regulatory regimes (Contractor, 1990; Hirsch, 1976; Hofstede, 1980; Hymer, 1976; Johanson & Vahlne 1977, 1990; Kogut & Singh, 1988; Zaheer, 1995).

Moreover, since greater service intensity implies more frequent and extensive interaction with customers the cost of interaction between the firm and its customers is further expected to increase with service intensity. This implies that service providers from SMOPEC are expected to face considerable challenges when competing with their large country counterparts on a global scale. In the following section some of the characteristic of these challenges are explored.

CONCEPTUAL FRAMEWORK

Technological Knowledge and Foreign Service Provision

Since firm-specific services are often based on firm-specific technological knowledge, the technical complexity of technology-intensive products requires frequent interactions with the customers (Hirsch, 1989; Almor & Hirsch, 1995). This assertion implies that service intensity and the level of technological knowledge are positively correlated as empirically shown by Almor et al. (2006) and others.

When analyzing the impact of technological knowledge level on the extent of foreign services provision two contradictory effects are at play. On the one hand, unique services based on proprietary technological knowledge are an enabler of greater service provision abroad (Aharoni & Hirsch, 1997). For firms providing fairly simpler "universal" services, location economies (such as the familiarity with local institutions, see Delios & Henisz, 2000) come to the forefront. Familiarity with business habits, regulations, culture, and consumer preferences are all expected to make domestic service suppliers advantaged compared to foreign ones. Yet, as the share of proprietary technological knowledge in products and their accompanied services increases, the relative importance of firm-specific services is likely to make foreign services providers less disadvantaged and allow them to compete successfully in foreign markets. This observation is true for manufacturers of service-intensive products as much as it is true for pure service providers (Delios & Beamish, 1999; Hashai & Almor, 2008; Dunning, 1977, 1988; Knight & Cavusgil, 2004; Oviatt & McDougall, 1994; Tseng, Tansuhaj, Hallagan, & McCullough, 2007; Zahra, Ireland, & Hitt, 2000). Greater levels of technological knowledge are therefore expected to allow service providers privileged access to foreign markets. Service providers with high levels of technological knowledge are likely to penetrate foreign markets more successfully and increase the share and dispersion of their foreign sales compared to service providers with low levels of technological knowledge. It is therefore hypothesized that:

Hypothesis 1. Technological knowledge level is positively correlated with the extent of foreign services provision.

On the other hand, greater technological knowledge may also hamper foreign services provision. Unique services based on proprietary technological knowledge are expected to be highly correlated with high levels of firm-specific services (Almor et al., 2006). This implies that greater levels of technological knowledge also require more frequent interaction with foreign customers in the processes of pre-sale, sale, and post-sale. The fact that such services are based on firm-specific knowledge implies that they often should be supplied via internalized entities (Kogut & Zander, 1993; Martin & Salomon, 2003a) and hence imply greater costs for internationalizing services providers (Aharoni, 1993). All in all, this implies that too high levels of technological knowledge may limit the extent of foreign services provision due to their associated costs, leading one to expect that at some point high levels of complex firm-specific technological knowledge may lead to less foreign service provision. This view is consistent with the observations of Martin and Salomon (2003b) and to the hypothesis that:

Hypothesis 2. After a certain level, technological knowledge level is negatively correlated with the extent of foreign services provision.

Service Standardization, Technological Knowledge, and Foreign Services Provision

Standardization of service provision enables firms to reduce the extra costs of providing a service abroad via the usage of third parties (Aharoni, 1996). As indicated above services can be classified as either universal or firm specific. Universal services can often be provided via indigenous firms in host countries. There are two reasons for this. One reason is that the knowledge required for such service providers to perform universal services is largely available and does not need to be specifically related to a specific type of technology. The other reason is that indigenous firms in host countries are not subject to the liability of foreignness (Hymer, 1976; Zaheer, 1995) and therefore are advantaged compared to foreign suppliers of universal services. In contrast, firm-specific services that are expected to be associated and based on firm-specific technological knowledge, are likely to be supplied by internalized entities of foreign services providers where firm-specific knowledge compensates for their liability of foreignness (Dunning, 1977, 1988).

Yet, there might be intermediate cases where services are not "purely" universal nor "purely" firm specific. As argued before, the provision of technology-intensive firm-specific services will likely limit the extent of foreign services provision at some point. Yet, assuming that a firm may turn its services to be less "firm specific" (but yet not purely universal), such a firm may reduce the limiting constraint of its service intensity.

Standardization of firm-specific services, by making such services documented or based on formal written rules and routines is likely to help firms to reduce the negative effects of service intensity on their extent of foreign services provision. Such standardization has two effects. It may allow firms to teach foreign employees in the host country to provide their services and hence reduce the costs of providing services by persons sent from abroad (these include the costs of flights, hotels, and other expenses occurring when technical persons are sent abroad). More importantly, it may enable firms to rely on third parties to reduce the costs of service provision aboard. This is because of the fact that specific knowledge how to provide technologically related services that is made more explicit can be taught more easily to third parties (Kogut & Zander, 1993; Martin & Salomon, 2003a). Standardization of services hence allows technology-intensive service providers to operate abroad with fewer constraints. It is therefore hypothesized that:

Hypothesis 3. Standardization of services positively moderates the linkage between technological knowledge level and foreign services provision.

Service Automation, Technological Knowledge, and Foreign Services Provision

An alternative way to overcome the negative effect of high levels of service intensity on firms' foreign services provision is by automating service provision. In contrast to standardization which, as argued before, facilitates the provision of technology-intensive services in the host country, automation of services reduces the costs of technology-intensive service provision from the home country. Service automation allows firms to provide their services via electronic means such as the Internet, specialized software, or other computer communication means. It therefore does not necessarily imply that the supplied services should be standardized and indeed such services may remain highly firm specific. Yet, the ability of the firm to use its own technical personnel from its home country (or a few existing foreign locations which are used as customer-support sites) allows to save much of the costs of establishing foreign subsidiaries abroad as well as the costs related to sending technical personnel overseas to provide services. It therefore follows that automation of service provision enables firms to reduce the extra costs of providing a service abroad (Aharoni, 1996; Nault, 1997) and hence allows service providers of technology-intensive services to reduce their disadvantages relative to indigenous service providers. Finally, it is therefore hypothesized that:

Hypothesis 4. Automation of services positively moderates the linkage between technological knowledge level and foreign services provision.

DATA AND MEASURES

The hypotheses were tested on a sample of 59 Israel-based knowledge-intensive service providers. The sample was derived from the full list of Israel-based knowledge-intensive firms constructed by the Dolev and Abramovitz Ltd. consulting firm. The Dolev and Abramovitz list includes about 400 Israeli knowledge-intensive firms that have reached the stage where they sell their products or services and represents the vast majority of the Israeli Hi-Tech sector. The Dolev and Abramovitz list is well recognized as a comprehensive resource for this sector in Israel.

Since the data needed for testing the hypotheses are usually unavailable in the financial reports of firms, interviews were used during which completed structured questionnaires were completed as the prime data collection method. The questionnaire underwent multiple pretests. The senior management of a random sample of 200 firms derived from the Dolev and Abramovitz list was approached. Overall, 170 interviews took place during the period January 2005–July 2006 (a response rate of 85%).

Out of the interviewed firms, 59 firms that have defined themselves as services providers were selected. The questionnaires included data relevant for each value adding activity, namely: R&D, production, sales, finance, and customer support. Firms defining themselves as "services providers" chose not to report on production activities. The sampled service providers belonged to the following sectors: IT services, Internet services, storage and data centers, cellular services, security services, telecommunications, and enterprise software.

In-depth focused interviews were conducted in order to ensure uniformity in the way the responses were interpreted. The use of a dedicated researcher minimized the potential for misinterpretation errors. The interviews were held with CEO/chairman or senior VP-level executives who had been involved with their firms since inception (or almost since inception) so as to enable them to provide detailed information on their firm's development over time. The usage of structured questionnaires was intended to elicit the views of the interviewee untainted by the interviewer's perceptions to the extent possible. In addition, a single person was in charge of coding the questionnaires in order to avoid a possible inter-coder bias. Wherever required additional data was complemented from secondary sources such as financial reports, financial newspaper archives, and web sites of the firms.

KEY MEASURES

Dependent Variable

The extent of *foreign services provision* was proxied by the percentage of services provided abroad (out of total sales).

Independent Variables

Technological knowledge level was proxied by the ratio of R&D expenditures to sales. *Standardization* of services was measured by a binary variable representing the extent to which firms have standardized their firm-specific knowledge by documenting it. As explained above the more explicit and less tacit services are, the greater is the ability of firms to use third parties to supply their services abroad (Kogut & Zander, 1993; Martin & Salomon, 2003a).

Automation of services was measured by a binary variable representing the ability of firms to provide services via the Internet, specialized software, computer communication means, etc. These data were self-reported by the firms in the sample.

Control Variables

Several control variables were used, including *firm size*, proxied by the number of employees. In essence, firm size is expected to be associated with economies of scale and hence allow for greater capability of foreign services provision (Aharoni, 1966; Caves, 1971, 1996; Cavusgil, 1984; Chandler, 1986, 1990; Porter, 1985).

Firm age was further controlled for where high-technology firms originating in Israel are expected to become more international as they grow and become older (Hashai & Almor, 2004) and for *market size* representing the global market size for each firm as reported by the firms in the sample. Greater global market size is expected to be positively correlated with greater extent of foreign services provision.

DESCRIPTIVE STATISTICS

Table 1 presents the descriptive statistics of the sample. On average the firms in the sample provide somewhat less that half of their services abroad (45%). These firms may be defined as technological knowledge intensive with an average ratio of R&D to sales of 23%. While the average firms size is quite small (86 employees) the range of size is quite wide spreading from 15 to 2,800 employees. In this respect, an interesting and puzzling observation is that for the firms in the sample there is a significant negative correlation between firm size and extent of foreign services provisions. A closer look at the data reveals that a few very large firms are mainly home biased while many small firms are virtually "born global" (Hashai & Almor, 2004; Knight & Cavusgil, 2004; Oviatt & McDougall, 1994). Out interpretation of this result (which is not expected to be universal) can be explained by the negative correlation ($r = -0.21$, $p < 0.01$) between firm size and technological knowledge level. This negative correlation implies that the larger Israeli service providers (Matrix, Ness, Malam, Yael, and others) are mostly providing fairly simple services. In this case location economies, connections to business networks, and familiarity of host markets (Delios & Henisz, 2000; Hymer, 1976; Zaheer, 1995) become the

Table 1. Descriptive Statistics ($N = 59$).

Measure	Mean	Standard Deviation	Minimum–Maximum
% of foreign sales	0.45	0.21	0.08–0.86
Technological knowledge level	0.23	0.12	0.05–0.54
Number of employees	86	402	15–2,800
Standardization	0.34	0.22	0–1
Automatization	0.21	0.25	0–1
Firm age (years)	7.2	6.3	5–28
Market size – US$ billions	2.5	12.3	1–90

most important thing for gaining competitive advantage, leading such firms to concentrate on their home markets. The smaller services providers are more technology intensive, thus given the arguments of Hypothesis 1 regarding technological knowledge and foreign services provision are more capable of offering their unique services abroad.

Table 1 further indicates that about a third of the firms in the sample have standardized the way they provide services and only a fifth reported on services automation. Finally, the analyzed firms are quite young (on average 7 years old) and cater an average market size of US$ 2.5 billion.

RESULTS

Results of cross sectional ordinary least squares (OLS) regressions are reported in Tables 2 and 3.

In Table 2, model 1 includes control variables only, model 2 includes the level of technological knowledge only, model 3 includes the level of technological knowledge squared, and model 4 also refers to the interaction between firm size and technological knowledge following the discussion in the descriptive statistics subsection.

Models 2–4 in Table 2 show a positive and significant relationship between the level of technological knowledge and the extent of foreign services

Table 2. Cross Sectional OLS Regressions ($N = 59$, Standardized Coefficients).

Independent Variable	Model 1	Model 2	Model 3	Model 4
Technological knowledge		0.22***	0.20***	0.22**
Technological-knowledge squared			−0.14**	−0.15**
Firm size	−0.14**			−0.12**
Standardization	0.06	0.07	0.06	0.05
Automation	0.03	0.03	0.04	0.03
Firm size × technological knowledge				0.04
Firm size × technological-knowledge squared				0.02
Firm age	0.16**	0.18**	0.17**	0.14*
Market size	0.08*	0.06	0.05	0.08*
Adjusted R^2	**0.12****	**0.21*****	**0.26*****	**0.28*****

*Statistically significant at 5%.
**Statistically significant at 1%.
***Statistically significant at 0.1%.

Table 3. Cross Sectional OLS Regressions – Standardization and
Automation Effects ($N = 59$, Standardized Coefficients).

Independent Variable	Model 5	Model 6	Model 7
Technological knowledge	0.21**	0.22**	0.22**
Technological knowledge squared	−0.13*	−0.14*	−0.12*
Firm size	−0.12**	−0.11**	−0.12**
Standardization	0.06	0.05	0.05
Automation	0.02	0.02	0.03
Standardization × technological knowledge	0.08*		0.05*
Standardization × technological knowledge squared	0.07*		0.03*
Automation × technological knowledge		0.06*	0.04*
Automation × technological knowledge squared		0.05*	0.05*
Firm age	0.16**	0.15**	0.12*
Market size	0.08*	0.09*	0.07*
Adjusted R^2	**0.31***	**0.29***	**0.30***

*Statistically significant at 5%.
**Statistically significant at 1%.
***Statistically significant at 0.1%.

provision, thus confirming Hypothesis 1. Models 3 and 4 show a negative relationship between the level of technological knowledge squared and the extent of foreign services provision thus supporting Hypothesis 2. No significant interaction effects are found between firm size and technological knowledge level thus refuting possible suspicious for firm size effect on the results.

As for the control variables, it can be seen that firm size is negatively correlated with the extent of foreign services provision. This is consistent with the earlier observations regarding firm size and foreign services provision. Firm age is positively correlated with the extent of foreign services provision implying that firms become more international as they mature. Finally, greater global market size is also associated with greater extent of foreign services provision as one may expect.

In Table 3, model 5 relates to the moderating effect of services standardization while model 6 refers to the moderating effect of service automation. Model 5 shows that while standardization by itself is not significantly correlated with the extent of foreign operations the interaction of this measure with technological knowledge and technological knowledge squared is positive and significant. This result confirms Hypothesis 3. Model 6 shows a similar result for automation, thus confirming Hypothesis 4.

Overall all the models presented in Tables 2 and 3 have fairly high R-squares and most F-values (of the whole regression) are statistically significant at $p < 0.1\%$. All average variance inflation factors (VIF) were considerably lower than the critical value of 10 (Neter, Wasserman, & Kutner, 1985), thus ruling out potential multicollinearity suspicions.

DISCUSSION AND CONCLUSION

This chapter has investigated the role of technological knowledge as a dominant determinant of the extent of foreign services provision of service multinationals originating from SMOPEC. The chapter hypothesizes and finds an inverted U-shaped relationship between the level of firms' technological knowledge and their extent of foreign services provision. This finding implies that, among Hi-Tech firms, services providers with limited technological knowledge as well as services providers with excess technological knowledge are likely to be less internationalized.

Our interpretation of this finding is that at low levels of technological knowledge, location economies, often tied to institutional aspects of operating in a given country, such as connections to business networks, knowledge of regulations, and familiarity with customer preferences comes to the forefront (Delios & Henisz, 2000; Hymer, 1976; Zaheer, 1995). As the level of technological knowledge increases, it compensates for the lack of location economies and enables foreign services providers to effectively compete with indigenous ones. Yet, when the level of technological knowledge becomes too high and its technological services become complex it becomes, once again, too costly for service providers to transfer their complex knowledge abroad (Kogut & Zander, 1993; Martin & Salomon, 2003b). Since services provision requires close interaction with customers the latter observation implies that contrary to manufacturers of products that may become exporters when their technological knowledge is highly complex (Martin & Salomon, 2003a), in the case of services providers such firms will become relatively more home-market biased.

Given this primary finding, the chapter further identifies that the standardization of services as well as their automation positively moderate the relationship between technological knowledge and the extent of foreign services provision. In other words, at any level of technological knowledge firms that are able either to standardize their technological knowledge (by means of its documentation) and/or automate it (by means of specialized software and computer communication devices) are more able to cater foreign customers than other firms. An important distinction here is that while standardization reduces the costs of providing services at the host country (requires less specialized employees or can be outsourced to third parties), automation reduces the costs of providing services from the home country (to the host country).

All in all this chapter has built a lot on the insights of Yair Aharoni for understating the internationalization patterns of services providers from a SMOPECs. In a series of studies Aharoni has touched upon important aspects presented in this chapter such as the identification of global services multinationals (Aharoni, 1993; Aharoni & Nachum, 2000), highlighting the pros and cons of small and medium enterprises (SMEs) as competitors of larger MNCs (Aharoni, 1994), looking on specific characteristics of SMEs such as their level of technological knowledge (Aharoni & Hirsch, 1996, 1997) and identifying the distance costs faced by multinationals originating from SMOPECs (Aharoni, 2000).

In fact, many other aspects of Aharoni's work can and should be used as a future extension of the current study. For instance, an analysis of relevant organizational structures and strategies of multinational services providers (Aharoni, 1996; Roberts, 1998) may shed an important light on the structures and strategies that facilitate or inhibit greater internationalization. An intriguing question in this respect is whether relatively more decentralized strategies (such as multi-domestic strategy) or relatively more centralized strategies (such as global strategy) allow for greater internationalization on behalf of multinational services providers. Another important question is to look into the process of such firms' internationalization, and identify possible enablers and impediments, in particular with respect to the decision whether to further expand globally or not (Aharoni, 1966).

Finally, given the title of this book, *The Future of FDI*, the current chapter puts emphasis on a new type of MNCs that are likely to become more dominant in the near future. If MNCs are currently conceived as large, industrial firms originating from large countries, this chapter argues that in the future a new type of MNCs is likely to emerge: small, technology-intensive services providers originating from small countries. The likelihood of such firms to become more dominant in the global economy seems quite high given the increased importance of services in our world (Aharoni & Nachum, 2000; Kolstad & Villanger, 2008) and the increased importance of technology as a facilitator of internationalization. Small, technology-intensive service providers from small countries until recently faced substantial obstacles compared to large, manufacturing firms originating from large countries in terms of global presence. Such firms were not able to exploit the economies of scale that larger firms have exploited. Such firms needed to bear the high costs of intensive interaction with end customers and were not able to build on a large home country to establish some captive market as they grow (due to their presence in a small economy). Yet, technological advances such as the Internet and other communication means as well as the sharp reduction in international transportation costs in the last few decades have changed many of these. Currently, small service providers from SMOPECs face lesser costs of finding and communicating with end customers in distant countries. Their technological advantages enable them to compensate for their location diseconomies and in many aspects the need to tailor specific services to end customers reduces the importance of economies of scale.

Global service multinationals, as a whole, and in particular global services multinationals originating from SMOPECs face very different internationalization challenges than those faced by large industrial firms originating in large countries (such as the need to closely interact with end customers). Furthermore, many of today's products are highly service intensive (reflected by the costs of firm-specific services, as exemplified in Fig. 1). Hence, scholars should devote more time to develop specific models that will inquire the process and outcomes of the internationalization of this new type of MNCs.

REFERENCES

Adler, N., & Hashai, N. (2007). Knowledge flows and the modeling of the multinational enterprise. *The Journal of International Business Studies, 38*, 639–657.

Agarwal, S., & Ramasawi, S. N. (1992). Choice of foreign market entry mode: Impact of ownership, location and internalization factors. *Journal of International Business Studies, 23*(1), 1–27.

Aharoni, Y. (1966). *The Foreign Investment Decision Process*. Boston, MA: Harvard University.

Aharoni, Y. (1993). Globalization of professional business services. In: Y. Aharoni (Ed.), *Coalitions and competition: The globalization of professional business services* (pp. 1–19). London: Routledge.

Aharoni, Y. (1994). How can small firms achieve competitive advantage in an interdependent world? In: T. Agmon & R. Drobnick (Eds), *Small firms in global competition* (pp. 9–18). Oxford: Oxford University Press.

Aharoni, Y. (1996). The organization of global services MNEs. *International Studies of Management & Organization, 26*(2), 6–23.

Aharoni, Y. (1999). Internationalization of professional services: Implications for accounting firms. In: D. Brock, M. Powell & C. R. (Bob) Hinings (Eds), *Restructuring the professional organization* (pp. 20–40). London: Routledge.

Aharoni, Y. (2000). Globalization and the small, open economy. In: T. Almor & N. Hashai (Eds), *FDI, international trade and the economics of peacemaking papers in honor of Seev Hirsch* (pp. 90–116). Rishon Lezion: College of Management Academic Division.

Aharoni, Y. (2004). The race for FDI in services – The case of the airline industry. In: P. Ghauri & L. Oxelheim (Eds), *European Union and the race for foreign direct investment in Europe* (pp. 381–406). Amsterdam: Elsevier.

Aharoni, Y., & Hirsch, S. (1996). The competitive potential of technology-intensive industries in developing countries. In: M. Svetlicic & H. W. Singer (Eds), *The world economy challenges of globalization and regionalization* (pp. 99–118). Hundmills, London and New York: Macmillan Press Ltd. and St. Martin Press Inc.

Aharoni, Y., & Hirsch, S. (1997). Enhancing competitive advantage in technology-intensive industries. In: J. H. Dunning, K. A. Hamdani, (Eds), *The new globalism and developing countries* (pp. 260–302). Tokyo, New York, Paris: United Nations University Press.

Aharoni, Y., & Nachum, L. (2000). *Globaization of services: Some implications for theory and practice*. London: Routledge.

Aliber, R. Z. (1970). A theory of direct foreign investment. In: C. P. Kindelberger (Ed.), *The international firm*. Cambridge, MA: MIT press.

Almor, T., Hashai, N., & Hirsch, S. (2006). The product cycle revisited: Knowledge intensity and firm internationalization. *Management International Review, 46*, 507–528.

Almor, T., & Hirsch, S. (1995). 'Outsiders' response to Europe 1992: Theoretical considerations and empirical evidence. *Journal of International Business Studies, 26*(2), 223–238.

Bhagwati, J. N. (1986). *Trade in services and developing countries*. 10th Annual Geneva Lecture (mimeo). London School of Economics, London.

Boddewyn, J., Marsha, J., Halbrich, B., & Perry, A. C. (1986). Service multinationals: Conceptualization, measurement, and theory. *Journal of International Business Studies, 17*, 41–57.

Buckley, P. J., & Casson, M. (1981). The optimal timing of a foreign direct investment. *Economic Journal, 91*, 75–87.

Buckley, P. J., & Hashai, N. (2004). A global system view of firm boundaries. *Journal of International Business Studies, 35*(1), 33–45.

Casson, M. (2000). *The economics of international business – A new research agenda*. Cheltenham, UK: Edward Elgar.

Caves, R. E. (1971). International corporations: The industrial economics of foreign investment. *Economica, 38*(1).

Caves, R. E. (1996). *Multinational enterprise and economic analysis* (2nd ed.). Cambridge, UK: Cambridge University.

Cavusgil, S. T. (1984). Differences among exporting firms based on their degree of internationalization. *Journal of Business Research, 12*(2), 195–208.

Chandler, A. D. (1986). The evolution of modern global competition. In: M. E. Porter (Ed.), *Competition in global industries*. Boston: Harvard Business School Press.

Chandler, A. D. (1990). *Scale and scope: The dynamics of industrial capitalism*. Cambridge, MA: Harvard University Press.

Contractor, F. J. (1990). Ownership patterns of U.S. joint ventures abroad and the liberalization of foreign government regulation in the 1980s: Evidence from the benchmark surveys. *Journal of International Business Studies, 21*(1), 55–73.

Delios, A., & Beamish, P. W. (1999). Geographic scope, product diversification, and the corporate performance of Japanese firms. *Strategic Management Journal, 20*, 711–727.

Delios, A., & Henisz, W. J. (2000). Japanese firms' investment strategies in emerging economies. *Academy of Management Journal, 43*(3), 305–323.

Dunning, J. H. (1977). Trade, location of economic activity and the MNE: A search for an eclectic paradigm. In: B. Ohlin, P.O. Hesselborn, P.M. Wijkman (Eds.), *The international allocation of economic activities, proceedings of a Nobel Symposium*, Stockholm: Macmillan.

Dunning, J. H. (1988). The eclectic paradigm of international production: A restatement and some possible extensions. *Journal of International Business Studies, 19*(1), 1–31.

Hashai, N., & Almor, T. (2004). Gradually internationalizing 'born global' firms: An oxymoron? *International Business Review, 13*, 465–483.

Hashai, N., & Almor, T. (2008). R&D intensity, value appropriation and integration patterns within organizational boundaries. *Research Policy, 37*(6–7), 1022–1034.

Hirsch, S. (1976). An international trade and investment theory of the firm. *Oxford Economic Papers, 28*, 258–270.

Hirsch, S. (1989). Services and service intensity in international trade. *Weltwirtschaffliches Archiv – Review of World Economics, 125*(1), 45–60.

Hofstede, G. (1980). *Culture's consequences: International differences in work-related values.* Beverly Hills, CA: Sage Publications.

Hymer, S. H. (1976). *The international operations of national firms: A study of direct foreign investment, 1960.* PhD. Dissertation, Sloan School of Management, Massachusetts Institute of Technology, Cambridge, MA.

Johanson, J., & Vahlne, J.-E. (1977). The internationalization process of the firm – A model of knowledge development and increasing foreign market commitment. *Journal of International Business Studies, 8*(1), 23–32.

Johanson, J., & Vahlne, J.-E. (1990). The mechanism of internationalisation. *International Distribution and Servicing Review, 7*(4), 11–24.

Knight, G., & Cavusgil, T. (2004). Innovation, organizational capabilities, and the born-global firm. *Journal of International Business Studies, 35*, 124–141.

Kogut, B., & Singh, H. (1988). The effect of country culture on the choice of entry mode. *Journal of International Business Studies, 19*(3), 411–423.

Kogut, B., & Zander, U. (1993). Knowledge of the firm and the evolutionary theory of the multinational corporation. *Journal of International Business Studies, 24*(4), 625–646.

Kolstad, I., & Villanger, E. (2008). Determinants of foreign direct investment in services. *European Journal of Political Economy, 24*, 518–533.

Martin, X., & Salomon, R. (2003a). Knowledge transfer capacity and its implications for the theory of the multinational corporation. *Journal of International Business Studies, 34*(4), 356–373.

Martin, X., & Salomon, R. (2003b). Tacitness, learning, and international expansion: A study of foreign direct investment in a knowledge-intensive industry. *Organization Science, 14*(3), 297–311.

Nault, B. R. (1997). Mitigating underinvestment through an IT-enabled organization form. *Organization Science, 8*(3), 223–234.

Neter, J., Wasserman, W., & Kutner, M. H. (1985). *Applied linear statistical models: Regression, analysis of variance, and experimental design.* Homewood, IL: Richard D. Irwin, Inc.

Oviatt, B. M., & McDougall, P. P. (1994). Toward a theory of international new ventures. *Journal of International Business Studies, 25*(1), 45–64.

Porter, M. E. (1985). *Competitive advantage.* New York: Free Press.

Roberts, J. (1998). *Multinational business service firms: the development of multinational organizational structures in the UK business services sector.* Aldershot, UK: Ashgate.

Sampson, G., & Snape, R. (1985). Identifying the issues in trade in services. *The World Economy, 8*, 171–181.

Teece, D. J. (1977). Technology transfer by multinational corporations: The resource cost of transferring technological know-how. *Economic Journal, 87*, 242–261.

Tseng, C. H., Tansuhaj, P., Hallagan, W., & McCullough, J. (2007). Effects of firm resources on growth in multinationality. *Journal of International Business Studies, 38*, 961–974.

Zahra, S., Ireland, D., & Hitt, M. (2000). International expansion by new venture firms: International diversity, mode of market entry, technological learning, and performance. *Academy of Management Journal, 43*, 925–950.

Zaheer, S. (1995). Overcoming the liability of foreignness. *Academy of Management Journal, 38*(2), 341–363.

PART IV
MNEs AND THE STATE

IF TEVA CHANGES ITS "NATIONALITY," WOULD ISRAEL'S ECONOMY BE AFFECTED?

Seev Hirsch

ABSTRACT

In their book Multinational Enterprises and the Global Economy, *John M. Dunning and Sarianna M. Lundan offer a generally accepted definition of the term multinational enterprise (MNE): "A Multinational or transnational enterprise is an enterprise that engages in foreign direct investment (FDI) and owns or, in some way controls value added activities in more than one Country" (Dunning & Lundan, p. 3). The title, however, may be misleading since it ignores the fact that each multinational has a home country as well as one or more host countries. Multinationals, in other words, have a nationality. It is the difference between the implications of home and host countries for the individual MNEs that the present chapter explores. It uses a case study involving Teva, Israel's flagship MNE, to address the question: "If Teva changed its nationality, would Israel's economy would be affected?"*

The hypothetical case of a change in Teva's nationality and its implications are employed to demonstrate the general validity of the concept of "Distance Premium," to examine the implication of

The Future of Foreign Direct Investment and the Multinational Enterprise
Research in Global Strategic Management, Volume 15, 357–377
Copyright © 2011 by Emerald Group Publishing Limited
ISSN: 1064-4857/doi:10.1108/S1064-4857(2011)0000015020

nationality to individual multinational business enterprises. The chapter explores the proposition that despite its declining effect, due to far reaching technological and political developments, the distance premium, continues to favor home country over host country locations and intra- over interorganizational value activities. The chapter goes on to examine expected changes in the distribution of rents generated by the MNEs between different stakeholder groups. It concludes that, with the exception of stockholders whose welfare is generally not affected by change of nationality, other stakeholders in the new home country gain at the expense of old home country stakeholders.

INTRODUCTION

The ideas for this essay came to me as I was putting the finishing touches to a report entitled "Crisis Moderates the Expansion of Israeli Multinationals." The report is part of an international initiative called Emerging Markets Global Players (EMGP), initiated and coordinated by Karl Sauvant, director of the Vale Columbia Center on Sustainable International Investment. The project ranks and analyzes the international operations of the leading multinational enterprises (MNEs) in so-called Emerging Economies.

The original version of the report contained 25 firms. A query by the coordinators concerned the *nationality* of certain firms, which listed a foreign country as the location of their head office. When questioned about their nationality, some firms stated that it was not Israel, despite the fact this is where their top management resided, and where the most important strategic decisions were believed to be taken.[1] The number of firms included in the report was subsequently reduced by 4 to 21. It was this experience that led us to pose the question: Does the nationality of MNEs affect the home country's economic welfare?

Why should IB scholars be interested in that question? If it can be shown that a change in nationality of MNEs can improve the economic welfare of the home country, then it follows that it makes sense for the home country's government to encourage foreign MNEs to become, in some sense, nationals and to dissuade local multinationals from changing their nationality. If, on the other hand, it can be shown that change of nationality leads to the deterioration in the home country's welfare, its government will presumably adopt the opposite approach.

Then there is the possibility that the nationality of an MNE is unrelated to its contribution to the home country's economic welfare. In fact it is quite likely that those who accept the premises of traditional trade economists about the determinants of comparative advantage will probably argue that it is impossible to generalize about the relationship between MNE's nationality and their contribution to the home country's economic welfare. MNEs, according to this way of thinking, locate their value-adding activities throughout the globe in such a way as to maximize their stockholders' after tax returns. This kind of calculation is unaffected by the nationality of different locations, except in the sense that it takes into account their tax regimes.

A related question is whether a change in the nationality of an MNE should be treated as a zero-sum game, for example, the loss of the old home country is equal to the gain of the new home country. Or alternatively, whether both countries can gain from such a move. In this case the question becomes one of who gains more and what can be done to increase the home country's share of the total gain.

To answer some of these questions we conduct what is known as a Gedankenexperiment. We ask a hypothetical question: "If Teva, the undisputed flagship of Israel's MNEs, changed its nationality, how would Israel's economic welfare be affected?" By posing the question in these terms we spare ourselves the tedious analysis of how the rents produced by the different value-adding activities of Teva are currently divided between the home country and the numerous host countries in the first place? We take the present division as given, accepting that it is determined by the relative economic power brought to bear by the different stakeholders involved in the activities of Teva or affected by them. If it can be shown how a *change* in Teva's nationality is likely to affect the welfare of its home country, then it follows that determination of MNEs nationality, in general, has public policy implications that deserve to be considered by both home and host countries.

The plan of the chapter is as follows.

The second section explores the relationship between received theories of IB and the political economy of foreign direct investment (FDI). It suggests a number of propositions that explain the intercountry distribution of economic rents generated by MNE activity and outlines the concept of MNE nationality. In the third section, the notion of MNE nationality is applied to Teva, Israel's leading MNE. After discussing Teva's international value-adding activities the analysis in the fourth section explores the likely effects of a change in the company's nationality on the economic welfare of its home country. Policy implications and suggestions for further research are considered in the concluding section.

ECONOMIC RENT AND THE DISTANCE PREMIUM – THEORETICAL CONSIDERATIONS

Our concern with the nationality of MNEs derives from the observation made by Geoffrey Jones that "… in the early twenty first century, ownership, location and geography still mattered enormously in international business. Indeed, in some respects they may matter more than in the past. Technological advances permitted different parts of the value chain to be made in different places, companies held portfolios of brands with different national heritages, but the nationality of a firm was rarely ambiguous, and usually a major influence on corporate strategy" (Jones, 2006, p. 29).

What does international business theory have to say about the relationship between MNEs' nationality and their value-adding capabilities? If we accept the basic premises of the OLI paradigm, MNEs should be regarded as instruments for generating economic rents. Since MNEs operate, by definition, in several countries, the latter have a legitimate interest in the international distribution of the value including the rents created by the MNEs' operations.

MNEs combine according to the OLI paradigm three types of advantages: ownership advantage, location advantage, and internalization advantage.[2] Ownership advantage is a firm attribute; it is a firm specific, proprietary asset, which enables its owners to earn rents – profits over and above those needed to keep them in their current business. Ownership advantage may consist of privileged access to resources, to markets, or knowledge. It may consist of access to physical resources, to exclusive rights of some kind that are only available to their owner and cannot be duplicated or otherwise taken away from him. Ownership advantage is intangible. It is not restricted to a specific location. It is transferable, at its owner's discretion, across national boundaries, to other countries, and to other organizations.

Location advantage is a country attribute. It is bound to a specific geographic area. It may consist of natural resources, a specific climate, or man-made institutions, such as a banking system, a physical or legal infrastructure, roads, electric grids, educational institutions, or health services. Location advantage is available to all residents of the location in question. They are, however, immobile. They cannot be transferred to other locations.

IB theory deals with situations where the owner or possessor of the ownership advantage is located in one country, while the location advantage is in another country or other countries. The ability to combine location advantage and ownership advantage, within a single business organization is the basis for FDI.

Internalization advantage is a transaction attribute. It pertains to the institutional form employed to combine ownership and location advantage. Internalization advantage is said to exist when it makes no economic sense to sell, license, or otherwise externalize the proprietary asset, embodying the ownership advantage. An MNE is established when the ownership advantage is exploited by its owner in a location, outside the home country, characterized by a location advantage.

This, rather detailed, restatement of the basic specifications of the OLI model, originally formulated by John Dunning explains why MNEs can be viewed as generators of economic rents. If the MNE possesses proprietary assets which it combines with access to economic resources enjoying a location advantage, by means of an organization it controls, the MNE can expect to generate economic rents, above normal profits, that is, profits higher than those generated under normal competitive conditions.

Next, we consider the question of location. Can any generalizations be made about the kinds of value activities undertaken by MNEs in their home country and in the host countries in which they operate, and on the rents generated by these activities? We contend that the choice of the country where MNEs locate their value-adding operations is influenced not only by location advantage considered above, but also by what we elsewhere labeled "Distance Premium (DP)" (see Hirsch, 2005).

DP is incurred whenever transactions are conducted in different countries. It is generated by the existence of systematic differences between the characteristics and costs of domestic and foreign interactions. Man-made trade barriers such as import duties and safety regulations constitute obvious examples of DPs. They are augmented by the need faced by parties based in the home country, and seeking to engage in international transactions, to employ more than a single language, to use different currencies and different credit mechanisms, to comply with multiple health and safety regulations, and to conform to the prescriptions of different legal systems. Thus, DP, which inevitably accompanies cross-border transactions, gives rise to what Stephen Hymer termed the "liability of foreignness" (Hymer, 1976).

Staffan Burenstam-Linder in "An Essay on Trade and Transformation" argued that trade intensity between pairs of countries decreases with what he termed "Economic Distance." He measured economic distance by the absolute difference in per-capita income between the two countries (see Buernstam-Linder, 1961). He showed that Scandinavian countries, which were characterized by economic proximity, traded with each other much more intensively than would be expected on the basis of their relative size and Geographic distance. Economic distance is in turn a proxy for differences in taste, which is of course a cultural phenomenon.

A related concept labeled "Psychic Distance" was developed by Johanson, Vahlne, and their associates from the "Uppsala School" (Johanson & Vahlne, 1977). Psychic distance results from lack of familiarity, which is, in turn, associated with subjective risk assigned to interactions between different entities. Interactions with foreigners seem more risky than interactions with local organizations due to their irreversible or irremediable nature. The willingness to commit resources to cross-border transactions is minimal at first when the organizations in question have little or no knowledge of each other. It increases with experience and growing familiarity, which are associated with decreasing levels of perceived risk and rising levels of mutual trust. It is possible to view Psychic Distance as a special case of DP. Both are results of ignorance and lack of prior knowledge. Both are subjective and both diminish as a function of experience, as organizations gain familiarity with cross-border interactions.

Additional insights into the effect of distance on business transactions are offered by Y. Aharoni in his book *The Foreign Investment Decision Process* (Aharoni, 1966, p. 306). Aharoni strongly recommends adding the following concepts and variables to the basic economic model of international investment:

1. The scarce resource in the large firm is not money but management time.
2. Information is not free of charge. The cost of information both in terms of money and the commitments created when additional data are acquired must explicitly be incorporated into the analysis.
3. The cost of organizational effort, changes in organizational policies, and decision rules are very costly in terms of both money and management time.

Aharoni's observations are consistent with the concept of DP. The initial foreign investment of an enterprise constitutes a departure from the traditional way of doing business. It requires investment of management time and other scarce resources in the acquisition of market information and in adapting the organization to the requirement of doing business in risky and unfamiliar environments. The foreign investment decision is a strategic decision involving a process that is considerably more complicated than the application of the investment evaluation procedures prescribed by the finance literature.

Aharoni distinguishes between decisions that are included in what he terms the "feasibility zone" and those outside it. In the early 1960s, international investments were generally outside the feasibility zone of the average US company. Foreign projects were simply not examined even if they offered extraordinary returns, because they were considered too risky. Inclusion in the feasibility zone required a change in the perception of risks involved in foreign operations and the realization by top management that serious negative consequences will follow, if it continues to ignore the opportunities associated with FDIs.

The level of DP has been considerably reduced in recent decade by technological developments in transportation and communication, which have dramatically reduced the costs of engaging in international business and the difference between domestic and international transactions. DP was also diminished due to international trade and investment agreements that led to the reduction of tariffs and other man-made barriers to international transactions, by harmonization of regulations. However, though much reduced since the end of the Second World War, DP continues to exist, and its persistence helps to explain some of the distinctive characteristics of international business transactions.

Hymer, Burenstam-Linder, Johanson and Vahlne, Hirsch, Aharoni, and other scholars focused on the effects of economic and psychic distance on the mode of international business transactions. The same concept can be also applied to intraorganizational relations, to the relationship between different units belonging to a single MNE, located in different countries. From the point of view of top management, the DP associated with decisions involving the home country are by definition smaller than those involving affiliates located abroad. By the same token the DP, associated with routine, day-to-day matters, is smaller than the DP associated with major strategic decisions, involving unfamiliar situations and nonexisting routines.

It may be argued, therefore, that the existence of DP favors home country locations, whenever decisions involving a choice between different units belonging to a single company have to be made. This proposition will be taken up again in the next section, which considers the specific example of Teva.

THE DP MODEL AND TEVA'S NATIONALITY

Teva is considered the flagship of Israel's MNEs. On its website Teva is described as "... a global pharmaceutical company specializing in the development, production and marketing of generic and proprietary branded pharmaceuticals as well as active pharmaceutical ingredients." Teva is among the top 15 pharmaceutical companies and one of the largest generic pharmaceutical companies.[3]

Its position in the world's pharmaceutical industry is illustrated in Table 1 which is adapted from UNCTAD's World Investment Report for 2008 (WIR). The table lists and ranks the 100 leading nonfinancial MNEs.

It lists the nine leading pharmaceutical companies included in the WIR by their foreign and total assets, sales, and employment. Of the nine global pharmaceutical firms, two are based in the United States, two in the United

Table 1. The Worlds' Leading Pharmaceutical Companies Ranked by TNI (2008).

Corporation	Home economy	Millions of US$ and Number of Employees						TNI ($)
		Assets		Sales		Employment		
		Foreign	Total	Foreign	Total	Foreign	Total	
1 AstraZeneca Plc	United Kingdom	36,973	46,784	29,691	31,601	54,183	65,000	85.4
2 Teva Pharmaceuticals	Israel	24,213	32,904	10,609	11,085	32,146	38,307	84.4
3 Roche Group	Switzerland	60,927	71,532	42,114	42,590	45,510	80,080	80.3
4 Novartis	Switzerland	43,505	78,299	40,928	41,459	48,328	96,717	68.1
5 Sanofi-Aventis	France	50,328	100,191	22,636	40,334	69,990	98,213	59.2
6 GlaxoSmithKline Plc.	United Kingdom	26,924	57,424	28,030	44,674	54,326	99,003	54.8
7 Pfizer Inc.	United States	49,151	111,148	27,861	48,296	49,929	81,800	54.3
8 Johnson & Johnson	United States	40,324	84,912	31,438	63,747	69,700	118,700	51.8
9 Bayer AG	Germany	25,696	73,084	24,979	48,161	53,100	108,600	45.3

Source: UNCTAD/Erasmus University database.
The world's top 100 nonfinancial TNCs, ranked by foreign assets (2008a, Annex Table 26).

Kingdom, two in Switzerland, and one each in Germany, France, and Israel. Teva is the smallest in terms of foreign assets though it is quite close to Germany's Bayer and United Kingdom's GlaxoSmithKline. Measured in terms of foreign sales and employment, Teva is some distance behind its competitors. Even the latest acquisitions, to be discussed below, are unlikely to have changed its ranking by these two measures.

The firms are also ranked by their Transnationality Index (TNI), which is calculated as a simple average of three ratios: foreign to total assets, foreign to total sales, and foreign to total employment. The index is commonly employed by international economists and business scholars to indicate the relative commitment by MNEs[4] to their cross-border value-adding activities. In terms of its TNI, Teva ranks number 2, close to Astra Zeneca PLC, which was formed by a merger between UK-based Zeneca and Sweden's Astra in 1999. Note that with the exception of Roche, a well-known Swiss pharmaceutical company, the TNI of the remaining companies is well below 80.

Having established Teva's multinational credentials, let us consider the company's nationality.

Paragraph 3 in Teva's Articles of Association that outlines the "Objectives and Purpose of the Company" states that "The Company's Center of Management shall be in Israel, unless the Board of Directors shall otherwise resolve, with a majority of three quarters of the participating vote" (see Teva's Annual Report, 2009). Teva's nationality is also manifested by the location of its head office and top management, including the CEO.

An additional illustration of what is meant by the designation of Teva as an Israeli corporation is given in Table 2, which shows data about the distribution of Teva's international activities. Foreign sales, that is, sales outside Israel, including exports, account for the bulk of the company's total sales. Only a fraction, less than four percent of its output is sold in the home country. On the other hand, close to thirty percent of Teva's assets are located in Israel, indicating that the share of Israel-based production is considerably larger than its share of sales. The distribution of employment similarly indicates that Israel-based production and other operations rate relatively higher than its share of Teva's global sales. The figures at the bottom of the table show that assets per employee in Israel are considerably higher than in foreign affiliates. Teva's Israeli operations are more capital intensive than its foreign operations.

By the end of 2009 Teva had 22 production sites worldwide, 7 in Israel, 11 in North America, and 4 in Europe. The geographic distribution of R&D was similarly skewed. Of 16 R&D sites, 6 were in Israel, 8 in the United States and Canada, and 2 in Europe.

Table 2. Teva: Total and Foreign Sales, Assets, and Employees
2007–2009.

Year	2007	2008	2009
Sales ($ million)			
Foreign	9,034	10,609	13,399
Israel	374	476	500
Total	9,408	11,085	13,899
% Israel/total	3.98	4.29	3.60
Assets ($ million)			
Foreign	1,723	2,722	2,682
Israel	792	977	1,084
Total	2,515	3,699	3,766
% Israel/total	31.49	26.41	28.78
Number of employees			
Foreign	22,378	32,146	28,788
Israel	5,534	6,161	6,301
Total	27,912	38,307	35,089
% Israel/total	19.83	16.08	17.96
Assets per employee ($)			
Foreign	76,995	84,676	93,164
Israel	143,115	158,578	172,036
% Israel/foreign	54	53	54

The crisis that afflicted the global economy during the years 2007–2009 did not elude Teva, though the effect was noted more in 2009 than in 2008. While sales continued to rise throughout the period, global assets and global employment declined in 2009. Note, however, that in Israel assets and employment continued to grow in both 2008 and 2009.

These statistics are consistent with the proposition that Teva's nationality is manifested by what may be termed a pro-Israeli bias in the choice of locations of value-adding activities. However, the explanation of the apparent preference for Israeli locations need not be sought in the realm of politics or nationalism. The DP model discussed in the second section suggests a perfectly rational explanation of Teva's international location decisions.

The DP model, which indicates how economic distance and the associated risks affect the choice of foreign locations, and modes of operations preferred by MNEs, is, as asserted in the second section, relevant to both inter- and intraorganizational relations. In the latter case it may be applicable to the relationship between different affiliates belonging to a single MNE, located in different countries. *Ceteris paribus*, the DP associated with decisions involving the home country is smaller than DP involving affiliates located abroad. By the same token the DP, associated with routine, day-to-day matters, is smaller than the DP associated with major strategic decisions, involving unfamiliar situations and nonexisting routines. Thus, the existence of DP favors home country locations whenever decisions involving a choice between different units belonging to a single company are being considered.

However, considering the infinitesimal likelihood that the *ceteris paribus* condition is ever met, this statement does not suggest that DP is likely to be the deciding factor in the decision process involving international locations. Cost considerations, political reasoning, risk factors, as well as straightforward cost/benefit calculations, may well outweigh the DP, and persuade management to favor non-Israeli options. The relative importance assigned by Teva to DP may nevertheless be inferred from the location decisions concerning its two major product groups, the generic and the innovative branded products.

Considering the generic products group first, we maintain that the DP associated with this group is relatively small and that this factor is reflected in Teva's strategy that based its growth strategy primarily on generic products. The strategy has been carried out largely through mergers and acquisitions, an approach that favors foreign locations, and not organic growth, which is often based on expanding home country operations.

Teva's major acquisitions in recent years included Sicor a US-based producer of generic injectibles, which was acquired in 2004 for $3.4 billion. Ivax, a leading supplier of respiratory products, as well as generic pharmaceuticals, was acquired in 2006 for $7.4 billion and Barr, yet another US-based producer of generic pharmaceuticals, was acquired in 2008 for $7.5 billion. Teva's most recent acquisition has been Ratiopharm, Germany's leading generics supplier, which was acquired for $4.95 billion in 2010. With the acquisition of Ratiopharm, Teva has become Europe's largest supplier of generics.

Coming back to the role of DP in explaining Teva's generic products strategy, it may be argued that Teva's strategic decision to seek a leadership role in generic pharmaceuticals, before engaging in innovative products, can be partly explained by the attempt to *minimize* the effects of the DP. The chemical properties of generic products are known, so are their medical characteristics. Reverse engineering can be employed to master the production technology, and published statistics can provide valuable information about the size of the market, the channels of distribution, the prevailing prices and many other relevant pieces of information needed for managing a business based on generic products. Many of the major risks that must be faced by suppliers of innovative products can be side-stepped or avoided by suppliers of generic products. Teva's management might have had these considerations in mind, when it initially embarked on its internationalization strategy in the mid-1980s.

Comparison between the decision processes involving the introduction of generic and branded products suggests that the DP is significantly higher in the case of the latter. Innovative products are much riskier. Technological problems must be overcome, complex sets of preclinical and clinical tests have to be performed, costly safety requirements must be satisfied, and numerous other hurdles must be overcome before a new product is approved by the authorities. Hundreds of millions US dollars must be invested before an innovative product can be introduced on the market. Failure to pass a single hurdle associated with the long approval chain may well mean that the entire project has to be abandoned.

The specifications of the "right" innovative product are not given. They must be developed following investments in progressively more costly experiments whose outcome is monitored and approved by rigidly run state agencies. It stands to reason that DP figures prominently in decision processes involving this kind of risk taking, when it is not known in advance whether the product can be produced, whether, if produced, it will perform according to expectations, whether it will pass all the clinical and safety hurdles, and if it does, whether it can be successfully marketed, at prices that will cover the enormous costs incurred, before the first revenue dollar is earned.

All these factors combine to raise the DP, which in the case of innovative products may be reduced by basing management decisions on information gathered from familiar, easily accessible sources, which it considers to be reliable and trustworthy on the basis of past experience. The history of Copaxone and Azilect, Teva's two innovative products, is consistent with this scenario.

Copaxone reduces the frequency of relapses of attacks suffered by patients suffering from multiple sclerosis, an illness afflicting the central nervous system. Copaxone was developed by Teva's scientists on the basis of research performed by Professor Sela, Professor Arnon, and Dr. Teitelbaum of the Weiztman Institute of Science, Rehovoth, Israel. It was first introduced in Israel in 1996. Introduction into the United States followed in 1997. European Union approval was obtained in 2001. By 2010,

Copaxone was being marketed in 52 countries. By mid-2010, Teva has managed to retain its monopoly over the product, which has a large global market as can be seen in Table 3, though the introduction of competing products in the near future cannot be ruled out. Introduction of generic versions will surely follow when patent protection lapses.

Azilect, Teva's other innovative drug reduces the manifestations of Parkinson's disease which, like Copaxone, is connected with the central nervous system. The global market for Azilect is considerably smaller than the market for Copaxone, which by 2009 accounted for about 20 percent of Teva's global sales. Azilect was originally developed by Professors Yudin and Finberg at the Technion, Israel's leading institute of Technology, at Haifa. With Lundbeck, its Swedish partner Teva took over the development and registration of the product, including the clinical trials and introduced it in 2005 initially in Israel, and shortly afterwards in the European Union, in 2005, and in the United States in the following year.

The company does not publish the profits it makes on individual products. Analysts agree, however, that Teva's innovative products, especially Copaxone, account for a major share of it total profits.

To summarize, we have shown that Israel's economy benefits from the value-adding activities carried out within its borders by Teva. These benefits

Table 3. Teva: Total Sales, Sales of Innovative Products, Shares, and Annual Growth Rates.

Year	2005	2006	2007	2008	2009
Sales ($ million)					
Total	5,250	8,408	9,408	11,085	13,899
Copaxone	1,177	1,414	1,713	2,263	2,826
Azilect	0	62	86	177	249
Share of innovatives (%)					
Copaxone	22.42	16.82	18.21	20.41	20.33
Azilect	0	0.73	0.91	1.59	1.79
Annual growth (%)					
Total		60.15	11.89	17.83	25.39
Copaxone		20.14	21.15	32.11	24.88
Azilect	*	*	39.63	105.23	41.08

Source: Teva's Annual Report.

are manifested by the fact that the share of Israel-based employment, assets, production, and R&D is larger than Israel's share of Teva's global sales, and that the capital intensity of Teva's Israel-based value-adding activities is higher than that of the company's foreign operations. We have also shown that Israel's economy appears to derive additional benefits from Teva's decision to manufacture its innovative products Copaxone and Azilect on the basis of R&D originating in Israel-based scientific institutions.

These conclusions can be generalized. They apply to the benefits that can be generated by the value-adding activities of MNEs in any country, regardless of the MNE's nationality. The issue addressed in this chapter pertains to a more specific situation, namely to the benefits that can be derived by the home country of an MNE from its nationality. The question, in other words is whether Israel's economy derives additional benefits from the fact that Teva is Israeli and not an American or a British MNE with Israeli operations? To address this issue we raise the question posed at the beginning of this chapter: If Teva *changed* its nationality, would Israel's economy be affected?

CHANGING TEVA'S NATIONALITY

The economic benefits that Teva offers its home country are self-evident. Israel's human, financial, and organizational resources are not large enough to sustain a home-based operation on a scale needed to be a leader of the global generic pharmaceutical products industry. It is the ability of Teva to engage in FDI, to acquire affiliates in the United States, Europe, Asia, Latin America, etc. Its ability to integrate the affiliates it acquires and to transform them into a cohesive unified organization, which enables the company to achieve the leadership position it has attained. Thanks to Teva, Israel is the home country of a global leader in generic pharmaceutical products. Without access to the resources mobilized by Teva around the globe, Israel would be at most a minor producer and exporter of pharmaceuticals.

Teva, however, does not have to be an Israeli company for Israel to benefit from the access that MNEs provide to global economic resources. While being the *home* country of Teva, Israel is the *host* country to affiliates of numerous foreign MNEs such as Intel, HP, SAP, and even competitors of Teva such as Merck. These MNEs, like Teva, make it possible for Israel to benefit from their value-adding activities and their access to global resources. To evaluate the economic effects of Teva's Israeli *nationality*, we must answer the question posed by the title of this chapter: "If Teva changed its nationality, would Israel's welfare be affected?"

Changing Teva's nationality means, for the purpose of our discussion, a change in the locus of decision making, that is, a change of the country where the top management team, including the CEO is located. As noted already, Teva's article of association specifies that such a change will have to be approved by at least three quarters of the company's board of directors. Considering the fact that numerous Israel-based companies have been acquired by foreign MNEs in recent years, this possibility cannot be ruled out.

A change in Teva's nationality would probably trigger some changes in the geographic distribution of the income earned by senior managers and in the taxes paid by them personally as well as taxes paid by the company. These changes are probably of minor importance, and will not be considered further. Our interest is primarily with the likely effects of a change of Teva's nationality on the geographic distribution of the company's value-adding operations. Specifically, is the change in nationality likely to be followed by the "migration" of value-adding activities, especially production and R&D from Israel to other countries?

Assuming that the location of Teva's production and R&D sites were determined on the basis of economic cost/benefit considerations in the first place, there is no reason to expect a change in nationality to bring about a change in location policy. However, as the analysis in the last section indicated, certain location-related decisions are sensitive to the DP. On the basis of this analysis we offer a number of propositions regarding the way the existence of DP affects the position of Israel-based senior managers in relation to their foreign-based counterparts:

1. Their claims on top management attention, on financial, and on other scarce resources will be considered before the claims of managers located abroad.
2. They will benefit from de facto "first refusal" rights, when Teva considers entry into new markets, new products, or new business areas.
3. When considering closure or transfer of production lines or discontinuation of products their interests will be given added attention.

These propositions are supported by the observations regarding the geographic distribution of Teva's production and R&D facilities. They are supported by the statistics that show that Israel-based production, R&D, and share of employment are larger than expected on the basis of Israel's size, market share, or other economic attributes. Moreover, the propositions are consistent with Teva's policy of basing the development and production of Copaxone and Azilect, its leading innovative products, on scientific research originating in two of Israel's leading scientific institutions: the Weitzman Institute and the Technion.

These propositions do not assume a deliberate policy of favoring claims by Israel-based managers. They are derived from the logic of the DP model that asserts that intercountry economic and psychic distance tends to be longer than intracountry economic and psychic distance and that the costs and perceived risks of intracompany interactions rise with economic and psychic distance. They are consistent with Aharoni's assertions that "... the scarce resource in the large firm is not money but *management time, that* information is not free of charge, and that its cost, in terms of money and the commitments created in making changes in organizational policies and decision rules, are very high" (Aharoni, 1966, p. 306).

The conclusion that follows from these observations is that a change in Teva's nationality will have adverse effects on Israel's economy. The short-run effects are likely to be minimal, assuming, as noted above, that the distribution of Teva's value-adding activities is based on economic consideration. In this case there is no reason to expect a change in location of affiliates engaged in R&D, in production, and in other value-adding activities, just because of the change in location of senior management.

In the long run, decisions on new products and new business lines are likely to be influenced by DP whose parameters will be determined in the new home country. After all, US or British universities are not inferior sources of ideas for new products. Decisions on transferring product lines to new locations, selling existing businesses, engaging in mergers and acquisition are all going to be made by a senior management team based in the new home country. The relatively low level of the DP affecting interactions with the new home country will inevitably steer some location decisions away from the old home country. Over a period of 10 or 20 years these decisions are bound to cumulatively change the balance of economic benefits in the direction of the new home country.

Bearing in mind the positive correlation between the DP level and innovation and its negative correlation with established routines, we expect the rate of change to be influenced by the share of the innovative products in the company's product portfolio. Given the association between the share of innovative products and the level of the risk and uncertainty, we expect a declining share of future innovative products to be located in the old home country.

Thus far no mention was made of capital costs or financial considerations in relation to possible changes in Teva's nationality. International finance literature recognizes the idea of "country risk" and its effect on companies' cost of capital (Campbell, 2004). It is indeed likely that Teva's cost of capital contains a risk premium reflecting its Israeli nationality as well as the location of its affiliates. A change of nationality is consequently likely to be reflected in the company's cost of capital. Note, however, that there is no reason to expect the "country risk" of Israel to be affected. The "country risk" associated with Teva's cost of capital will continue to reflect the location of the company's value-adding activities. Capital markets are likely to view investments in the company as more or less risky, only if they expect a change in its nationality to be associated with location decisions affecting its value-adding activities.

The cost of capital has a direct bearing on the economic welfare of Teva's stockholders. The company's shares are listed on the American Stock Exchange (NASDAQ) and on the Tel Aviv Stock Exchange (TASE). Trade in the shares on either exchange is open to Israeli and non-Israeli stockholders alike. An active arbitrage market prevents significant price variations between the two stock exchanges.

We do not offer predictions regarding the likely response of Israeli and non-Israeli stockholders to a change in Teva's nationality. Both groups are likely to adapt their holdings to their belief in the inherent abilities of future management teams, to find the appropriate balance between product strategies and location decisions, given expected developments in the global pharmaceuticals markets. Risk lovers will probably prefer Teva's current nationality to remain unchanged. Risk haters are likely to opt for nationality change that will reduce the country risk element associated with Teva's cost of capital.

The second section that dealt with the characteristics of MNEs in general described them as rent-generating organizations. The divisions of the rents generated by Teva between different groups of stakeholders are relevant in the context of nationality change. The term refers to stockholders who were considered in some detail above, and to several other groups including senior managers, junior managers, other employees, suppliers and, last but not least, the government that is regarded as the custodian of the public interest. In each case it is appropriate to distinguish between stakeholders residing in the old and new home countries.

Senior managers of the old home country are as a group likely to be the big losers from the change of nationality. They lose income and they lose power as the geographic locus of "big" decision-making shifts between countries. The remaining stakeholders based in Israel lose out as well, as they cease to enjoy the benefits associated with the implicit right of first refusal, as more product lines get shifted abroad, and as new innovative products are developed and produced in the new home country rather than in the old one. The government too is likely to lose tax revenues associated with the change in location of the company's head office.

While losing in relative terms, compared with their counterparts from the new home country, Israeli stakeholders may actually gain in absolute terms, if the change of nationality is accompanied by a sufficiently large increase in overall growth rate. There is, however, no reason to expect such a development in the first place unless we believe the article of association, cited earlier, which requires Teva's locus of decision making to be based in Israel, to counter the economic interests of its stockholders.

DISCUSSION

This chapter discusses the benefits that MNEs offer to the countries in which they operate and the ways they are distributed among stakeholders. Employing the terminology of Dunning's OLI model, we observe that the presence of MNEs in a country enables it to benefit from the combination of the ownership advantage provided by the MNE in question and location advantage conferred by the resources available in its territory. These benefits are not static. They enhance each other over time, as the company translates its proprietary knowledge into value-adding activities, which employ and upgrade local labor and other production factors.

In the process of operating integrated value-adding activities in several countries MNEs create economic rents – profits over and above those needed to keep them in their particular line of business. Distribution of the rents between the different stakeholders reflects their relative bargaining power. Our analysis has shown that the stakeholders located in the home country are poised to derive a disproportionately large share of the rents generated by the MNEs, due to the effect of DP that raises the costs of interrelative to intracountry interactions. The DP similarly raises interorganizational relative to intraorganizational costs of interaction. The DP, in summary, favors home country locations as well as interactions within the organization.

The DP translates into specific advantages enjoyed by home country value activities of the MNE. Ideas for new products and lines of business are more likely to be sought locally than abroad. Local affiliates enjoy (informally) the right of first refusal, when new business ventures are being considered. Proposals by home country managers for new lines of business are getting preferential attention. On the other hand, locally produced marginal product lines are likely to be given another chance before being transferred abroad or disposed of altogether.

Change in the distribution of the rents generated by the MNE following its change of nationality between stakeholders is predictable. New home country stakeholders including managers, suppliers, employees, and the government are expected to gain while their counterparts in the old home country are expected to lose. Regardless of their country of residence, stockholders, unlike the other stakeholders, are expected to gain from a decline in the "country premium" and to lose if it increases.

The expected public policy response to this conclusion is to encourage the establishment of home-based MNEs and to discourage the change of nationality by local MNE. This, however, is easier said than done, bearing in mind the OECD's injunctions against discrimination between incoming and outgoing FDI, and given the likelihood of retaliation by foreign governments.

In the early 1960s, Pinhas Sapir, the legendary minister of Finance, known at the time as Father of Israel's industry, was asked by the CEO of the then government owned Israel Chemicals Corporation to approve a 10 million US dollars investment, in the acquisition of an Italian company engaged in bromine production. The request was promptly denied. The reason: "Our mission is to develop Israel, not Italy." This response, inspired by typical mercantilist thinking that regards capital outflow as bad for the economy, causing loss of foreign exchange and increasing unemployment, has been quite common. Israel, like many other middle-income countries has traditionally sought to encourage incoming FDI, reasoning that it promotes economic development by importing technology, providing local employment and capital inflows, while replacing imports and increasing exports. Outgoing FDI was, as noted above, frowned upon.

Over time this attitude has begun to change. Teva's experience, augmented by that of Finland's Nokia and Switzerland's Roche and Novartis demonstrates that with their access to global human, financial, physical, and organizational resources and markets MNEs reduce the barriers that hamper cross-border trade, investments, and other inter- and intrafirm transactions. They thus effectively extend the economic size of their home countries and enable them to reap the benefits of specialization and of scale economies way beyond their boundaries. The flip side is that Teva's nationality can be changed overnight, either by being bought by foreign MNE, or by simply moving its head office and some senior executives to another country. Most Israelis will probably agree that this is a risk worth taking, and that the laws allowing free movement of FDI in either direction should be retained.

Finally, some thoughts about a related phenomenon that may be labeled "The MNE Paradox." MNEs extend the economic borders of the countries in which they operate, while simultaneously diminishing the effective sovereignty of their governments. Extension of economic reach is achieved through the control of value-adding affiliates in different countries. The MNEs are able to combine labor, capital, and other resources from different countries with proprietary assets such as technological, marketing, and managerial knowledge, to produce goods and services enjoying simultaneous ownership, location, and internalization advantages. In the absence of MNEs, the global list of enterprises exhibiting these characteristics and their value would be diminished. MNEs are therefore rightly regarded as net contributors to global economic welfare in general, and to their home country's economic welfare, in particular.

On the negative side we count the diminution of sovereignty of the countries in which MNEs operate. Countries wishing to benefit from the presence of home as well as foreign-based MNEs must be prepared to submit to the conditions that they impose, albeit informally. MNEs are unlikely to accept limitations on their right to transfer capital in and out of the country, they are unlikely to accept laws or taxes, or other practices that discriminate against them, or that depart too obviously from some generally acceptable norms. They have two powerful tools at their disposal: intracompany pricing and the threat (often only implicit) of exit, as well as of nonentry. These tools are available to all MNEs, including outgoing MNEs. The knowledge of their existence is normally sufficient to steer governments' policies and ad-hoc decisions especially of small counties, in directions that are acceptable to the MNEs.

Governments in general, and home country governments in particular, cannot be expected to like these kinds of limitations on their freedom of action, that is, on their sovereignty. Indeed, Vernon's "Vernon R Sovereignty at bay: the multinational spread of U.S. enterprises" reflects the widespread concerns over the implications of the growing imbalance between the MNE's and the nation states in which they operate (Vernon, 1971). However, as long as they are unable to agree on a set of rules of conduct and on the structure of the institutions that will enforce them, nation states are likely to continue to adhere to modes of behavior that are consistent with MNEs' expectations.

NOTES

1. Our definition of a firm's nationality is consistent with that employed by G. Jones: "place of registration and ... the company's 'seat' (*siège social*) defined as the place where the central administration and direction is located." He goes on to state "... But where the place of incorporation does not coincide with the place where the direction is actually exercised, the latter is normally taken in many Continental legal systems" Jones (p. 8).

2. An early version of the "OLI Paradigm" was included in Dunning (1977, pp. 395–414). The latest version of the OLI paradigm which was published in Dunning and Lundan (2008, pp. 95–103) is different in some respects from the early version.

3. See Internet site Teva Pharmaceutical Industries Ltd.

4. See, for example, UNCTAD's World Investment Report (2008), from where the figures in Table 1 are taken.

REFERENCES

Aharoni, Y. (1966). *The foreign investment decision process.* Boston: Division of Research, Harvard Business School, Harvard University.

Buernstam-Linder, S. (1961). *An essay on trade and transformation.* Stockholm: Almqvist & Wicksell.

Campbell, H. (2004). Country risk components, the cost of capital, and returns in emerging markets. In: S. Wilkin (Ed.), *Country and political risk: Practical insights for global finance* (pp. 71–102). London: Risk Books C29.

Dunning, J. M. (1977). Trade, location of economic activity and the MNE: A search for an eclectic approach. In: B. Ohlin, P. U. Hesselborn, & P. M. Wijkman (Eds), *The international allocation of economic activity, Proceedings of a Nobel Symposium,* Stockholm (New York, Holmes & Meier Publishers, Inc.).

Dunning, J. M., & Lundan, S. M. (2008). *Multinational enterprises and the global economy* (2nd ed.). Cheltenham, UK: Edgar Elgar.

Hirsch, S. (2005). Internationalization, distance barriers and home country size, lessons from the World Investment Report 2005. *Insights, 5*(4), 8–12.

Hymer, S. (1976). *The international operations of national firms: A study of direct foreign investment.* Ph.D. dissertation (1960). MIT Press, Cambridge, MA.

Johanson, J., & Vahlne, J. E. (1977). The internationalization process of the firm – A model of knowledge development and increasing market commitments. *Journal of International Business Studies, 8*(1), 23–32.

Jones, G. (2006). *Nationality and multinationals in historical perspective.* Working Paper HBS no. 06-052.

Vernon, R. (1971). *Sovereignty at bay, the multinational spread of U.S. enterprises.* London: Longman.

UNCTAD. (2008). *World Investment Report,* Geneva.

THE IMPACT OF FOREIGN DIRECT INVESTMENT ON LOCAL FIRMS: WESTERN FIRMS IN EMERGING MARKETS

Pervez N. Ghauri and Rebecca Firth

ABSTRACT

This study focuses on the impact of foreign direct investment (FDI) on local firms in host economies. We examine both backward and forward linkages and their effects on domestic firms. Data collection was undertaken over a three-year period whereby qualitative in-depth interviews were carried out with senior managers in UK headquarters, subsidiaries and 'linked' local firms in order to facilitate a multi-perspective approach to examining this topic. Results indicate that linkages do exist, contrary to earlier belief. The main factors which facilitate linkage formation were found to be subsidiary-related variables, mainly the mode of entry into the local market, subsidiary autonomy, level of embeddedness and subsidiary role. It was also found that government regulation and policy had some impact on the formation of linkages. Over time the impact on local firms was found to be positive with increased employment, productivity and significant upgrading of skills and competencies. The key contribution of this chapter is to extend the literature on linkages to consider services while developing a conceptual

The Future of Foreign Direct Investment and the Multinational Enterprise
Research in Global Strategic Management, Volume 15, 379–405
Copyright © 2011 by Emerald Group Publishing Limited
ISSN: 1064-4857/doi:10.1108/S1064-4857(2011)0000015021

framework in this area. Overall, our study confirms the importance of the subsidiary in linkage formation and also shows how the externalities occurring from linkage formation in the service sector may benefit local firms and subsequently aid local economic development as a whole.

Keywords: FDI; domestic firms; linkages; western firms; emerging markets

INTRODUCTION

The impact of foreign direct investment (FDI) on local firms in host countries has been seen as a growing policy concern in recent years (Driffield & Noor, 1999; Oosterhaven, Eding, & Stelden, 2001; UNCTAD, 2001; Giroud, 2007). FDI as a whole is often considered positive for host economies and has been frequently examined from a broad spectrum of angles. Researchers, however, are now becoming specific in identifying the ways through which benefits of FDI may manifest themselves, focusing on linkages and resultant productivity spillovers (Javorcik, 2004; Gorg & Strobl, 2001; Girma, 2001; Aitken & Harrison, 1999). The formation of linkages is one such strategy by which multinationals (MNEs) can produce positive externalities benefiting host country (Rodriguez-Clare, 1996; Girma et al., 2001; Javorcik, 2004; Ivarsson & Alvstam, 2005).

China is a particularly interesting emerging economy in which linkages can be examined. China was the largest recipient of inward FDI in Asia and indeed of all the developing nations in 2007; services, high-tech industries and high-value-added industries attracted $84 billion worth of FDI in China. China has abundant human capital, both skilled and unskilled, increasing the likelihood that innovation will emerge from China. Moreover, China is also abundant in natural resources and is frequently known as the 'world's factory'. There are thus clear incentives for service MNEs to locate and subsequently form linkages in this market. Studies focusing on emerging markets have recognised that the need for spillovers occurring from linkage formation may be even greater in these economies where the level of economic development is generally lower than in developed nations and the potential for positive gain and improvement is larger (Jindra, Giroud, & Scott-Kennel, 2009; Hansen, Pedersen, & Petersen, 2009).

Linkages have been investigated from a variety of theoretical perspectives including industrial economics, development and various international business perspectives, but studies have invariably concentrated on manufacturing. Historically, linkages are more likely to occur in manufacturing due to the high input intensity and tangible nature of processes in the sector. Suppliers providing tangible inputs to MNEs (backward linkages) are essential to the production process in manufacturing. Downstream relationships of multinational subsidiaries, such as distributors or marketing firms (forward linkages), are less tied to manufacturing per se. There is hardly any literature on linkages in services. This is surprising given the fact that the services sector represents the largest share of global FDI flows, accounting for 62% of estimated world inward FDI stock in 2006, up from 49% in 1990. Manufacturing firms are increasingly deterred from investing in Asia, in particular, because of higher costs of labour compared to other emerging markets which leaves an opportunity for the investment for service firms (UNCTAD, 2008, pp. 9–42). The services literature highlights the idea that the structure of services is changing. Internationalisation of services and the proposition that services and manufacturing are becoming increasingly intertwined means that increasing elements of service provision are becoming more tangible than in the past (Coombs, 1999; Aharoni, 1996). This indicates that there may be potential for both tangible and intangible inputs in service industries, and this increases the relevance of forming backward and forward linkages for companies.

There are a number of contextual, theoretical and methodological gaps which can be identified in existing studies on the impact of FDI in emerging markets. Contextual gaps include a lack of work on FDI in China and a limited number of studies examining linkages over time following the period of FDI and how they develop. Theoretical gaps concern the limited number of studies focusing on the service sector. The methodological gaps that can be pinpointed are the lack of qualitative, in-depth methods used to look at linkages and a lack of work that looks at all entities which may be involved in the linkage formation process, including the MNE headquarters (HQ), the subsidiary, the supplying entity, and policy makers as suggested by Aharoni (1981). This chapter aims, firstly, to review the current literature on the impact of FDI and linkages and examine how this may be applied to services; and, secondly, to examine, through empirical work what exactly the impact of FDI in services is and how this may change over time. The possible impact of FDI on host-country firms is evaluated through studying linkages with local firms. Finally, we will discuss the implications of this research for policy makers as well as the limitations and areas for further research.

A REVIEW OF THE LITERATURE

The literature on the impact of FDI and linkages 'can be described as emergent' (Giroud & Scott-Kennel, 2006) and 'murky' (Lall, 1980). The most overarching definition comes from Lall (1980) who describes linkages as:

> Direct relationships established by firms in complementary activities which are external to 'pure' market transactions (i.e. anonymous buyers and sellers exchanging goods in discrete transactions at prices determined in competitive markets).

The importance of research into linkages is slowly being realised, and further clarity is being brought to an area which is sometimes misunderstood and in which there has been conflicting empirical evidence. The relevance of linkages in today's economy cannot be overestimated; there are benefits for MNEs', local firms' and host economies' economic development. The importance of cross-border linkages is confirmed by the fact that one-third of world trade today is between MNEs and their foreign alliance partners (UNCTAD, 2004; Hansen et al., 2009). The potential benefits accruing from FDI may be even more significant in 2011 as we are grappling with a world economic crisis. Although the number of linkages may be curtailed during a recession, existing relationships and positive spillovers should be extended and maximised.

Investigation into the role of linkages on host-country economies began with the work of Hirschman (1958) who took an industrial economic view. More recent work has concentrated primarily on backward linkages in manufacturing industries (Kiyota, Matsuura, Urata & Wei, 2008; Iguchi, 2008; Giroud, 2007). Lall's (1980) pioneering study identified several different types of linkages that occurred and were present in his study of FDI of truck manufacturers into India. These linkages ranged from establishment linkages where MNEs would provide direct assistance to local firms to set up an operation, through to linkages which aimed to facilitate the upgrading of local firms through financial, informational and training support. Due to work accruing as a response to this study, we now have a clearer idea of the types of linkages that exist.

Linkages have been examined in relation to head-office-level factors and market-level factors. These include the MNE sourcing strategy and a preference towards a global or local strategy (Aharoni, 1996; Kelegama & Foley, 1999; Ivarsson & Alvstam, 2005; Scott-Kennel, 2007), the nature of the product and the technology involved (Lim & Fong, 1982; Wong, 1992; Ivarsson & Alvstam, 2005) and the industrial sector of the MNE (UNCTAD, 2001;

Giroud & Mirza, 2005). Market-level factors include the influence of government policy and regulation (Aharoni, 1980, 1981; Lim & Fong, 1982; Brown, 1998; Li & Yeung, 1999) and the nature of the host economy in facilitating these types of relationships.

The importance of the subsidiary in linkage formation cannot be overestimated. The level of autonomy and subsidiary roles of the MNE in the host country has been examined, and a common argument remains that the higher the level of subsidiary autonomy, the more likely linkage formation and resultant spillovers will be (Castellani & Zanfei, 2002; Iguchi, 2008; Jindra et al., 2009). The more active the subsidiary and the more 'scope' given to it by the parent, the more independent it can be in forming local linkage relationships and facilitating spillovers (Martin & Bell, 2006; Santangelo, 2009). In this context, it can be argued that 'centres of excellence' and particularly innovative subsidiaries will be more likely to form linkages, and these types of linkages are likely to be the most enduring, high-quality linkages because the subsidiaries are more creative and undertake activities that involve a greater range of local inputs (Frost, Birkinshaw, & Ensign, 2002; Jindra et al., 2009; Cantwell & Iguchi, 2005). Early work argued that the level of centralisation or decentralisation of an organisation as well as the level of control may impact on the level of autonomy; in terms of services which are generally seen as being more footloose and decentralised (Enderwick, 1992), autonomy in the subsidiary may be even greater. Subsidiaries can, thus, be seen as the main actors in the linkage formation process and a dynamic and active force behind relationships formed in the host country. This is related to the idea of embeddedness of the subsidiary in the local market and in external networks (McAleese & McDonald, 1978; Chen & Chen, 1998; Driffield & Noor, 1999; Belderbos & Capannelli, 2001; Chen, Chen & Rku, 2004). Embeddedness can be said to reflect subsidiary scope and roles, whereby more embedded competence-creating/exploratory-natured subsidiaries can be expected to produce more linkages (Santangelo, 2009; Holm & Pedersen, 2000).

An MNE's organisational structure has also been identified as a key determinant of linkage formation. This may be established in part via the entry mode of an MNE in a new foreign market (McAleese & McDonald, 1978; Belderbos & Capannelli, 2001; Chen et al., 2004; Javorcik, 2004). Acquisition or joint venture (JV) may enable the simultaneous acquisition of a readymade network of suppliers or at least enhanced access to local firms indicating that linkage formation may be more likely. Greenfield entry on the other hand may force the investing MNE to go about forming linkages unaided, from scratch.

Linkage studies have been undertaken in both less developed countries (LDCs) (Brannon et al., 1994; Brown, 1998; Kelegama & Foley, 1999) and developed countries (Angel, 1994; Barkley & McNamara, 1994; Belderbos & Capannelli, 2001; Castellani & Zanfei, 2002). Results are mixed for linkage studies in LDCs although it is generally assumed that there are impediments to forming linkages in LDCs because the infrastructure and absorptive capacity of local firms is not as well developed to allow local firms to benefit from externalities coming from MNEs. Studies of linkages in LDCs also highlighted the heavy role of government regulation which may have impacted the results regarding linkage-forming propensity of firms.

The effects of linkages can be split into two main types: (1) direct productivity effects and employment creation and (2) indirect effects (Hansen & Schaumburg-Muller, 2006). The first type occurs when a local firm sees an increase in output or profit indicating an overall increase in productivity usually as a result of heightened business opportunities with the linked MNE. The indirect effects may include less tangible benefits such as knowledge transfer, innovation, and technology transfer from the MNE, all of which are deemed positive for the local.

LINKAGE FORMATION IN SERVICES

Studies of linkages in manufacturing have been relatively common in comparison to studies on linkages in services. This may be because of the tendency to see services as 'footloose' and having few tangible inputs (Enderwick, 1992), thereby reducing the likelihood of the formation of (at least) backward linkages. The propensity of service firms to use suppliers is reduced if one subscribes to this view. However, a number of scholars working on the service industries have noted the changing nature of services in the world economy (Evangelista, 2000; Howells, 2004). Because of this shift there may now be increased impetus for service firms to source through both backward and forward linkages.

Services have created a powerful role for themselves in many economies. The importance of linkages in services will always be key because of the role services have to play in 'satisfying the demands from manufacturing' (O'Farrell & O'Loughlin, 1981). In this study of linkages in services, the authors (O'Farrell & O'Loughlin, 1981) examine service linkages to manufacturing firms in Northern Ireland. They look primarily at the low-value service activities such as office cleaning, security etc. The aim of their paper was to examine the value of local service inputs in Northern Ireland, the types of service linkages and the locations of the suppliers. They looked at the impact of linkages from a development perspective, hoping ultimately to show development occurring as a result of their aforementioned aims. Findings suggest that in terms of the distribution of inputs sourced, 42% are sourced locally (within 20 miles of each plant). Nachum and Keeble (2003) examine linkages formed within clusters in the media sector between foreign affiliates and indigenous firms in London. The media sector is largely made up of service functions. No service-sector-specific results were found. However, findings did indicate that foreign affiliates formed lower levels of linkages because they internalised many functions that would commonly be outsourced or supplied externally making them more isolated from the cluster generally. Therefore, participation in a cluster by subsidiaries is shown to increase embeddedness and enhance linkage formation. This finding again confirms the importance of the embedded and active subsidiary in the formation of linkage relationships.

Due to the lack of empirical work on the impact of FDI and linkages in services, our conceptual framework has been developed primarily based on manufacturing studies (see Fig. 1). This is then applied to service sector case studies, the aim being to see which factors most strongly affect linkage formation and how exactly linkages are affected. The literature on FDI and linkages can be broken up into 'influential' areas on linkage formation. These include factors relating to the MNE, factors relating to the subsidiary in the host country, factors relating to host-country conditions themselves and factors relating to the 'linked' company (primarily domestic suppliers).

METHODOLOGY

The methodology used to measure the impact of FDI and linkages has been notoriously difficult. There have been four main kinds of studies (Giroud & Scott-Kennel, 2006). Case studies have allowed a description of firms and their linkage relationships (Lim & Fong, 1982; Awuah, 1997; Ivarsson & Alvstam, 2005; Okada, 2004). Case studies have been useful for looking at linkages in depth and have allowed us insights into depth and scope of linkages as well as effects which we would not gauge from quantitative studies. There have been industry-level studies (Kelegama & Foley, 1999; Dries & Swinnen, 2004) and survey-based studies (O'Farrell & O'Loughlin, 1981; Belderbos & Capannelli, 2001; Gorg & Ruane, 2001; Scott-Kennel, 2001; Giroud, 2003). There have also been studies using panel-level data and

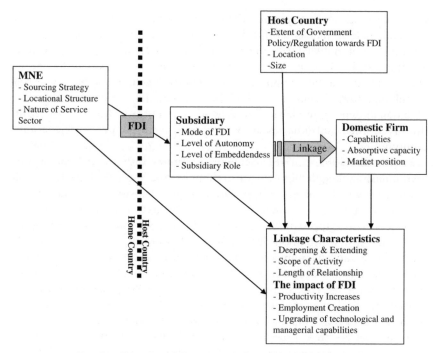

Fig. 1. Conceptual Framework for Linkage Formation.

input–output tables. These studies have, however, not been able to capture the complexities of linkages.

The measurement used up until now has involved calculating a percentage of total raw material and components sourced in the host economy local procurement ratio (Belderbos & Capannelli, 2001) and other similar calculated approaches, but the problems with these approaches are that this type of measurement does not include service suppliers and can only be collected at a single point in time so we do not know 'whether the length of time spent in the host economy is a determinant factor for backward linkages' (Giroud & Scott-Kennel, 2006).

Service MNEs were chosen and initially identified using the Thompson One Banker Deals database to identify which firms had undertaken substantial FDI in China. Subsequently, further online research was done to make sure that the firms identified met the minimum requirements of the study, that is, they were in services, were headquartered in UK and had undertaken FDI in China. Theoretical sampling has been used where 'a certain level of knowledge of the case is already present' (Flick, Kardorff, & Steinke, 2004). As this is an exploratory study, we decided to use an inductive and qualitative approach (Eisenhardt, 1989; Yin, 2003; Ghauri & Gronhaug, 2000; Eisenhardt & Graebner, 2007). This research is therefore based on in-depth interviews with respondents from two British service firms (the HQ, their subsidiaries in China and their suppliers in the host economy).

Eisenhardt (1989, p. 548) argues case studies should be used and are 'particularly well-suited to new research areas' and are 'useful in early stages of research' which makes this approach apt for a study on the impact of FDI in services. The case is made up of at least three interviews with senior managers lasting approximately an hour. In total six interviews were carried out for the case selected, one interview was done with the UK HQ, one with the Chinese subsidiary and one or more with Chinese-based suppliers of the subsidiary. We prepared three separate interview guides based on our framework for the HQ, subsidiary and suppliers, respectively. This enabled us to cross check the same issues in a relevant manner, tailored to each type of firm, thus improving the quality of the answers we received. At least two interviewers were present at every interview in order to improve the reliability and consistency of questioning. Most interviews were conducted in English; however, an interpreter was present in case needed and did intervene with one supplier interview. All interviews were digitally recorded and then transcribed by the authors personally, continually cross checking with the interview notes.

A systematic analysis was undertaken using a computer-assisted qualitative data analysis (CAQDAS) software N*vivo. The use of N*vivo as argued by Sinkovics, Penz and Ghauri (2005, 2008) saves time, increases reliability by reducing human error and allows the potential of unexpected insights without losing rich textual narratives (Ghauri, 2004; Ghauri & Firth, 2009). This enabled us to use a variation on template analysis (King 2004), whereby a number of codes or 'nodes' were created from the conceptual framework and each interview analysed according to these categories. The percentage of text in each node relating to a certain variable was considered, but also the context and quality of information of each node due to the fact that some respondents talked more about certain variables than others; from this an interpretation of the data is made by the researchers.

HSBC IN CHINA

The Hong Kong & Shanghai Banking Corporation (HSBC) is one of the largest financial service organisations in the world. With over 9,500 offices in 85 countries and territories in Europe, Asia Pacific, the Americas, the Middle East and Africa, it is an internationally active and dynamic organisation. Its sheer size alone allows it many advantages compared to its smaller competitors. The head office is located in London. Worldwide there are approximately 335,000 employees working in different areas of the business. It positions itself using the slogan 'the world's local bank,' emphasising its strength of being to leverage a global network whilst adapting to local markets. The HSBC subsidary in Shanghai, China was established in 1865 one month after the company was set up in Hong Kong and has had a continuous presence in China ever since. It was the first foreign bank since 1949 to be granted a banking license and has the largest network of any foreign bank with 62 outlets at the start of 2008 with more being planned. HSBC takes a regional focus concentrating on the four major cities of Beijing, Shanghai, Shenzhen and Guangzhou, where majority of the population and wealth is situated, and this suits the types of banking which HSBC primarily offers, that is, corporate and commercial banking and premier personal banking.

HSBC has a linkage and management stake in Pacific Credit Card Centre (PCCC) which qualifies as a horizontal linkage. It leverages its relationships with this local company in order to run its credit card business. Regulations prevent foreign banks from running credit card operations in China and from acquiring more than 19.9% of local enterprises. Therefore, the relationship with PCCC enables HSBC to get around the regulation regarding credit cards because PCCC is a semi-independent unit of a local bank Bank of Communications (BOCOM), in which HSBC has a minority stake of 19.9%. This is not a traditional linkage because in a sense it has been deliberately 'manufactured' by HSBC so that should regulations change regarding acquisitions, the credit card business will have already been set up and ready to be internalised between BOCOM and HSBC. There are about 3,000 employees at PCCC with about 50 from BOCOM, 16 from HSBC and all the rest new recruits. PCCC is a growing business with approximately 2.6 million customers, which is expected to double next year.

HSBC also has a linkage relationship with BOCOM. This is the fifth largest bank in China and is state owned. It was founded in 1908 and now has its head office in Shanghai. BOCOM is highly innovative and successful in China and 'was the first to implement shareholding system for its capital and mode of ownership form; the first to command an organisational structure based on market rules and cost/return rules; the first to introduce competition into the banking industry in China; the first to introduce assets/liability ratio management and apply it for regulating business operations and risk; the first to build new bank/enterprise relationships based on two-way selection; and the first commercial bank to integrate banking, insurance and securities businesses' (www.bankcomm.com.hk 2008). In 2008 BOCOM was leading the way for China's banking development and reforms. Itself an MNE, it has branches in New York, Tokyo, Singapore, Seoul, Frankfurt and Macau as well as a representative office in London. HSBC owns the maximum allowed 19.9% of BOCOM, having paid around 1.9 billion US dollars, currently making this a JV and horizontal linkage relationship. Slowly HSBC will be allowed to acquire more and more as the rules relax. Today the Chinese Ministry of Finance remains the largest shareholder. It is a nationwide bank. It has 50,000 staff members, 2,800 branches, and represents 145 cities in China.

KINGFISHER PLC/B&Q IN CHINA

Kingfisher plc is a company which owns a number of DIY and home improvement outlets. It began in 1983 as part of now dissolved holding company Woolworths. They run a total of seven brands including B&Q (United Kingdom, Ireland, China ...), Castorama (France & Poland), Brico Depot (France, Poland & Spain), Screwfix (UK), Koçtas (Turkey), Trade Depot (United Kingdom) and Hornbach (Austria, Czech Republic, Germany, Luxembourg, Netherlands, Romania, Slovakia, Sweden, Switzerland). It has over 800 stores spread over these countries and around 70,000 employees in total with approximately 6 million customers visiting a store each week. Kingfisher is Europe's leading home improvement retailer and the world's third largest. Kingfisher reported sales of 9.36 billion in February 2008, just over half of which was generated outside the United Kingdom. The B&Q brand in the United Kingdom has been publicly suffering in the past couple of years, a situation which is bound to get worse with the latest economic downturn of 2008–2009. However, B&Q has quite successfully entered the Chinese market and was the market leader in 2005 following its acquisition of German chain OBI in China. It also relatively recently expanded into Korea. B&Q in Asia originated with the opening of a store in Nankan in Taiwan in 1996 via a JV with Testrite. After the opening of the second store, they began to look towards China and opened the first store in Shanghai in June 1999. Although there is strong competition in China and profits are currently not expected to be level with B&Q in the United Kingdom, there is potential for steady growth. There are currently about 65 stores in China with potential for even more in the 'big box' retail category. The core cities of operation are Shanghai, Beijing, Shenzhen and Guangzhou.

Nippon Paint is the leading paint and coatings manufacturer in Asia. It has been a supplier of B&Q China for some time. It has recently opened it seventh new plant in China. Nippon paint produces paints and coatings for the industrial, automotive, architectural and DIY sectors. Nippon paint has an overall strong presence in Asia with over 20 manufacturing plants in the region and a global network of over 20 countries. Asia, however, remains the companies' strongest focus. The company was originally founded in 1881 in Japan, but it was not until 1994 when Nippon Paint China was formally established. Nippon paint has been innovative in its product development, introducing the 'flexceed' printing plates which can be developed in water and has a water-borne recycling system. Nippon Paint has also been clever in identifying its target market, for example, acquiring more than a 70% share in the motorcycle coatings market in Vietnam. It launched the colour tinting system first in China, installing more than 800 of these systems across the country, as well as offering over 1,000 colours and shades changing the whole paint industry in China. Nippon Paint has been supplying B&Q directly in China since they entered the market in 1999. Three percent of their total sales come from the business generated with B&Q. Nippon Paint is currently the biggest supplier of B&Q and is the market leader in paints and coatings in China, most likely because it was the first such company to locate to China giving them first-mover advantage (Director Supply Chain: Nippon Paint).

Another B&Q supplier in China, Kohler, is primarily known for the manufacture of kitchen and bathroom interiors; however, it also has a global power business and a hospitality and real estate business. Kohler has more than 50 manufacturing locations worldwide and there are more than 32,000 Kohler employees working on six continents. The business in China is focused on the supply of high-end kitchen and bathroom interiors and they distribute the full range of Kohler plumbing products throughout the PRC. Kohler was founded in 1873. In 1980 Kohler received orders from five major hotels in China – the first sales in China by an international plumbing products company since the 1930s. The Kohler office in China was established about a decade ago, and they have been supplying B&Q for the past three years (National Sales Manager: Kohler, China). Kohler recently strengthens its commitment to the Chinese market with a JV in 2007 with YinXiang Ltd in Chongquing to produce engines. Kohler has some competitors such as TOTO from Japan, and American Standard and Roca from Spain, but Kohler is currently the leading brand. In China about 90% of five-star hotels use the Kohler brand (National Sales Manager: Kohler, China).

FINDINGS

The Impact of FDI and Linkages Formation

Evidence of linkage formation has been found by both case companies. Although a thorough examination of only a handful of suppliers has been undertaken in further depth, extensive linkage formation was identified by interviewees (see Table 1). These were supply relationships that were mentioned during the interviews or in secondary data; however, only a couple of the most important suppliers were then interviewed further.

For B&Q in China, vertical backward linkages with input suppliers is the primary form of linkage, HSBC on the other hand have noticeably stronger horizontal linkages with a tendency to go for a more collaborative approach. This may be due to the difference in subservice sector of the two chosen cases as B&Q is a business that is highly input driven, whereas HSBC relies primarily on intangible inputs to drive the business forward. The complexity of the market may also be a factor affecting the type of linkage decision, as HSBC has chosen to strengthen its linkage relationships by taking an equity stake in many of its linked domestic firms. This is perhaps also to give a level of security and reassurance when operating in a physically distant market. Many of its linkages are with local firms who were less known to HSBC, and therefore taking a stake ensures there is an added level of control over joint activities when a horizontal linkage is formed. B&Q in China has identified their 'top' and most important suppliers as being global ones. This may be related to issues of trust and quality control for key products. However, the data suggests that the majority of less key suppliers are local.

For both HSBC and B&Q, subsidiary factors appear to be the main influences on (a) where linkages are formed and (b) whether linkages are global or local. The mode of FDI, the level of autonomy and the subsidiary role in particular are found to be the most frequent and likely influences on linkage formation, particularly local linkage formation. The subsidiary influence is pivotal in the decision of whether firms will form linkages or not.

Table 1.   Evidence of Linkage formation in HSBC & B&Q.

Firm	Linkage	Sector	Type of Linkage		Nature of Relationship
HSBC China	WPP	Advertising	Global	Forward	$800 mn global contract
	Household	Administrative services	Global	Backward vertical	Acquired for $14.2 bn
	Bank of Communications (BOCOM)	Banking	Local	Horizontal	19.9% ownership
	Pacific Credit Card Centre	Banking	Local	Backward vertical	Owned by BOCOM
	Ping' an Insurance	Insurance	Local	Horizontal	19.9% ownership
	Bank of Shanghai	Banking	Local	Horizontal	8% ownership
	Shanxi securities	Fund management	Local	Horizontal	19.9% ownership
	MOW	Risk management consultancy	Global	Backward vertical	Global contract
	IBM	IT solutions	Global	Backward vertical	Global contract
B&Q China	Nippon Paint	Paint manufacturer	Global	Backward vertical	Asia contract
	Kohler China	Bathroom manufacturer	Global	Backward vertical	Standard supply
	ICI	Paint manufacturer	Global	Backward vertical	Standard supply
	American Standard	Bathroom manufacturer	Global	Backward vertical	Standard supply
	Haier	Electronics	Local	Backward vertical	Standard supply
	SCS	Quality control	Local	Backward	Standard supply

B&Q in China assumed that linkage formation was more fraught with difficulties because of its lack of ability to find a JV partner; in all of these cases it was indicated that a JV would have been the preferred method of entry, but this was not possible. In the case of HSBC in China, a curious situation has occurred whereby despite not being able to find a full JV partner (only being able to acquire 19.9% of BOCOM) they have used horizontal linkage formation almost as a substitute for a JV partner, acquiring a high level of security and local expertise through the horizontal linkage. Therefore, mode of establishment with a JV partner is shown to be preferable and more beneficial in terms of forming vertical backward linkages with suppliers, but in rare cases a positive situation can occur whereby horizontal linkages can actually be facilitated by the lack of ability to find a JV partner.

In terms of the level of autonomy, evidence shows that subsidiaries with high levels of autonomy and in particular innovative subsidiaries such as centres of excellence are more likely to form linkages. HSBC and B&Q in China are a good example of this. Related to subsidiary autonomy is the role of the subsidiary. Results have shown that the more innovative a subsidiary is and the more country-specific functions it undertakes, the more likely linkage formation is. This is exemplified in HSBC China, where products are highly adapted to the Chinese market. Other aspects of the conceptual framework which were found to be important and to be noted were the nature of the service sector; for example, B&Q, which has more tangible inputs overall, formed more linkages with suppliers because of the tangibility of their products and government regulation. The other aspects of the framework, although mentioned as influential factors, were not particularly found to show any impact or linkages.

Changes in Depth Linkages with Host-Country Firms over Time

Firstly, it is necessary to properly define what we mean by the deepening of linkages in this chapter. Deepening refers to the effort an MNE puts in to 'expand the *number* of suppliers that meet the requirements of foreign affiliates in terms of cost, quality and timely delivery, and/or help *existing* suppliers improve their capabilities in one or more areas' (UNCTAD, 2001, p. 140).

The deepening of linkage relationships over time is shown visually in Tables 2 and 3, and the analysis is subsequently explained further in the text. The tables show the authors' subjective view of the extent to which deepening of linkages has occurred, extension of the scope of activity has occurred and the extent of commitment of HSBC and B&Q to the linkage relationship according to evidence found in the MNE HQ, subsidiary and supplier interviews. N*vivo has been used firstly to systematically locate evidence, to consider the frequency of text which has been located but also relevance of what is actually said. These two levels of evidence have been analysed in all levels of the case interviews.

HSBC in China has exhibited a high level of both deepening linkage relationships (see Table 2). All levels of interviews acknowledge this although the subsidiary gave the strongest evidence of this trend. Deepening was most prevalent which shows a commitment to existing suppliers rather

Table 2.   Changes in Linkage Characteristics Over Time for HSBC China.

Firm	HSBC in China			
Linkage Characteristics	MNE HQ Interview +/−	Subsidiary Interview +/−	Supplier Interviews +/−	Summary of Evidence
Deepening[a]	+ +	+ + +	+ + +	High levels of upgrading plus equity investment in suppliers
Scope of activity	−	+ + +	+ + +	Keen interest in expanding collaboration in many areas with suppliers
Length of relationship	−	+ + +	+ + +	Relationships are generally long lasting and are not changed due to JVs

Note: + + indicates a level of perceived evidence which is medium; + + + indicates a level of perceived evidence which is high; and − indicates that no evidence was found.
[a]Deepening is defined as the efforts by firms to deepen and upgrade existing linkages by helping to improve supplier capabilities (UNCTAD, 2001, p. XXV).

Table 3.   Changes in Linkage Characteristics Over Time for B&Q China.

Firm	B&Q in China			
Linkage Characteristics	MNE HQ Interview +/−	Subsidiary Interview +/−	Supplier Interviews +/−	Summary of Evidence
Deepening	−	−	+	Low upgrading
Scope of activity	+ + +	+ + +	+ + +	Increased scope of activity
Length of relationship	+ +	+ + +	+ + +	Significant commitment to keeping existing suppliers

Note: + indicates a level of perceived evidence which is low; + + indicates a level of perceived evidence which is medium; + + + indicates a level of perceived evidence which is high; and − indicates that no evidence was found.

than to form too many new linkages. Suppliers undertook a wide range of activities with HSBC in terms of the scope of linkages, and relationships are overall perceived to be long lasting.

In case of B&Q in China, there are low levels of deepening in terms of investment and upgrading of local suppliers; however, they did make efforts to increase the number of linkages and the scope of activity undertaken by suppliers which involved a wide range of inputs as well as installation services (see Table 3). They were frequently using supply contracts in China to produce products which are then exported back to Europe. They had also made a significant commitment to keep relationships going with suppliers once linkages were formed with contracts initially lasting a year which were in most cases renewed.

The Impact of FDI on Domestic Firms

Productivity Increases

One of the main impacts of FDI on local suppliers can be the productivity increases they experience as a result of certain benefits of the relationship. In the case of HSBC China, where horizontal linkages have been formed, there have been very obvious signs of productivity increases. PCCC was essentially created by HSBC under the guise of belonging to BOCOM to create a credit card business. PCCC is actively expected to increase productivity and grow week by week and is given resources to enable it to do this:

> We've done many things from using Mickey Mouse to Tiger Woods to help us. Bonus points to get gifts. Air miles across all airlines have merchant discounts. Special operators, like HSBC Champion Golf Events we won awards; we've been on Tele here helping us on the FIFA awards, we had a great day with Tele. I can draw you a card volume, these actually are out of date. You see how quickly we are growing. January, February and March, April, May, so it's about 2.6 million there and we ought to have about 4 million by the end of the year. (PCCC CEO China)

There is also evidence that the productivity increase in PCCC may be directly due to the linkage relationship with HSBC:

> They've never seen this sort of growth. So even for HSBC people, this is new learning for them as well. Across China, on cards, most of the banks have found foreign partners. The difference with our relationship we believe, is there's more than just this, it's more than just this small equity holding. There are 60 areas of cooperation. So that's why I believe this is actually a stronger relationship. (PCCC CEO China)

The story is a very similar one in terms of the productivity increases of BOCOM itself. BOCOM was already very strong prior to its linkage with HSBC with over 50,000 staff and 2,800 branches represented in over 145 cities in China. Since the linkage with HSBC:

> HSBC now as part of the team I think we emphasize more on returns and efficiency of the investment, on return of the equity and on return of the risk assets, on the

effectiveness of the customer base, on making use of the resources, how to improve the
rate of return... ... ...We have achieved from zero to now 300,000 customers, each of
which has at least a million deposits with us. So that's the indirect profit we got from
HSBC because of the people here. (BOCOM CEO China)

There is also some evidence that HSBC have been influential in allowing
BOCOM to acquire some assets in Hong Kong to which they otherwise
would have not had access.

The B&Q case in China mirrors HSBC's experience in the sense that there
have been significant productivity gains for local suppliers. Kohler takes
8–9% of its total business from sales with B&Q, which is growing because as
B&Q have opened up new stores this has given them access to new segments
of the market; B&Q grew initially from 1 store to 59 stores in China and
another 50 stores in Hong Kong. Kohler's relationship with B&Q allows
them to expand the distribution of their products to Hong Kong and
Taiwan as well as improving sales via this route. Admittedly, B&Q is a very
large customer for Kohler. Nippon Paint supplies through B&Q in China,
Taiwan and Hong Kong as well. About 3% of Nippon Paints sales come
from B&Q in China; however, the increase in productivity is less notable
than for Kohler because their main customers are primarily in the
automobile sector and this is their main focus.

Employment Creation
Another indicator of the success of a company is whether or not it can
afford to take on new employees. It is argued, this in turn also benefits the
standard of living and thus local economy. PCCC in China has employed at
least 3,000 new employees through the setting up of the credit card linkage
with HSBC:

It's crazy, crazy, crazy. From 0 staff to there, this is also a few months out of date we
have 3,000 now. We expect 4,000 by the end of the year. So it's very very rapid growth.
(PCCC CEO China)

Equally, BOCOM has a handful of senior executives from HSBC now
working to improve their personal banking business in addition to the
existing staff of 50,000 and 20–25 new managers as well as the appointment
of a new deputy CEO. At HSBC itself:

We have 2250 staff here at the moment, last year we added 750 staff and grew our head
count by 57%, this year we'll add 1000 staff. Our ratio of local staff to expatriate is now
96% local and the 4% will continue to shrink. (CEO HSBC China)

It is important to note that the majority of staff are local employees because this is better for the local economy overall as gains directly go back into the local environment.

Upgrading of Technological and Managerial Capabilities
HSBC in China has contributed significantly to the upgrading of local enterprises on both the technical and managerial side of the business. The supplying entities confirm the HQ and subsidiary initiative which has been taken up to help improve their capabilities in many areas. The HSBC China case is an excellent example of how benefits can accrue via FDI and linkage formation. In the B&Q China case, education and learning seems to be the main form of upgrading which has taken place, but there is little technical upgrading occurring (Table 4).

Table 4. Evidence of Upgrading Occurring in HSBC and B&Q in China.

Firm/Interview	Upgraded Technological Capabilities	Upgraded Managerial Capabilities
HSBC UK HQ	'Technical service agreement' to improve different aspects of operations	Governance, audit, compliance, risk management, operating management, asset liability management, corporate card
HSBC China subsidiary	– Product sophistication – Treasury side – Overseas network – Monetary investments – 'Technical services agreement' to ensure knowledge transfer and transfer of best practice – Introduction of credit cards to BOCOM – Development of personal banking business – Trade finance and cash management systems	– Consultants working in areas like credit risk management, audits, and HR to transfer HSBC experience to BOCOM – How to utilize efficiency gains from the partnership – Training workshops for product training, joint-training seminars, treasury and cash management training, trade finance – Upgrading of service standards
BOCOM China	'Technical service agreement' allows HSBC to put employees, consultants and advisors into BOCOM	– Consultants in HR department, one in risk management, one in management accounting, then one in audit

Table 4. (*Continued*)

Firm/Interview	Upgraded Technological Capabilities	Upgraded Managerial Capabilities
	Allows BOCOM to ask for more resources – Credit card business – Customer segmentation – Introduction and development of two new brands – 'Process re-engineering initiative'	– Improved transparency of the bank – dealing with investors and analysts – Risk management – Marketing skills – Planning ,marketing, retail risk and product development in retail banking – Change in structure of the bank to functional line management style – Developed two or three risk management tools from HSBC – Branch remodelling and branch distribution
PCCC China	TSA with 60 + initiatives Technical capability on risk management, HR management and training & legal compliance Call centre	Establishment of a marketing department Establishment of central data centre Whole credit card business Codes of conduct
B&Q China	No evidence of upgrading	Manager training Auditing of suppliers to check quality Education on CSR
Nippon Paint China	No evidence of upgrading	Educating on CSR Auditing from B&Q
Kohler China	No evidence of upgrading	Training on sales systems, B2B systems and finance processes

DISCUSSION AND CONCLUSIONS

This research has focused on discovering the impact of FDI and linkage formation in the service sector. We have discussed two cases of firms that have invested in China and analysed the types of linkages they have formed, the impact of FDI, changes over time and the effect on domestic firms. This study has confirmed that linkages do exist in the service sector confirming the findings of Nachum and Keeble (2003) and O'Farrell and O'Loughlin

(1981). Our main observation from this exercise has been that linkage formation and its effects differ significantly depending on the service subsector and the country. Differences in patterns of linkage formation have previously been observed by region and level of economic development of the market (Giroud, 2003). These findings reveal a difference in type of linkage formation in terms of commitment to the market. The one trend that supersedes the type of firm is the importance and influence of the subsidiary in the formation of linkages. This finding concurs with previous research which argues subsidiaries often act as 'listening posts' for linkage opportunities. They may be more important than the MNE HQ for identifying, searching for and evaluating these opportunities (Castellani & Zanfei, 2002). In particular, the level of autonomy of the subsidiary has been highlighted in this study as an influential determinant on linkage formation; this finding concurs with manufacturing studies which argue the same (Jindra et al., 2009; Santangelo, 2009). This may be even more of an important influence in services as autonomy can be said to be high as a result of the footloose, decentralised nature of service firms (Enderwick, 1992). The subsidiary role in general has been found to be of a significant influence on linkage formation and deepening. As in the HSBC China case, innovative subsidiaries which can be considered centres of excellence are more likely to form successful linkages (Holm & Pedersen, 2000).

Traditional schools of thought on services have implicitly implied that there may be less potential for linkages in the service sector due to the primarily intangible nature of the product they offer (UNCTAD, 2004). We argued that this is not the case. Our case studies show the contrary: although both case companies showed a propensity to form linkages, HSBC not only had a tendency to form more linkages with local firms but also to form higher quality, more committed types of linkages. This can be seen by HSBC's likelihood of deepening linkages and their long-term investment in local firms. Also, their tendency towards upgrading of local suppliers is strong, especially in China where they have over 60 initiatives helping to upgrade local firms. B&Q, on the other hand, despite requiring a higher number of tangible inputs to operate show significantly less commitment in the quality of their linkages. It can be argued, therefore, that service subsector and the type of industry may reveal different patterns of linkages, but this may be more due to their particular expansion strategy rather than due to the difference in service subsector per se.

The nature of the market is clearly an influential factor here. Policy in China on the percentage that can be acquired by foreign entities restricts full acquisitions and, therefore, arguably restricts the inheritance of linkages by investing MNEs and forces firms to seek linkage opportunities independently. Our study shows that policy makers in China increasingly demand that foreign firms investing in China contribute towards knowledge development of local firms.

The recommendations of this research are, therefore, for companies to do a thorough analysis of markets before entry and to attempt to develop and build relationships prior to entry or through JVs in complex markets, and, moreover, to comply and adapt to rules and regulations and policy by the local governments as suggested by Aharoni (1980, 1981). This will not only facilitate entry but also convince the local government of good intentions of the foreign firm. Moreover, in China, it is essential in order to recreate the security and local knowledge traditionally obtained from JV partners. The policy implications for local governments are, therefore, to extend policy to actively promote linkage formation, particularly in relation to the MNE subsidiary in the country. A number of measures could be taken such as the provision of information about suppliers available and matchmaking MNE subsidiaries and local suppliers together, highlighting the benefits to be gained from local suppliers such as technology upgrading. MNE sub-sidiaries should be encouraged to provide training to local suppliers in return for incentives, and the encouragement of linkage formation through financial policy incentives for subsidiaries. This research highlights the need for specific linkage promotion programmes where possible in countries such as China.

The limitations of the study are that we were not able to consider and compare specific service subsector using any great number of cases because of the constraints of our sample. If more countries or more MNEs were included, perhaps this could be an area for future work. It would be interesting to investigate larger samples in specific service subsectors in conjunction with the examination of the impact of FDI and linkage formation in different countries. On the whole, the main contribution of this research has been to bring to light the impact of FDI and linkages in service and develop a conceptual framework from which to view this topic. It has attempted a comparative approach across service subsectors and analysed data collected from both the leading and linked enterprises, considering the impact from the supplier perspective as well as the MNE HQ and subsidiary perspective. The more practical contributions are to further inform host-country governments on how, specifically, MNEs form linkages through FDI so they are aware of how best to understand and handle invested MNEs in order to encourage and promote linkages and the positive impact of local firms.

ACKNOWLEDGEMENT

The authors would like to thank Economic and Social Research Council (ESRC- RES-000-23-0840) for funding this research.

REFERENCES

Aharoni, Y. (1980). The state-owned enterprise as a competitor in international markets. *Columbia Journal of World Business, 15*(1), 14–22.

Aharoni, Y. (1981). Performance evaluation in state-owned enterprises: A process perspective. *Management Science, 29*(11), 1340–1347.

Aharoni, Y. (1996). The organization of global service MNEs. *International Studies of Management and Organization, 26*(2), 6–23.

Aitken, B. J., & Harrison, A. E. (1999). Do domestic firms benefit from direct foreign investment? Evidence from Venezuela. *The American Economic Review, 89*(3), 605–618.

Angel, D. P. (1994). Tighter bonds? Customer–supplier linkages in semiconductors. *Regional Studies, 28*(2), 187–200.

Awuah, G. B. (1997). Promoting infant industries in less developed countries (LDCs): A network approach to analyse the impact of the exchange relationships between multinational companies and their indigenous suppliers in LDCs' efforts to boost infant industries' development. *International Business Review, 6*(1), 71–87.

Barkley, D. L., & McNamara, K. T. (1994). Local input linkages: A comparison of foreign-owned and domestic manufacturers in Georgia and South Carolina. *Regional Studies, 28*(7), 725–737.

Belderbos, R., & Capannelli, G. (2001). Backward vertical linkages of foreign manufacturing affiliates: Evidence from Japanese multinationals. *World Development, 29*(1), 189–208.

Brannon, J. T., et al. (1994). Generating and sustaining backward linkages between Maquiladoras and local suppliers in Northern Mexico. *World Development, 22*(12), 1933–1945.

Brown, R. (1998). Electronics foreign direct investment in Singapore: A study of local linkages in "Winchester City". *European Business Review, 98*(4), 196–210.

Cantwell, J., & Iguchi, C. (2005). Effects of backward linkages to local suppliers development path: The case of the Malaysian electrical and electronics industry. In: A. Giorud, A. T. Mohr & D. Yang (Eds), *Multinationals and Asia: Organisational and institutional relationships* (pp. 54–71). London: Routledge.

Castellani, D., & Zanfei, A. (2002). Multinational experience and the creation of linkages with local firms: Evidence from the electronics industry. *Cambridge Journal of Economics, 26*(1), 1–25.

Chen, H., & Chen, T. J. (1998). Network linkages and location choice in foreign direct investment. *Journal of International Business Studies, 29*(3), 445–467.

Chen, T.-J., Chen, H., & Rku, Y. H. (2004). Foreign direct investment and local linkages. *Journal of International Business Studies, 35*(4), 320–333.

Coombs, R. (1999). *Innovation in services: Overcoming the service–manufacturing divide.* The Netherlands: Nijmedgen Business School.

Dries, L., & Swinnen, J. F. M. (2004). Foreign direct investment, vertical integration, and local suppliers: Evidence from the polish dairy sector. *World Development, 32*(9), 1525–1544.

Driffield, N. N., & Noor, A. H. M. (1999). Foreign direct investment and local input linkages in Malaysia. *Transnational Corporations, 8*(3), 1–25.

Eisenhardt, K. M. (1989). Building theories from case study research. *Academy of Management Review, 14*(4), 532–550.

Eisenhardt, K. M., & Graebner, M. E. (2007). Theory building from cases: Opportunities & challenges. *Academy of Management Journal, 50*(1), 25–32.

Enderwick, P. (1992). The scale and scope of service sector multinationals. In: P. C. Buckley (Ed.), *Multinational enterprises in the world economy: Essays in honour of John Dunning*. England: Edward Elgar.

Evangelista, R. (2000). Sectoral patterns of technological change in services. *Economics of Innovation and New Technology, 9*(3), 183–221.

Firth, R., & Ghauri, P. N. (2010). Multinational enterprise acquisitions in emerging markets: Linkage effects on local firms. *European Journal of International Management, 4*(1/2), 135–162.

Flick, U., Kardorff, E. V., & Steinke, I. (2004). *A companion to qualitative research*. London: Sage.

Frost, T., Birkinshaw, J. M., & Ensign, P. C. (2002). Centres of excellence in multinational corporations. *Strategic Management Journal, 23*, 997–1018.

Ghauri, P. N. (2004). Designing and conducting case studies in international business research. In: R. Marschan-Piekkari & C. Welch (Eds), *Handbook of qualitative research methods for international business* (pp. 109–124). Cheltenham, UK: Edward Elgar.

Ghauri, P. N., & Firth, R. (2009). The formalization of case study research in international business. *Der Markt, 48*(1–12), 29–40.

Ghauri, P. N., & Gronhaug, K. (2000). *Research methods in business studies* (4th ed.). Harlow, England: Prentice Hall.

Girma, S., et al. (2001). Who benefits from foreign direct investment in the UK? *Scottish Journal of Political Economy, 48*(2), 119–133.

Giroud, A. (2003). *Transnational corporations, technology and economic development: Backward linkages and knowledge transfer in South East Asia*. Cheltenham, UK: Edward Elgar.

Giroud, A. (2007). MNE vertical linkages: The experience of Vietnam after Malaysia. *International Business Review, 6*(2), 159–176.

Giroud, A., & Mirza, H. (2005). *Factors determining input linkages between local suppliers and foreign subsidiaries in South East Asia*. Working Paper. University of Bradford, UK.

Giroud, A., & Scott-Kennel, J. (2006). *Foreign-local linkages in International Business: A review and extension of the literature*. Academy of International Business, Guanghua School of Management, Peking University.

Gorg, H., & Ruane, F. (2001). Multinational companies and linkages: Panel-data evidence for the Irish electronics sector. *International Journal of the Economics of Business, 8*(1), 1–18.

Gorg, H., & Strobl, E. (2001). Multinational companies and productivity spillovers: A meta-analysis. *Economic Journal, 111*(475), 723–739.

Hansen, M. W., Pedersen, T., & Petersen, B. (2009). MNC strategies and linkage effects in developing countries. *Journal of World Business, 44*, 121–130.

Hansen, M. W., & Schaumburg-Muller, H. (2006). *Transnational corporations and local firms in developing countries: Linkages and upgrading.* Copenhagen: Copenhagen Business School Press.

Hirschman, A. O. (1958). *The strategy of economic development.* New Haven, CT: Yale University Press.

Holm, U., & Pedersen, T. (2000). *The emergence and impact of MNE centres of excellence: A subsidiary perspective.* London: Macmillan.

Howells, J. (2004). Innovation, consumption and services: Encapsulation and the combinatorial role of services. *Service Industries Journal, 24*(1), 19–36.

Iguchi, C. (2008). Determinants of backward linkages: The case of TNC subsidiaries in Malaysia. *Asian Business and Management, 7*(1), 53–73.

Ivarsson, I., & Alvstam, C. G. (2005). Technology transfer from TNCs to local suppliers in developing countries: A study of AB Volvo's truck and bus plants in Brazil, China, India, and Mexico. *World Development, 33*(8), 1325–1344.

Javorcik, B. S. (2004). Does foreign direct investment increase the productivity of domestic firms? In search of spillovers through backward linkages. *The American Economic Review, 94*(3), 605–627.

Jindra, B., Giroud, A., & Scott-Kennel, J. (2009). Subsidiary roles, vertical linkages and economic development: Lessons from transition economies. *Journal of World Business, 44*, 167–179.

Kelegama, S., & Foley, F. (1999). Impediments to promoting backward linkages from the garment industry in Sri Lanka. *World Development, 27*(8), 1445–1460.

King, N. (2004). Using interviews in qualitative research. In: C. S. Cassell & G. G. Symon (Eds), *Essential guide to qualitative methods in organizational research* (pp. 11–22). London: Sage.

Kiyota, K., Matsuura, T., Urata, S., & Wei, Y. (2008). Reconsidering the backward vertical linkages of foreign affiliates: Evidence from Japanese multinationals. *World Development, 36*(8), 1398–1414.

Lall, S. (1980). Vertical inter-firm linkages in LDC's: An empirical study. *Oxford Bulletin of Economics and Statistics, 42*(3), 203–226.

Li, X., & Yeung, Y. M. (1999). Inter-firm linkages and regional impact of transnational corporations: Company case studies from Shanghai, China. *Geografiska Annaler Series B, Human Geography, 81*(2), 61–72.

Lim, L. Y. C., & Fong, P. E. (1982). Vertical linkages and multinational enterprises in developing countries. *World Development, 10*(7), 585–595.

Martin, A., & Bell, M. (2006). Technology spillovers from foreign investment (FDI): The active role of MNC subsidiaries in Argentina in the 1990s. *Journal of Development Studies, 42*(2), 678–697.

McAleese, D., & McDonald, D. (1978). Employment growth and the development of linkages in foreign-owned and domestic manufacturing enterprises. *Oxford Bulletin of Economics and Statistics, 40*(4), 321–339.

Nachum, L., & Keeble, D. (2003). MNE linkages and localised clusters: Foreign and indigenous firms in the media cluster of Central London. *Journal of International Management, 9*(2), 171–192.

O'Farrell, P. N., & O'Loughlin, B. (1981). The impact of new industry enterprises in Ireland: An analysis of service linkages. *Regional Studies, 15*(6), 439–458.

Okada, A. (2004). Skills development and interfirm learning linkages under globalization: Lessons from the Indian automobile industry. *World Development, 32*(7), 1265–1288.

Oosterhaven, J., Eding, G. J., & Stelden, D. (2001). Clusters, linkages and interregional spillovers: Methodology and policy implications for the two Dutch mainports and the rural North. *Regional Studies, 35*(9), 809–822.

Rodriguez-Clare, A. (1996). Multinationals, linkages, and economic development. *The American Economic Review, 86*(4), 852–873.

Santangelo, G. D. (2009). MNCs and linkage creation: Evidence from a peripheral area. *Journal of World Business, 44*, 192–205.

Scott-Kennel, J. (2001). *The impact of foreign direct investment on New Zealand industry.* Unpublished Ph.D. thesis. University of Waikato, New Zealand.

Scott-Kennel, J. (2007). Foreign direct investment and local linkages: An empirical investigation. *Management International Review, 47*(1), 51–77.

Sinkovics, R. R., Penz, E., & Ghauri, P. N. (2005). Analysing textual data in international marketing research. *Qualitative Market Research, 8*(1), 9–38.

Sinkovics, R. R., Penz, E., & Ghauri, P. N. (2008). Enhancing the trustworthiness of qualitative research in international business. *Management International Review, 48*(6), 689–713.

UNCTAD. (2001). *World investment report: Promoting linkages.* New York: United Nations.

UNCTAD. (2004). *World investment report: The shift towards services.* India: Bookwell.

UNCTAD. (2008). *World investment report: Transnational corporations & the infrastructure challenge.* New York: United Nations.

Wong, P. K. (1992). Technological development through subcontracting linkages: Evidence from Singapore. *Scandinavian International Business Review, 1*(3), 28–40.

Yin, R. K. (2003). *Case study research: Design and methods.* Thousand Oaks, CA: Sage.

APPENDIX. TABLE SHOWING COMPANY RESPONDENTS INTERVIEWED

Case Type		Companies and Respondents		
Chinese cases	1	HSBC UK (Head of Strategic Finance)	HSBC China (Chief Executive Officer China)	– Bank of Communications (Executive Vice President) – PCCC Card Centre (CEO)
	2	Kingfisher UK (Head of Corporate Development)	B&Q China (Senior Director Buying Support)	– Nippon Paint (Director, Supply Chain Management) – Kohler (National Sales Manager – Retail)

THE REGULATORY FRAMEWORK FOR INVESTMENT: WHERE ARE WE HEADED?

Karl P. Sauvant

ABSTRACT

Governments throughout the world have sought, and are seeking, to attract foreign direct investment (FDI) and, for that purposed, have liberalized their national regulatory frameworks for FDI and established a strong international investment law regime. However, there are signs that, as a result of a number of important developments (which are being discussed in some detail in this chapter), governments are re-evaluating their stance toward FDI, or at least certain types of it. This re-evaluation has found its expression in a number of regulatory changes that may eventually lead to a regime that balances the rights of investors and host countries in a manner that places more emphasis on maintaining policy space for host-country governments while still protecting foreign investors.

Keywords: Foreign direct investment (FDI); multinational enterprises (MNEs); international investment law

The Future of Foreign Direct Investment and the Multinational Enterprise
Research in Global Strategic Management, Volume 15, 407–433
Copyright © 2011 by Emerald Group Publishing Ltd
All rights of reproduction in any form reserved
ISSN: 1064-4857/doi:10.1108/S1064-4857(2011)0000015022

As Yair Aharoni has pointed out, "globalization compels almost all firms to organize all value-added activities in a global manner" (Aharoni, 2010, p. 42). Globalization has, in no small measure, been driven by foreign direct investment (FDI). While world FDI flows averaged US $ 50 billion during the first half of the 1980s, they had reached US $ 2.1 trillion in 2007 (before declining, I would say temporarily, to US $ 1.1 trillion in 2009, on account of the financial crisis and recession) (Table 1).[1] These flows, undertaken by more than 80,000 multinational enterprises (MNEs), had accumulated to a stock of some US $ 19 trillion in 2009. The FDI stock generated in this manner, via 800,000 plus foreign affiliates, produces estimated sales of goods and services of some US $ 30 trillion, a figure that compares with world exports of US $ 16 trillion (one-third of which consists of intrafirm trade). These figures refer only to control exercised by parent companies through FDI. Control over firms abroad can, of course, also be exercised through various nonequity forms (e.g., management contracts, technology and franchising agreements), in this manner (probably considerably[2]) expanding the scope of international production falling under the common governance of MNEs.

Be that as it may, FDI has become more important than trade in delivering goods and services to foreign markets, integrating not only markets but also national production systems through an internal international division of labor of MNEs. This creates an integrated international production system – the productive core of the globalizing world economy. Moreover, since FDI consists of a bundle of tangible and intangible assets (including capital, employment, technology, skills, access to markets), it can play an important role in a country's development effort.[3]

At the same time, the landscape of the world FDI market is changing. In particular, firms headquartered in emerging markets are becoming important players, with, among them, state-controlled entities (especially state-owned enterprises and sovereign wealth funds (SWFs)) rising in importance. This, in turn, contributes to a reassessment of the costs and benefits of FDI in general, considering that such investment is, after all (from the perspective of governments), just a tool to advance their growth and development.

Given the role that FDI plays in the world economy and can play in national development, it is important to understand how this investment is regulated, both at national and international levels. And since the international regulatory framework for investment has become an important parameter for national policy and rule making in this area, the following discussion focuses on the characteristics and development of the international investment regime.

Table 1. Selected Indicators of FDI and International Production, 1990–2009.

Item	Value at Current Prices (Billions of Dollars)				Annual Growth Rate (Percent)				
	1990	2005	2008	2009	1991–1995	1996–2000	2001–2005	2008	2009
FDI inflows	208	986	1,771	1,114	22.5	40.0	5.2	-15.7	-37.1
FDI outflows	241	893	1,929	1,101	16.8	36.1	9.2	-14.9	-42.9
FDI inward stock	2,082	11,525	15,491	17,743	9.3	18.7	13.3	-13.9	14.5
FDI outward stock	2,087	12,417	16,207	18,982	11.9	18.4	14.6	-16.1	17.1
Income on inward FDI	74	791	1,113	941	35.1	13.4	31.9	-7.3	-15.5
Income on outward FDI	120	902	1,182	1,008	20.2	10.3	31.3	-7.7	-14.8
Cross-border M&As[a]	99	462	707	250	49.1	64.0	0.6	-30.9	-64.7
Sales of foreign affiliates	6,026	21,721	31,069[b]	29,298[c]	8.8	8.2	18.1	-4.5[b]	-5.7[c]
Gross product of foreign affiliates	1,477	4,327	6,163[d]	5,812[e]	6.8	7.0	13.9	-4.3[d]	-5.7[e]
Total assets of foreign affiliates	5,938	49,252	71,694[f]	77,057[f]	13.7	19.0	20.9	-4.9[f]	7.5[f]
Exports of foreign affiliates	1,498	4,319	6,663[g]	5,186[g]	8.6	3.6	14.8	15.4[g]	-22.2[g]
Employment by foreign affiliates (thousands)	24,476	57,799	78,957[h]	79,825[i]	5.5	9.8	6.7	-3.7[h]	1.1[i]
Memorandum									
GDP (in current prices)	22,121	45,273	60,766	55,005[j]	5.9	1.3	10.0	10.3	-9.5[j]
Gross fixed capital formation	5,099	9,833	13,822	12,404[j]	5.4	1.1	11.0	11.5	-10.3
Royalties and license fee receipts	29	129	177	na	14.6	8.1	14.6	8.6	na
Exports of goods and services	4,414	12,954	19,986	15,716[j]	7.9	3.7	14.8	15.4	-21.4

Source: UNCTAD, based on its FDI/TNC database (www.unctad.org/fdistatistics); UNCTAD, *GlobStat;* and IMF, *International Financial Statistics,* June 2010. UNCTAD (2010).

Note: Not included in this table are the values of worldwide sales by foreign affiliates associated with their parent firms through nonequity relationships and of the value of sales of the parent firms themselves. Worldwide sales, gross product, total assets, exports, and employment of foreign affiliates are estimated by extrapolating the worldwide data of foreign affiliates of TNCs from Austria, Canada, the Czech Republic, Finland, France, Germany, Italy, Japan, Luxembourg, Portugal, Sweden, and the United States for sales; those from the Czech Republic, Portugal, Sweden, and the United States for gross product; those from Austria, Germany, Japan, and the United States for assets; those from

Austria, the Czech Republic, Japan, Portugal, Sweden, and the United States for exports; and those from Austria, Germany, Japan, Switzerland, and the United States for employment, on the basis of the shares of those countries in worldwide outward FDI stock.

[a]Data are available only from 1987 onwards.

[b]Data for 2007 and 2008 are based on the following regression result of sales against inward FDI stock (in millions of dollars) for the period 1980–2006: sales = 1,471.6211 + 1.9343* inward FDI stock.

[c]Data for 2009 based on the observed year-over change of the sales of 3,659 TNCs' foreign operations between 2008 and 2009.

[d]Data for 2007 and 2008 are based on the following regression result of gross product against inward FDI stock (in millions of dollars) for the period 1982–2006: gross product = 566.7633 + 0.3658* inward FDI stock.

[e]Decline in gross product of foreign affiliates assumed to be the same as the decline in sales.

[f]Data for 2007 and 2008 are based on the following regression result of assets against inward FDI stock (in millions of dollars) for the period 1980–2006: assets = −3,387.7138 + 4.9069* inward FDI stock.

[g]Data for 1995–1997 are based on the following regression result of exports of foreign affiliates against inward FDI stock (in millions of dollars) for the period 1982–1994: exports = 139.1489 + 0.6413* FDI inward stock. For 1998–2009, the share of exports of foreign affiliates in world export in 1998 (33.3%) was applied to obtain the values.

[h]Based on the following regression result of employment (in thousands) against inward FDI stock (in millions of dollars) for the period 1980–2006: employment = 17,642.5861 + 4.0071* inward FDI stock.

[i]Data for 2009 based on the observed year-over change of the estimated employment of 3,659 TNCs' foreign operations between 2008 and 2009.

[j]Based on data from IMF, *World Economic Outlook*, April 2010.

THE NATIONAL REGULATORY FRAMEWORK

At the national level, many host countries, and especially emerging markets,[4] have special laws and regulations in place that govern FDI, typically complemented by provisions in other laws and regulations (e.g., concerning taxation). The story of national FDI regulation, at least since the mid-1980s, is one of creating a favorable climate for this investment: countries have progressively liberalized the conditions for the entry of MNEs into their markets (e.g., by opening sectors to foreign investors); facilitated the operations of these enterprises (e.g., by abolishing performance requirements); and provided various protections to MNEs and their foreign affiliates (e.g., against arbitrary nationalizations). The data compiled by UNCTAD since 1992 document this story convincingly: out of a total of 2,748 regulatory FDI changes made by countries across the world during the period 1992–2009, 89 percent were in the direction of making the investment climate more favorable to foreign investors (Table 2).

These regulatory changes have been accompanied by active efforts to attract FDI. Virtually all countries have an investment promotion agency at the national level, and many have such agencies also at the provincial and even city levels. There may be some 8,000 agencies in existence today worldwide,[5] making the world market for FDI highly competitive. Typically, these agencies seek to attract as much FDI as possible to their shores, although an increasing number also have become more focused by targeting investors that can make a particular contribution to the host economy, in line with its overall development objectives. Financial, fiscal, regulatory, and other incentives are an important tool for this purpose, even though the effectiveness of such incentives is often questionable (see UNCTAD, 1996).

In addition, a rising number of home countries of MNEs (including virtually all developed countries, but also more and more emerging markets) facilitate the internationalization of their firms and even provide support to their MNEs to expand abroad (see Buckley, Clegg, Cross, & Voss, 2010, pp. 243–276; De Beule and Van Den Bulcke, 2010, pp. 277–304), ranging from the provision of information about investment opportunities abroad, to the financing of feasibility studies, to the offering of insurance of investments against political risk.[6] This reflects the expectation of governments that, to remain internationally competitive in an open world economy, their firms increasingly need to acquire a portfolio of locational assets that provides them with better access to markets and resources of various kinds.

Table 2. National Regulatory Changes, 1992–2009.

Item	1992	1993	1994	1995	1996	1997	1998	1999	2000	2001	2002	2003	2004	2005	2006	2007	2008	2009
Number of countries that introduced changes	43	56	49	63	66	76	60	65	70	71	72	82	103	92	91	58	54	50
Number of regulatory changes	77	100	110	112	114	150	145	139	150	207	246	242	270	203	177	98	106	102
Liberalization/promotion	77	99	108	106	98	134	136	130	147	193	234	218	234	162	142	74	83	71
Regulations/restrictions	0	1	2	6	16	16	9	9	3	14	12	24	36	41	35	24	23	31

Source: UNCTAD database on national laws and regulations. UNCTAD (2010).

Note: Compared with reporting on these numbers in previous WIRs, the wording in the table has changed from "more favorable" to "liberalization/promotion" and from "less favorable" to "regulations/restrictions."

All in all, the national regulatory regime for FDI in host and home countries is today very favorable to foreign investors – probably more favorable than at any time in history. In particular, the manufacturing and natural resources[7] sectors are largely open to such investment, although the liberalization process in the services sector has not gone equally far. In addition, countries actively seek to attract FDI, and home countries support the internationalization process of their firms through various means. One of these means is the establishment of a strong international investment law regime.

THE INTERNATIONAL REGULATORY FRAMEWORK

As the principal capital-exporting countries and homes to most MNEs, the developed countries have been the principal advocates and drivers of the establishment of a strong international investment law regime. Reflecting their interests, they sought rules that protect the investments made by their firms abroad and, beyond that, facilitate their operations in foreign markets, both in terms of market entry and managing their foreign affiliates on a day-to-day basis. At the same time, it was expected that such a regime would encourage the flow of investment to countries that were seen as lacking a strong rule of law in the investment area, that is, especially the developing countries (and, later, the economies in transition).

As in the trade area, the construction of this investment regime began with bilateral treaties, in particular friendship, commerce, and navigation (FCN) treaties and, since 1959,[8] bilateral investment treaties (BITs); by the end of 2009, there were about 2,750 BITs and some 250 free trade agreements with substantial investment chapters (UNCTAD, 2010, p. 81). The international investment law regime also consists of various regional,[9] interregional,[10] and partial multilateral[11] agreements (collectively "international investment agreements" – IIAs). In the absence of a comprehensive multilateral agreement on investment, the international investment law regime today consists therefore of a patchwork of rules, including voluntary instruments,[12] that is multilayered and multifaceted.

Not surprisingly, furthermore, most IIAs reflect the interests and priorities of the developed countries as the traditional home countries of MNEs. In particular, they typically provide distinct protections for the post-entry treatment of foreign investors, including fair and equitable treatment, full protection and security, treatment otherwise in accordance with the international minimum standard, and prompt, adequate, and effective compensation in case of expropriation. Most modern investment agreements also provide investors a direct right to enforce these protections through investor–state arbitration. More recently, a growing number of these instruments also seek to facilitate the entry and operations of investors, most importantly by granting national treatment at the pre-establishment phase and most-favored-nation treatment.[13]

In other words, the international investment law regime focuses largely on the rights of investors and the responsibilities of host countries, enforceable under international law. From that perspective, the regime today is open, stable, and predictable; provides for transparent rules for the treatment of foreign investors and their foreign affiliates; and can be enforced if need be. In fact, one could argue that the international investment law regime is stronger than the international trade regime, as it can be enforced directly by investors, as opposed to investors having to go through their governments in order to settle claims if and when they feel aggrieved. To quote Thomas Waelde:

> Investment treaties [...] have built, indubitably, one of the most effective and truly legal regimes within the fragmented and mostly quite rudimentary institutional frameworks for the global economy. Comparable in terms of legal character and effectiveness to the WTO regime, the international investment regime is arguably more advanced, as it fully incorporates the most important and directly affected non-state actors. In a longer-term perspective, claimants (and their lawyers), who are essentially driven by private interests, help ensure greater compliance and effectiveness for the treaties and their underlying objectives than can or is achieved by exclusively inter-state implementation procedures. It also goes beyond the prospective-remedy-only sanction available under the WTO (Waelde, 2009, p. 514).

FACTORS DRIVING CHANGE

These are the characteristics of the *current* international regulatory framework for FDI. However, a number of developments are underway that have an impact on the nature of this framework. Six are particularly noteworthy.

- *A changing appreciation of the quality of FDI.* While all governments continue to seek FDI as it can make a contribution to growth and development, a number of them are paying more attention to the *quality* of the investment they seek to attract, in terms of both the mode of entry of investment and the extent to which it has sustainable development characteristics.

As to the first consideration, relatively little attention was paid in the recent past to whether foreign investors entered a market through greenfield projects (i.e., the establishment of new production facilities) or through mergers and acquisitions (M&As)[14] – both were seen as bringing the bundle of tangible and intangible assets associated with FDI that are important for development (see UNCTAD, 2000; Globerman & Shapiro, 2010, pp. 22–44). In a number of countries, however, certain M&As are increasingly regarded with reservation. The principal reasons include that M&As merely represent a change in ownership and are often accompanied by restructuring (and hence frequently involve a reduction in employment if not the closing down of some production capacities), while greenfield investments create new productive capacity and hence employment.[15] More importantly, when cross-border M&As target firms in sensitive sectors (which can range from military hardware to critical infrastructure and sectors central to economic development) or national champions (in any industry), the political reaction can be particularly strong.[16] This changing attitude toward M&As is important as M&As are the principal form of market entry for foreign investors in developed countries and an increasingly important form of market entry also in emerging markets.

As to the extent to which FDI has sustainable development characteristics, the objective of a number of governments is no longer just to obtain *more* such investment, but rather *sustainable FDI*. "Sustainable FDI" is defined here as FDI that contributes as much as possible to economic, social, and environmental development and good governance (especially in terms of a mutually beneficial distribution of benefits associated with an investment[17]), while remaining profitable for the investing firms. While a number of governments have traditionally targeted investment that contributes particularly to economic development, the other dimensions of this concept have typically received less attention.[18] This seems to be changing, especially as regards the social dimension of the concept but also the environmental one (see in this context also UNCTAD, 2010).

The broader implication of this development is that some types of FDI are no longer being considered as equally welcome, that is, a number of governments are taking a more differentiated attitude toward the characteristics that incoming FDI takes[19] – a fact (as will be discussed below) that is reflected in changes in the regulatory framework for foreign investment.

- *The rise of emerging market MNEs.* Adverse reactions to incoming M&As can be even stronger when the acquirer is a firm headquartered in an emerging market.[20] While traditionally the developed countries as a group have always been the most important host countries (absorbing by far more than half of all investment flows), the bulk of this investment came from other developed countries and was easily accepted.[21] But with the rise of emerging-market MNEs,[22] this picture is changing. FDI flows from emerging markets have become important, having reached US $ 351 billion in 2008, around seven times the average of world FDI outflows during the first half of the 1980s. On average, emerging markets accounted for 11 percent of global FDI outflows during 1995–2000; that share rose to 14 percent during 2003–2008. Even during the crisis year of 2008, when outflows from developed countries declined by almost 20 percent, those from emerging markets rose by 4 percent; in 2009, while outflows from developed countries plummeted by nearly half, those from emerging markets declined only by a bit more than one-fifth. As a result, the share of emerging markets in world FDI flows rose to 16 percent in 2008 and 25 percent in 2009.[23] These aggregate data mirror, of course, the growth in foreign assets of MNEs headquartered in emerging markets (of which there are over 20,000 (*ibid.*, p. 17)), and whose value has risen faster than the assets of their competitors headquartered in the industrialized world. In 2008 (the latest year for which these data are available), the foreign assets of the 100 largest MNEs from developing countries rose by 12 percent over the previous year, while the corresponding growth rate for the world's 100 biggest MNEs (overwhelmingly from industrialized countries) was only 1 percent (*ibid.*, p. 18).[24]

This rise of MNEs headquartered in emerging markets changes the global FDI landscape. It remains to be seen how long it will take for the developed countries to accept these new competitors on equal terms (as investment treaties demand), or whether they will seek to impose new restrictions on entry, particularly when it takes the form of M&As in high-profile sectors. The integration of these new global players in the world FDI market is a difficult process, especially when they are different (or operate differently) from established MNEs.

One of these differences is that, in the case of a number of the new home countries, the most important players include state-controlled entities – in particular state-owned enterprises and, increasingly, SWFs. In the case of China (an extreme case), some 80–90 percent of outward FDI flows and stock are controlled by state-controlled enterprises.[25] This aspect has given rise to special concerns (justified or not) about, for example, whether state-controlled entities pursue noncommercial objectives when investing abroad, benefit from nontransparent favorable government treatment, or lack proper governance and accountability structures. As a result, some countries such as Australia, Canada, Germany, and the United States have become more cautious about sovereign FDI.[26]

The broader implication of the rise of emerging-market MNEs is that a growing number of emerging markets – among them Brazil, China, India, and Russia (the BRICs), but also such countries as Chile, Mexico, Egypt, South Africa, Malaysia, the Republic of Korea, Singapore, and Thailand – see themselves no longer only as *host* countries but also as *home* countries, with implications for the international investment policies that they are pursuing. At the same time, host countries may exhibit some skepticism when it comes to the growing importance of emerging-market MNEs, especially when these are state-controlled entities.

- *Rising attention to national interest.* Another implication of the rise of emerging-market MNEs and the more differentiated attitude of governments to the form that incoming FDI takes is that considerations of "national interest" (and related concepts, such as "national security" and "essential security interests") have become more important in recent years, with these concepts not always clearly distinguishable from each other, and individual countries focusing on different aspects of them.

This is particularly true for a number of developed countries, but it also is beginning to extend to a number of emerging markets. For example, in the post-9/11 United States, essential security concerns related to FDI have achieved greater saliency, as have concerns over foreign control over critical infrastructure. Such concerns are particularly evident when, in the case of M&As, the prospective acquirer is headquartered in a country that may be considered a strategic competitor of the United States (as is China), or is based in a country whose political allegiances are viewed with some suspicion (e.g., some Islamic states) and/or is a state-controlled entity. For Western and Central European countries, "national security" concerns may reflect political fears of domination by investors from some countries (e.g., Russia and increasingly China) or concerns of threats to the "national interest" posed by foreign takeovers of national champions in key industries. For Russia, in turn, "national interest" or "security" concerns may emerge from investments related to the exploitation of natural resources or investment in firms controlling military technology. For some emerging markets, such as China, "national security" is being defined primarily in terms of economic development and hence focuses on strategic industries seen as crucial to continuing growth. And in yet other contexts, such as Argentina in the wake of its 2001–2002 economic crisis, "essential security" concerns have come to be associated with that nation's right to take emergency actions in the wake of domestic turmoil.[27] What is common to all these approaches is that the underlying security threat to the nation is intentionally left undefined. This is not surprising, as governments want to have the flexibility to define "national interest" and similar concepts in relation to specific circumstances, without being straight-jacketed by pre-established definitions and commitments.

The broader implication of this development is that a number of developed countries that, in the past, sought strict international investment disciplines are now seeking greater flexibility and more policy space for themselves (an approach championed in the past principally by developing countries), in order to be able to pursue policies and take actions that they consider necessary – and enshrine this approach in their national regulatory frameworks and IIAs.

- *The rise of investment disputes.* Since the international investment law regime allows for investor–state disputes, it is not surprising that the number of cases in which investors feel aggrieved by actions taken by host countries is rising. (In fact, it is surprising that this has not occurred earlier and that there are not more such disputes, considering the number of MNEs and foreign affiliates that exist.[28]) The number of treaty-based international investment disputes has risen dramatically in recent years, with more than half of the 357 known arbitration cases having arisen between the beginning of 2004 and the end of 2009 (Fig. 1). Crucially, these disputes involve not only emerging markets as respondents (as was perhaps originally thought), but also developed countries, including the United States,[29] as host countries, and they can lead to substantial awards against respondent countries.[30]

Both the number of disputes as well as the types of claims being made in them are giving rise to second thoughts on the part of IIA signatories, many of which did not expect the types of challenges to government regulation or even judicial actions that are emerging in the course of treaty-based arbitrations. Complaints that state parties to investment treaties are increasingly put on the defensive in investor–state claims and that, even when states win the underlying disputes, the threat of litigation produces an untoward regulatory chill, have become a common refrain among a number of nongovernmental organizations, including in developed countries. There is also a perception that, although the goal of the investment regime was to promote harmonious and predictable rules, investor–state arbitral decisions have not led to consistent international investment law, even producing inconsistent rulings arising under strikingly similar facts.[31] The high profile of some investor–state

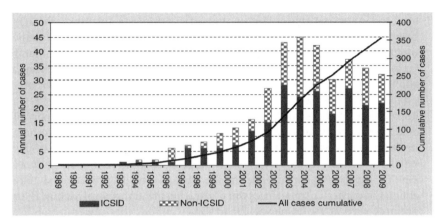

Fig. 1. Known Investment Treaty Arbitrations (Cumulative and Newly Instituted Cases), 1989–2009 (Number). *Source:* UNCTAD (2010, p. 84).

decisions and the adverse attention drawn to a number of them that implicate policy questions have also undermined the contention that international arbitrations will successfully depoliticize such matters.

The broader implication of these developments is that governments of developed countries, led by the United States, are becoming more conscious of their status as *host* countries[32] and, in that position, potentially subject to claims against them. As a result, governments are becoming more skeptical of their decisions to delegate the right to initiate investment disputes to private third-party beneficiaries and more concerned about the consequences of such delegation on their continuing right to regulate in the public interest. This, in turn, further influences the attitude countries take to the content of international investment obligations.

- *Doubt about whether IIAs lead to more FDI.* There are also growing questions as to whether one of the principal purposes of IIAs is being achieved, namely the goal of increasing FDI flows, especially to emerging markets, with the help of investment treaties. Empirical research to date has not established a clear relationship between such agreements and FDI flows.[33] This is not surprising, as factors relating to host countries' economies (especially market size and growth, the quality of the infrastructure, skills, innovatory capacity) are by far the most important FDI determinants, and it is therefore difficult to isolate any IIA-specific effects.[34] It is also not surprising given the fact that most IIAs are premised on the assumption that a good regulatory framework (as established by IIAs) is sufficient to encourage MNEs to go forward with their investments; this ignores the fact that, at best, the (national and international) regulatory framework can only be enabling – but unless the economic determinants allow for profitable investments, it is very unlikely that FDI will take place.[35] Moreover, IIAs, as a rule, do not provide for active measures by home country to encourage their firms to invest abroad (and especially in emerging markets or at least in the least developed countries), or to help institutions in host countries to acquire the capacity to attract foreign investors. In fact, although IIAs presume that the protection of investment and the removal of governmental barriers to free capital flows would enhance such flows, the treaties themselves were not necessarily intended to promote such flows, at least as far as some capital-exporting countries are concerned.[36] They were, at best, signaling devices to encourage investors to seek out those host countries with a favorable investment climate.

The broader implication of this development is that, if IIAs do not necessarily lead to more investment flows, governments may become less inclined to make investor-protection and liberalization commitments – or even conclude such agreements in the first place.

- *Doubts about whether outward FDI is a good thing for home countries.* As mentioned earlier, all developed countries and a growing number of developing countries facilitate or even support the outward investment of their firms. However, doubts have occasionally arisen in a number of developed countries as to whether outward FDI is indeed beneficial for home countries.[37] Trade unions in particular are concerned about the export of jobs seen as being associated with outward FDI; and such concerns are particularly potent during times of economic crisis and high levels of unemployment. While a number of studies have shown that outward FDI is beneficial to home countries, at least on balance and for developed home countries,[38] the public debate in the United States and Europe at times assumes differently. Most recently, for example, offshoring has led to calls in the United States to restrict this kind of activity (see, e.g., Politi, 2010; Cohen, 2010). There have also been threats by some in the US Congress to block the approval of BITs and free trade agreements (or even to withdraw from existing agreements, including the North American Free Trade Agreement (NAFTA)) (see, e.g., Palmer, 2010). In Western Europe, outward investment in general has occasionally come under fire in some countries, under the heading of "delocalization"; at least in one instance, the president of one country is reported to have linked the provision of aid to some firms to these firms repatriating from abroad some production facilities, or keeping the production of certain products at home (see, e.g., Hall, 2010).

In the case of emerging markets that have become important outward investors, doubts of this kind do not seem to have become prominent so far, although it would not be surprising if they should become at one point in the future. After all, most emerging markets do not have all the production capacities they need to provide their citizens with an advanced standard of living. Hence, investment abroad to create production capacities there could easily lead, at one point, to a backlash against outward FDI in emerging markets, even though such investment is in the interest of the firms involved as they need (as mentioned earlier) a portfolio of locational assets to remain internationally competitive.

The broader implication of this situation is that there is a tension between the objective of MNEs to maximize their global (or at least regional[39]) competitiveness, on the one hand, and the objective of governments to maximize the performance of their territorially bound economies, on the other hand. The establishment of regulatory frameworks for FDI in light of a sometimes somewhat fragile consensus about the benefits of outward FDI for home countries needs to take this tension into account.

These are all developments that, in various ways, influence national and international FDI rule making. They show that governments look at FDI with fresh eyes as regards the costs and benefits that it brings to them, not only in terms of its contribution to economic development, but also in terms of serving broader national objectives. The following section shows that this revaluation of at least certain types of FDI is beginning to find its expression in national and international regulatory frameworks and their implementation.

THE CHANGING REGULATORY REGIME FOR FDI

As a result of these developments, a number of countries have introduced changes or "clarifications" in their national regulatory regime that provide them with more leeway to deal with incoming investments, especially when these are undertaken by state-controlled entities and are taking the form of M&As. Significantly, the erstwhile strongest supporter of open national rules and a strong international investment law regime is leading this change.[40] In the United States, the Foreign Investment and National Security Act (FINSA) of 2007 and its subsequent implementing regulations strengthened the role of the Committee on Foreign Investment in the United

States (CFIUS) as a screening mechanism for incoming FDI under national security aspects. CFIUS has the authority to review and investigate covered transactions and to negotiate, impose, and enforce conditions necessary to mitigate any threat to national security presented by any such transaction. A transaction will be investigated if, among other things, it involves a foreign government-controlled entity and if it would result in control of any critical infrastructure and could impair national security. Neither "national security" nor "critical infrastructure" is defined precisely. Germany, too, changed its law on foreign investment in 2009, to allow the government to review certain takeovers by firms from outside the European Economic Area. Australia and Canada tightened or "clarified" their regulations in 2008 and 2009, respectively, emphasizing that M&As by foreign state-controlled entities will receive special attention. France identified at the end of 2005 a number of sectors in which FDI is restricted. The Commission of the European Community, for its part, initiated in 2008 a process of consultations, with a view toward arriving at a common approach toward SWFs. The OECD, too, undertook a similar process and arrived in 2008 at "Guidelines for Recipient Country Investment Policies Related to National Security" (see OECD, 2009). Outside the OECD area, Russia adopted in 2008 a law that established procedures for foreign investments in companies of strategic importance for national defense and security, and China (which always had a list of encouraged, restricted, and prohibited projects for foreign investors) introduced during 2006–2008 a review process in light of national economic security considerations. Finally, the IMF decided in 2007, prodded by developed countries, to identify best practices for SWFs; as a result, and with the participation of representatives of SWFs, "Generally Accepted Principles and Practices" (see International Working Group of Sovereign Wealth Funds, 2008) (the "Santiago Principles") were adopted in 2008, reflecting "appropriate governance and accountability arrangements as well as the conduct of investment practices by SWFs on a prudent and sound basis" (ibid., p. 4).

As can be seen from the dates of these various initiatives, the great majority of them were initiated before the world financial crisis and recession struck in late 2008. In fact, during the crisis, state-controlled entities were often regarded as "white knights" that bailed out in particular financial institutions in distress, and countries heeded the calls of the Group of 20 to refrain from FDI protectionism (G8 leaders' declaration, 2009). However, once countries have emerged fully from the crisis while, on the other hand, SWFs and state-owned enterprises amass even higher foreign exchange earnings and seek to invest them in equities,[41] it is likely that the fears related to them will reassert themselves and will be reflected in national and international regulatory instruments.

More broadly, during the crisis and recession, countries sought more capital to help them emerge from the recession; in other words, inward FDI was particularly welcome. At the same time, as long as unemployment remains high in key home countries, the question of offshoring of services is likely to remain a topic for discussion; in other words, outward FDI could potentially be restricted or at least discouraged. However, once countries have emerged from the recession and once unemployment has declined, some of the other considerations discussed earlier as they relate to the cost/ benefit calculation of governments regarding FDI are likely to reassert themselves, especially when it comes to M&As targeting national champions or other enterprises considered important to the national economy (e.g., in natural resources[42]). For the same reason, it may also well be that further liberalization, especially in sensitive services sectors, may slow down.

Partly as a result of legislative changes, countries – especially (but not only) developed ones, but including all those mentioned earlier – have also strengthened their capacity to screen FDI projects, typically focused on M&As. In the case of the United States, for example, the number of filings with the CFIUS rose, between 2001 and 2008, from 55 to 155, and the number of investigations grew from 1 to 23 (Fig. 2).

In 2008, 15 percent of CFIUS filings led to investigations. While the number of notifications declined in 2009 to 65,[43] the number of investigations rose to 25, representing about 40 percent of the filings – a substantial increase. It should be noted that these types of examinations of M&As, in the United States and elsewhere, are typically not subject to judicial review but rather take place within the "black box" of discussions within the relevant government agencies, thereby reducing the transparency of the decision-making process and regulatory framework.

The change toward a more circumscribed treatment of foreign investors and more policy space for governments in light of a changed cost/benefit calculation on the part of governments is also beginning to be reflected in international investment agreements and, with that, is bound to influence the international investment law regime in general. In particular, leading countries such as Canada and the United States are now concluding IIAs with more limited protections for investors and greater scope for governmental action, including through broad exceptions. Changes to United States' IIAs include a narrower definition of fair and equitable treatment and reduced scope for investors to claim that they have been the victims of a regulatory taking (United States' Model BIT, 2004). Canada has opted for

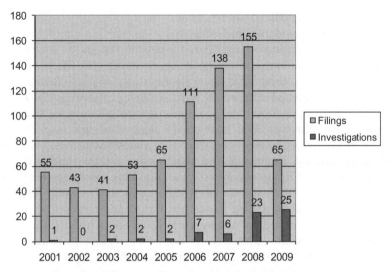

Fig. 2. CFIUS Filings and Investigations, 2001–2009. *Source:* US Treasury
Department, available at: www.ustreas.gov.

an ample list of general exceptions from IIA protections inspired by those
contained in Article XX of the General Agreement on Tariffs and Trade
(GATT) (see Canadian Model BIT, 2004; General Agreement on Tariffs and
Trade). These changes lessen the risk of unpredictably broad interpretations
of investment protections by investor–state arbitrators. Most importantly,
some countries, such as the United States, are turning to a "self-judging"
essential security exception intended to oust certain disputes, at the option
of the respondent state, from investor–state arbitration altogether. Given
the fact that "essential security" is left undefined, such an exception
from arbitrability potentially undermines the entire edifice of international
investment law.

More generally, the countries worldwide that introduced during 2006–
2007 at least one change making their investment climate less welcoming for
foreign investors accounted for 40 percent of world FDI flows (Sauvant,
2009, p. 240).

While the policy changes in China and Russia concerned all FDI, those in
most developed countries paid special heed to state-controlled entities as a
class of investors, introducing differential treatment for them. The latter also
applies to the initiatives by the European Commission, the OECD, and the

IMF, even if they remain voluntary. They are justified largely on the basis of national security considerations, in particular the fear that the FDI activities of state-controlled entities, especially in the case of M&As, are driven not so much by commercial but rather by political considerations. This may well be the case, but to date there is no systematic evidence to show that (be it for SWFs and state-owned enterprises from emerging markets or developed countries); that is, it is difficult to show that a substantial number of investment decisions would not have been undertaken by private firms in the same situation on the basis of commercial considerations alone.

In any event, the changes in the national and international regulatory frameworks for FDI go beyond specific considerations regarding state-controlled entities. They show that governments are searching for a new balance between the rights and responsibilities of governments and foreign investors at both the national and international levels, driven by the various developments discussed earlier.

Among these developments, probably none is more important than the blurring of the traditional distinction between *developed* "capital-exporting" and *developing* "capital-importing" countries. To be sure, developed countries have always been (and still remain) the principal host countries for FDI – but this FDI originated overwhelmingly in other developed countries; any issues that arose in connection with this investment could be discussed and settled in the framework of the OECD, on the basis of the instruments of that organization. What is new for developed countries is the rising influx of FDI from emerging markets. While emerging markets continue to remain primarily host countries,[44] the rise of their own MNEs is likely to bear on their perspective on the international investment law regime as governments in a growing number of emerging markets are now paying more attention to their status as capital exporters, as their firms, some of which have become major international players,[45] invest abroad.

Both developed countries and emerging markets now need to balance their positions as home and host countries, and hence their objectives: as home countries, they seek a strong international regulatory regime that protects foreign investors and facilitates their operations; as host countries, they seek an international regulatory regime that leaves them sufficient policy space for their right to regulate in the public interest. It is a tension that finds its expression in the negotiation of IIAs.

This tension is exemplified by changes in the model BITs and actual investment treaties of the United States and China, as both are today simultaneously the leading capital-exporting (home) and capital-importing (host) countries among, respectively, the developed countries and the emerging markets (see, e.g., Alvarez, 2009, pp. 943–975). United States' IIAs began as very strong investor protection devices, as laid out in their clearest form in the 1984 US model BIT and the IIAs based on it (see Alvarez, 2008; Vandevelde, 2008–2009, pp. 283–316).[46] Once the United States became a respondent in treaty-based international investment claims after the conclusion of NAFTA, it gradually circumscribed or even dropped various protections in order to maintain the regulatory space it needed to pursue its own policy objectives and limit the possibility that claims could be brought against it; this evolution is captured in the 2004 US model BIT and the IIAs based on it (see Alvarez, 2008; Vandevelde, 2009a). Chinese IIAs, for their part, began as relatively weak investor protection devices, but then moved in the direction of the strongly investor-protective US model of 1984 (as Chinese investors invested in significant numbers and amounts abroad) – only to move, in its latest BITs, toward the US position of less expansive formulations on such a key protection standard as fair and equitable treatment (Alvarez, 2008).

The extent to which two leading capital exporters and importers of the world, China and the United States, are now groping to find the right balance that reflects their positions as both host and home countries, are concluding separate investment agreements with increasingly similar provisions and are even negotiating one as between themselves, gives rise to the hope that, eventually, and despite the proliferation of IIAs, the "spaghetti bowl" of agreements will eventually coalesce around agreed terms that respect the need of investors for the rule of law and fairness of process and the right of governments to regulate in the public interest. Perhaps this will occur in the framework of a multilateral agreement on investment that enshrines a new balance of the rights and responsibilities of the various stakeholders in the regime and promotes sustainable FDI, and, thereby, as Aharoni put it, attempts to "determine the optimum balance between the incentives necessary to attract FDI and the regulation required to defend the pubic interest" (Aharoni, op. cit., p. 56).

ACKNOWLEDGMENT

This contribution draws partly on Karl P. Sauvant and Jose E. Alvarez, "Introduction: international investment law in transition", in Jose E. Alvarez and Karl P. Sauvant, with Kamil Ahmed and Gabriela del P. Vizcaino, eds., *The Evolving International Investment Regime: Expectations, Realities, Options* (New York: Oxford University Press, 2011).

I gratefully acknowledge helpful comments by Seev Hirsch, Ucheora Onwuamaegbu, Srilal Perera, and Ravi Ramamurti, as well as the help of Wouter Schmit Jongbloed in the finalization of this manuscript.

NOTES

1. UNCTAD (2000). This source, or earlier editions of it, has also been used for the following data, unless otherwise indicated.

2. No systematic data exist on the importance of such nonequity forms; but in some industries (e.g., hotels), they are widespread.

3. See, e.g., UNCTAD (1999), Moran (2006, 2011), Dunning (1994, pp. 23–51), and Dunning and Lundan (2008). However, it should be noted that national policies are important to maximize the positive effects of FDI and minimize any negative ones.

4. "Developed countries" are all members of the Organisation for Economic Co-operation and Development (OECD), minus Chile, Mexico, the Republic of Korea, and Turkey. "Emerging markets" are all economies that are not members of the OECD, plus Chile, Mexico, the Republic of Korea, and Turkey. "Developing countries" are all emerging markets that do not belong to the Commonwealth of Independent States and South-East Europe. See UNCTAD (2000) for individual members of these groups.

5. Millennium Cities Initiative and Vale Columbia Center on Sustainable International Investment, 2009, p. 1. For a review of the performance of these agencies at the national level, see IFC (2009).

6. On political risk, see MIGA (2009). For an example of how the institution of one country, the United States, has handled political risk, see Kantor, Nolan, and Sauvant (2011).

7. In the natural resources sector, the involvement of MNEs often takes forms other than FDI (e.g., production-sharing agreements, management contracts); however, in either case, control over the assets involved is typically in the hands of foreign investors.

8. When the first BIT, between the Federal Republic of Germany and Pakistan, was concluded.

9. Most important among them, the North American Free Trade Agreement, Chapter Eleven.

10. Most important among them various OECD instruments, including OECD (1961), OECD (1976b), and the Energy Charter Treaty, Part III, Articles 10–17.

11. Especially the Agreement on Trade-related Investment Measures (TRIMs) and the GATS. The latter is particularly important as some two-thirds of FDI consists of services FDI. See also the Multilateral Investment Guarantee Agency, established in 1988 in the framework of The World Bank Group.

12. For example, the OECD (1976a).

13. For a discussion of international investment law, see, e.g., Salacuse (2010), Muchlinski, Ortino, and Schreuer (2008), Muchlinski (2007), Dolzer and Schreuer (2008), and Reinisch (2009). For critical views, see, e.g., Van Harten (2007), Alvarez (2008, 2011), Sornarajah (2004, 2008, pp. 39–80, 2010, ch. 16).

14. Although some countries, like Australia and Canada, have since long screened large M&As.

15. The advantages and disadvantages of M&As vs. greenfield FDI are discussed, in great detail, in UNCTAD (2000) and Globerman and Shapiro (2010).

16. See, e.g., the attempted acquisition of Unocal (United States) by CNOOC (China) or the rumored acquisition attempt of Danone (France) by PepsiCo (United States).

17. This is particularly relevant in the natural resources sector, especially in light of swings in the prices of such resources and the distribution of the resulting revenues.

18. Indicative of this are the results of a survey of investment promotion agencies undertaken in 2010 by the Vale Columbia Center on Sustainable International Investment (2010) regarding the extent to which these agencies pay attention to sustainable FDI; see VCCWAIPA at www.vcc.columbia.edu

19. It may be indicative of this that arbitral tribunals have weighted in on the definition of "investment" for ICSID jurisdiction purposes, including discussing whether contribution to development is an essential element; see, e.g., *MHS v Malaysia* and the annulment decision.

20. See, e.g., the discussions surrounding the acquisition of Arcelor by Mittal, Lenovo's acquisition of the PC division of IBM, and Tata's bid for Corus; see Sauvant (2009, pp. 215–272).

21. Developed countries continue to attract most FDI, although in 2009 emerging markets attracted almost half of the world's FDI inflows as the economies of these countries remained more resilient in the wake of the financial crisis and recession.

22. See UNCTAD (2009), Sauvant, Mendoza, and Ince (2008), and Sauvant and McAllister, with Maschek, op. cit. In fact, in 2008, outward FDI flows from China were higher than the average of world FDI flows during the first half of the 1980s.

23. Calculated on the basis of data from UNCTAD (2010).

24. To a certain extent, of course, this reflects the lower level of assets from which the former started as outward investors, compared with the latter.

25. See Cheng and Ma (2007, p. 15). (It should be noted that a number of developed country state-owned entities undertake FDI as well.) For a discussion of China's outward FDI, see Davies (2010).

26. See the discussion below.

27. On Argentina, see, e.g., Alvarez and Khamsi (2009, pp. 379–478). The lessons of Argentina have apparently been taken to heart by others; see, e.g., the latest Canadian Model BIT (permitting "prudential" measures with respect to the banking sector) and the US latest BIT (including a self-judging essential security clause). For discussion, see Mendenhall (2011).

28. Depending on the applicable IIA, foreign affiliates and, indeed, individual investors in affiliates, may be able to initiate disputes.

29. By the end of 2009, at least 81 governments (49 of developing countries, 17 of developed countries, 15 of economies in transition) had been or were involved in treaty-based arbitrations; investors from developed countries had initiated the overwhelming number of claims. See *ibid*.

30. See e.g., CME (2003), awarding CME Czech Republic B.V. US $ 269,814,000 in damages for breach of an investment treaty.

31. For a discussion of Argentina cases, see Alvarez and Khamsi, op. cit.

32. As is suggested by the United States' divisive debates over the content of its US model BIT. See "Report of the Subcommittee on Investment of the Advisory Committee on International Economic Policy regarding the Model Bilateral Investment Treaty" (2009).

33. The most important studies are contained in Sauvant and Sachs (2009). As a recent study observed: "... the literature on BITs is stalemated on whether they actually increase FDI..." (see Tobin & Busch, 2010, pp. 1–42). The same study observed however also that BITs might make free trade agreements more likely and, in this manner, indirectly influence FDI flows. Perhaps one of the reasons for this finding is that corporate counsels seem to be relatively unfamiliar about the existence of BITs – at least this is the result of a survey of US MNEs; see Yackee (2011).

34. For a discussion of the FDI determinants, see UNCTAD (1998, chap. IV); and Dunning and Lundan (2008). Some countries, attract considerable amounts of FDI, e.g., Brazil even though it has not ratified any of the BITs it had negotiated.

35. Conversely, even when the regulatory framework is not very good, FDI will take place if profitable investment opportunities exist. For example, investments in the mining sector took place in the Congo even during the country's civil war.

36. As Vandevelde observed for the United States: "When the BIT program was inaugurated in the Carter Administration, the United States had seen the BITs as a means of building a body of state practice consistent with its view of customary international law while protecting existing stocks of investment. In part because of concerns that labor otherwise would oppose the agreements, United States BIT negotiators initially had made clear not only to potential United States BIT partners but to Congress as well that there was no evidence that BITs would lead to increased outward investment flows. By the early 1990s, however, the promotion of democracy and market economics in the transitional economies was a major foreign policy objective and BITs were regarded as a means of promoting outward investment"; Vandevelde (2009b, p. 45). As this observation suggests, the promotion of FDI was not a goal when the US BITs program began in the 1970s. However, over time, the argumentation changed, and eventually BITs were justified in the United States as a means of investment promotion.

37. See, e.g., O'Murchu and Cienski (2010), who report that the move "has drawn sharp criticism from both workers and members of the European parliament."

38. See, e.g., Moran (2011, section VII), Globerman and Shapiro (2008, pp. 229–271), and Visser (2006, pp. 343–358).

39. As Rugman (2005) shows, most MNEs are primarily regional in their operations.

40. The developments discussed in this paragraph are documented in Sauvant (2009), and are therefore not individually referenced here.

41. SWFs are estimated to control about US $ 4 trillion dollars (Sovereign Wealth Fund Institute, 2010), given certain assumptions; see Jen (2007).

42. See, e.g., the preliminary decision of the Government of Canada to block the acquisition of PotashCorp (Canada) by BHP Billiton (Australia) in November 2010; see Beattie and Simon (2010).

43. The decline may have been the result of the lower number of cross-border M&As into the United States on account of the crisis and the decline of FDI inflows;

that number fell from 1,297 in 2007 to 1,117 in 2008, to 710 in 2009, and 293 during January to May 2010; in terms of value, cross-border M&As into the United States declined from US $ 165 billion in 2007 to US $ 40 billion in 2009 (see http://www. unctad.org/Templates/Page.asp?intItemID=5545&lang=1); FDI flows into the United States declined from US $ 324 billion in 2008 to US $ 130 billion in 2009 (UNCTAD, 2010, p. 167). It is not known how many cross-border M&As that were intended or initiated did not go forward because of the new regulatory framework in the United States.

44. The inward FDI flows of emerging markets were roughly an average of US $ 650 billion during 2007–2009, while their outward flows during the same period were an average of US $ 310 billion; the inward FDI stock of emerging markets was US $ 5.4 trillion in 2009, compared with an outward stock of US $ 3 trillion; see UNCTAD (2010, annex tables 1 and 2).

45. The four BRICs (Brazil, Russia, India, China) alone accounted for more than a third of FDI outflows from emerging markets during 2007–2009; see *ibid.* For rankings of the largest MNEs based in the BRICs, see www.vcc.columbia.edu.

46. The full text of 1984 US model BIT can be found in Vandevelde (1992).

REFERENCES

Aharoni, Y. (2010). Reflections on multinational enterprises in a globally interdependent world economy. In: K. P. Sauvant, G. McAllister & W. A. Maschek (Eds), *Foreign direct investment from emerging markets: The challenges ahead.* New York: Palgrave Macmillan.

Alvarez, J. E. (2008). The evolving foreign investment regime. *American Society of International Law.* Available at http://www.asil.org/ilpost/president/pres080229.html.

Alvarez, J. E. (2009). Contemporary foreign investment law: An 'Empire of Law' or the 'Law of Empire'? *Alabama Law Review, 60,* 943–975.

Alvarez, J. E. (2011). The once and future foreign investment regime. In: Arsanjani, M., Cogan, J. K., Sloane, R. D. & Wiessner, S. (Eds), *Looking to the future: Essays on international law in honor of W. Michael Reisman.*

Alvarez, J. E., & Khamsi, K. (2009). The Argentina crisis and foreign investors: A glimpse into the heart of the investment regime. In: K. P. Sauvant (Ed.), *Yearbook on international investment law and policy 2008–2009.* New York: Oxford University Press.

Beattie, A. & Simon, B. (2010). Race for resources tests trade openness. *Financial Times,* November 6/7.

Buckley, P. J., Clegg, L. J., Cross, A. R., Voss, H., et al. (2010). What can emerging markets learn from the outward direct investment policies of advanced countries? In: K. P. Sauvant, G. McAllister & W. A. Maschek (Eds), *Foreign direct investment from emerging markets: The challenges ahead* (pp. 243–276). New York: Palgrave Macmillan.

Canadian Model BIT. (2004). Available at: http://www.international.gc.ca/trade-agreements-accords-commerciaux/assets/pdfs/2004-FIPA-model-en.pdf.

Cheng, L. K., & Ma, Z. (2007). China's outward FDI: Past and future. July 2007. Available at: http://www.nber.org/books_in_progress/china07/cwt07/cheng.pdf.

Cohen, W. S. (2010). Obama and the politics of outsourcing. *Wall Street Journal,* October 12.

CME Czech Republic B.V. v. Czech Republic. (2003). UNCITRAL. Available at http:// ita.law.uvic.ca/documents/CME-2003-Final_001.pdf.

Davies, K. (2010). Outward FDI from China and its policy context. *Columbia FDI Profiles*, October 18. Available at www.vcc.columbia.edu.

De Beule, F., & Van Den Bulcke, D. (2010). Changing policy regimes in outward foreign direct investment from emerging markets: From control to promotion. In: K. P. Sauvant, G. McAllister & W. A. Maschek (Eds), *Foreign direct investment from emerging markets: The challenges ahead*. New York: Palgrave Macmillan.

Dolzer, R., & Schreuer, C. (2008). *Principles of international investment law*. New York: Oxford University Press.

Dunning, J. H. (1994). Re-evaluating the benefits of foreign direct investment. *Transnational Corporations*, 2(1), 23–51.

Dunning, J. H., & Lundan, S. M. (2008). *Multinational enterprises and the global economy*. Cheltenham: Edward Elgar Publishing.

Energy Charter Treaty (ECT). Available at www.encharter.org.

G8 leaders' declaration. (2009). Responsible leadership for a sustainable future. *L'Aquila*, G8 Summit 2009. Available at: http://www.g8italia2009.it/static/G8_Allegato/G8_Declaration_08_07_09_final,0.pdf.

General Agreement on Tariffs and Trade. Available at http://www.wto.org/english/docs_e/ legal_e/06-gatt_e.htm.

Globerman, S., & Shapiro, D. M. (2008). Outward FDI and the economic performance of emerging markets. In: K. P. Sauvant, K. Mendoza & I. Ince (Eds), *The rise of transnational corporations from emerging markets: Threat or opportunity?* Cheltenham, UK: Edward Elgar.

Globerman, S., & Shapiro, D. (2010). Modes of entry by Chinese firms in the United States: Economic and political issues. In: K. P. Sauvant (Ed.), *Investing in the United States: Is the US Ready for FDI from China?* Cheltenham, UK: Edward Elgar.

Hall, B. (2010). France to rein in state-backed groups. *Financial Times*, August 4.

IFC. (2009). *Global investment promotion benchmarking 2009: Summary report*. Washington, DC: World Bank.

International Working Group of Sovereign Wealth Funds. (2008). Sovereign Wealth Funds: Generally accepted principles and practices, 'Santiago Principles'. Available at http:// www.iwg-swf.org/pubs/gapplist.htm.

Jen, S. (2007). How big could Sovereign Wealth funds be by 2015? *Morgan Stanley Global Economic Forum*, May 4. Available at: www.morganstanley.com.

Kantor, M., Nolan, M. D., & Sauvant, K. P. (Eds). (2011). *Reports of overseas private investment corporation determination*. New York: Oxford University Press.

Mendenhall, J. (2011). The evolution of the essential security exception in U.S. trade and investment agreements. In: Sauvant, K. P., Sachs, L. E., Jongbloed, W. & Schmit, P. F. (Eds), *Sovereign investment: Concerns and policy reactions*. New York: Oxford University Press.

MIGA. (2009). *World investment and political risk 2009*. Washington, DC: MIGA.

Millennium Cities Initiative and Vale Columbia Center on Sustainable International Investment. (2009). *Handbook for promoting foreign direct investment in medium-size, low-budget cities in emerging markets*. New York: MCI and VCC. Available at www.vcc.columbia.edu.

Moran, T. H. (2006). *Harnessing foreign direct investment for development: Policies for developed and developing countries*. Washington: Center for Global Development.

Moran, T. H. (2011). *Foreign direct investment and development: Launching a second generation of policy research. Avoiding the mistakes of the first, re-evaluating policies for development and developing countries.* Washington: Peterson Institute for International Economics.

Muchlinski, P. (2007). *Multinational enterprises and the law* (2nd ed.). New York: Oxford University Press.

Muchlinski, P., Ortino, F., & Schreuer, C. (Eds). (2008). *The Oxford Handbook of International Investment Law.* New York: Oxford University Press.

North American Free Trade Agreement. Chapter Eleven. Available at http://www.ustr.gov/trade-agreements/free-trade-agreements/north-american-free-trade-agreement-nafta.

O'Murchu, C., & Cienski, J. (2010). Twinings to move tea plant to Poland. *Financial Times,* November 9.

OECD. (1961). *Code of liberalisation of capital movements.* Paris: OECD.

OECD. (1976a). Guidelines for multinational enterprises. In: *Declaration on international investment and multinational enterprises.* Paris: OECD.

OECD. (1976b). *Declaration on international investment and multinational enterprises.* Paris: OECD.

OECD. (2009). Guidelines for recipient country investment policies relating to national security. Recommendation adopted by the OECD Council on 25 May 2009. Available at http://www.oecd.org/dataoecd/11/35/43384486.pdf.

Palmer, D. (2010). U.S. lawmakers launch push to repeal NAFTA. *Washington Post,* March 4. Available at: http://www.reuters.com/article/dUSTRE6233MS20100301.

Politi, J. (2010). Bill on overseas jobs raises hopes and fears in US. *Financial Times,* September 27.

Reinisch, A. (2009). *Recent developments in international investment law.* Paris: A. Pedone.

Report of the Subcommittee on Investment of the Advisory Committee on International Economic Policy regarding the Model Bilateral Investment Treaty. (2009). Available at http://www.state.gov/e/eeb/ris/othr/2009/131098.htm.

Rugman, A. (2005). *The regional multinationals.* Cambridge, UK: Cambridge University Press.

Salacuse, J. W. (2010). *The law of investment treaties.* New York: Oxford University Press.

Sauvant, K. P. (2009). Driving and countervailing forces: A rebalancing of national FDI policies. In: K. P. Sauvant (Ed.), *Yearbook on international investment law and policy 2008–2009.* New York: Oxford University Press.

Sauvant, K. P., & Sachs, L. E. (Eds). (2009). *The effect of treaties on foreign direct investment: Bilateral investment treaties, double taxation treaties and investment flows.* New York: Oxford University Press.

Sauvant, K. P., Mendoza, K., & Ince, I. (Eds). (2008). *The rise of transnational corporations from emerging markets: Threat or opportunity?* Cheltenham, UK: Edward Elgar.

Sornarajah, M. (2004). *The international law of foreign investment* (2nd ed.). Cambridge: Cambridge University Press.

Sornarajah, M. (2008). A coming crisis: Expansionary trends in investment treaty arbitration. In: K. P. Sauvant & M. Chiswick-Patterson (Eds), *Appeals mechanism in international investment disputes.* New York: Oxford University Press.

Sornarajah, M. (2010). Toward normlessness: The ravages and retreat of neo-liberalism in international investment law. In: K. P. Sauvant (Ed.), *Yearbook on international investment law and policy 2009/2010.* New York: Oxford University Press.

Sovereign Wealth Fund Institute. (2010). Available at: http://www.swfinstitute.org

Tobin, J. L., & Busch, M. L. (2010). A bit is better than a lot: Bilateral investment treaties and preferential trade agreements. *World Politics, 62.*

UNCTAD. (1996). *Incentives and foreign direct investment.* Geneva: UNCTAD.

UNCTAD. (1998). *World investment report 1998: Trends and determinants.* Geneva: UNCTAD.

UNCTAD. (1999). *World investment report 1999: Foreign direct investment and the challenge of development.* Geneva: UNCTAD.

UNCTAD. (2000). *World investment report 2000: Cross-border mergers and acquisitions and development.* New York: UNCTAD.

UNCTAD. (2009). *World investment report 2006: FDI from developing and transition economies. Implications for development.* Geneva: UNCTAD.

UNCTAD. (2010). *World investment report 2010: Investing in a low-carbon economy.* Geneva: UNCTAD.

United States' Model BIT. (2004). Available at: http://www.state.gov/documents/organization/117601.pdf.

Vale Columbia Center on Sustainable International Investment. (2010). Investment promotion agencies and sustainable FDI: Moving toward the fourth generation of investment promotion. Report of the findings of the Survey on Foreign Direct Investment and Sustainable Development undertaken by the Vale Columbia Center on Sustainable International Investment (VCC) and the World Association of Investment Promotion Agencies (WAIPA) June 25, 2010. Available at www.vcc.columbia.edu.

Van Harten, G. (2007). *Investment treaty arbitration and public law.* New York: Oxford University Press.

Vandevelde, K. (1992). *United States investment treaties policy and practice.* Boston: Kluwer.

Vandevelde, K. J. (2009a). A comparison of the 2004 and 1994 U.S. Model BITs: Rebalancing investor and host country interests. In: K. P. Sauvant (Ed.), *Yearbook on international investment law and policy 2008–2009.* New York: Oxford University Press.

Vandevelde, K. J. (2009b). *U.S. international investment agreements.* New York: Oxford University Press.

Visser, H. (2006). Outward foreign direct investment: Is it a good thing? In: G. Meijer, W. J. M. Heijman, J. A. C. van Ophem & B. H. J. Verstegen (Eds), *Heterodox views on economics and the economy of the global society.* Wageningen: Wageningen Academic Publishers.

Waelde, T. W. (2009). Improving the mechanisms for treaty negotiation and investment disputes: Competition and choice as the path to quality and legitimacy. In: P. S. Karl (Ed.), *Yearbook on international investment law and policy, 2008–2009.* New York: Oxford University Press.

Yackee, J. W. (2011). How much do U.S. corporations know (and care) about bilateral investment treaties? Some hints from new survey evidence. *Columbia FDI Perspective.*

AUTHORS' BIOGRAPHIES

Yair Aharoni is professor emeritus, Tel Aviv University. During his long and distinguished academic career, Aharoni served as the first dean of the faculty of management at Tel Aviv University, was instrumental in establishing several MBA and executive development programs, and served as rector of the College of Management in Israel. Aharoni held visiting appointments in several European and US universities and occupied chairs at different times in Tel Aviv University, Harvard Business School, and Duke University. For his academic achievements, he was awarded both the Landau Prize and the Israel Prize in management science.

Aharoni's books in Hebrew include *The Functions and Role of Directors* (1963); *Accounting for Management* (1974, 1978, 1980); *Structure and Conduct in Israeli Industry* (1975); *State Owned Enterprises in Israel and Abroad* (1979); *Business Strategy* (1982); and *The Political Economy of Israel* (1992). His books in English include *The Foreign Investment Decision Process* (1966); *Business in the International Environment* (1977); *Markets, Planning and Development* (1977); *The No-Risk Society* (1981); *The Management and Evolution of State-Owned Enterprises* (1986); *Israel's Political Economy: The Dreams and the Realities* (1991). In addition to these and other books and monographs, he has published more than 100 papers and chapters in books and written more than 150 cases.

Dr. Paloma Almodóvar is senior lecturer in management in Complutense University of Madrid. She has a PhD in strategy management and masters in advanced data analysis and modeling. She teaches international business and strategic management and her research has been published in refereed journals. She has been recognized with five national awards, all of them for her research about the internationalization of Spanish companies. Dr. Almodóvar has been visiting fellow at the Rotman School of Management (University of Toronto, Canada), CEIBS (Shanghai, China), Bío-Bío University (Chile), University of Auckland (New Zealand), and Henley Business School (University of Reading, UK). Her research interest is focused on international business, paying special attention to entry-mode choices, regionalization strategies, and born-global firms.

Tamar Almor, associate professor, currently serves as dean of students and lectures at the School of Business Administration, The College of Management. She specializes in business strategy, international entrepreneurship, and international business, which she teaches to MBA students. She is a member of the editorial board of "Management International Review" and has published tens of articles in leading journals such as *International Business Review*, the *Journal of International Business Studies*, and *Management International Review*. She also has edited three books.

Joshua B. Bellin is a research fellow at the Accenture Institute for High Performance, based in Boston. He has intensively researched international operating models in a diverse set of industries including electronics and high tech, retail, oil and gas, and telecommunications. His insights have been published in the *Wall Street Journal, MIT Sloan Management Review*, and *Strategy and Leadership*, among other publications.

Peter J. Buckley, professor of international business and director of the Centre for International Business, University of Leeds was president of the Academy of International Business (2002–2004). He is currently chair of the European International Business Academy. In 2010, he was awarded a Cheung Kong Scholar Chair Professorship by the University of International Business and Economics (UIBE), Beijing.

Timothy M. Devinney (BSc, CMU; MA, MBA, PhD, Chicago) is professor of strategy at the University of Technology, Sydney. He has published 6 books and more than 70 articles in leading journals including *Management Science, The Academy of Management Review, Journal of International Business Studies, Organization Science*, and the *Strategic Management Journal*. He is a fellow of the Academy of International Business, a recipient of an Alexander von Humboldt Research Award and a Rockefeller Foundation Bellagio fellow. He is past-chair of the International Management Division of the AOM and associate editor of *AOM Perspectives*, director of the SSRN international management network, and coeditor of the *Advances in International Management Series* (Emerald).

Fragkiskos Filippaios is currently the Director for Postgraduate Development and Accreditations and a Senior Lecturer in International Business at Kent Business School, University of Kent. Previously he was the International MBA Course Director at Kingston Business School, Kingston University London holding the responsibility for all international MBA programmes offered by Kingston University London, in Russia, Greece, Cyprus and India. The academic year 2007/2008 he was the Ministry of

Economy and Finance Senior Research Fellow at the Hellenic Observatory, European Institute, London School of Economics, where he still is a Visiting Fellow. His research interests are on the roles of subsidiaries of Multi-national Enterprises, the location strategies of multinationals' subsidiaries, the role of technology in the multinational group and the empirical assessment of Foreign Direct Investment.

Rebecca Firth completed her PhD at Manchester Business School, UK. Her research interests are in the area of interfirm linkages, particularly in relation to Asian economies and their impact on economic development. Additionally, she has a keen interest in qualitative research. She has previously studied at The University of Leeds, Dresden University of Technology, and Hong Kong University of Science and Technology. She now works in economic development consulting specializing in tourism, culture, and heritage.

Jens Forssbaeck is an associate professor of corporate finance at Lund University School of Economics and Management. He holds a PhD in finance from Copenhagen Business School, Denmark, and an MSc in economics from Uppsala University, Sweden. He has previously been a visiting researcher at universities in France, the Netherlands, and the United Kingdom. His main research interests lie in the areas of international finance and various micro- and macroeconomic aspects of financial markets and institutions.

Pervez N. Ghauri completed his PhD from Uppsala University in Sweden where he also taught for some years. He has since worked in University of Groningen, Netherlands and Manchester Business School, UK. At present, he is professor of international business at King's College London, UK. Recently, he was also awarded an honorary doctorate by Turku school of Economics and Management. He has published more than 20 books and numerous articles in journals such as *Journal of International Business Studies, British Journal of Management, Journal of World Business*, and *Management International Review*. He is editor-in-chief for *International Business Review* and editor for Europe for *Journal of World Business*.

Stéphane J. G. Girod, is a Research Fellow at the Accenture Institute for High Performance which he joined in January 2008 upon completion of his doctorate at the Said Business School, University of Oxford. At Accenture, he led the international operating model research project. His research and consulting activities focus on the organizational strategy and organizational transformation of developed-market and emerging-market multinational enterprises. He has lectured at Indiana University, Bocconi University, and Aalto University among others, and his works have appeared in leading peer-reviewed and practitioner journals. He is based in London.

Niron Hashai is a senior lecturer and head of strategy and entrepreneurship at the School of Business Administration, The Hebrew University. His research interests are the theory of the multinational enterprise and determinants of the internationalization process, with special emphasis on knowledge intensive firms. He has published extensively in top-tier international business and innovation journals and serves on the editorial board of the *Journal of International Management*.

Seev Hirsch is professor emeritus of international business at the Leon Recanati Graduate School of Business Administration, Tel Aviv University. He was the School's second dean and was Jaffe Professor of International Trade since 1981. He joined Tel Aviv University in 1965, after getting his MBA and doctorate at the Harvard Business School in Boston. Prior to becoming an academic, he was a member of Kibbutz Maagan Michael. He published numerous books and articles on international trade, foreign direct investment, multinational enterprises, economic relations of the European Community, and on economic aspects of peace making.

Arie Y. Lewin is professor of strategy and international business at Duke University, Fuqua School of Business and is director of the Center for International Business Education and Research (CIBER). He is elected fellow of the Academy of International Business, and The Organization Management and Theory Division of the Academy of Management awarded Professor Lewin the first Joanne Martin Trailblazer Award at the 2008 Annual Meeting. Professor Lewin is visiting research professor at IESE (2005–2008) and RSM Erasmus University (1998 till date) where he is also ERIM senior fellow. He was editor-in-chief (2002–2007) of *Journal of International Business Studies* (JIBS); founding editor-in-chief of *Organization Science* (1989–1998), and the convener of the acclaimed Organization Science Winter Conference (1994 till date). His research interests center on strategic renewal of organizations encompassing studies of adaptation and selection as coevolutionary systems, emergence of new organizational forms, and adaptive capabilities that distinguish between innovating and imitating organizations. He is the lead PI for the multiyear international Offshoring Research Network (ORN) project that focuses on companies in transition to globalizing their organizations, business functions, processes and services by tracking firm strategies, experiences, and future plans related to global delivery of all business functions and administrative and technical work. Current research focuses on the globalization of innovation.

Lilach Nachum is professor of international business. Her major professional interests and expertise are the theory of the MNE and the distinctiveness of these firms as an organizational form, their location decisions, and strategy. Her research in these areas is summarized in two books and a number of articles, published in journals such as *Management Science*, *Strategic Management Journal*, and the *Journal of International Business Studies*, among others. She is a board member of the *Journal of International Business Studies*, *Global Strategy Journal*, *Management International Review*, and the *Journal of International Management*.

Lars Oxelheim holds a chair in international business and finance at the Lund Institute of Economic Research, Lund University and is affiliated with the Research Institute of Industrial Economics (IFN), Stockholm, and with the Fudan University, Shanghai. Lars Oxelheim is chairman of the Swedish Network for European Studies in Economics and Business (SNEE). He has authored or edited some 35 research monographs and authored a number of research articles published in international business, finance, and economic journals. His recent research monographs include *Corporate Decision-Making with Macroeconomic Uncertainty* (Oxford University Press), *Markets and Compensation for Executives in Europe* (Emerald Group Publishing), *National Tax Policy in Europe – To Be or Not to Be* (Springer Verlag), *Corporate and Institutional Transparency for Economic Growth in Europe* (Elsevier), *How Unified is the European Union?* (Springer Verlag), *European Union and the Race for Inward FDI in Europe* (Elsevier), and *Money Markets and Politics – A Study of European Financial Integration and Monetary Policy Options* (Edgar Elgar). Lars Oxelheim is a frequently invited keynote speaker and adviser to corporations and government agencies.

Marina Papanastassiou is professor at the Department of Strategic Management and Globalization at the Copenhagen Business School in Denmark and a part-time professor at Háskólinn á Bifröst in Iceland. Her research interests focus on the global innovation strategies of multinational corporations. Her research is extensively published in international refereed academic journals and chapters in books, and she has coauthored three books with Robert Pearce. In 2002, she served as the president of the European International Business Association (EIBA).

Ruth Rama is research professor at the Department of Economics, Spanish Council for Scientific Research (CSIC), Madrid, since 1988. Before coming to CSIC, she was a consultant for the Centre on Transnational Corporations of the United Nations, the OECD, and the FAO. She has published in the fields of multinational enterprises' strategies, patenting, and organization of R&D in food and drink multinationals, internationalization of R&D, and local networks of multinationals. She is the editor of a book titled *Multinational Agribusinesses*.

Ravi Ramamurti is CBA Distinguished Professor of International Business and Director of the Center for Emerging Markets, at Northeastern University, Boston. He obtained his MBA from the Indian Institute of Management, Ahmedabad and his DBA from Harvard Business School. He has been a visiting professor at Harvard Business School, MIT Sloan School of Management, IMD, Switzerland, The Fletcher School at Tufts University, and the Wharton School (University of Pennsylvania). Over three decades, his research and consulting have focused on the strategy of firms operating in, or from, emerging economies. His last book was *Emerging Multinationals in Emerging Markets* (Cambridge University Press, 2009), and he has published extensively in the leading management journals. He has been a consultant to several international agencies and to state-owned and private firms in many countries. In 2008, he was elected a fellow of the Academy of International Business.

Alan M. Rugman is professor of international business at the Henley Business School of the University of Reading. He is director of research in the School of Management. Previously he held the L. Leslie Waters chair of International Business at the Kelley School of Business, Indiana University (2001–2009). Dr. Rugman has published widely: his recent books include: *Inside the Multinationals*, reissued by Palgrave Macmillan on its 25th anniversary in 2006; *The Regional Multinationals* (Cambridge University Press, 2005); *Regional Aspects of Multinationality and Performance* (Elsevier/Emerald, 2007); and *Rugman Reviews International Business* (Palgrave, 2009). He has served as a consultant to major private-sector companies, research institutes, government agencies, and as an outside advisor on free trade, foreign investment, and international competitiveness to two Canadian prime ministers. From 2004 to 2006, Mr. Rugman served as president of the Academy of International Business (AIB).

Karl P. Sauvant is the founding Executive Director of the Vale Columbia Center on Sustainable International Investment, Senior Research Scholar and Lecturer in Law at Columbia Law School, Co-Director of the Millennium Cities Initiative, and Guest Professor at Nankai University, China. Until July 2005, Dr. Sauvant was Director of the United Nations Conference on Trade and Development's (UNCTAD) Division on Investment, Technology and Enterprise Development (DITE), the focal point in the UN system for matters related to foreign direct investment (FDI) and technology, as well as a major interface with the private sector.

While at the UN, he created, in 1991, the prestigious annual *World Investment Report*, of which he was the lead author until 2004. He is the author of, or responsible for, a substantial number of publications on issues related to economic development, FDI and services. In 2006, he was elected an Honorary Fellow of the European International Business Academy. He received his Ph.D. from the University of Pennsylvania in 1975.

SUBJECT INDEX